STRATEGIC TOOLS FOR SOCIAL ENTREPRENEURS:
ENHANCING THE PERFORMANCE OF YOUR ENTERPRISING NONPROFIT

STRATEGIC TOOLS FOR SOCIAL ENTREPRENEURS:
ENHANCING THE PERFORMANCE OF YOUR ENTERPRISING NONPROFIT

J. Gregory Dees
Jed Emerson
Peter Economy

JOHN WILEY & SONS, INC.

This publication is designed to provide accurate and authoritative information in regard to the subject matter covered. It is sold with the understanding that the publisher is not engaged in rendering legal, accounting, or other professional services. If legal advice or other expert assistance is required, the services of a competent professional person should be sought.

Library of Congress Cataloging-in-Publication Data

ISBN: 0-471-15068-1

Printed in the United States of America.

10 9 8 7 6

WILEY NONPROFIT LAW, FINANCE, AND MANAGEMENT SERIES

The Art of Planned Giving: Understanding Donors and the Culture of Giving by Douglas E. White

Beyond Fund Raising: New Strategies for Nonprofit Investment and Innovation by Kay Grace

Budgeting for Not-for-Profit Organizations by David Maddox

Careers in Fundraising by Lilya Wagner

The Complete Guide to Fund Raising Management by Stanley Weinstein

The Complete Guide to Nonprofit Management by Smith, Bucklin & Associates

Critical Issues in Fund Raising edited by Dwight Burlingame

Cultivating Diversity in Fundraising by Janice Gow Pettey

Faith-Based Management: Leading Organizations that are Based on More than Just Mission by Peter Brinckerhoff

Financial and Accounting Guide for Not-for-Profit Organizations, Sixth Edition by Malvern J. Gross, Jr., Richard F. Larkin, John H. McCarthy, PricewaterhouseCoopers LLP

Financial Empowerment: More Money for More Mission by Peter Brinckerhoff

Financial Management for Nonprofit Organizations by Jo Ann Hankin, Alan Seidner and John Zietlow

The First Legal Answer Book for Fund-Raisers by Bruce R. Hopkins

Fund-Raising Fundamentals: A Guide to Annual Giving for Professionals and Volunteers by James M. Greenfield

Fundraising Cost Effectiveness: A Self-Assessment Workbook by James M. Greenfield

Fund-Raising Regulation: A State-by-State Handbook of Registration Forms, Requirements, and Procedures by Seth Perlman and Betsy Hills Bush

Grantseeker's Budget Toolkit by James A. Quick and Cheryl S. New

Grantseeker's Toolkit: A Comprehensive Guide to Finding Funding by Cheryl S. New and James A. Quick

Grant Winner's Toolkit: Project Management and Evaluation by James A. Quick and Cheryl S. New

High Impact Philanthropy: How Donors, Boards, and Nonprofit Organizations Can Transform Nonprofit Communities by Kay Sprinkel Grace and Alan L. Wendroff

High Performance Nonprofit Organizations: Managing Upstream for Greater Impact by Christine W. Letts, William P. Ryan, and Allen Grossman

Improving the Economy, Efficiency, and Effectiveness of Nonprofits: Conducting Operational Reviews by Rob Reider

Intermediate Sanctions: Curbing Nonprofit Abuse by Bruce R. Hopkins and D. Benson Tesdahl

International Fund Raising for Nonprofits by Thomas Harris

International Guide to Nonprofit Law by Lester A. Salamon and Stefan Toepler & Associates

Joint Ventures Involving Tax-Exempt Organizations, Second Edition by Michael I. Sanders

The Law of Fund-Raising, Second Edition by Bruce R. Hopkins

The Law of Tax-Exempt Healthcare Organizations, Second Edition by Thomas K. Hyatt and Bruce R. Hopkins

The Law of Tax-Exempt Organizations, Seventh Edition by Bruce R. Hopkins

The Legal Answer Book for Nonprofit Organizations by Bruce R. Hopkins

The Legal Answer Book for Private Foundations by Bruce R. Hopkins and Jody Blazek

A Legal Guide to Starting and Managing a Nonprofit Organization, Third Edition by Bruce R. Hopkins

The Legislative Labyrinth: A Map for Not-for-Profits, edited by Walter Pidgeon

Managing Affordable Housing: A Practical Guide to Creating Stable Communities by Bennett L. Hecht, Local Initiatives Support Corporation, and James Stockard

ManagingNonprofits.org by Ben Hecht and Rey Ramsey

Mission-Based Management: Leading Your Not-for-Profit in the 21st Century, Second Edition by Peter Brinckerhoff

v

Mission-Based Management: Leading Your Not-for-Profit in the 21st Century, Second Edition, Workbook by Peter Brinckerhoff

Mission-Based Marketing: How Your Not-for-Profit Can Succeed in a More Competitive World by Peter Brinckerhoff

Nonprofit Boards: Roles, Responsibilities, and Performance by Diane J. Duca

Nonprofit Compensation and Benefits Practices by Applied Research and Development Institute International, Inc.

The Nonprofit Counsel by Bruce R. Hopkins

The Nonprofit Guide to the Internet, Second Edition by Michael Johnston

Nonprofit Investment Policies: A Practical Guide to Creation and Implementation by Robert Fry, Jr.

The Nonprofit Law Dictionary by Bruce R. Hopkins

Nonprofit Compensation, Benefits, and Employment Law by David G. Samuels and Howard Pianko

The Nonprofit Handbook, Third Edition: Management by Tracy Daniel Connors

The Nonprofit Handbook, Third Edition: Fund Raising by James M. Greenfield

The Nonprofit Manager's Resource Dictionary, 2e by Ronald A. Landskroner

Nonprofit Organizations' Business Forms: Disk Edition by John Wiley & Sons, Inc.

Planned Giving: Management, Marketing, and Law, Second Edition by Ronald R. Jordan and Katelyn L. Quynn

The Private Foundation Answer Book by Bruce Hopkins and Jody Blazek

Private Foundations: Tax Law and Compliance by Bruce R. Hopkins and Jody Blazek

Program Related Investments: A Technical Manual for Foundations by Christie I. Baxter

Reengineering Your Nonprofit Organization: A Guide to Strategic Transformation by Alceste T. Pappas

Reinventing the University: Managing and Financing Institutions of Higher Education by Sandra L. Johnson and Sean C. Rush, Pricewaterhouse-Coopers LLP

The Second Legal Answer Book for Nonprofit Organizations by Bruce R. Hopkins

The Second Legal Answer Book for Fund Raisers by Bruce R. Hopkins

Social Entrepreneurship: The Art of Mission-Based Venture Development by Peter Brinckerhoff

Special Events: Proven Strategies for Nonprofit Fund Raising by Alan Wendroff

Starting and Managing a Nonprofit Organization: A Legal Guide, Third Edition by Bruce R. Hopkins

Strategic Communications for Nonprofit Organizations: Seven Steps to Creating a Successful Plan by Janel Radtke

Strategic Planning for Nonprofit Organizations: A Practical Guide and Workbook by Michael Allison and Jude Kaye, Support Center for Nonprofit Management

Strategic Tools for Social Entrepreneurs by J. Gregory Dees, Jed Emerson, and Peter Economy

Streetsmart Financial Basics for Nonprofit Managers by Thomas A. McLaughlin

A Streetsmart Guide to Nonprofit Mergers and Networks by Thomas A. McLaughlin

Successful Marketing Strategies for Nonprofit Organizations by Barry J. McLeish

Successful Corporate Fund Raising: Effective Strategies for Today's Nonprofits by Scott Sheldon

The Tax Law of Colleges and Universities, 2e by Bertrand M. Harding

Tax Planning and Compliance for Tax-Exempt Organizations: Forms, Checklists, Procedures, Third Edition by Jody Blazek

The Universal Benefits of Volunteering: A Practical Workbook for Nonprofit Organizations, Volunteers and Corporations by Walter P. Pidgeon, Jr.

Trade Secrets for Every Nonprofit Manager by Thomas A. McLaughlin

Values-Based Estate Planning: A Step-by-Step Approach to Wealth Transfers for Professional Advisors by Scott Fithian

To Peter F. Drucker and John W. Gardner, for their visionary work on behalf of the nonprofit community, for showing us what's truly possible when we commit ourselves to achieving our highest aspirations, and for demonstrating through their work and their lives that people are the most important asset of them all.

FOREWORD

Enterprise drives much of human endeavor, from the neighborhood business to the corporate giant, from the church bake sale to the healthcare conglomerate. Social sector leaders today need to understand social enterprise in order to help their organizations further their missions. In a society where the call is for collaboration, for leading beyond the walls, and for making the wise use of the people and tangible resources of the institution, the ways and means of enterprise must be learned.

The social entrepreneur holds unique advantages over entrepreneurs in other circumstances. With mission as the guiding star, the social entrepreneur can organize and deploy diverse resources. The social entrepreneur can engage volunteers, customers, partners, and investors through a logical business plan that furthers the organization's mission. In the social sector, success in the enterprise equals significance through changed lives and healthy communities.

Although the social entrepreneur has the advantage of a mission that inspires, this entrepreneur must also meet the challenges of developing and rewarding people, of working in collaboration and partnership with other organizations and the community, and of meeting the competitive challenges most businesses face daily.

In 1989 Peter F. Drucker published a notable article in the *Harvard Business Review*. Many who read the title—"What Business Can Learn from Nonprofits"—thought it was a misprint. Drucker wrote that social sector organizations set the standards to be emulated when it comes to strategy, the effectiveness of the board, and the mobilization and productivity of knowledge workers. *Strategic Tools for Social Entrepreneurs* shares the entrepreneurial techniques perfected in the business community as well as social sector models of innovation and results. In five years the lessons from the social sector may well change the way enterprise in all three sectors is developed and managed. Now is the time for social sector leaders to use every tool available to them and to apply those tools to further the organization's mission, serve its customers, and build community.

Not every nonprofit organization needs to operate an enterprise. At the same time, every nonprofit leader needs to know when enterprise is the right tool to further the organization's mission. As we employ the tools we need to futher the mission of our organizations, we may move closer to our vision of a country of healthy children, strong families, decent housing, good schools, and work that dignifies, all embraced by the inclusive, cohesive community. May your organization use *Strategic Tools for Social Entrepreneurs* to help us get a little closer.

Frances Hesselbein
Chairman of the Board of Governors
The Peter F. Drucker Foundation for Nonprofit Management

PREFACE

Ewing Marion Kauffman (Mr. K) was a successful businessman and former owner of the Kansas City Royals baseball club. When he started his foundation (the Ewing Marion Kauffman Foundation), he initially planned to devote his substantial accumulated wealth to helping children and youth become productive members of society. This meant initiating a variety of programs in the Kansas City region to help young people develop moral and ethical behaviors, stay free from drugs and alcohol, be prepared to enter school ready to learn, and successfully graduate from high school, trade school, or college.

After a few years of operating these four programs within the foundation, Mr. K decided that he needed to do more to help children, youth, and their families become more self-sufficient. Because Mr. K had always been an entrepreneur—and because he had turned his own modest personal savings into a fortune through hard work and an unbounded entrepreneurial spirit—it was natural for him to believe that, by encouraging and accelerating entrepreneurship in America, he could achieve this goal. After several months of careful study, he came to the conclusion that his foundation should be a leader in teaching and promoting the concepts of entrepreneurship to children, youth, and adults—and he set about turning that idea into a reality.

Under the leadership of Michie Slaughter, Kurt Mueller, Bob Rogers, Lou Smith, Ray Smilor, Marilyn Kourilsky, Rhonda Holman, and many others, the Kauffman Center for Entrepreneurial Leadership at the Ewing Marion Kauffman Foundation has developed and funded many innovative and groundbreaking programs to teach entrepreneurship to youth and adults. While the early work in this area was focused entirely on for-profit enterprises, as time went on Mr. K noticed that the same skills and attitudes seen in successful for-profit entrepreneurs were also prevalent in many successful nonprofit leaders. At Mr. K's urging, the foundation soon began to devote its significant resources to developing, supporting, and encouraging entrepreneurs who practice in the nonprofit sector as well.

We have met many wonderful, inspiring, dedicated and courageous social entrepreneurs over the years—many of whom are written about in this book. Nonprofit organizations have always been faced with a dilemma: how to balance the competing needs for providing necessary services to clients who could not afford to pay for them. For years, nonprofits have relied on the financial largesse of the government, corporations, foundations, and individuals to generate operating and program funds. Without these traditional sources of funds, most nonprofits would not exist today. Over the past decade, however, many of these traditional sources of funds have dried up. According to an Independent Sector study, federal government spending on programs of concern to nonprofits (not including assistance to individuals) has decreased by more than $30 *billion.*

In response to these trends, more and more nonprofit organizations are beginning to consider new and different ways to generate the funds they need to operate. Indeed, for many organizations, social enterprise—the adoption of entrepreneurial behaviors and techniques by nonprofit organizations—is rapidly becoming a necessity for survival rather than just another management buzzword. Instead of viewing the world of business as the enemy, many nonprofits are beginning to learn how to take business skills and frameworks and apply them within a community context to create social value.

Make no mistake about it: This is really hard work. For the most part, social entrepreneurship is not a science that can be simply copied from the for-profit world—nonprofits *are* different. That is exactly why this book exists. Not only will *Strategic Tools for Social Entrepreneurs* help social entrepreneurs determine how and when for-profit entrepreneurial skills can help them achieve meaningful results and create social value for their clients, it will provide them with all the tools and resources necessary to put these important concepts into practice.

Mr. Kauffman died in 1993. His legacy lives on, however, through the work of his foundation, and through the lives of all the people he has touched over the years. Mr. Kauffman would be pleased that entrepreneurs—both for-profit and nonprofit—are working together now more than ever before to create a better world. As Mr. K said: "All the money in the world cannot solve problems unless we work together. And if we work together, there is no problem in the world that can stop us as we seek to develop people to their highest and best potential."

We hope this book is a practical tool to help you fulfill *your* potential to create meaningful social value for your clients.

Steve Roling
Ewing Marion Kauffman Foundation

ACKNOWLEDGMENTS

Nothing like this gets accomplished without family support. Whatever talent I bring to this project was first nurtured by my parents, Geneva Evelyn and James Harold Dees. The patient and loving support of my wife, Betty Ann Probst, was essential to its successful completion. She is my shining star and best friend. Accordingly, my work on this book is dedicated to the memory of my father who passed away before he could see the finished product, to my mother's continuing health, and to many more years in the warm embrace of my wife.

On a more specific level, I want to thank my good friend Steve Roling at the Kauffman Foundation. This was his idea and he should be held fully responsible! It continues to be a rare treat to work with Jed Emerson and Peter Economy. Jed's unique combination of passion, intelligence, experience, and receptivity make him the very best kind of colleague and coauthor. Peter has a wonderful gift for making complex concepts accessible and for keeping a major project, such as this, on track. Susan McDermott, our editor at Wiley, has been very supportive and encouraging. All of our authors have demonstrated not only their expertise but also their patience and flexibility as we worked to make sure themes and concepts were integrated across the chapters. I am particularly grateful that Melissa Taylor and Beth Anderson agreed to take on the challenge of composing chapters with Jed and me. They made us look good. I am also deeply grateful for all of the friends and colleagues who encouraged and supported my work on social entrepreneurship. It would be futile to attempt a complete list here. Many colleagues from McKinsey, Yale, Harvard, MACED, Stanford, and Duke have served as role models, coaches, mentors, cheerleaders, and intellectual partners. Numerous social entrepreneurs and philanthropists have helped me understand the power and limits of bringing business concepts into this arena. Together, these friends, colleagues, and social entrepreneurs gave me the strength to persist when others were telling me that working on social entrepreneurship was fundamentally misguided, unimportant, or unwise from a career point of view. This has proven to be the most satisfying work of my life.

J. Gregory Dees

I would like to thank the project team who made this book, and its predecessor, possible. Finding folks with whom one can not only work but enjoy the process of work is something to be valued, and I greatly appreciate each member's wit and patience. Greg has been a personal colleague and mentor who has had a major impact on my ability to maintain enthusiasm in the face of institutions and individuals who do not naturally welcome challenge and change. Peter's feedback has contributed to making my own words say what I mean as opposed to what I thought I was saying. And Steve's unrestrained backing of my work and life journey has been exceptional. I would also like to thank Beth Anderson and Melissa Taylor, whose leadership in writing our chapters in this book was significant and whose great attitude made for a fun writing process—critical to both the generation of good ideas and presentation of "readable" text when sculpting the thoughts of three authors.

I would like to offer my sincere and personal thanks to Paul Brest and Susan Bell, both of the William and Flora Hewlett Foundation. My senior fellowship with the Foundation has been critical to my development of next-wave ideas and has provided me a path to future applied theory and practical thinking. Their unwavering support has been central to my transitioning from traditional social entrepreneurship and venture philanthropy to blended value pursuits of even deeper levels of potential importance. Their unbridled enthusiasm for my emergent notions of reality has provided me with more room to grow than many others ever have the good fortune to explore—and I deeply appreciate it, all the while skipping along the edge.

Special thanks must also go to Carol Guyer, a wonderful mentor and matriarch of progressive philanthropy. Carol's lifetime of experience has contributed much to my own work and thinking. I am deeply grateful for her friendship.

Finally, I would like to thank the many folks who have seen my "stand-up number" or listened to me rant in a meeting and allowed me the courtesy of expressing my raging frustration, enthusiasm, and love for those attempting to maximize value of all kinds—within nonprofits, business, and (dare I say) government. Your gracious accommodation of my presentation and verbal eccentricities is appreciated more than you know, and in the future I will try to use fewer swear words in expressing my thoughts (with the operative word being "try"!).

Get out and climb mountains, adopt abandoned animals, change the world, and be peace!

Jed Emerson

I would like to thank my coeditors Greg Dees and Jed Emerson both for their patience and for freely imparting their great knowledge and insights on the topic of social entrepreneurship. I would also like to thank our guest authors for being so responsive to the needs of this long-term project—it's been a real pleasure working with each one of you. A special thanks to Alison Carlson for first introducing me to the project team, to John Tyler, Suzanne Mathes, and Karen Owens at EMKF who many times dropped everything to help out, and to our editors at John Wiley & Sons—Susan McDermott and Alexia Meyers—for helping to develop this book and bring it to fruition. And thanks most of all to Steve Roling at EMKF for inviting me to join the team and for supporting my efforts. Your ongoing leadership on this project has been inspiring, and I'll always be grateful to you for allowing me the privilege of being a part of this book.

Peter Economy

ABOUT THE AUTHORS

J. Gregory Dees is Adjunct Professor of Social Entrepreneurship and Nonprofit Management at Duke University's Fuqua School of Business, and Entrepreneur-in-Residence with the Kauffman Foundation's Center for Entrepreneurial Leadership. Prior to coming to Duke, he served as the Miriam and Peter Haas Centennial Professor in Public Service at Stanford University's Graduate School of Business where he was the founding codirector of the new Center for Social Innovation. Most of Greg's academic career was spent at Harvard Business School where he helped launch the Initiative on Social Enterprise. In 1995, he received Harvard Business School's Apgar Award for Innovation in Teaching in recognition of his new course on "Entrepreneurship in the Social Sector." Greg took a two-year leave from Harvard to work on economic development in central Appalachia at the Mountain Association for Community Economic Development in Berea, Kentucky. He previously taught at the Yale School of Management and worked as a management consultant with McKinsey & Company. When not teaching at Duke, Greg and his wife make their home in Louisville, Kentucky.

Jed Emerson has been active in community and social work since the mid-1970s, spending the past decade focusing his efforts on the areas of social entrepreneurship and venture philanthropy. Jed is cofounder of the Roberts Enterprise Development Fund, Senior Fellow with the William and Flora Hewlett Foundation, and a lecturer with the Center for Social Innovation at the Graduate School of Business at Stanford University. Jed also served as the Bloomberg Senior Research Fellow at Harvard Business School.

In 1996, he coedited and wrote numerous chapters in *New Social Entrepreneurs: The Success, Challenge and Lessons of Social Purpose Enterprise,* published by The Roberts Foundation in San Francisco, CA. Jed is well known for his writings and public speaking. Other articles and writings of his may be found at the Fund's website (*www.redf.org*). The *Nonprofit Times* selected Jed in both 1998 and 2000 as one of the "50 Most Influential People in the Nonprofit Sector" in recognition of his advocacy and advancement of concepts such as social return on investment, social enterprise, and innovative approaches to philanthropy. Jed holds masters degrees in both social work and business administration.

Peter Economy is the bestselling business author of numerous works including *Leadership Ensemble: Lessons in Collaborative Management from the World's Only Conductorless Orchestra, Managing For Dummies, At the Helm: Business Lessons for Navigating Rough Waters,* and many others. He is Associate Editor for the Drucker Foundation's award-winning magazine *Leader to Leader,* home-based business expert for the AllBusiness.com website, and consulting editor for *Bob Nelson's Rewarding Employees.* He was formerly Director of Administration for Horizons Technology, Inc., a San Diego based software development firm, and Vice President for project management and operations for a nationwide computer services firm. Peter has a Bachelor of Arts degree with majors in economics and human biology from Stanford University and is currently pursuing MBA studies at the Edinburgh Business School.

Steve Roling, Senior Vice President of the Ewing Marion Kauffman Foundation of Kansas City, Missouri, has spent his professional career involved in various for-profit and nonprofit organizations. While still in graduate school he was resident director of Butterfield Youth Services—a residential treatment facility for at-risk youth. He then joined the staff of former U.S. Senator Tom Eagleton (D-MO) as a legislative assistant in Washington, D.C. for six years. He returned to his home state of Missouri to become a banker for four years before he spent six years as Publisher of the *Kansas City Business Journal.* For the last 10 years, Roling has worked for the Ewing Marion Kauffman Foundation, and is currently responsible for the foundation's Youth Development investments. Steve and his wife Judi have two daughters. Stephanie is a nurse at Mount Sinai Hospital in New York City and Susie is a junior at The Catholic University of America. Steve Roling has both an undergraduate and graduate degree from the University of Missouri–Columbia.

Beth Battle Anderson is a Senior Research Associate in social entrepreneurship and nonprofit management at The Fuqua School of Business at Duke University. She works closely with Professor J. Gregory Dees, under whom she previously served as Research Associate and Acting Director at the Center for Social Innovation at Stanford Graduate School of Business. While pursuing her MBA at Stanford, Beth spent a summer as an Associate with McKinsey & Company. Prior to business school, she worked for five years in the nonprofit sector, first within the grassroots Olympic Movement and subsequently at an outdoor education center for people with disabilities. Beth received her BA in Classics from Williams College.

Jill Blair is a founding Principal of BTW Consultants–*informing change,* a consulting firm based in Berkeley, CA, that works with nonprofit and philanthropic organizations. The services provided include evaluation, program development, information systems design, needs assessments, and organizational planning. As a consultant to nonprofits and philanthropy, Jill works both locally and nationally on program design, strategic assessment, and evaluation. She has worked on policy and program issues related to the lives of children and youth for more than 15 years, in the public, private, and philanthropic sectors. In 1990, Jill served as Special Assistant to the Chancellor of the New York City Public Schools, and was responsible for designing and implementing the nation's first school-based condom availability program for AIDS prevention. Among the projects that Jill is currently directing are two evaluations of innovative program models, a foundation incubator, and an organizational capacity grants initiative. She is also working with the Charles and Helen Schwab Foundation on facilitating the design of a capacity building initiative for California substance abuse treatment programs in San Mateo County.

Kay Sprinkel Grace, CFRE, is a San Francisco-based organizational consultant, providing workshops and consultation to local, regional and national and international organizations in campaign strategies, case and board development, staff development, and other issues related to leadership of the fund raising process. Her clients include schools, universities, health and human services organizations, arts and cultural organizations, and those concerned with the environment and other issues. She is an acclaimed and popular trainer of boards and staffs, and has provided mentoring to countless people entering or working in the development profession. She has been a member of the faculty of The Fund Raising School (Center on Philanthropy, Indiana University) since 1980, and serves on its advisory board.

She is the author of *Beyond Fund Raising: New Strategies for Nonprofit Innovation and Investment* (John Wiley & Sons, 1997) and co-author, with Alan Wendroff, of *High Impact Philanthropy: How Donors, Boards, and Nonprofit Organizations Can Transform Communities,* released by John Wiley & Sons in January, 2001. She has published articles for *Fund Raising Management,* and the journal of the National Society of Fund Raising Executives, and is a regular columnist for the publication *Contributions.* She has participated in the development and production of three videotapes for the National Center for Nonprofit Boards, and is the author of their best-selling booklet and audiotape, *The Board's Role in Strategic Planning.*

Her BA and MA are from Stanford University, where she served two years (1992–94) as the first woman Volunteer Chair of the Stanford (Annual) Fund. She served for three years as chair of the University of San

Francisco Institute for Nonprofit Organization Management Advisory Board, and is on the board of the Women's Philanthropy Institute and the Djerassi Resident Artist Program (Woodside, California). She lives in San Francisco and is passionate about her grandchildren, art and her photography.

Shirley Brice Heath is a Faculty Affiliate of the Center for Social Innovation at Stanford University. Professor Heath's passion for social entrepreneurship and community grew out of her work on youth language and culture. Her ArtShow video features entreprising nonprofits that use the arts to engage young people. She has taught social entrepreneurship at Stanford and consults internationally on issues related to social entrepreneurship, youth, community, and the arts. Heath is also the recipient of the prestigious MacArthur Fellowship (also called the "genius" award).

James Heskett is Professor Emeritus at the Harvard Business School, cochair of the faculty for the school's program in Strategic Perspectives in Non-Profit Management, and faculty chair of the Denali Initiative in Social Entrepreneurship. He is a director of several organizations, including WeGo.com, a company offering Internet-based support services to associations and other nonprofit organizations, and has authored a number of books, articles, and cases, among which are many based on the experiences of nonprofit organizations.

Jerry Kitzi is the president of Social Venture Partners of Greater Kansas City. SVP—GKC is an exciting model of venture philanthropy designed to grow philanthropy and strengthen the nonprofit sector. It provides investors a hands-on opportunity to combine their financial investments with their business expertise to address the day-to-day growth issues of the nonprofits they select for investment. Before helping to launch SVP—GKC, Kitzi served as the vice president, Youth Development division, with the Ewing Marion Kauffman Foundation where he was responsible for overall planning, coordination, and implementation of the Youth Development division's approved operating and grant-making strategies. Kitzi also served as the executive director of Adolescent Resources Corporation in Kansas City, a nonprofit organization dedicated to improving the quality of life for teenagers and their families.

Melissa A. Taylor is a PhD candidate at the Martin School of Public Policy and Administration at the University of Kentucky. Prior to pursuing her PhD full-time, she was a research associate for the Stanford University Graduate School of Business where she focused on nonprofit issues.

She was formerly the director of the Entrepreneurship Initiative at the Mountain Association for Community and Economic Development (MACED), a nonprofit organization in Berea, Kentucky.

Fay Twersky is a founding Principal of BTW Consultants–*informing change,* a consulting firm based in Berkeley, CA, that works with nonprofit and philanthropic organizations. The services provided include evaluation, program development, information systems design, needs assessments, and organizational planning. Fay has worked as a consultant for more than ten years and is nationally recognized for her work in assessing community economic development initiatives. She develops strategies for tracking both the social impacts and economic progress of nonprofit enterprises funded by the Roberts Foundation. In 1996, Fay coedited the book, *New Social Entrepreneurs: The Success, Challenge and Lessons of Non-Profit Enterprise Creation.* More recently, Fay has authored and coauthored several articles that describe efforts to develop sustainable client tracking systems as well as new lessons being learned from the successes and failures of social entrepreneurship. In addition to her work in the field of social entrepreneurship, Fay directs program and initiative evaluations in the fields of community and economic development, public health, education, criminal justice, and adolescent services. Locally and nationally, Fay trains practitioners and funders in community-oriented evaluation and needs assessment research.

Betty Henderson Wingfield of Executive Development Associates is an independent consultant, executive coach, facilitator, and keynote speaker in the areas of executive development, leadership and management development, and organizational change. As an independent consultant, Betty has enjoyed the opportunity of working with the private and public sectors.

Prior to becoming an independent consultant, Betty was Senior Manager of Human Resources Training and Development at BankBoston in Boston, MA. She led the development and implementation of BankBoston's innovative Acceleration Leadership Program (ALP) for the top 200 executives. During her tenure at the bank, she was honored for her leadership skills and focus on client satisfaction. She was a key contributor to most of the major strategic change initiatives within the organization.

Before joining BankBoston, Betty was Regional Director of the Ronkin Educational Group in Framingham, MA, where she was responsible for day-to-day operations of the regional office. From 1987–1992, she was Regional Training Manager for WWGroup, Inc., covering eastern Massachusetts and Rhode Island. Her career has also included program development for the YWCA of Pomona Valley, California, and various teaching assignments in public education.

In 1998, Betty spent a month in Fontainbleau, France, at INSEAD, the European business school, studying in the Advanced Management Program. She graduated from Winston-Salem State University with a BS degree in Education and continued her graduate studies in Urban Education at California State University in Los Angeles.

CONTENTS

Editor's Introduction

Innovation and entrepreneurship are thus needed in society as much as in the economy, in public-service institutions as much as in business. . . . What we need is an entrepreneurial society in which innovation and entrepreneurship are normal, steady, and continuous.

> —Peter F. Drucker, *Innovation and Entrepreneurship: Practice and Principles*

In the ever-renewing society what matures is a system or framework within which continuous innovation, renewal, and rebirth can occur. . . . Renewal is not just innovation and change. It is also the process of bringing the results of change in line with our purposes.

> —John W. Gardner, *Self-Renewal: The Individual and the Innovative Society*

The importance of entrepreneurship and innovation in the social sector has long been acknowledged by leading thinkers. Yet remarkably little has been written on a very practical level specifically to help social sector leaders become more effective social entrepreneurs. If you visit the entrepreneurship or business section of any bookstore, you will find dozens of books to guide business entrepreneurs but few, if any, to guide social entrepreneurs.

This is an embarrassment.

The first book in our two-book series, *Enterprising Nonprofits: A Toolkit for Social Entrepreneurs* (John Wiley & Sons, Inc., 2001), was designed to fill this gap. But it was just a start; this book takes our work a giant step further. It provides you with strategic frameworks, tools, and concepts to improve your entrepreneurial effectiveness. Both of these books are the fruits of a conversation that started at the Kauffman Foundation's Center for Entrepreneurial Leadership in the spring of 1998. The conversation was about how we could help nonprofit leaders draw on the lessons and tools that have come out of decades of research on business entrepreneurship.

In order for this book to be effective, we knew that it would have to meet several special requirements. It would have to:

- Be grounded in the best thinking about effective entrepreneurship.
- Modify that thinking to make it appropriate for use in the social sector.
- Integrate that thinking with the best ideas about nonprofit management.
- Take a very practical "hands-on" approach.
- Be accessible to readers with no prior business training.

In sum, we decided to produce a down-to-earth toolkit to help social sector leaders hone their entrepreneurial skills and, thereby, serve their social missions even more effectively. We are not trying to turn nonprofits into businesses. Rather, our goal is to help forward-thinking nonprofit leaders learn from business, be more enterprising, and have greater positive, long-term impact in their chosen fields. This is very much a "how-to" book, grounded in research on and experience with entrepreneurs in both sectors.

WHAT IS SOCIAL ENTREPRENEURSHIP?

Before telling you about the content and format of this book, we had better define our subject matter, particularly for those who are not familiar with our work in *Enterprising Nonprofits.* For us, social entrepreneurship is not about starting a business or becoming more commercial. It is about finding new and better ways to create social value.

ENTREPRENEURSHIP IS. . .

Since economist Jean Bapiste Say first coined the word "entrepreneur" some 200 years ago, numerous distinguished and learned people have provided their definitions of the word. If we distill down all the thinking on what makes someone an entrepreneur, however, we would be left with this definition:

> *Entrepreneurs are innovative, opportunity-oriented,*
> *resourceful, value-creating change agents.*

WHAT MAKES SOCIAL ENTREPRENEURS DIFFERENT?

Social entrepreneurs are different from business entrepreneurs in many ways. The key difference is that social entrepreneurs set out with an explicit social mission in mind. Their main objective is to make the world a better place. This affects how they measure their success and how they structure their enterprises.

The best measure of success for social entrepreneurs is not how much profit they make but the extent to which they create social value. Social entrepreneurs act as change agents in the social sector by:

✔ *Adopting a mission to create and sustain social value.* For social entrepreneurs, the mission of social improvement is critical, and it takes priority over generating profits. Instead of going for the quick fix, social entrepreneurs look for ways to create lasting improvements.

✔ *Recognizing and relentlessly pursuing new opportunities to serve that mission.* Where others see problems, entrepreneurs see opportunities. Social entrepreneurs have a vision of how to achieve their goals, and they are determined to make their vision work.

✔ *Engaging in a process of continuous innovation, adaptation, and learning.* Social entrepreneurs look for innovative ways to assure that their ventures will have access to needed resources and funding as long as they are creating social value.

✔ *Acting boldly without being limited to resources currently in hand.* Social entrepreneurs are skilled at doing more with less and at attracting resources from others. They explore all resource options, from pure philanthropy to the commercial methods of the business sector, but they are not bound by norms and traditions.

✔ *Exhibiting a heightened sense of accountability to the constituencies served and for the outcomes created.* Social entrepreneurs take steps to assure they are creating value. They seek to provide real social improvements to their beneficiaries and their communities as well as an attractive social and/or financial return to their investors.

Social entrepreneurs seek out opportunities to improve society and they take action. They attack the underlying causes of problems rather than simply treating symptoms. And, although they may act locally, their actions have the very real potential to stimulate global improvements in their chosen arenas, whether that is education, health care, job training and development, the environment, the arts, or any other social endeavor.

TWO BOOKS AND A WEBSITE

Enterprising Nonprofits offered an essential toolkit that covers the core elements of effective social entrepreneurship. It was designed to engage, challenge, and help even the most experienced readers. It provided readers with a starting point for understanding and applying the core concepts of social entrepreneurship, and it covered a range of core topics including defining your mission, identifying opportunities, mobilizing resources, exercising accountability, managing risks, understanding customers, being innovative, handling your finances, and developing a plan. We supplemented the book with a website to provide you with information about resources and support available to social entrepreneurs. You can find the site directly at *www.enterprisingnonprofits.org* or through the Kauffman Foundation's EntreWorld website (*www.EntreWorld.org*). The EntreWorld site serves as a resource for entrepreneurs around the world.

Strategic Tools for Social Entrepreneurs adds more tools to the toolkit offered in *Enterprising Nonprofits*. The tools in this book focus on a wide range of strategic issues. Part I is entitled "Creating Value and Assessing Performance." Successful social entrepreneurs need strategic vision that has the potential to create greater social value than their competitors create and that will be attractive to collaborators, staff members, board members, funders, and the community being served. We have chapters on each of these areas, closing the section with a chapter on gathering performance information that really matters. You cannot tell whether you are creating value unless you track your performance. Part II is about strategies for "Growing and Exploring New Directions." It tackles two of the most common strategic issues facing enterprising nonprofits: developing viable earned income strategies and deciding how to build on your initial success. It also provides tools for managing the change process that is inherent in social entrepreneurship, particularly when the entrepreneur is operating in an existing organization. We close with a chapter on maintaining an entrepreneurial mind-set as you grow.

THE STYLE OF THIS BOOK

This book follows the same format as its predecessor. It has been designed to be used, not just read. Although each author has his or her own style of writing, we required some common elements of style. We wanted to make it easy for you to locate what you need and to apply the relevant ideas to your current situation. Specifically, we have used lots of headings, bullet points, charts, and summaries to make specific topics readily visible. We have even placed icons in the margin to highlight particularly important items. The icons we use are as follows:

*core
concept*   An important new concept or framework

*tool of
the trade*   A framework or technique for applying core concepts

practical tip   A tidbit of advice on effective and cost-conscious use of the tools

reality check   An in-depth example illustrating the application of a tool

gem of wisdom   A relevant quote from a person of great experience or wisdom

red flag   A potential problem, risk, trap, or complication

action step   Specific activities allowing readers to put concepts and tools to use

concept check   A review of concepts and tools previously introduced

Our efforts to create a practical and "user-friendly" book went well beyond formatting devices. We urged our authors to use examples and case studies in order to bring their concepts, frameworks, and tools to life. The examples were chosen for their power in illustrating particular key points. But remember: In this context, they are teaching tools, not endorsements of specific organizations. All organizations have their strengths and weaknesses. The examples chosen for this book tend to focus on the strengths and lessons we feel may be of use to you.

Of course, the ultimate value of this book lies in your ability to apply the tools we offer to your own situation and see improved performance as a result. If that does not happen, we have failed. No number of bullet points, icons, or examples will do this for you. You have to do it for yourself, but we can help. At key points in the text, our authors challenge you to put their ideas to the test, and they guide you through the process by offering exercises, checklists, and action steps. Of course, good entrepreneurial management cannot be reduced to formulas or cookbook-style recipes. Our frameworks can point you in the right direction, but you will definitely need to adapt what our authors suggest to your specific situation. Keep in mind that in order to make the material in this book most relevant to your own situation, you may well need to improvise on the themes of a given chapter. Improvisation is consistent with the spirit of entrepreneurship. For every practical tool in this book, our authors have endeavored to provide sufficiently detailed explanations, so that you can improvise on the details while remaining true to the underlying logic of the core ideas. In case our explanations do not go far enough, we have included For Further Reading in the Appendix. The books and articles that you find there give you an opportunity to dig more deeply into the subject matter of each chapter.

SUMMARY

Far too many "how-to" and "self-help" books are purchased with good intentions and high spirits but end up sitting on the shelf, unused. We will be deeply disappointed if that is the fate of this book. We have worked hard to make it practical and easy to use. However, if you take what it says seriously, it may require you to change your mind-set, adopt new behaviors, and develop new skills. We hope the process will be fun, and we are confident that it will be rewarding, if you see it through, but we know it will not be easy. Give this book a try and tell us, via our website, how well it works for you. We welcome your suggestions and comments. Besides, all the royalties from the sale of this book and *Enterprising Nonprofits* will flow back to the Kauffman Foundation in order to support work on social entrepreneurship.

We wish you the best in your entrepreneurial endeavor, and remember, fortune favors the prepared mind—so use this book and build learning organizations that will help you achieve your dreams and those of your community. The best is yet to come!

PART I

CREATING VALUE AND ASSESSING PERFORMANCE

Chapter 1

DEVELOPING A STRATEGIC SERVICE VISION

James L. Heskett, Professor Emeritus, Harvard Business School

IN THIS CHAPTER

Understanding the strategic service vision
Defining the value equation
Involving multiple constituencies in the strategic service vision
Satisfying conflicting constituencies
Considering the implications for social entrepreneurs

Social entrepreneurs come from a wide variety of backgrounds, they have widely varying interests, and they apply their talents to an equally broad set of challenges. But those who are *truly* successful share at least one thing in common: They have a strategic service vision. Consider these people:

- Dr. Byrnes Shouldice—treating wounded soldiers in World War II, and applying principles learned from veterinary and pediatric medicine—found that patients who take responsibility for their own recovery early in the process not only recover faster but recover with a greater degree of success. He built an extremely successful medical/surgical service around the idea.

- Commissioner William Bratton—as head of the New York Police Department from 1994 to 1996—developed a strategy around the concept that crime could be managed and that a police force should measure, manage for, and reward results rather than effort—a concept that bordered on the heretical among many criminologists and sociologists at the time. As a result, New York City became one of the safer U.S. cities after only a few short years under his leadership.

- Frances Hesselbein—as executive director of the Girl Scouts of the USA between 1976 and 1991—led the organization through a transformation centered around the concept of the individual girl as the client, with all planning, organization, and implementation directed toward helping each Girl Scout achieve her full potential. The organization achieved these goals while broadening its ethnic and racial constituency.

- Bill Strickland, Jr.—founder of the Manchester Craftsman's Guild in his native Pittsburgh—has implemented a vision intended to help at-risk youth achieve recognition in their community through the study, production, and display of art in a setting in which excellence in surroundings as well as execution communicates a stronger set of messages than their more traditionally oriented public school teachers were able or willing to do.

core
concept

While these social entrepreneurs represent different backgrounds, interests, and efforts directed to varied challenges, they all share a common philosophy, something I have called a *strategic service vision*—a set of ideas and actions that maximizes the leverage of results over efforts directed toward well-defined targets and supported with highly focused operating strategies.[1]

Entrepreneurs, whether in the for-profit or the social sector, build visions around core ideas. At the outset of their efforts, however, they are unable to foresee and plan all elements of strategies with which to achieve their goals. As James Collins and Jerry Porras have suggested in their book, *Built to Last,* they try a lot of things and keep what works.[2] The end result is made up of a number of self-reinforcing, internally consistent elements—a thing of beauty. But we often forget that the process by which it is achieved requires not only great ideas but the willingness on the part of a leader with stamina and determination to engage in a great deal of trial and error, another common trait of social entrepreneurs.

Having a framework to guide such trial and error can make the process more efficient. Hence the importance of the concept of a strategic service vision. This framework has evolved from my efforts to document factors in the success of outstanding entrepreneurial endeavors, those that have literally changed the standards for performance in their chosen fields. The original inspiration for this effort was an opportunity to observe the workings of a hospital in the suburbs of Toronto, Canada.

The Shouldice Hospital was and is a highly focused institution. It does one thing well: It fixes one type of hernia experienced predominantly by men, the inguinal hernia. And it does it with a recurrence rate that is about one-twelfth the rate of the average of North American hospital. It has come to represent the apotheosis of a social "focused factory," using a term from the production management literature to denote an organization, process, or facility designed to do one thing very well.[3] It places a great deal of emphasis on self-help and camaraderie among patients, offering a social as well as a medical experience. In fact, many of its patients don't want to leave the hospital at the end of their three to four day stay. The working lifestyle of its employees is also addressed, with an emphasis on counseling as opposed to some of the more menial nursing tasks and a regular operating schedule for surgeons. And to complement the strategy, the "hospital" is much like a country club, equipped with facilities to encourage patients to exercise constantly in order to hasten their recovery.[4]

Although social entrepreneur Byrnes Shouldice and his successors may not have known it, as the hospital's strategy slowly took shape over several decades, it had developed a number of concepts that illustrate what I have come to call a strategic service vision, a framework that has now been tested against best practice in many organizations and actually used as the basis for developing strategic direction for profit-making and not-for-profit organizations alike.

THE STRATEGIC SERVICE VISION

Entrepreneurs employing a strategic service vision target their markets very carefully, both in demographic and in psychographic terms. For years demographics (age, education, income, etc.) have been used for this purpose, probably because the information, while not always of high relevance, was more accessible. Recently more effort has been made to collect information regarding psychographics (lifestyle, likes and dislikes, fears, etc.), which can have higher relevance than demographics. For example, at Shouldice, it is important to know a person's height-to-weight ratio as well as general health characteristics in order to assess the risks associated with a surgical procedure. The hospital screens for these factors, often recommending a diet to overweight aspirants for the operation. However, Dr. Byrnes Shouldice learned early on that many of his patients selected his treatment, originally carried out in a house in downtown Toronto, because of word of mouth about the effectiveness of patients taking charge of their own recovery, beginning with their walk from the operating table on his arm.

SHOULDICE HOSPITAL'S OPERATING STRATEGY

Today Shouldice Hospital is not for all clients, particularly those who do not wish to travel to Toronto, those who don't have the time to become involved in the Shouldice experience, those who are not interested in the social aspect of the service, and those who are not particularly risk-averse. For them, same-day outpatient surgery at or near their home is preferable. But nearly 8,000 people make the trek to Toronto from all over the world annually, often queuing for weeks on the hospital's waiting list to do so.

As a result, Shouldice has positioned itself to meet the needs of a targeted group of clients who self-select (both physically and psychologically) into its service.

Nor is Shouldice for all employees. Surgeons work in teams and perform essentially the same relatively simple operation over and over. They have to take a great deal of pride in their work, enjoy working with patients, value regular operating hours, and have a high tolerance for boredom. Staff members self-select themselves into Shouldice just as patients do.

For patients, Shouldice offers both a high probability of operating success and an enjoyable social experience. For employees, it offers a high-quality, team-oriented, somewhat democratic working environment at above-market wages. These are neither products or services; they are results. One of the real lessons from observing this organization over time is that, consciously or not, it has developed a service concept (similar to a business definition) based on results, not products or services. It reflects what clients of a wide range of organizations have told us repeatedly: that they primarily buy results, not products or services.

core concept   In order to achieve these results, Shouldice has designed a process for achieving them, something we have come to term an operating strategy. Further, it's an operating strategy that leverages results over costs.

For clients, Shouldice involves them in their medical procedure from start (self-diagnosis) to finish (self-recovery). In the meantime, it creates a social atmosphere in which patients counsel each other and provide peer pressure for involvement in activities requiring exercise, critical to recovery. This is economic in two ways: It both costs little and actually substitutes client labor for staff labor. The hospital's focus on one kind of operation assures the repetitive work that contributes to outcome quality throughout medicine. For staff, Shouldice defines jobs that are pleasant, encourage teamwork, and provide ample compensation for regularly scheduled work. The result is a productive and relatively low-cost leveraging of results over costs for both clients and staff.

SHOULDICE HOSPITAL'S SOCIAL DELIVERY SYSTEM

All of this is supported by a service delivery system designed to complement the operating strategy. It starts with the physical facility, a former estate situated on ample, well-manicured grounds. And it continues with furnishings not reminiscent of a hospital as well as devices, such as stairways with low risers, to facilitate patient mobility and exercise.

Real social entrepreneurship addresses each of the several constituencies important to a not-for-profit organization. In the case of Shouldice, for example, we have seen how it has been applied to both patients and staff. The needs of families of young children being treated at Shouldice are addressed as well, with free accommodations provided for them. In the spirit of the strategic service vision, it should be noted that this also reduces care costs for a group of patients who often require a great deal of attention; their parents provide the care.

tool of the trade Dr. Byrnes Shouldice and his successor provide a working example of the strategic service vision, diagrammed in Exhibit 1.1. Since becoming aware of Shouldice, I've encountered a select group of entrepreneurs who understand implicitly these concepts and employ them to deliver superior results at low cost, proving that quality doesn't have to be traded off against costs in delivering a service. In fact, in a majority of cases, the handful of "breakthrough" service organizations they have created has actually changed the rules by which service is delivered in their respective industries, whether for-profit or social in purpose.

The strategic service vision provides a framework for developing a set of shared "core" values, practices, and measures as part of an overall

	Target Market	Service Concept	Operating Strategy	Service Delivery System
Patients	Well "connected" to medical info network	High-quality, low-cost medical outcomes	Effective medical techniques	Non-hospital, country club setting
	"First movers"	Memorable social experience	Focus on doing one thing well	Only a few ties that encourage exercise, recovery
	Value time, well-being	Membership in a life-long "club"	High involvement of carefully-screened patients	
	Reliant on recommendations of others		Quality control: Doctors fix own mistakes	-Recreation
				-Communal, TV, phone
	Ambulatory		Profit sharing incentives	-Extensive walking paths
	"Low risk" surgery candidates			Building design to facilitate climbing stairs
Employees	Competent	Regular hours	Controlled schedule	Communal dining
	Non-innovative	Good pay	Job sharing	Pleasant working environment
	Seeking "non-medical" lifestyle	A "high satisfaction" environment	Good pay/good margins	
		Good jobs	Teaming	

EXHIBIT 1.1 Shouldice Hospital—Strategic Service Vision

strategy. But how do entrepreneurs implement the strategy? For this we focus on the operating strategy and a concept my colleagues and I have come to call the value equation.

THE VALUE EQUATION

Whether purchasing a product or service, entering into an employment agreement, or making a grant to a not-for-profit organization, people want value. But just what is value? While social entrepreneurs rarely take time to define it, they implicitly understand and endeavor to deliver it. The *value equation,* based on extensive observation, makes an effort to define it. It can be depicted as:

core concept

$$\text{Value (for clients, staff, volunteers, donors, etc.)} = \frac{\text{Results} + \text{Process Quality}}{\text{Cost} + \text{Ease of Access}}$$

This doesn't, of course, include all the considerations involved in a particular transaction, but it highlights the most important ones. The experience of the New York Police Department, under the leadership of Commissioner William Bratton between 1994 and 1996—which we'll refer to throughout this section—clearly illustrates these concepts.[5]

PUTTING THE VALUE EQUATION TO WORK AGAINST CRIME

reality check

Even though crime in New York City had peaked in 1990, it was still a major concern as the Giuliani administration took over on January 1, 1994. The city had the reputation of being a high-risk environment for citizens and visitors alike. Citizens wanted reduced crime. But ironically, most of the police department's measures for performance had to do with effort (number of 911 calls answered, speed of response, etc.) instead of results. In fact, police departments around the world were being run primarily to deliver effort, largely based on a conclusion—supported by criminologists and sociologists, and others—that crime was largely a product of economic conditions such as high unemployment and low income and could not be managed to lower levels. Many on the department's police force, including a number of Bratton's 76th Precinct commanders, agreed. His challenge was to convert an organization managed for effort to one managed for results.

Bratton's first challenge was to redefine the responsibilities of precinct commanders to place primary emphasis on crime reduction, something that might seem remarkable to those not knowledgeable about police work. The next challenge was to populate the position with commanders who believed it *could* be done and to transfer to other jobs those who didn't think a 10 percent reduction in crime could be achieved in the first year. Results rather than effort thus became the focus for citizens and employees alike. This required, among other things, measuring for results (percentage reductions in major crimes), giving people the tools to achieve them (better equipment, better information, and better procedures and policies), and recognizing people for achieving them.

red flag   But results at all costs? As one of Bratton's predecessors commented, crime could have been reduced under his administration. All that would have been required would have been a suspension of the Constitution, something that few citizens would tolerate. This raises the issue of process quality, the second element of the value equation.

THE ROLE OF PROCESS QUALITY

Process quality has received perhaps more attention than any other element of the value equation, primarily from a number of researchers interested in service marketing.[6] The primary findings of this research are that there are five elements of service quality of greatest importance to customers. They are:

core concept

1. Dependability (doing things you say you will do)
2. Timeliness (doing them when you say you will do them)
3. Authority (doing them in ways that tell customers you know what you are doing)
4. Empathy (doing them with an eye to the needs of customers)
5. Tangible evidence (doing them in a way that lets customers know a service has been performed).

Elements of process quality clearly place limits on ways that a police department might deliver value to its constituents, particularly if the constituents include citizens under suspicion and even criminals.

reality check   At the NYPD, it led to the creation of an initiative to counter police brutality, an initiative that was incomplete at the time of Bratton's departure from the department but one whose importance was underlined by several recent incidents of alleged police brutality in New York. The initiative led directly, however, to a revised curriculum at the Police Academy for new recruits, one stressing the

(continued)

importance of techniques for carrying out one's duty without crossing process quality boundaries. Going one step further, the department was attempting to change the civil service exam structure for police work, stressing the importance of attitude among applicants, many of whom were applying for police work under the misguided motives of obtaining greater power and being allowed to carry (and possibly use) weapons.

In poll after poll, citizens stressed the importance of being able to have a police presence in their neighborhoods. This was a reaction to "squad car" patrolling in which teams of police covered wide areas in vehicles, rarely spending much time in any one neighborhood and becoming familiar with residents. In one way or another, citizens were stressing the importance of low "access costs," costs required to access a service. In this case, the cost might be measured in terms of time required to arrive at the scene of a crime or the time required to call for police help. But of course access to police assistance often does come at a price, the price of additional personnel. In the case of the NYPD, it had to be achieved within a relatively constant (and at times even a declining) budget.

This required the use of new techniques to reduce the cost of policing and the number of personnel needed to deliver a particular result. The subsequent "reengineering" of the department led to a number of improvements designed to free up a larger proportion of personnel to patrol the streets of New York. For example, legal processes were redesigned to allow police personnel to testify in trials by remote video, rather than spending hours (often on overtime compensation) waiting on the pleasure of a judge and the court to hear their testimony. Perhaps the most sweeping redesign of processes intended to concentrate police activity on the most-needed crimes and locations involved the creation of ComStat, a computer-driven information system combining information about the location of criminals, crimes, and instruments of crime, the three factors providing the most predictive capability regarding potential crimes and ways of preventing them before they might occur. This system, combined with weekly meetings to discuss results and specific initiatives designed to achieve them, led to a significant refocusing of the department's efforts on crime "hot spots," in itself a controversial means of achieving greater "customer access" to protection.

Repeatedly, the department encountered political obstacles to its need to reapportion effort and human resources to those areas of highest crime. The argument that a reduction in crime in one part of the city contributed to a better quality of life throughout the city too often fell on deaf ears when received by politicians who perceived a potentially high political risk if they were to concur with schemes that could involve the diversion of police coverage from their neighborhoods to high-crime areas.

This fact suggests the complexities that arise when a complex network of constituencies must be served, typical of many nonprofit organizations. Compared to the typical customer-supplier-investor set of important for-profit constituencies, most not-for-profit managers have a far more complex set of needs to serve. Nevertheless, value equation thinking can help in sorting out the constituencies and their needs in ways contributing to effective decision making. In the case of the NYPD, effort was brought to bear on high-crime areas by assigning newly minted Police Academy graduates to those areas before they received their more permanent assignments to other precincts in the city. Where there is a will and a strong enough need, there is often a way.

THE BOTTOM LINE

The value equation–oriented approach to policing in New York City produced dramatic results, far exceeding the expectations of the mayor's office and academic critics of the effort. Over three years, the department achieved a 50 percent reduction in major crimes, far greater and far sooner than that experienced in other parts of the United States, providing some support for the belief that crime can be managed. The accomplishment has become somewhat obscured by the fact that other major cities are now achieving significant reductions in crime as well. What is not as well known is the fact that a number of cities have adopted the practices and measures associated with the NYPD's value equation. Many have actually employed the former commissioner and members of his staff as consultants to help them implement results-oriented, value-driven methods.

In this case, the benefits for citizens are clear: greater safety at affordable costs. Evidence suggests that those citizens in high-crime areas have experienced a greater improvement in safety than those in other precincts. How about other constituencies? The police have received more support for and interest in their work. Larger numbers have been freed up to do the kind of on-the-ground work needed to understand neighborhood challenges and crime sources. The city has benefited in a number of ways, not the least of which are increasing revenues from tourism, rising occupancy of both office and residential space, a higher tax base, and a higher bond rating that has produced lower interest costs on the city's outstanding debt. The mayor obtained a platform on which to run for higher political office. Businesses have found it easier to attract talent to the city. In fact, probably only criminals have found it hard to detect value in the strategy, particularly in view of the fact that a serious effort has been made to increase the quality of arrests, leading to actual jail time in cases of conviction.

Commissioner Bratton's entrepreneurial ideas have changed the face of police work around the world. Other cities have attempted to implement his ideas with varying degrees of success. They have found that social entrepreneurship requires more than groundbreaking ideas. It requires someone with the vision, energy, and perseverance to lead in the implementation. Social entrepreneurs most often understand the needs of clients. Those who are truly successful fashion strategic service visions for each of several important constituencies, including donors, clients, volunteers, and communities, to name just a few.

INCORPORATING MULTIPLE CONSTITUENCIES IN A STRATEGIC SERVICE VISION

What does this all have to do with a typical not-for-profit in which donors and volunteers assume roles as important constituents? A great deal, if the enthusiasm of not-for-profit managers for these concepts is any indication.

Both the strategic service vision and the value equation are eliciting growing interest among donors. Greater emphasis is being placed on results and indicators of success in achieving them. Of special interest are ways of leveraging results over costs, whether the costs represent operating costs funded by donors or the costs of clients in accessing the service. The number of articles addressing the issue of administrative costs in relation to total grant budgets of nonprofits is an indication of a growing concern with the efficiency and the effectiveness with which grant money is being distributed. Concepts associated with the strategic service vision and value equation address this concern.

Clients of nonprofits have equal interest in obtaining results and the process quality by which the results are achieved. Too often they face undependable, untimely responses to their needs from people whose expertise they question, no matter how empathetic the service worker, whether volunteer or employee. Like the patients at Shouldice Hospital, many would gladly take a participative role in improving both results and process quality associated with the services they receive. They are rarely asked to do so.

Volunteers have a special set of needs involving both results and process. Their zeal is often high, perhaps too high. Their expectations for ways in which they might serve may be even higher. They want to be involved in "meaningful" work, too often at times that are convenient to them rather than the organization. Here the management of the strategic service vision and value equation probably means managing expectations, creating more effective screening devices to ensure that the right volunteers are selecting themselves into the organization, and organizing responsibilities for maximum involvement on a continuing basis.

Communities too have a myriad of needs that they attempt to satisfy through a handful of highly successful nonprofits in their midst. Here the challenge for the nonprofit is to resist the temptation of trying to "save the world," instead accepting only those new need-based challenges that fit the service concept of the organization—attempting, like Shouldice, to do one or a very few related things very well. The highest priorities here have to be given to both market focus (serving a narrow range of constituents and needs) as well as operating focus (doing a few things well over and over). Although this may sound less exciting than the typical nonprofit strategy that inspires volunteers and leaders alike, it is the stuff that produces long-term service success and organization viability.

SATISFYING CONSTITUENCIES WITH CONFLICTING NEEDS

What do you do when important constituencies have conflicting needs? Or when an operating strategy designed to produce maximum value for one constituency clearly reduces the value of the outcome for another?

Satisfying all constituencies simultaneously often is impossible. It's at this point that tough decisions have to be made, decisions based in part on a ranking of the importance of various constituencies. It's better to rank them on a rational basis using factors implied by the strategic service vision.

gem of wisdom

Frances Hesselbein, when she was executive director of the Girl Scouts of the USA, used to say that every organization needs to understand who its customers are and what they need. At the Girl Scouts, she was fond of saying "The donors are not the customers. Volunteers are not the customers. The customer is each Girl Scout, whom we try to help realize her full potential." This provided the organization with its mission. Time after time, she used the simplest but most compelling language to remind others in the organization of the fact that it was, under her leadership, "mission-focused, values-based (as described in the Girl Scout Promise and Law), and demographics-driven (to denote an important goal of making sure the transformation of the organization included greater diversity in membership and staff)."[7]

Social entrepreneurs not only make tough choices and communicate them effectively. They also find ways of allocating resources in ways that satisfy several constituencies simultaneously, another way of leveraging results over effort.

For example, out of lack of financing or the need to funnel most funds into the production of immediate results, many nonprofits give too little attention to the systems by which services will be delivered—information systems, physical facilities, locations, and other design features. Too often the service delivery system does not support and complement either the operating strategy or the service concept. Volunteers and staff alike are forced to wear the "hairshirt" of the nonprofit. Worse yet, clients get the idea that they deserve only secondhand, second-rate support systems. Too often such inadequacy is worn as a badge of honor by staff concerned about becoming too ostentatious in the eyes of their donors, clients, and others.

One of the most successful community-centered nonprofits, the Manchester Craftsmen's Guild in Pittsburgh, is housed in a facility of world-class design with pleasant spaces surrounding an impressive outdoor fountain. The facility is like an oasis in the middle of what has been a nondescript light industrial area rebuilt after the inner-city riots of 1968. Potential donors as well as staff and at-risk high school students participating in the guild's programs are served gourmet-style meals prepared in the chef training kitchens of the guild's sister organization, the Bidwell Training Center, located in the same building. Why the fountain? William Strickland, executive director of both organizations and world-class social entrepreneur, is quick to point out that for people who have rarely experienced excellence in anything, the architecture as well as the food is especially important in creating a culture of excellence and high expectations that program participants will be expected to fulfill while in the program and to take with them when they leave. The architecture, food, and other tangible evidence of excellence are very effective fundraising mechanisms as well. The final reason has to do with the strategic service vision for staff members. Strickland says simply, "We also have a fountain because I wanted a fountain." Not one donor has complained.

If the fountain and other elements of Manchester Craftsmen's Guild's service delivery system were isolated examples, its vision would not be fulfilled. Instead, excellence in the service delivery system at the guild complements high standards, careful measurement, results-based efforts, and a highly targeted set of clients, staff, and donors.[8]

IMPLICATIONS FOR SOCIAL ENTREPRENEURS

The strategic service vision and value equation frameworks for examining opportunities and converting them to useful results have a number of implications for social entrepreneurs, including the following 10:

1. Successful social institutions are expected and asked to do too many things, with the attendant risk of loss of focus. Thus, the following questions are of special importance: Have you clearly defined the target of your organization's efforts? Have you dealt with the most difficult question of all: Which clients will we not serve? Often the most important role of a social entrepreneur is that of saying no to such requests.

2. It's important to target clientele, staff, donors, and other important constituents on the basis of both demographic and psychographic

dimensions. It is not enough to do so on the basis of education or income. Attention also has to be paid to how such constituents think, what they need psychologically, and how they live.

3. By defining an organization's purpose in terms of results produced for important constituencies, as opposed to just products or services, social entrepreneurs build focus into the very definition of the "business."

4. Successful social entrepreneurs understand that an organization's purpose and activities need to be positioned in relation to the needs of important constituencies and the degree to which those needs are already being met by other organizations.

5. Ways of implementing breakthrough entrepreneurial ideas are delineated in terms of operating strategies designed to leverage results for important constituents over the costs (in terms of time, money, and other resources) needed to deliver the results. In this regard, social entrepreneurship often involves asking the question "What will we not do to satisfy a client or other constituent?"

6. Elements of an organization's service delivery system (information systems, facilities, locations, etc.) complement other elements of the strategic service vision and the operating strategy in highly successful strategies.

7. Successful social entrepreneurs ensure that front-line staff have the capability (including support systems, facilities, and decision-making latitude) to deliver the results and the process quality (dependability, timeliness, authority, empathy, and tangible evidence) desired by important constituents.

8. Having ensured that resources are directed to delivering results to targeted constituencies, social entrepreneurs concentrate on issues of process quality, cost, and the ease of access to their organizations' services, ensuring maximum value.

9. What gets measured is what gets managed. Important measures, controls, and sources of recognition reflect an organization's concentration on delivering results for important constituents. Successful social entrepreneurs ensure that these cornerstones for effective performance are in place.

10. Great ideas are not envisioned whole. Social entrepreneurship has a great deal to do with stamina and endurance while the pieces of a strategic service vision are put into place through a process of trial and error.

gem of wisdom

     An old marketing saw tells us that "Customers don't buy quarter-inch drills, they buy quarter-inch holes." The lesson here for profit-making organizations is that if you think you are in the business of delivering quarter-inch drills, you run the risk of being put out of business by someone who devises a method for making holes more effectively and efficiently. The lesson is just as important for enterprising nonprofit entrepreneurs.

Failure to define the mission of the organization in terms of results for each of its important constituencies can produce a strategy irrelevant to the needs of clients, the most important constituency of all. The leadership of Shouldice Hospital understands this. The former Commissioner of the New York City Police Department understands it. Frances Hesselbein and her associates at the Girl Scouts of the USA understood it. And Bill Strickland and his colleagues at the Manchester Craftsmen's Guild understand it. And in one way or another, those associated with every leading service organization my associates and I have studied over the past 20 years understand it. The challenge for all of us is to act on this understanding.

SUMMARY

Developing a strategic service vision is just as important for nonprofit organizations as it is for their for-profit counterparts in the private sector. The strategic service vision provides a framework for developing a set of shared "core" values, practices, and measures as part of an overall strategy.

Key points to remember are:

✔ Truly successful social entrepreneurs have a strategic service vision.

✔ A strategic service vision is a set of ideas and actions that maximizes the leverage of results over efforts directed toward well-defined targets and supported with highly focused operating strategies.

✔ Entrepreneurs employing a strategic service vision target their markets very carefully, in both demographic and psychographic terms.

✔ People want value. The value equation is used to define value for clients, staff, volunteers, donors, and other stakeholders.

✔ There are five key elements of service quality: dependability, timeliness, authority, empathy, and tangible evidence.

✔ The strategic service vision and value equation frameworks have a wide range of implications for social entrepreneurs.

Notes

1. For a more extensive discussion of the concept, see James L. Heskett, "Lessons in the Service Sector," *Harvard Business Review,* March–April 1987, pp. 118–126.
2. James C. Collins and Jerry I. Porras, *Built to Last* (New York: HarperBusiness, 1994), pp. 140–168.
3. For a more complete discussion of the focused factory concept, see C. Wickham Skinner, "The Focused Factory," *Harvard Business Review,* May–June 1974, pp. 113–121.

4. Shouldice Hospital and its strategy is described in some detail in James L. Heskett, *Shouldice Hospital Limited,* case no. 9-683-068 (Boston: HBS Publishing, Inc., 1983).
5. For a more complete description of this situation, see James L. Heskett, *NYPD New,* case no. 9-396-293 (Boston: HBS Publishing, Inc., 1996).
6. The most extensive of this work is reported in Leonard L. Berry, A. Parasuraman, and Valarie A. Zeithaml, "The Service-Quality Puzzle," *Business Horizons,* September-October 1988.
7. See James L. Heskett, *Girl Scouts of the USA (A),* case no. 9-690-044 (Boston: HBS Publishing, 1989), for a more complete description of what this social entrepreneur was able to achieve.
8. Strategies devised and implemented by Strickland at Manchester Craftsman's Guild are documented in James L. Heskett, *Manchester Craftsman's Guild and Bidwell Training Center,* case no. MCG005 (Boston: HBS Publishing, 2000).

Chapter 2

DEVELOPING AN ENTREPRENEURIAL COMPETITIVE STRATEGY

Jerry Kitzi, President, Social Venture Partners of Greater Kansas City

IN THIS CHAPTER

Understanding your competitive environment

Assessing your strengths and weaknesses

Selecting a competitive strategy

If you are involved in the exchange of goods and services, no matter what the supporting structure looks like, there is competition. There is competition for customers and clients, be they poorest of the poor or the sickest of the sick. There is competition for resources, be they government contracts, foundation grants, charitable donations, or the discretionary income of the potential customer or client. Competition now comes in all shapes and sizes, markets are much more diverse, and technology has dramatically changed the playing field.

In the not-for-profit sector, it is no longer acceptable to look at the word "competition" and shrug it off as a concept foreign to the mission-driven nature of the sector; not-for-profits are just as competitive as the next guy—or at least they should be. Competition, at its best, directs resources to their best use and clients to the best programs. It can lead to continuous improvement in performance and stimulate innovation. Competition helps the organization select strategies that focus on where and how to create the most value relative to others who are engaged in similar activities. These are all very positive attributes of competition.

core concept   *"Becoming competitive"* in the positive sense means, first, being smart about dealing with all the competition you face now and are likely to face in the future and then selecting a strategy that lets you focus on where and how you can *create the most value relative to others who are engaged in similar activities.* The latter may well involve more creative forms of collaboration. Healthy competition will encourage collaboration when and only when it makes sense to collaborate—the driver becomes superior performance (relative to mission objectives).

This kind of competition is good for society and for the social entrepreneurs. If someone else can serve your clients better than you can or just as well at a lower cost, you are doing them and society a disservice if you don't improve your own performance. Otherwise, you should simply get out of the way and let your potential clients go to the better provider. This kind of competitive orientation can lead organizations that are not the best to strive to become the best and those that are at the top to work hard to stay there. Being competitive in this positive way is a moral imperative, not just a practical necessity.

Accepting the inevitability of competition is the easy part (okay, the *relatively* easy part). The difficult part is understanding your competitive environment, assessing your relative strengths and weaknesses, and selecting a competitive strategy that will lead to success. These are the topics that we will address in detail in this chapter.

UNDERSTANDING YOUR COMPETITIVE ENVIRONMENT

It is impossible to have a conversation about business—for profit or not for profit—without recognizing and accounting for competition. There is quite a bit of discussion, as we move into the twenty-first century, about "who" the competition is and isn't. As a quick review:

✔ The business sector, sometimes called the "private sector," "for profit," or "market," is focused on the health and well-being of its primary constituents—its investors and owners. It is not designed to attend to the human needs of society. Yet there are more and more for-profits with a social mission emerging in the not-for-profit sector.

✔ The second sector, sometimes called the "public sector" or "government"—be it federal, state, or local—is specifically designed to include provisions to account for the well-being of society. Government has the ability to contract with either the for-profit sector or not-for-profit sector to achieve desired outcomes.

✔ The third sector, sometimes called the "independent" or "not-for-profit" sector, formed to address the needs of the underserved by typical market or government means.

According to Gene Wilson, senior vice president, Ewing Marion Kauffman Foundation, the private sector has been and continues to be the largest employer of labor in the United States at about 75 percent of the workforce. Government is next at about 16 percent, and not-for-profits follow, just under 9 percent.[1] Although small, this last sector has been realizing tremendous growth, increasing at a rate four times faster than the overall growth of the U.S. economy since 1970. It is currently estimated that not-for-profit, tax-exempt organizations have an estimated $500 billion in revenue and earn more than $100 billion in revenue each year in the United States.

CHANGING LANDSCAPES

If you are a not-for-profit provider of services, other providers with a similar mission and services in your market are considered your competition. For example, a YMCA providing youth services in an area of town is in competition with a Boys and Girls Club in the same area of town. There is competition for clients, volunteers, and of course funding.

The "blurring" of the sectors suggests in general terms, new entrants into the market from nontraditional sources. If you are a not-for-profit provider of services, there also may be competition from the for-profit sector. The blurring also suggests that not-for-profits can and are competing in for-profit markets. However, even with all the renewed talk about blurring, competition in any market between or among sectors has been around for a long time. Consider Yale University versus the State of Connecticut in 1898.

In the 1860s, the university had come to the conclusion that it had an opportunity to provide additional services for its students—housing, food services, and so forth—that could be more convenient by being located on campus. In 1869 the university completed construction of significant dormitory space for the student population.

However, this move angered local businesspeople, many of whom owned and/or operated local boardinghouses, restaurants, and other businesses that were geared toward a student market. The competition for this student market continued, and the relationship between the town of New Haven and the university became very strained.

In response, the town passed a special law that required the university to pay sales tax on anything and everything not directly related to education in the strictest sense. The townspeople declared what we now refer to as "unfair competitive advantage." Tensions grew and the university filed suit. The tax was eventually overturned in 1898 by what was then called the State Supreme Court of Errors, and the university maintained its tax-exempt status.

So, if competition between the sectors is not new, then why the increased attention now? A number of changes in our society that have occurred as we wound down the twentieth century are contributing to the blurring. Perhaps the greatest single push is related to the change in government. William P. Ryan wrote in his article "The New Landscape for Nonprofits":

> *For most of this century, society's caring functions were the work of government and charities. Government provided some services and philanthropy filled in the gaps. Since the Great Society days of Lyndon Johnson, nonprofits and government have worked together in a deliberate partnership. Under this arrangement, public agencies awarded contracts to nonprofit providers in large part because of what they were: reputable, committed, like-minded community institutions. Until fairly recently, many public agencies effectively prohibited for-profits from competing for those contracts precisely on the grounds of what they were: profit seeking, socially suspect, self-centered businesses. Government agencies are [now] outsourcing a greater proportion of work, and they are awarding contracts to providers not because of what they are but because of what they can do.[2]*

As a result, what was once considered a closed market has now become wide open, and competition rules the day. No longer is it not-for-profit organizations competing against other not-for-profit organizations. Today it's not-for-profit organizations bidding against other not-for-profits, for-profits, and even government entities not wanting to see their jobs lost by elected officials eager to outsource their work. Even the high-risk, difficult populations—the homeless, welfare moms, juvenile offenders, students from underfinanced urban public schools—are now aggressively sought by larger for-profit corporations.

Today there is greater demand for "results" not only from public agencies but from charities as well. The public got tired of hearing about $200 hammers, $300 toilet seats, the welfare state, a failing public education system, and all the rest. The public also got fed up with the scandals involving their favorite charities. The United Way scandal of a few years ago and constant media attention to the misuse of funds by religious leaders and televangelists broke trust. The public wanted better results and accountability for tax dollars *and* charitable gifts.

As a result of that collective frustration, changes occurred. The Government Performance and Results Act of 1993 and United Way of America's Outcome Measures Initiative *Measuring Program Outcomes: A Practical Approach* have literally transformed the way thousands and thousands of government agencies and not-for-profit organizations approach their work.[3] Decisions are now based on cost and value created—changes in conditions, behaviors, or level of satisfaction of the client(s).

Finally, the changing face of philanthropy related to the New Economy—venture philanthropy and e-philanthropy—and the huge transfer of wealth from one generation to the next at the beginning of the twenty-first century influenced an additional change in the not-for-profit sector. The emphasis on earned income and alternative sources of revenue to diversify funding took many not-for-profits into for-profit markets, where they are competing successfully.

According to James Austin of Harvard Business School, the so-called commercialization of universities has motivated many high-powered research colleges and universities, more than ever before, to generate revenues from their areas of competitive advantage. In the area of basic sciences, patents by universities in 1969 ranged between 25 to 50 per year. By 1989 that figure rose to 200 to 900 patents. The University of California generated $63 million in revenue related to patents in 1996 and Stanford, $43 million. Total discretionary funds generated by patents for budgets in major research universities grew from approximately 1 percent in 1969 to 8 to 9 percent by 1996.[4] "Patent or Perish" is replacing "Publish or Perish."

There are countless examples of youth-serving organizations, the faith community, schools, arts programs, and the like that have shed the image of "charities in need" and have become competitive players in for-profit markets.[5]

However, introducing the mind-set of earned income may represent a significant culture shift and should not be taken lightly. There also are a number of legal issues that should be considered, such as exempt function income and dual use of assets or facilities. You must take your organization through either the Internal Revenue Service's "organizational test" or "operational test" to determine if the activities of the organization still fall under exempt status.

There is no longer a very distinct line in terms of who can play in what market and for what purpose. The determining factors for success are focused more and more on results, and organizational structure is taking a backseat in terms of importance. As a result, industry analysis becomes increasingly important to keep a competitive position in the market. Competition should be viewed as a tool to help you achieve better results versus the perception of a struggle with heartless competitors.

INDUSTRY ANALYSIS

The process of developing a competitive strategy begins with an analysis of the playing field you are attempting to enter or are currently engaged in. Fundamentally, a competitive strategy requires a thorough understanding of the acceptable standards or levels of value that are expected in your particular market or industry. In the for-profit sector, where quantifiable measures such as average profitability for an industry exist, determining a competitive strategy is a much cleaner process. The not-for-profit sector has much softer measures.

core concept Simply stated, an *industry analysis* is a process of mapping your environment. Where are you going? Who's traveling with you? Who is trying to enter the picture? What are the barriers?

COMPETITIVE STRATEGY FRAMEWORK

tool of the trade Certain factors of analysis used in the for-profit sector are applicable in the not-for-profit sector. Michael Porter presents one of the best models of industry analysis in his book *Competitive Advantage: Creating and Sustaining Superior Performance.*[6] With Porter's work as a guide, you can use the model in Exhibit 2.1 to help you analyze your organization and its position and/or potential in the market. If you were pursuing an earned income strategy, Porter's book would be extremely helpful in assessing your potential in a given market.

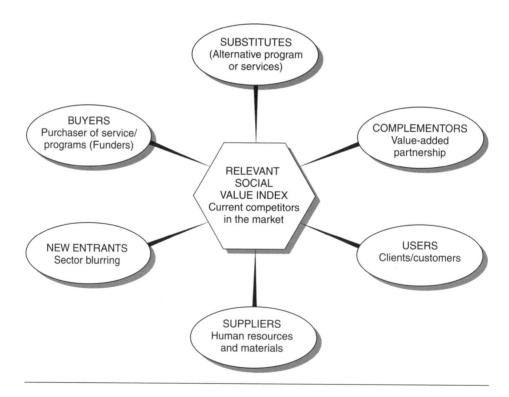

EXHIBIT 2.1 Understanding your competitive environment industry analysis model.

Relevant Social Value

Determining the degree of social value created by a particular service or product is subject to many different interpretations and priorities. It is therefore important to try to identify the value created relevant to other offerings that are similar in nature. The value of your service is then also measured against the priorities in your community. It is important to determine the acceptable or expected social value of a service or product and its place in the overall priorities of the community within which you operate.

Next, an analysis of the cost for the service or product is needed to have a full understanding of the relevant social value. Providing a service or product that delivers a better outcome but at a cost that is greater than what the market is willing to bear will not necessarily help you gain competitive advantage. A clear picture of the cost and benefit of your program or service positions you to determine how to develop a competitive strategy for customers, resources, or both.

Urban school districts keep data on reading scores, math scores, dropout rates, graduation rates, percentage of graduates going on to college, and much more. This information is very useful for districts trying to develop strategies to improve scores and rates. Likewise, it is very useful for competitors such as private schools competing for students in the same demographic market. If the average graduation rate for public schools in an urban area is 60 percent and a private school can boast of a graduation rate of 75 percent for the same target population, then there is competitive advantage for the private school. The social value created is higher than the social value created by the public schools. The analysis has relevance because the value is similar in nature.

Attractiveness is further determined by the cost of the service to the buyer. (In this scenario, the buyers are the parents of the students or donors providing scholarships.) For years parents were willing to pay the added premium (tuition) for private education because the perceived value was worth the added cost compared to the tax-supported public education system. When school vouchers appeared on the scene in the 1990s, private schools, which had been competing well, gained a substantial competitive advantage for the students when cost was leveled for parents.

Again, the market is always changing, and as a result valuation of a service or product is always changing. Using the same education scenario, new entrants in the market in the late 1990s such as charter schools and for-profit education management businesses such as Edison Schools increased the competition for students and placed greater emphasis on positioning the service relative to the expected value. Private schools lost competitive advantage because charter schools positioned themselves to create the same social value as private schools but without the added cost of tuition.

Finally, there are also opportunities to set the relevant social value for certain industries where there currently isn't a quantifiable measure. For example, most people perceive organizations like scouting, Campfire, and 4H as having good social value. People generally perceive positive value based on their own experience or general observations of the benefit youth realize by participating. But what are the measures? There are no standards for levels of "leadership attained" or "acting more responsible." Yet there is competition among the players in the market for the youth (users) as well as contributions from donors (buyers). Scouting gains a temporary advantage every time an Eagle Scout award is referenced in relation to the celebrity status of past presidents, senators, astronauts, and captains of industry, etc.

Michael Porter says, "Competitive strategy must grow out of a sophisticated understanding of the rules of competition that determine an industry's attractiveness. The ultimate aim of competitive strategy is to cope with and ideally, to change those rules in the firm's favor."[7]

Therefore, when no generally acceptable or easily quantifiable measure of relevant social value exists, create one! Create your competitive advantage and demand for your service or product before someone else sets the standard. In the true spirit of entrepreneurship, determine at least a qualitative measure of the value created by your service or product so a marketing strategy can help establish you as the leader in the industry. It is smarter to set the pace than respond to it.

action step   List in the center of the model the value created by your service or product. Next, list the other players in the market who are trying to deliver value that is relative to what you are creating. This is the core of your map—the first step in understanding your competitive environment.

New Entrants

Market needs change with time. New entrants into markets are a regular occurrence albeit heavily influenced by the barriers to entry. Take, for example, the area of human services. The Welfare Reform legislation of 1996 (specifically, Temporary Assistance to Needy Families, TANF) further advanced the trend of privatization and outsourcing. As a result, there has been a significant increase in the number of for-profits bidding on contracts for services from government agencies. There are a number of private-sector entities in the mix. At this point, no one is bigger than aerospace manufacturing giant Lockheed Martin. According to Audrey Rowe, senior vice president and managing director of Children and Family Services for ACS Corporation, formerly known as Lockheed Martin IMS, "The public sector wanted more business-like approaches and results. We believe we can successfully bid for contracts that allow us to use our strengths—advanced technology systems, and streamline processes to get the desired results for the contractor and our shareholders."[8]

Lockheed Martin acts on basic assumptions and sound business practice. It uses its primary asset—advanced technology systems—and employs the best and the brightest from their fields of expertise, provides excellent training and development, and streamlines processes in areas that have been traditionally encumbered by government process and hierarchy.

In Baltimore City, for example, Lockheed Martin successfully bid for the state's child support collection contract. The barriers to entry were minimal, so the company quickly staffed up and opened offices complete with the information technology systems that created superior efficiencies. At the end of the first year, it had achieved its goals for collection. In the process, Lockheed Martin saved the government $2 million and achieved the return projected to shareholders. All that despite having provided 4 percent salary increases for staff and advanced staff development opportunities—a luxury in the not-for-profit sector.

action step   Take a view of the landscape and analyze the possible new entrants into your market. List them in the "New Entrants" area of the model.

What is different about their makeup and approach? Will current policy being debated at the local, state, or national level open up the market to new entrants? What are the barriers to new entrants (things like community acceptance and reputation)? Can you compete or at least hold your share?

Buyers

There is tremendous competition for the financial resources needed to sustain and grow a social enterprise. It is extremely important to know who you are competing against for philanthropic grants, government contracts, private charitable donations, membership fees, United Way funding, tax credits, and corporate giving, as a few examples. How much money is available in your community? What are the priorities of perceived social need? One quick place to look is the funding priorities of your local United Way. The volunteer process of United Way provides a fairly reliable reflection of what community members see as the most important issues they would like their gifts directed toward. Also try the published reports of foundations, many of which are now located on the Internet, to see priorities in charitable giving.

You also must project your clients' ability to use what, if any, discretionary revenue they have at their disposal. Small focus groups can help you determine if your service has a perceived value that people are willing to pay for. Likewise, it is important to determine if discretionary money is being used to purchase a substitute product or service.

Many organizations are also seeking alternative sources of funding; commercial loans, lines of credit, social venture capital funds, and cause-related marketing are just a few examples. These are more difficult, especially if you are a new start-up and don't have assets to show. What bank wants the publicity of foreclosing on a sweetheart public charity? But there are more and more new sources of buyer power being generated from the wealth of the New Economy, and people like you are competing for them.

List the known buyers (funders) of the services or product you are providing in the "Buyer" area of the model. Who are the sources of revenue for your competitors? List any potential buyers who are interested in the value created but not yet engaged in the purchase of services being offered by you or your competitors. And keep in mind the buying power of the user if scholarships or sliding-fee scales are associated with your programs or services.

Users

It is important to clarify that customers, in this sense, mean the *users* of the service or product. Since many, many social enterprises offer services or products that are subsidized, the buyers or funders of those services or products are also referred to as the customers—they are buying the service for those in need who do not have the means to pay. Here customer means the end user—the person for whom the benefit is intended.

Whether you are a nursing home, day-care center, school, place of worship, homeless shelter, or art gallery, someone else wants the same people you are intending to serve or sell. Sure, there is client creaming and patient dumping. But the minute you think no one else wants your clients is the minute you start your decline. You cannot count on customer loyalty if you have developed a mind-set of "They need us" or "No one else wants them."

red flag
The social value created by your service or product has to have relevance to the user. The need you are addressing may have the highest priority of the community. It may represent a significant area of interest to buyers such as foundations or government. But it also has to have relevance to the user.

For example, traditional youth-serving organizations have long offered programs and services for school-age youth during after-school hours and the summer months. The goal of most of the organizations was to contribute to the positive development of youth. Many of the larger organizations, such as Boys and Girls Clubs, 4H, scouting, Campfire, and the Ys, offered training for youth workers and specific programs for youth emphasizing leadership development, educational opportunities, and recreation, to name a few.

During the 1970s and 1980s, the rise of drug use, crime, violence among juvenile offenders, and a more public awareness of teenage pregnancy created a huge demand for the development of prevention programs across the country. Many of these same youth-serving organizations were viewed as logical distribution channels for these programs. Foundations, government agencies, and other funding entities invested heavily to try to offset these alarming trends.

However, the prevention programs were marketed to the buyers, not the users. Prevention programs were perceived as a needed resource for troubled youth. Little attention was paid to understanding the target market's wants or needs. Kids didn't want programs and services designed to "fix them" or "prevent" them from being kids. The more emphasis placed on prevention, the greater interest in what they were being prevented from. Middle and late stages of adolescence are times of experimentation, active learning, and a search for identity. Youth didn't want prevention; they wanted to participate in meaningful activities during after-school hours and summer months. So they stopped showing up.

Dorothy Stoneman and a group of colleagues and youth started the first YouthBuild program in East Harlem in 1978. The purpose of the YouthBuild program is "to unleash the positive energy of youth and unemployed young adults to rebuild their communities and their own lives with a commitment to work, education, responsibility, and family."[9]

Dorothy Stoneman asked, "If I put myself behind you, how would you change the community, what would you do?" The youth said *they* wanted to fix up their neighborhood. Youth wanted to participate. Other social entrepreneurs started asking the same kind of questions, and youth themselves started social enterprises in response to unmet needs. Young people ages 16 to 24 acquire construction skills, complete a high school education, and receive leadership training while rehabilitating or constructing new housing for low-income and homeless people in their communities. Participants spend alternate weeks on the job site and in school. The program promotes involvement in a positive peer group and in the community.

By the early 1990s the program had been replicated across the country in 11 cities. YouthBuild USA was founded in 1990 to coordinate the expanding network. By the end of 1999 there were approximately 129 YouthBuild program sites in 40 states. The proposed federal appropriation for fiscal year 2000 was $75 million. Stoneman is now president of YouthBuild USA and a recipient in 1996 of a MacArthur Fellowship.

Today there are a significant number of new youth development organizations like YouthBuild, Youth Volunteer Corps, Youth as Resources, Youth on Board, Youth Service America, and Young Audiences that are youth led or youth driven. Their central theme is participation in meaningful activities rather than prevention from doing something.

action step List the demographics of the target population (users) for your market by the "User" area of the model. Part of your industry analysis should involve surveying users to make sure you are creating value relevant to their wants and needs.

Suppliers

The greatest asset you can have in your social enterprise is your human resources—the people who get it done, both in terms of executive leadership and line staff. There is a great deal of job-related stress and typically low pay associated with the public and not-for-profit sector. There is high turnover in many fields.

Well-trained competent staff are recruited just as hard by for-profits and not-for-profits alike. Lockheed Martin attributes its success in part to the rigorous training and development of staff recruited from the rank and file of government and not-for-profit organizations.

Program volunteers are another extremely valuable resource. Just because they offer their time, energy, and passion without compensation doesn't mean they should be undervalued or overlooked. Someone else is just as needy for volunteer help. Consider the cost of the resources for the training and coaching to position them for effectiveness.

Board members are vital to your organization's success, and good ones are highly recruited and often sit on more than one board at a time. In many communities the not-for-profit sector has not done a good job of recruiting and developing adequate numbers of board members who can contribute their expertise, perform governance functions, and raise or contribute financial resources for a social enterprise.

Fixed costs of materials, space, and other supports are resources that figure into the relevant social value of your service or product. For example, many foundations seeking research and evaluation services opt for less expensive services but with perceived similar value (credibility) offered by not-for-profit organizations or even for-profit organizations rather than the traditional providers—universities. The high cost of administrative overhead tacked on to most university proposals became a barrier to their competitiveness, in spite of their lower staff costs for graduate assistants.

action step   List the sources for the various types of human resources needed for your service or program in the "Suppliers" area of the model. Staff and volunteers from your competitors are a source. Schools and universities, volunteer coordinating organizations, and listings on the Internet as e-philanthropy expands are additional sources.

Many enterprising not-for-profits are merging or developing shared back-room partnerships as a way of lowering costs and gaining competitive advantage. Make note of any of your competitors who use this method of cost control.

Substitutes

There are always substitutes for your product or service. Keeping with the youth services example used earlier, youth-serving organizations that provide programming during nonschool hours and summer months are competing with television, the Internet, video games, the underground economy, amusement parks, gangs, or kids just hanging out with their friends. All of these substitutes are in essence competition for programs or services offered by youth-serving organizations. Again, ask: Does the value created by your service or product generate enough interest by your customer (user) to compete against substitutes?

 List any of the potential substitutes in the "Substitutes" area of the model. There are numerous sources of survey data and market research regarding what your target population (user) is doing with its time (and money). Colleges and universities, Gallup polls, marketing firms, and other sources on the Internet all have research data or market survey information. Determine how attractive the substitutes listed are compared to your offerings.

Complementors

An additional factor to consider in an industry analysis that is gaining more and more relevance relates to what Adam Brandenburger and Barry Nalebuff call "complementors" in their book *Co-opetition.* They define a complementor as "a complement to one product or service that makes the first one more attractive. Hot dogs and mustard, cars and auto loans, television shows and *TV Guide,* fax machines and phone lines, digital cameras and color printers, catalogs and overnight delivery services . . . these are just some of the many, many examples of complementary products and services."[10]

Is there a potential partnership or alliance that adds value to your service or product that improves your competitive position? Is there a complementor out there that could benefit from your service as much as you can benefit from its service? Is there a way to make the partnership profitable for both parties in terms of social value created and resources generated?

For example, the result of welfare-reform legislation was a mandate for welfare recipients to reenter the workforce. Both for-profit and not-for-profit providers sought out government contracts to provide job training and job readiness services. A significant complementor to the service provider is child care. The traditional barrier to low-income families staying in the workforce is affordable child care. A government contract is usually a higher source of revenue to the child-care provider than the subsidies provided by foundations and United Way.

Therefore, the two providers complement one another. Together, their proposal is more attractive to the buyer—in this case, a state government that understands the importance of finding solutions to the child-care barrier. And the relationship is also more attractive to the user—the welfare recipients who have concerns for quality child care while they are preparing to reenter the workforce. The relationship with the complementor improves the competitive position of the job training program relative to the value created by the other competitors in the market who may not be offering a value-added service. And the proposal creates more demand for the complementor—the child-care provider who now is positioned for fees from a potentially more lucrative funding source.

action step List in the "Complementor" area of the model potential partnerships or alliances that create value added for both parties. Who would benefit from a partnership with you while at the same time increase the value of the service or product you are offering?

The industry analysis model is a significant tool to help you understand your competitive environment. Use the completed map of the environment to help develop your competitive strategies. What do you have to do to increase market share or compete against "new entrants" to your market? How should you market your services in a way that makes them more attractive than the potential "substitutes"? How do you increase the value of your service or product so it becomes more attractive to your "buyers" and "users"? What can you do to make yourself more attractive to suppliers? And where are the potential partnerships with "complementors" that improve your position in the market?

You and your planning group should answer these questions when determining your competitive strategies. But before you determine your strategy, you first must determine your relative strengths, weaknesses, and development needs to become competitive.

ASSESSING YOUR STRENGTHS AND WEAKNESSES

The next step in determining competitive strategy is to assess your relative strengths and weaknesses. Numerous resources offer methods of organizational assessment. Most usually offer variations of a SWOT analysis—Strengths, Weaknesses, Opportunities, and Threats. The strengths and weaknesses refer to the internal capability. The opportunities and threats are external factors or environmental conditions that could impact the work of the organization. Let's take a look at two key assessments: the organizational assessment, and the service delivery assessment.

ORGANIZATIONAL ASSESSMENT

For the purposes of competitive strategy, any analysis or assessment must be done in the context of the market you are in and in relation to the competitors in your market. And it is important to account for the subjectivity of assessment. Senior management is usually overly optimistic about weaknesses, small samples can skew feedback, and any strength taken to an extreme can become a weakness.

tool of the trade   First assess the overall strengths and weaknesses of the organization. Simple techniques involve creating a list of the most-valued functions of the organization—an internal audit. This list will provide a general assessment of the organization's capabilities. For example:

✔ *Governance.* Rate the capability of the board. What is the composition in terms of professional need, diversity, and so on? How well does the board perform its functions, and what is the level of commitment to the mission?

✔ *Management and organization.* Rate the capability of leadership and senior staff. Analyze the structure, policies, reporting systems, and guiding principles.

✔ *Culture.* Are there organizational values and beliefs, an entrepreneurial spirit, and a commitment to outcomes? Is there an environment where all associates, volunteers, and advisors know that their contribution is making a difference?

✔ *Strategic thinking/planning.* Do you have clarity of mission, outcomes, and strategies? Are there marketing plans and processes for the evaluation of the organization's effectiveness?

✔ *Resource development.* Do you have viable fund development, reporting, and communication plans? How good are your vendor/supplier relationships, partnerships, and alliances? Do you have fee structures and other earned income potential?

✔ *Financial management and reporting.* Rate the financial controls. Do you have an annual budget, monthly financial reports, annual or semiannual audits, adequate insurance, and timely reporting to appropriate sources?

✔ *Marketing and promotion.* Have you done a market analysis? Do you have a marketing plan, process for customer feedback, and/or focus group surveys? Are your communication materials consistent with marketing plan and strategies?

✔ *Human resources management.* Do you have good personnel policies, updated job descriptions, annual performance reviews, professional development opportunities, and compensation and benefits that are competitive within your market? Do you provide quality orientation activities and training for volunteers?

✔ *Physical plant and equipment.* Do you have the technology to create efficiencies and effectiveness (quick access to information, rapid response, quality control, financial accountability, etc.)? Are your facilities safe and inviting to customers, and do they facilitate a positive working environment? Does your program-related equipment exceed quality standards, and is it well maintained?

The examples just mentioned can provide valuable insight into the general strengths and weaknesses of the organization. It does little good to tack on programs and services if the core of the organization is weak and fragile. Yet the not-for-profit sector is notorious for being undercapitalized. Work to strengthen the primary functions of the organization as a part of your competitive strategy. Rate yourself or have others—users, buyers, suppliers, complementors, and even competitors—rate you on a strong to weak scale (1=strong, 5=weak).

SERVICE DELIVERY ASSESSMENT

The next step is to do a more specific assessment of your programs or services. This assessment is more specialized to the market within which you are operating. Make a list of the attributes of your service or program that are highly valued. Create this list by observing competitors' offerings in the market as well as your own. Use the completed Industry Analysis to study what your competitors seem to value in relation to service delivery. Add in the perspective of the "buyers" and "users" as you create your list. Use the strong–weak scale and determine your rating.

tool of the trade   The list will be specific to your service or product. What is highly valued in the delivery of child-care services will be different from what is highly valued in the delivery of services for the homeless. However, some potentially transferable categories include:

✔ *Effectiveness.* Rate the relative social value created by the service or programs in terms of changes in behavior, condition, or level of satisfaction for the user. How does it compare to your competition?

✔ *Cost.* Are there average fees to the customer for the service or product? How do your fees compare to those of the competition?

✔ *Personnel.* Rate the capabilities of managers and staff—teachers, counselors, coaches, volunteers, and others—associated with the service or program. Does your competition have better-trained or more qualified providers?

✔ *Convenience.* Consider your location, facilities, and times that facilitate high customer usage. How do the factors compare to the competition's user rates?

✔ *Quality.* Are you providing the highest-quality service or product relative to the target population and cost?

Again, these are just a few general examples. Get as specific as you can in analyzing all aspects of the programs or services that your organization offers. You must have a thorough understanding of the strengths and weaknesses of the organization and its programs and services prior to developing a competitive strategy. It does little good to tack on programs and services if the core of the organization is weak and fragile. You may find that the best strategy may be limited to strengthening your organization to come up to a level of competition with the rest of the pack.

The general wisdom among strategists is to build strategy on your strengths rather than devoting scarce resources to fix your weaknesses. However, serious weaknesses must be dealt with for the organization to be healthy.

red flag   Finally, involve your buyers, users, suppliers, complementors, and perhaps your competitors in the assessment process. Keep in mind that not all the feedback you get from these constituent groups will be positive. Don't take it personally, but do take it seriously, and build your strategies accordingly.

SELECTING A COMPETITIVE STRATEGY

Whether you are a 100-year-old agency delivering services to the poor or a brand-new start-up working for a cleaner environment in the twenty-first century, your mission statement is the single most important document to keep you—and your employees, volunteers, board members, customers, clients, and other stakeholders—competitive, focused, and energized.

Once you and your team—including your board—are clearly focused and committed to the mission, you can then identify *how* to compete, with *whom* to compete, and for *what*. The mission is the foundation upon which you build all of your strategies and marketing plans. It reflects what you and your board value most.

However, mission alone is clearly not enough. *Competitive strategy ultimately is determined by how you plan to create the greatest value within your competitive environment.*

POSITIONING

You should have been able to recognize, based on the findings from the Industry Analysis and Organizational Assessment, some of the unique features of your programs, services, and/or the organization itself that actually differentiates you from the pack. Being the leader in achieving the best results for your clients or customers at the lowest cost to buyers is the preferred position. However, it may not be the best competitive strategy that will provide sustainable growth over time. Identify your position in terms of cost and results. List the specific factors that further differentiate you from your competition.

The Positioning Matrix in Exhibit 2.2 is designed to help you in the process of identifying your competitive strategy.

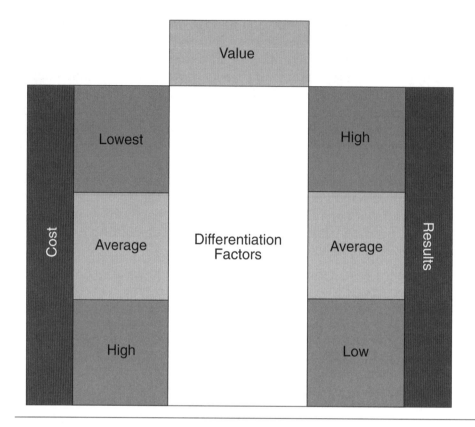

EXHIBIT 2.2 Positioning matrix.

Cost Strategies

Your buyers are interested in purchasing the best possible results for the best price. According to Porter, "A firm has cost advantage if its cumulative cost of performing all value activities is lower than competitors' costs."[12]

What is your position in relation to the rest of the competition in terms of cost? Are you lower, higher, or about average? If you are lower, you can develop strategy around sustaining the leader position in efficient costs for programs and services. If you are average or higher, you may want to pursue strategies to lower costs. To be more competitive, you must analyze the things that are driving your costs up and develop cost-reduction strategies accordingly.

Again, some of the costs, whether they are fixed (like rent) or variable (like office supplies), are fairly standard for all nonprofits. Others will be very specific to your particular program or service. You and your team should be able to list them and identify strategies to lower costs in a number of areas. Try looking at the following:

action step

✔ *Human resources.* The primary costs for nonprofits are human resource costs. Salary and benefits account for the largest percentage of program costs. And a shortage of labor can contribute to higher costs by driving up the price you have to pay to attract talented and committed workers. Where are you in the salary range for workers relevant to your program and services? Are you lower in human resource costs but experiencing high turnover? Are there ways for you to incorporate paraprofessionals or volunteers? For example, Habitat for Humanity is in competition for resources to do affordable housing with community development corporations, also dedicated to developing affordable housing for low-income families. Habitat drastically reduces the labor cost by using volunteers in the construction of homes, thereby giving it a cost advantage over its competitors.

✔ *Materials/supplies.* Materials and supplies needed in the delivery of programs and services is another significant cost for most nonprofits. Identify the materials and supplies associated with your programs and services. Are there ways to lower your costs? Are there opportunities for group purchasing with other providers, donated materials, or other cost-reduction strategies? For example, the Guadalupe Center, a human service organization in Kansas City, Missouri, recognized the high costs associated with the delivery of meals and snacks for the hundreds of children, youth, and senior citizens participating in its programs. The center launched a culinary arts/catering service as a strategy to lower its food costs. The culinary arts program trains workers who are then placed in the catering service that provides snacks and meals to the child-care center, charter school, and senior center at a reduced cost compared to previous arrangements. The catering service also provides additional earned income from private catering activity to apply against administrative costs linked to the center.

✔ *Volume and usage ratios.* Decisions about contracts for services from government sources, United Way, or other donors often focus on the cost per client ratio. What does it cost to provide service to one client? Increasing the volume of clients or customers served helps to reduce the cost ratio. However, many times the ratio is predetermined, as in the case of child-care services—with licensing tied to the proper adult-to-child ratio guideline. Are you offering classes to an average audience of six when you could get the same results with a class size of 60? Can the use of technology increase your reach? Are there other innovative ways to reduce your cost ratio by increasing your volume?

✔ *Partnerships and alliances.* Are there partnerships, alliances, or outsourcing strategies that could lower your costs? Is there a complementor that increases the potential for results without being an added cost to your organization? Are there innovative ways to alter the form or volume of materials or services from suppliers that reduce their cost, resulting in lower cost to you? Can a strategic partnership increase revenue for your service or product?

There are other elements of your programs or services that add value, but at a price. Look to the list of value activities produced for the Strengths and Weaknesses assessment. What action can be taken to help support using cost advantage as part of your competitive strategy?

Results Strategies

You also may seek to develop strategy by being the industry leader in achieving desired results. Having quantifiable measures for changes in behavior, condition, or level of satisfaction by the user of services is critical for a strategy in this area.

Where did you position yourself in the matrix? Are you the industry leader, just average, or struggling to achieve results? If you are the leader, what are the actions you can take to sustain your position over time? If you are in the middle of the pack, what actions can you take to get better results? Some of the same drivers of cost can contribute to achieving desired results. Consider the following:

✔ *Human resources.* Do you have the human resources necessary to achieve desired results? Are staff and or volunteers adequately trained and qualified to achieve results? Are there diversity issues being overlooked? Is there a learning curve that will eventually allow service providers to achieve desired results? Does the culture reward innovation and customer service? What actions could you incorporate that will improve the delivery of program and services for better results?

✔ *Materials and supplies.* Are the materials and supplies appropriate for your audience? Are you using technology to your advantage in the delivery of educational services, customer tracking, and so on? Even the best trainers get mediocre results with poor curricula. Poor facilities, bad timing, and safety issues all take away from attendance and effective program delivery.

✔ *Volume and usage ratios.* Have your cost-cutting efforts increased volume but reduced the individualized attention the customers sought? The nature of the sector calls for more individualized attention for better outcomes. Are your classes too large? What actions can you take to improve in this area?

✔ *Partnership and alliances.* Did you recognize a complementor in the Industry Analysis or Strengths and Weaknesses assessment that has the potential to improve your results? Is there a logical partnership or alliance with an organization that saves you cost but delivers value added to your service and ultimately better outcomes for the client? Does the organization have a partnership and alliance policy?

Differentiation Factors

Besides being the leader in your industry for delivering results or cost advantage, another factor differentiates you from the rest of the competition—your market niche. Your market niche can be influenced by the uniqueness of the program or service, the way you market it, unique use of technology, etc. You should have been able to recognize some of these factors as you progressed through the Industry Analysis and Strengths and Weaknesses assessment. They are the things that make you uniquely qualified or a perfect fit to deliver the program or services you are offering. Once identified, your competitive strategy should build on these assets. Take some time to consider the following:

- ✔ Quality
- ✔ Reputation
- ✔ Target market

Quality. There really is no substitute for quality programs and services. For-profit markets do a better job of weeding out poor-quality products or services. Customers simply don't buy them. However, market discipline does not do as good a job weeding out inefficient, ineffective, or poor-quality *human* services. Highly subsidized services don't have to meet the market test as rigorously because funding streams don't usually get firsthand information about the quality of the service or product they are buying for the underserved. And there is little user power, since often the people in need have little, if any, choice in selecting services available.

There is also concern that the privatization and outsourcing movement will further jeopardize the delivery of quality products or services. This concern is based on the perception that for-profits are only in it for the money and, if push comes to shove, when government programs experience cuts, the private sector contractors will pass along those cuts to the customer in the form of poor quality rather than accepting smaller profit ratios. However, for-profits, perhaps better than not-for-profits, understand the importance of quality. Consider the words of Audrey Rowe of ACS Corporation, formerly known as Lockheed Martin IMS, when asked the question about the tension between quality and profit: "We carefully analyze our costs and the offering of the government agency. If we don't believe we get an acceptable return and deliver a quality service, then we make the decision to walk away and seek out other opportunities. We will not sacrifice quality or return—our reputation is based on it!"[13]

Again, quality is broadly defined in terms of target population and cost. As an example, there is a perceived difference in quality when you compare staying at the Ritz as compared to Motel 6. Yet there is room for both in the marketplace. And Motel 6 risks losing its customer base if it doesn't deliver a quality product and service. If you want to be competitive, you have to have a commitment to quality.

Reputation.   Closely linked to quality is reputation. The reputation organizations have in the community is a significant asset or liability depending on the nature of the reputation. Quality programs and services, trusting relationships in the community, collaborative efforts, and good communication and outreach all contribute to reputation.

Most not-for-profits offer services in a neighborhood. Some may offer services in a satellite location, such as a school building, or as part of a collaborative effort with another not-for-profit. For the most part, however, they are single-site locations (although the Internet may dramatically change the way services are delivered and to whom). You may not have the lowest costs, but because of your reputation in the community you actually may be positioned to be the most attractive program or service to users and buyers. Therefore, the reputation you have in the neighborhood can better position you with clients and buyers while creating barriers to new entrants.

Target market.   Are you going for a broad or a narrow target market? The uniqueness of the clients and customers you are attempting to serve actually may provide a differentiation factor. Are you dealing with a population that no one else is attempting to serve? Is there a subset in the population that no one else has tried to serve or is uniquely qualified to serve?

YouthBuild was mentioned earlier in this chapter. YouthBuild is one of the leaders in the market in terms of creating value through the results it gets with youth. However, the organization also has one of the highest cost ratios in the industry. It positions itself as creating great results for a very difficult population—school dropouts and adjudicated youth—at a cost that may seem high but actually is much lower than the substitute: incarceration. YouthBuild's competitive strategies have helped to create greater sustainability in the form of a multi-million-dollar appropriation in the federal budget.

Results and cost are the two primary factors that differentiate you from your competition. The above-mentioned factors also may provide you a unique position in the market and an opportunity to develop a competitive strategy that reflects that asset. Are there other factors unique to what you do, how you do it, or where?

As an example of how an organization looks using the Positioning Matrix, consider an organization mentioned earlier—Habitat for Humanity.

Habitat creates good, affordable housing opportunities for low-income families. Habitat competes in a market with community development corporations and for-profit urban redevelopment corporations.

Habitat has positioned itself to compete on a number of different fronts. The new homeowner (user) values the product—a good affordable home—and is involved in the building process (results). The volunteers (suppliers—labor) value the experience—a well-organized program that creates a very real sense of accomplishment and giving back to the community. Volunteer labor also lowers the cost of building the house (cost). The contributors and donors (buyers) have a sense of creating social value when they witness service in action (volunteers) and homeowners who are thrilled with the end result. The product has high value to all the stakeholders.

Since the primary resource is volunteer labor, Habitat has a significant cost advantage over the competition. Habitat takes advantage of the unique features that differentiate it from the literally hundreds of community development corporations (CDCs; not-for-profits) and other related entities that develop housing for the working poor in both rural and urban core settings. Granted, the CDCs have a different strategy to get to their goals of housing. But from a distinctive market niche, Habitat has competitive advantage because of results, cost, and the unique differentiating factor of the spirit of giving back created by its volunteer strategy.

Millard Fuller, the founder of Habitat for Humanity, was admittedly surprised at the success of Habitat. His vision back in the 1970s was to eliminate poverty housing in the rural South and in developing countries. Today, thanks in large part to an estimated 200,000 volunteers, Habitat constructs on the average of one house per hour somewhere in the world each and every day of the week. There are more than 1,400 independent Habitat for Humanity affiliates in the United States and more than 150 affiliates working in 800 locations in 53 other nations.

Once you have identified the direction you want to take in terms of positioning your programs and services, you have to assess the sustainability of your strategy. Keep in mind the simple fact that others will follow. Review and push your strategies in order to maintain superior performance.

SUMMARY

Competitive strategy is ultimately determined by how you plan to create the greatest value within your competitive environment. The nature of the sector is about creating value for those in need. Being the leader in achieving desired results is the primary driver in competitive strategy. Cost is also a significant factor in creating strategy that can position your organization for sustainability in the future. Finally, being creative in determining the factors that differentiate you from the pack and building on those factors is fundamental to competitive strategy. Use the tools to help you outline your direction, set a goal, and develop the strategies you believe are doable and sustainable.

- ✔ Competitive strategy ultimately is determined by how you plan to create the greatest value within your competitive environment.

- ✔ An industry analysis is a process of mapping your environment and determining your organization's position and/or potential in the market.

- ✔ The sectors will continue to be blurred. Success is focused more on results and less on structure.

- ✔ Determine the acceptable or expected social value of a service or program and its place in the overall priorities of the community within which you operate.

- ✔ When no generally acceptable or easily quantifiable measure of relevant social value exists, create one!

- ✔ It does little good to tack on programs and services if the core of the organization is weak and fragile. Make an honest assessment of how you stack up.

- ✔ Whenever possible, try to build strategies on your strengths rather than to devote scarce resources to fixing your weakness.

- ✔ Being the leader in achieving the best results for your client or customer at the lowest cost to buyers is the preferred position for competitive advantage.

- ✔ Competition is a natural occurrence. At its best it directs resources to their best use and clients to the best programs for the ultimate outcome—results!

Notes

1. Information presented by Gene Wilson, Senior Vice President Ewing Marion Kauffman Foundation, to ALADN, National Association for Academic Librarians, March 1999. Data for Mr. Wilson's presentation was gathered from *Giving USA Report,* 1998 and *Independent Sector Almanac,* 1998.
2. William Ryan, "The New Landscape for Nonprofits," *Harvard Business Review,* January–February 1999, p. 128.
3. The guide to outcomes measurement is found in the United Way publication, *Measuring Program Outcomes: A Practical Approach,* Item number 0989, United Way of America, 1996.
4. These points excerpted from a presentation by James Austin at the Independent Sector Spring Research Forum: *Crossing the Borders, Collaboration & Competition Among Nonprofits, Business and Government,* March 1999.

5. Numerous examples are presented in *New Social Entrepreneurs: The Success, Challenge and Lessons of Nonprofit Enterprise Creation,* Jed Emerson and Fay Twersky, (San Francisco: Roberts Foundation, 1996).
6. The Competitive Strategy Framework used in this chapter is influenced by the Industry Analysis model presented by Michael E. Porter, *Competitive Advantage: Creating and Sustaining Superior Performance,* (New York: The Free Press, 1985) p. 5.
7. Ibid, p. 4.
8. Interview with Audrey Rowe, Senior Vice President & Managing Director, ACS Corporation (formerly Lockheed Martin IMS), March 1999.
9. Interview with Dorothy Stoneman, Executive Director, Youth Build USA, July 1999.
10. Adam M. Brandenburger and Barry J. Nalebuff, *Co-opetition,* (New York: Doubleday, 1998) p. 12.
11. Michael E. Porter, *Competitive Advantage: Creating and Sustaining Superior Performance,* (New York: The Free Press, 1985) p. 12.
12. Ibid, p. 97.
13. Interview with Audrey Rowe, Senior Vice President & Managing Director, ACS Corporation, (formerly Lockheed Martin IMS), March 1999.
14. Information compiled from Habitat for Humanity's *Annual Report,* 1998.

Chapter 3

COOPERATIVE STRATEGY: BUILDING NETWORKS, PARTNERSHIPS, AND ALLIANCES

Jerry Kitzi, President, Social Venture Partners of Greater Kansas City

IN THIS CHAPTER

Creating a cooperative strategy
Recruiting willing and able partners
Negotiating with partners
Managing the partnership

In today's complex, ever-changing world, the need for complex solutions for society's ills requires new forms of enterprises, partnerships, and alliances for greater effectiveness. Social entrepreneurs are leading the way as the sector changes to meet these complex needs. The intentions of the sector are not changing—creating social value—but the business practices and relationships needed in this new day and age *are* changing.

Developing a cooperative strategy is as important as developing a competitive strategy in response to these changes. Partnerships create opportunity to expand reach, achieve better outcomes, realize better uses of resources, and improve your position in the market.

Specific skills are associated with cooperative strategies and managing partnerships. Assessing viable partnership opportunities, developing effective negotiating skills, and developing measures of accountability with new partners are just a few examples of the entrepreneurial toolbox needed for you to be effective in the twenty-first century. The bottom line is that you and others can be better together.

CREATING A COOPERATIVE STRATEGY

As Brian O'Connell states in *Building Coalitions, Collaborations, Alliances, and Other Partnerships:*

> *From the beginning of Independent Sector (IS), we began to receive inquires about coalition building and over the years the interest escalated. This was not idle curiosity but a pervasive and growing need to figure out how to create coalitions, collaborations, federations, and other partnerships necessary to deal with the increasing complexity of needs in our communities and nation. Increasingly people are finding that their causes are linked to others, and that solutions are not possible without allies.[1]*

There are a variety of cooperative strategies and structures—all based on relationships—and there is a continuum of involvement and commitment based on the type of strategy and structure you choose. However, the first step in building a relationship in any form of a cooperative strategy begins with you.

There must be:

✔ Clarity of purpose

✔ A clear recognition of the benefits and risks

✔ An appreciation by the board and the executive for the time and energy it takes to work in any new relationship to accomplish a common goal

✔ A sincere commitment to a cooperative strategy in order to accept the changes that might occur as roles and responsibilities shift in relation to services delivered

The decision for partnerships is generated most often from *within* the organization, and, most often, it's a planned strategy. If you are trying to grow, stay competitive, or gain competitive advantage as well as to discover innovation within your own organization, a cooperative strategy is one of the best tools to get it done.

MOTIVATION AND BENEFITS

In her book *Forging Nonprofit Alliances*, Jane Arsenault suggests that this simple question be answered during the strategic planning process:

> *Given the specific environment in which we operate, can we more effectively deliver on our mission statement by working together with one or more partner organizations, or by working alone?[2]*

A thoughtful process that includes an analysis of the opportunities and threats that are present or predictable in the foreseeable future combined with a careful look at your organization's strengths and weak-nesses should allow you to answer that question. You also can engage in a much deeper analysis using the Industry Analysis model described in Chapter 2.

Motivation

It is important to be clear about your motivation for choosing a cooperative strategy in order to effectively determine who your partners should or could be and how to position yourself in the negotiation processes that will follow.

Do you form or join a network, partnership, or collaboration because you see a role for your organization in an effort that will produce greater results for the customer or client in need? Are you one of the missing pieces that, when added to the puzzle of complex services, help to complete the picture? Or is your motivation more internal? Are your services or products better by adding a particular partner(s)? Is it smarter to contract out rather than add a program area for which you don't currently have staff or other resources?

It may be a little idealistic to think that every social entrepreneur is forming partnership and alliance strategies solely for the purpose of improving outcomes for those in need. The reality is that it's often about money. In many cases, an organization joins a collaborative effort because it provides the organization an opportunity to generate new revenue.

Being clear about your motivation for entering into a partnership can help you be better focused when searching for partners, accepting offers, or stating your position in a negotiation process. The last thing you would want to do is misrepresent your position to a potential partner.

Cooperative Strategy Benefits

Forming relationships with other organizations/suppliers provides numerous benefits. Some examples of potential benefits include:

✔ *Expand your capability.* A partner(s) may increase your capacity to serve your customers through value-added services, facilities, technology, and so on. As an example, many youth-serving organizations, limited by their own facilities, are now partnering with schools to provide after-school programs and services. Expanded capability improves your competitive position for grants and contracts.

✔ *Extend your reach.* A partner(s) may provide access to more customers and clients for your services. As an example, a local Head Start program partners with a local community health center. The children in the Head Start program get needed health screening and services and the health center adds families to its client population. Extended reach increases your share of a potential market and provides an improved competitive position.

✔ *Lower your cost.* A partner(s) may create cost savings for particular services that improve your offerings to customers. By adding an established partner, you can eliminate the added cost inefficiencies of start-up—learning curve, new equipment, staff training and development, and so forth. Partners also may share costs, thereby lowering administrative overhead.

✔ *Provide more effective services or products.* A partner(s) may offer services or products that, when combined with your offerings, improve the chances for desired outcomes. A unique combination of complementary offerings can create a service of greater perceived value, such as in the case of child-care services added to the site of a job-training program.

✔ *Gain increased access to additional resources.* A partner(s) may increase your access to grants or contracts, volunteers, technical expertise, or media exposure.

✔ *Improve your credibility.* Partners from either the for-profit or the not-for-profit sector actually may improve your standing based on the value of their name and reputation. You may gain competitive position based on the association with an established, well-respected business organization or institution.

Cooperative strategies are effective ways of establishing relationships that can help bring about desired results. It begins with you answering this basic question:

> *Can we deliver on our mission statement more effectively by working together with one or more partner organizations or by working alone?"*

You must be clear about your motives for seeking or accepting external relationships. You and your board must consider the benefits and implications for the work required for whatever type of partnership you are entertaining. At the very least, the board should carefully consider policies that support cooperative strategies. Support for such policies creates the freedom for the executive to actively network and seek out partnerships that improve the bottom line.

Ultimately, in this day and age, the nature of the work practically demands some form of external relationship to get the job done. We truly can be better together.

FORMS AND FUNCTIONS

You have probably been at a meeting, conference, or some social gala where the featured speaker, addressing the topic of collaboration, provided the following definition: "An unnatural act between two or more consenting organizations."

It gets a laugh because collaboration in a competitive environment isn't generally considered to be a natural act. However, there is increasing pressure—especially from buyers such as foundations and government agencies—for multiservice collaborations to cover the complex needs of those at risk. But the term "collaboration" is used loosely. It's great to say you are collaborating with XYZ organization, but often it's more something people *say* they are doing than what they *actually* are doing.

Sharon Lynn Kagan of the Busch Center in Child Development and Social Policy of Yale University offers the following definition of *collaboration:*

core concept

> *Organization and inter-organization structures where resources, power, and authority are shared and where people are brought together to achieve common goals that could not be accomplished by a single individual or organization independently.*[3]

Simply stated, collaboration means sharing resources, power, and authority for a common goal. Now think about the last time you said or heard someone say "We are collaborating" with someone. Were they really willing to share resources? Were the decisions of the collaborative effort truly primary and each own agency's needs secondary? The fact is, many people say they are in collaboration but they may be far from it.

Arthur Himmelman produced an expanded definition of multiorganizational working relationships in his monograph, *Communities Working Collaboratively for a Change.*[4] In it he offers practical categories of working relationships. (See Exhibit 3.1.)

A variety of forms for interorganizational relationships can add value to your organization. Using Himmelman's work as a starting point, it's critical to recognize that each level of relationship involves a greater degree of trust and communication. And, as in any relationship, trust takes time to build and grow. Rosabeth Moss Kanter, in her article "Collaborative Advantage: The Art of Alliances," describes the best business alliances as being similar to the best marriages.[5] They go through stages of courtship, engagement, shared responsibilities, and so on. Consider some of the following structures when analyzing potential for partnership.

Networks

Arthur Himmelman defined networking as exchanging information for mutual benefit. A common example of this type of strategy is making and receiving referrals with a partner to provide value-added services to clients. There need not be a memorandum of understanding or other formal document mandating this form of cooperative strategy. However, it still requires a level of trust. You are sending your clients to some other organization to receive services you believe they need—probably services that you do not provide—in order to help your clients get the results

	Networking	Coordination	Cooperation	Collaboration
Definition	Exchanging information for mutual benefit	Exchanging information and altering activities for mutual benefit and to achieve a common purpose	Exchanging information, altering activities, and sharing resources for mutual benefit and to achieve a common purpose	Exchanging information, altering activities, sharing resources, and enhancing the capacity of another for mutual benefit and to achieve a common purpose
Relationship Characteristics	Informal Initial level of trust, limited time availability, and a reluctance to share turf	Formal Dedicated time, higher levels of trust, and some access to each other's turf	Formal Substantial amount of time, high levels of trust, and significant access to each other's turf	Formal Substantial time commitments, very high levels of trust, and extensive areas of common turf
Resources	No interagency sharing of resources required	Controlled by the individual organization	Limited sharing of resources (may require written or legal agreement)	Full sharing of resources, risks, rewards, and responsibilities

EXHIBIT 3.1 Communities working collaboratively for a change.

they desire. Your reputation is at stake with that referral—if the clients get treated badly, it reflects back on you. Therefore, there needs to be some form of relationship—trust in that person or organization's ability to deliver a quality service or product.

Other examples of networking relate to the sharing of information for the purposes of planning new community partnerships or innovations in service delivery. Sharing trends in client services and needs, sharing accomplishments with new approaches, or sharing failures from specific approaches in order to improve the overall delivery system for better outcomes all require some level of trust and commitment on the part of participants.

For example, a coalition forms to address the needs and concerns of early childhood care and education providers in a community. Coalition members are concerned about workforce preparation and retention. Members brainstorm approaches and share strategies in order to design a better training and development system. Members also may consider a strategy for advocating for legislation that could address financing issues—resulting in better pay and subsequent improved retention of the workforce. Members in this scenario share information for the purpose of creating benefit for *all* participants, including themselves.

Coordination

Multiservice partnerships often are managed more easily by a coordinating agency. These intermediaries or lead agencies accept the role of facilitating communication among participants, holding participating organizations accountable for results, reporting back to funding sources on progress toward goals, and, in certain circumstances, actually providing subcontracts with participating organizations for specific services.

Many examples exist of coordinated efforts that do not involve the use of a coordinating agency or an intermediary organization. In these scenarios, each participating organization takes responsibility for its particular piece of the service under a measure of mutual accountability. In effect, each organization holds itself and each other participating organization accountable to create systems or services that become more user friendly or effective. There is no one single organization monitoring progress but rather a collective or mutual understanding and expectation.

Participation in coordinated service partnerships requires high degrees of trust and commitment. There are high expectations for referral and performance, and participants become more dependent on each other for overall outcomes achieved.

It is often necessary to have responsibilities detailed in writing, such as in a memorandum of understanding (MOU). In the HomeFront case (see page 50), the partners called their written document a Commitment to Service Agreement. Whatever the term, a formal written document usually provides a rationale for the relationship and explicit expectations of each participating entity. The MOU can help clarify the meaning of words used in the negotiation of work responsibilities. The old "You do this and I'll take care of that" method leaves lots of room for interpretation and potential hard feelings down the road.

red flag   Don't be afraid to get it in writing!

If there is going to be any exchange of resources between entities, a legal agreement or contract is in order. The agreement should detail the terms and conditions of the relationship. The scope of services, time lines, rates of exchange, dissolution clauses, and more should be clearly stated and usually prepared and reviewed by your attorneys and theirs. This is a must in this type of collaborative relationship.

Cooperation

At one end of a continuum, the form and function described in the definition of cooperation by Himmelman can be practiced with a formal legal agreement between partnering organizations or contract for services. In essence, you contract with another organization whose specialty is a service that, when united with your organization's offerings, make for better outcomes for the customer and clients.

CASE STUDY

HOMEFRONT

The Coalition for Community Collaboration is a multidisciplinary network of approximately four hundred family-serving organizations, institutions, businesses and individuals. The Coalition works to build and strengthen the capacity of the Kansas City metropolitan area to better serve families. The Coalition established a Family Congress as a means of creating a forum for families to voice their concerns/needs.

One of the recommendations that gained considerable support among the membership was the need for a central phone number for families to call with concerns and questions about parenting. A group of family service organizations which were members of the coalition responded to the call from the Family Congress. They agreed to form a partnership that would establish a central phone number for the metropolitan area.

Callers would be referred to participating organizations that provided the type of information or services requested and closest to the callers' geographic area if a visit was needed. One of the participating organizations, Heart of America Family Services, stepped forward and offered to serve as the coordinating organization—fielding the calls and making the appropriate referrals. The pilot program—which was promoted by the local PBS broadcasting affiliate, KCPT—quickly generated a call volume of approximately 500 calls per month.

Based on the success of the pilot, funding was secured for continuation of the phone line and staff support. The partners implemented a plan for increased publicity, and responses from families have been very positive. Only those organizations agreeing to a set of performance standards, indicated by signing a "Commitment to Service Agreement," are listed on the publicity materials and referred by the coordinating organization, Heart of America Family Services.

Contracts may be with other not-for-profit organizations or with for-profits. The changing nature of this work—or "blurring of the sectors," as it is now called—has been characterized by a significant number of for-profits entering into the traditional not-for-profit domains. (This is discussed in greater detail in Chapter 2.) The public is also demanding more businesslike approaches for more efficient use of tax dollars. As a result, more government agencies at the local, state, and national level are awarding contracts to for-profit businesses to manage caseloads of welfare recipients, rebuild inner-city neighborhoods, remove trash, and manage our schools.

In many of these cases, the for-profits will turn around and contract with local not-for-profits in order to capitalize on their assets: local trust, a trained and culturally sensitive workforce, and accessible facilities. The for-profits have a huge advantage in terms of resources and cash flow to outbid the small not-for-profits for these contracts. However, you can successfully negotiate significant subcontracts provided you are able to value your assets high enough to make the partnership viable for you.

Another significant consideration in contract services is the issue of control. There are countless examples of excellent innovations in service delivery, curriculum with proven potential, or new program ideas that have died or remained obscure because of the issue of control. Who gets the credit? Who owns the intellectual property? Who owns the copyright? Who gets the patent? These questions define the battlefield of control that pits partner against partner—all in the name of "common good."

It's somewhat understandable especially in some situations, where millions of dollars in product revenue are potentially at stake. Consider the biotechnology field. There may be a series of legal agreements between a major university's research department, for-profit biotech firm(s), venture capital investors, and public funding agency(s)—all expecting the discovery of a protein that will save humankind and fill their coffers.

Strategies that involve legal agreements or contract for services are more complicated and require high levels of trust and commitment. Yet they also provide tremendous opportunities to benefit your organization and the customers you serve.

At the other end of the continuum of forms of cooperative relationships are examples based on a simple verbal agreement—a simple "You do such and such and we will do this and that." In these examples there is usually not an exchange of resources, but it may be the beginning of a relationship that eventually leads to a greater degree of trust and accountability. And, of course, there are any number of examples along the continuum that create the right blend of formality and accountability relevant to the depth of trust and commitment between partners.

Collaboration

Collaboration is without question the most difficult form of strategy for working relationships if held strictly to the definition of Himmelman and Kagan. The characteristics—sharing resources, power, and authority—demand the greatest commitment from the participants, and collaboration requires the most fundamental sacrifices of power and control.

In a collaborative relationship, the organization's priorities are secondary to the collaborative's priorities. It is very difficult for boards of directors—the people who are the last resort for fiduciary responsibility for the organization—to release already scarce resources to another entity (the collaborating group) without some say or control over how those resources will be used. Many have tried, and most have resorted to coordinated efforts or contract services to avoid such a dilemma.

Unfortunately, it is this very mind-set that undermines collaborative relationships in the first place. According to Himmelman:

> *Organizations that enter into collaborations with a commitment to sharing power must understand the true meaning of the word share. It is not about someone having to give up their power or someone else taking it. Organizations should begin with a understanding that the power needed to have the capacity to produce the intended results must be shared among all players without one being dominated or controlled by another. A commitment to sharing power resolves the contradiction between giving and taking.*[6]

It is more likely that organizations that say they are working collaboratively with someone actually mean they are trying to cooperate and work in sync with others. When push comes to shove, nearly all of the structures of so-called collaboratives fit within the cooperation and coordination categories.

There are many examples of relationships that form to increase or sustain social value, and there are plenty of examples of not-for-profits developing relationships with other like-minded enterprises—in both the for-profit and not-for-profit sectors. The structures for these relationships vary in one form or another but generally are designed to increase revenue or help gain efficiencies and effectiveness. Regardless of the structure, organizations can be better together.

RECRUITING WILLING AND ABLE PARTNERS

Forming lasting partnerships with other individuals and organizations means working through a quality recruiting process that identifies likely partners, introduces you to them, and then is able to convince them into joining with you.

GETTING STARTED

Good partnerships can be characterized as good relationships between two or more people with mutual self-interests. The easiest way is to start with the relationships you have and explore the possibilities. Who, from within your circle of professional work relationships, would be a likely partner to help you improve services? Who would add value to what you do? Who could you add value to?

Coalitions, task forces, councils, or any other similarly named group that has, as its primary purpose, the creation of a forum for like-minded individuals to network and discuss issues relevant to their common vision is another excellent place to look for potential partners. These networks of committed, like-minded people are the R&D ground for the sector. Innovations that emerge from brainstorming and multiservice partnerships that offer more comprehensive or better-coordinated services usually spring up out of these types of gatherings. Also, by working on projects together in these networks, you get a better idea about whom you might want to contract with for services that will improve your offerings rather than trying to start such services yourself.

Assess potential partners on past performance. The will may be there, but the ability may be weak. Look at their materials to make sure there is fit with your organization. Be careful to avoid drifting from your mission for the sake of partnership. And keep in mind the analogy of partnerships being like marriages. They may look great up front, but once the honeymoon is over and the real work begins, things may look very different. Take the time to develop the relationship!

action step

If you are seeking partnership, you should have a plan for making first contact. If you know the enterprise you want to partner with, find out where there is a relationship between the organizations—you and the other executive, relationships among board members, other leadership, and so on. Consider the following steps:

✔ *Create a climate for partnerships.* Clearly stated policies—agreed to by the board—should set the stage for partnerships and alliances. These policies should be established and reviewed as part of the organization's planning processes. The policies should be broad enough so the executive is free to pursue partnership opportunities without the burden of cumbersome processes of review.

✔ *Create a plan for contact.* Know whom you want to pursue and what you are seeking. Be clear up front before making contact about what you hope to gain from the partnership. Establish a contact person(s), time line, setting, and so on.

✔ *Create a positive meeting environment.* Try to build off existing relationships in requesting a first meeting where you will express interests. Offer to host the meeting in a suitable location (your place)—provided, of course, it would not create a perceived disadvantage for your potential partner.

✔ *Create a negotiating team.* Whether you are considering an agency consolidation or the development of a simple memorandum of understanding for a network of providers, form a negotiation team. The team could be you and another colleague (staff or board member) if it is a simple negotiation with another organization about referral, for example. Or it could be a larger team with select staff, board members, legal counsel, and so forth if it is a substantial negotiation regarding new structures and legal entities.

Unlimited opportunities exist just outside your door or website for value-added partnerships. The first place to start is with the professional working relationships you have already cultivated. Second, explore possibilities within the networks aligned with your work. Finally, brainstorm with board and staff to list those to whom you can add value or who could add value to your efforts.

CROSSING THE SECTORS

Most of the discussion to this point has centered on cooperative strategies within the not-for-profit sector. Many of the networks and coalitions that serve as a forum for generating new ideas, a neutral setting for debate, and a common space for building relationships are comprised of organizations driven by a social mission. Usually the majority of contract services are developed with other socially driven organizations.

Cause-related Marketing

However, the changing face of philanthropy has created additional opportunities for social entrepreneurs. Generally speaking, corporate giving by socially responsible businesses is still alive and well in this country. Firms still encourage their employees to "give back" through corporate volunteerism programs. What has changed is the way businesses are providing financial resources. Corporate giving programs, even in light of the strength of the markets in the late 1990s, were changing for a number of reasons. Regardless of the reason, the fastest-growing form of corporate giving is now termed "cause-related marketing."

Other variations of cause-related marketing opportunities in cross-sector partnerships exist, such as licensing agreements and transaction-based promotion—partnerships that provide resources to socially driven efforts while also creating improved public image for socially minded businesses. Many major corporations are jumping on the bandwagon that seems to have started with American Express and its efforts to support the restoration of the Statue of Liberty.

American Express donated approximately $1.7 million toward the effort to restore Ellis Island and the Statue of Liberty, based on a percentage of purchases by users of their American Express card. American Express reported the use of its bankcard increased by 28 percent in the year it introduced the campaign (1983) as compared to the previous year.

And online shoppers probably have noticed the growing number of sites, like Amazon.com, that provide an opportunity to determine where

CASE STUDY

JIM FRUCHTERMAN AND ARKENSTONE

reality check

Jim Fruchterman was one of the founders of Calera Recognition Systems, a high-tech company specializing in optical character recognition (OCR) in California's Silicon Valley. Jim and his partners raised $25 million from venture capital firms to launch Calera. The business has been very successful and has since merged to form CAERE Corporation (a company that was acquired by ScanSoft, Inc., in 2000).

Along the way Jim became very motivated to produce technology equipment specifically targeting physically challenged people but found very little interest among the same venture capital firms he had been successful with in the past. In most cases the market for this population was too small to produce the kind of returns venture capital firms specializing in high technology were accustomed to. Jim chose to start Arkenstone—a not-for-profit high-technology firm specializing in OCR—anyway. Arkenstone was able to produce and sell reading machines for the blind at about half the cost of anyone else in the for-profit market. From there Arkenstone expanded into other special needs areas.

Today, some 10 years later, Arkenstone has a budget of approximately $5 million, with more than 90 percent of total revenue generated by product sales. Arkenstone has a workforce of 35 people, many of whom were engineers, marketing executives, and production managers from the more lucrative for-profit high-tech firms of Silicon Valley.

Jim attributes the success of Arkenstone to his committed colleagues, staying focused on the mission, and strategic partnerships and alliances. For example, the more scanners, chips, and the like, that Jim was able to acquire through cause-related partnerships, the more prices were lowered, thereby increasing his reach to those in need at home and in the workplace. A few examples:

- Intel recently provided $1 million worth of product donation (chips). Intel realized an excellent opportunity to act on its commitment to corporate social responsibility. In the process, an engineer with Arkenstone developed a tactile version of Intel's logo so even the blind could be reminded, "Intel inside."
- Sony provided a single copy of its digital map technology at cost, $35,000. Sony, as a commitment to their corporate social responsibility, then provided permission to Arkenstone to make copies for the production of talking maps for the blind at a much more realistic price of $500 each.
- IBM has offered technology development contracts that allow Arkenstone to market new products at a low cost, with recognition going to IBM for supporting the technology development.
- Hewlett-Packard has donated scanners.

(continued)

The relationship Jim had with a board member of Calera—who was also an executive with Intel—led to the partnership agreement with Intel and an eventual product donation. Many other examples of strategic applications of cause-related marketing partnerships and contracts with for-profits and government agencies began as simple relationships built from within the networks Jim is connected to in Silicon Valley.

the percentage of sale designated for donation to charitable cause should be directed.

Cause-related marketing in all its forms has literally exploded, going from $75 million in 1988 to over $535 million by 1997, according to an article in *Time* magazine.[7] Even local hometown businesses are getting into the act. When asking the question of partnership opportunities, expand the horizon to include business partners as well.

Risks

You and your board must consider very carefully the pluses and minuses in any partnership strategy or structure. There is an "ethical line" that must be considered before serious negotiations take place. You have to gauge—no matter how difficult to measure—the value of the relationship, either financial or programmatic, in comparison to the value of a mission sacrificed. Keep in mind that it takes years to develop organizational integrity and trust with the stakeholders and customers and clients you are attempting to serve.

 red flag   What are the potential risks associated with the proposed partnership? For example, what do the large corporations whose businesses produce potentially harmful although unintended consequences do in the name of corporate social responsibility—say, the manufacturing giant whose emissions pollute the air or water, the paper mill that reduces forestry, tobacco companies, beer distributors?

Should the university accept the research grant from the tobacco company? Should the small college accept the scoreboard with the beer distributor's logo on it? Should the environmental protection advocacy group license their logo to the furniture manufacturer?

Alan Andraesen, in "Profits for Nonprofits: Find a Corporate Partner," cautions nonprofits about the potential negative consequences by making alliances with corporations:

✔ *Wasted resources.* Building a cause-related marketing alliance requires a lot of time and effort. If the venture fails, the nonprofit organization, which probably has a small staff and limited resources, may find that it has seriously compromised other activities relating to its mission.

✔ *Reduced donations.* Individuals and foundations may reduce their donations if they think that the nonprofit does not need their help anymore or if they are turned off by the nonprofit's ties to the for-profit world.

✔ *"Tainted" partners.* Many corporations enter into relationships with nonprofits because they want to bask in the glow of their esteemed partners. In some cases, however, a partnership with a tainted for-profit corporation may prevent a nonprofit from carrying out its mission.

✔ *Contrary marketing.* A corporate marketer may use tactics that conflict with a nonprofit's image and strategy.

✔ *Structural atrophy.* The nonprofit can come to rely too excessively on corporation funding.[8]

Once you step outside the confines of your own organization, you invite risk. But is that risk any more dangerous than standing still? Are you and your board clear about the ethical line you are willing to draw, in light of the potential resources? Have you done the right due diligence in relation to your proposed partner?

These are critical questions to ask as you and your board consider a cooperative strategy in cross-sector partnerships. Careful planning, skillful negotiations, and clarity of expectations (in writing) can improve your chances for organizational benefit while at the same time help you avoid any negative consequences.

NEGOTIATING

We are engaged in some form of negotiation from the time we get up until the time we go to bed. Who is taking the kids to the soccer match after school? How much for that old chair at the garage sale? Where are you going for lunch? What is the percentage of sales that will be contributed to your organization in exchange for the rights to your logo in a cause-related marketing negotiation?

Any time you are interacting with another person(s) for the purpose of exchanging something of value, there is negotiation. And there are skills that can make you a more effective negotiator.

NEGOTIATING STYLES

What kind of negotiator are you? Are you a win-at-any-cost type of negotiator? Or are you a kinder, gentler negotiator more concerned with avoiding conflict and creating harmony? This isn't to suggest that any style is wrong, for most of us have different styles and incorporate them according to the situations we find ourselves in.

A practical book about negotiation is *Getting to Yes,* by Roger Fisher, William Ury, and Bruce Patton of the Harvard Negotiation Project.[9] This resource, and a follow-up piece by Fisher and Danny Ertel, *Getting Ready to Negotiate: The Getting to Yes Workbook,* can help you improve your skills. Consider this excerpt from *Getting to Yes:*

> *Whether a negotiation concerns a contract, a family quarrel, or a peace settlement among nations, people routinely engage in positional bargaining. Each side takes a position, argues for it, and makes concessions to reach a compromise. When negotiators bargain over positions, they tend to lock themselves into those positions. The more you clarify your position and defend it against attack, the more committed you become to it. The more you try to convince the other side of the impossibility of changing your opening position, the more difficult it becomes to do so. Your ego becomes identified with your position. You now have a new interest in "saving face"—in reconciling future action with past positions—making it less and less likely that any agreement will wisely reconcile the parties' original interests.[10]*

It is also essential to recognize how negotiation styles have changed over time. Bill Breslin, of the Program on Negotiation Clearinghouse at Harvard Law School, believes organizations are shifting to more of a problem-solving style of negotiating. He says, "The history of negotiation is tied into labor-management relations, which were formal and ritualistic. There has been rapid evolution in the field. The last ten years have seen a shift towards shared problem solving."[11]

Fisher, Ury and Patton explain the distinctions in Exhibit 3.2.

tool of the trade   If the order of the day is partnership for solving complex problems, then negotiation becomes an even more critical skill. Today there is a shift to more of a problem-solving style of negotiation. However, many, many negotiators still are using older methods. You first have to know your own style. Take a profile instrument. Second, you must broaden your skill set. A number of books and training opportunities are available to help you hone your skills. Last, and this will be discussed in greater detail in the next section, negotiate as a team—you and a board member or other colleagues from your organization. Better together applies to teamwork in negotiation too.

SUCCESSFUL METHODS

As mentioned earlier, an entrepreneurial culture that promotes seeking out opportunities for cooperative strategies increases your organization's chances for success. Identify potential partners, develop an action plan, and establish a negotiation team as appropriate. The team should:

Soft	Hard	Principled
Participants are friends.	Participants are adversaries.	Participants are problem-solvers.
The goal is agreement.	The goal is victory.	The goal is a wise outcome reached efficiently and amicably.
Make concessions to cultivate the relationship.	Demand concessions as a condition of the relationship.	**Separate the people from the problem.**
Be soft on the people and the problem.	Be hard on the problem and the people.	Be soft on the people, hard on the problem.
Trust others.	Distrust others.	Proceed independent of trust.
Change your position easily.	Dig in to your positions.	**Focus on interests, not positions.**
Make offers.	Make threats.	Explore interests.
Disclose your bottom line.	Mislead as to your bottom line.	Avoid having a bottom line.
Accept one-sided losses to reach agreement.	Demand one-sided gains as the price of agreement.	**Invent options for mutual gain.**
Search for the single answer: the one *they* will accept.	Search for the single answer: the one *you* will accept.	Develop multiple options to choose from; decide later.
Insist on agreement.	Insist on your position.	**Insist on using objective criteria.**
Try to avoid a contest of will.	Try to win a contest of will.	Try to reach a result based on standards independent of will.
Yield to pressure.	Apply pressure.	Reason and be open to reason; yield to principle, not pressure.

Source: Roger Fisher, William Ury, and Bruce Patton, *Getting to Yes*

EXHIBIT 3.2   Negotiating methods and styles.

✔ Be clear on the goals of the organization and the objectives for each negotiation.

✔ Clarify roles and responsibilities for each member of the team. Who will do background due diligence? Who will make contacts? Who will present specific details, attend sessions, and so on?

✔ Debrief following each negotiation session—review notes, discuss observations, strategize for next sessions.

tool of the trade

Before you begin negotiations, consider the four methods for conducting successful negotiations offered by Fisher, Ury, and Patton in *Getting to Yes:*

1. *Separate the people from the problem.* Negotiators are people, not abstractions. They have emotions, interests, perceptions, and different styles of communication. Try to stay focused on the problem you are attempting to resolve without personalizing it to "members of the other side."

2. *Focus on interests, not positions.* Negotiators will state their position, something they have decided on. Interests are what caused them to so decide. They are the underlying concerns, needs, desires, and fears that negotiators are trying represent in their positions. Get to them and you have a better chance of problem-solving a win-win solution.

3. *Invent options for mutual gain.* Try to avoid focusing on narrowing the gap between positions and instead focus on broadening the options available. Brainstorm without judging, search for mutual gain, and make the decision-making process as easy as possible.

4. *Insist on using objective criteria.* Try to use criteria that are reflective of industry standards, scientific merit, or market value. Focus less on what you are willing or unwilling to accept and more on standards of fairness, community practice, or precedent.[12]

Uneven Playing Fields

We would all like to think negotiations could go smoothly to the benefit of all parties in the name of common good. However, the playing field is not always as level as we might hope. Consider this example:

Representatives of a small community development corporation (CDC) with a solid reputation in an older, racially and economically diverse community had been trying for years to get the local housing authority to change its focus regarding the deteriorating conditions of one of its old public housing development—"the projects." Newly announced funding from the department of Housing and Urban Development (HUD) created the opportunity for local leaders including the CDC to propose a plan for demolition of some units (reduced density), renovation of other units, and new construction for a mixed blend of public use and market-rate housing.

The CDC had tenant approval and the strong support of homeowners near the projects who wanted "anything" done. Local civic leadership also was willing to come on board in support of this innovative vision. The planning time line was too short for the CDC, which didn't have the staff expertise to put together the plans for architecture, financing, and other necessary areas that would increase the chances for a successful bid. They needed a partner.

They approached a for-profit corporation about a partnership. The for-profit had the cash flow, in-house expertise, and necessary connections to put together a financing package that could assure a favorable review of the approximately $20 million proposal. Besides the "social value" that would be realized in the community, significant resources (revenue) would be available through developer fees. The two parties entered into *negotiation. The not-for-profit, in its mind, had little bargaining power. Its assets were the community support and local relationships. The for-profit recognized the assets of the CDC and agreed to partner—but with a 90 percent–10 percent split of developer fees. The CDC was hoping for a 51 percent–49 percent split. The CDC countered, but the for-profit again offered 90 percent–10 percent or nothing.*

The window of opportunity was closing for the CDC. While it contemplated going it alone, it was afraid it just didn't have the horses to run a race this big. It accepted the 90 percent–10 percent split.

A number of years invested in working the housing authority, meeting with the community, educating civic leaders, and developing public goodwill came down to a couple of hundred thousand dollars in fees, some resentment, and significant lessons learned. The for-profit worked well with the not-for-profit and walked away with well over $1 million in fees.

The negotiations in this case were much more involved than what was described. The point of the case is to stress that partnerships are, more often than not, unequal. Foundations say they want to partner with not-for-profit organizations. It's not an equal partnership. Large for-profits elect to partner with not-for-profits. It's not an equal partnership. Larger not-for-profits choose to partner with smaller not-for-profits. It's not an equal partnership.

Fisher, Ury, and Patton suggest that you develop a BATNA—a Best Alternative to a Negotiated Agreement—before beginning a negotiation, especially with potential partners who appear to be more powerful.

The BATNA works by establishing in advance your "bottom line." This does sound contradictory to what has been offered so far—it is! This is your backup plan, your plan B, C, or D, when everything else doesn't go as planned. This position does lock you in and removes new possibilities that might be generated in principled negotiation. However, there is power in walking away. Consider the advice of Fisher, Ury, and Patton:

gem of wisdom

People think of negotiating power as being determined by resources like wealth, political connections, physical strength, friends, and military might. In fact, the relative negotiating power of two parties depends primarily upon how attractive to each is the option of not reaching agreement.[13]

Successful entrepreneurs do not leave negotiations to chance. Excellent teams, supportive environments, facilitated processes, and sound principles are all attributes of successful negotiations. You should be seeking substantive gain for all partners through a respectful process. In the end, any method that accomplishes this goal along with maintaining and/or strengthening the relationships between the partners is the ideal.

Keep in mind that you probably will enter into negotiations some time in the future with the same people you are negotiating with today. Repeat business happens more often than business through new partnerships. The people you are trying to crush today will be back. Likewise, the trusting win-win relationships you build today are likely to produce win-win situations in the future.

Which scenario would you prefer?

MANAGING THE PARTNERSHIP

The negotiation team may have developed an excellent agreement that has the potential to benefit partners and clients. But all contracts get played out on the front line where line staff, who are closest to the customer, have to develop the relationships with line staff from the partnering organization.

Either organization waving the memorandum of understanding in the face of staff will do little to produce results.

ROAD MAP FOR SUCCESS

First, did you include a representative(s) from the specific area affected by the partnership agreement in the planning process? Did you consider your theory of change if new or radically different services or products are to be offered? Consider the ten commandments for implementing change from Todd D. Jick's book, *Managing Change: Cases and Concepts.*

tool of the trade

1. Analyze the organization and its need for change.
2. Create a shared vision and common direction.
3. Separate from the past.
4. Create a sense of urgency.
5. Support a strong leader role.
6. Line up political sponsorship.
7. Craft an implementation plan.
8. Develop enabling structures.
9. Communicate, involve people, and be honest.
10. Reinforce and institutionalize change.[14]

Note: If the partnership entails changing the structure dramatically, such as a merger, an agency consolidation, or a newly created holding company, you may want to review the strategies in *Forging Nonprofit Alliances* by Arsenault for greater depth of detail.[15]

COMMUNICATION

One of the keys to building strong relationships is communication. Establish clear lines of communication both inter- and intraorganization. How will decisions be made and how will results of decisions made be communicated? Will line staff have open lines of communication for providing feedback on successes and barriers to performance? Will you establish methods for electronic communication for all stakeholders?

Trusting relationships are built through open and honest communication. Taking the time to develop a communication plan can help you avoid stumbling blocks in any new cooperative strategy. Address issues and concerns up front and in a timely manner. Establish an issues resolution process so staff know the appropriate channels for raising concerns before they fester.

PARTNER ACCOUNTABILITY

Once agreements are signed and staff are prepared, the process for determining progress and accountability begins. Today's entrepreneurial mind is geared to results, not activity.

Traditionally, not-for-profits have declared "effectiveness" in relations to units of service provided, patient visits, documents published, and so forth. The push from government, venture philanthropists, and the corporate sector is for results—the intended changes from the services offered. Harold S. Williams, Arthur Y. Webb, and William J. Phillips write in their book, *Outcome Funding:*

> *A common reaction from people in social and human services is that theirs is a "soft" area in which target specificity is simply not possible. How do you measure prevention? How do you quantify self-esteem? . . . While these questions are noble, they miss the point. It is possible, as well as desirable, to define performance targets for virtually all programs funded by government.*[16]

It isn't enough that an agency provided job-training classes. Did the client get a job? It isn't enough that 30 students attended an education program. Did their knowledge or skill level improve?

United Way of America is also supporting this shift with local United Way agencies across the country. Thousands of not-for-profits are going through "outcomes" training. United Way's manual, *Measuring Program Outcomes: A Practical Approach,* does an excellent job of distinguishing among input, outputs, and outcomes.[17]

The emergence of venture philanthropy—philanthropies emulating a venture capital approach with their investments in not-for-profit organizations compared to the more traditional charitable gift—are also looking for results, not activity. Therefore, the shift in accountability boils down to holding partners accountable for outcomes, not activity.

red flag

Hold people accountable for results, not activity.

BENCHMARKS

With that said, we now have to recognize that this complex society we have been talking about assures us that no one single provider is going to change the world. No one single partner has the key to unlock the chain of events that have created the circumstances in which the customer/client is now mired. Therefore, outcomes are actually the longer view and benchmarks indicate progress toward those outcomes.

The benchmarks are the performance measures that become the barometer by which you can measure the progress of your partners or by which you will be measured by contractors and/or investors. Just like outcomes, benchmarks have to be agreed on by both parties in the negotiation process. Likewise, a process for reviewing contract deliverables should be agreed on in the negotiation process (including realistic time lines for results).

Keep in mind that early wins build momentum. Establishing benchmarks early on that are achievable and fundamental to growth can create a culture of accomplishment and success. That's not to say that you should lower the standard of services or expected outcomes for the client. It does suggest that you start small, build on success, celebrate achievements, and recognize those who contribute to your success.

PERIODIC ASSESSMENT

Regular assessment can help identify barriers to achieving benchmarks. Often times an exploration as to why results have not been achieved will reveal problems with the delivery of a service, changes needed in basic assumptions, or alteration of product design. All these considerations, and others, are especially true if the product or service is associated with a new enterprise in a start-up mode.

red flag

Just because a partner fails to meet a benchmark, it doesn't mean you walk away or never offer a contract again. It does mean that it is time for some careful scrutiny as to why the benchmark wasn't reached.

Such partnerships can be compared to the work of venture capital investors and new start-up businesses. Christine W. Letts, William Ryan, and Allen Grossman write in their article, "Virtuous Capital: What Foundations Can Learn from Venture Capitalists":

The venture capital firm and the start-up begin building their relationship around financial and organizational projections, which then act as a set of performance measures. The measures, which can include cash flow, sales, profits, or market share, are continually updated to reflect the start-up company's progress and the market conditions. Clear objectives give the investors and the start-up managers a focus for their working relationship.[18]

Determine quantifiable benchmarks that can be assessed periodically (quarterly). In the start-up phase, these benchmarks may need to be adjusted. But remember, "Clear objectives give the investors and the start-up managers a focus for their working relationship." It's not about saying "*They* aren't performing." It's about "*We* are not getting the results we were projecting. Let's find out why and adjust." If you keep that point in mind, the partnership has a chance to get the desired results.

Partnerships can improve results and increase revenue. Make sure the people most affected by a new partnership are consulted and involved in the negotiation process. Their insight will be invaluable, and their buy-in is absolutely necessary for the partnership to work.

Create an environment that promotes communication. Keep your partners informed and establish mechanisms for feedback. Partners must be held accountable for meeting expectations. In this day and age, expectations in the not-for-profit sector means results. Be very clear about the difference between activity—units of service, patient visits, people in attendance, brochures printed—and results. Results are the change in knowledge, attitude, behavior, or level of satisfaction by the end user—the customer or client.

Remember, the customer in this situation is the person benefiting from the service or product. The other customer in the not-for-profit sector is the investor or contracting agency. Social entrepreneurs understand that return on investment means valuing the results you are able to deliver for both the investor and customer.

Finally, be clear about benchmarks and outcomes and the processes you will use to assess them in the negotiation process. Clarity will help the relationship withstand the pressures inherent in this work. So here is another variation of the better-together concept. We can be better together—as long as we agree on what "better" means. Negotiation skills are critical to answering that question.

SUMMARY

Networking with other organizations and building partnerships and alliances offers you the opportunity to leverage your own organization—

multiplying its effectiveness, extending its reach, and helping limited human and financial resources go much farther. Start small and build on success. Establish benchmarks that allow partners to see progress and recognize barriers to success. Create opportunities for early wins and celebrate your achievements.

✔ Be clear about your motivation and the potential benefits and risks in choosing a cooperative strategy in order to effectively determine who your partners should/could be.

✔ The board should establish policies that support cooperative strategies in order for the executive to have the freedom to actively network and seek out partnerships that improve the bottom line.

✔ Collaboration means sharing resources, power and authority for a common goal.

✔ Multiservice partnerships are generally managed more easily by a coordinating organization.

✔ Coalitions, councils, or any other similarly named group that has, as its primary purpose, the creation of a forum for like-minded individuals to network and discuss issues relevant to their common vision are excellent places to look for potential partners.

✔ The fastest form of corporate giving is in cause-related marketing.

✔ Any time you are interacting with another person for the purpose of exchanging something of value, there is negotiation.

✔ There has been a rapid evolution in the field of negotiating toward shared problem-solving.

✔ Excellent teams, supportive environments, facilitated processes, and sound principles are all attributes of successful negotiations.

✔ Today's entrepreneurial mind is geared to results, not activity.

✔ Results are the change in knowledge, attitude, behavior, or level of satisfaction by the customer/client.

Notes

1. Brian O'Connell, "Building Coalitions, Collaborations, Alliances and Other Partnerships," An Occasional Paper of the Lincoln Filene Center for Citizenship and Public Affairs, Tufts University, Medford, Massachusetts, May 1997, p. 5.
2. Jane Arsenault, *Forging Nonprofit Alliances* (San Francisco: Jossey-Bass, 1998) p. 5.
3. Sharon L. Kagan, *United We Stand: Collaboration for Child Care and Early Education Services,* (New York and London: Teachers College Press, 1989) p. 32.
4. This exhibit was excerpted from Arthur T. Himmelman's monograph, "Communities Working Collaboratively for a Change," 1996 Revised Edition.
5. The importance of relationship and the comparison of business alliances to "best marriages" is described in greater detail in the article by Rosabeth Moss Kanter, "Collaborative Advantage: The Art of Alliances," *Harvard Business Review,* July 1994.

6. Excerpt taken from an interview with Arthur T. Himmelman, President, Himmelman Consulting, September 1999, regarding his monograph, "Communities Working Collaboratively for a Change," Copyright 1992, Revised 1996.

7. Information was excerpted from Daniel Kadlec's article, "Companies Are Doing More Good, and Demanding More Back," *Time* magazine—The New World of Giving, May 1997, p. 63.

8. Adapted from "Profits for Nonprofits: Find a Corporate Partner," Alan R. Andreasen, *Harvard Business Review,* November–December 1996.

9. Roger Fisher, William Ury, and Bruce Patton, *Getting To Yes,* Second Edition (New York: Penguin Books, 1991).

10. Ibid, p. 3.

11. Interview with Bill Breslin, Program on Negotiation Clearinghouse, Harvard Law School, June 1999.

12. Adapted from *Getting To Yes,* Second Edition, Roger Fisher, William Ury, and Bruce Patton, (New York: Penguin Books, 1991).

13. Ibid, p. 102.

14. Todd D. Jick, *Managing Change: Cases and Concepts,* (Massachusetts: Richard D. Irwin, Inc., 1993) p. 195.

15. An in-depth discussion about the strategies relative to mergers of nonprofit organizations can be found in Chapter 6 of the book by Jane Arsenault, *Forging Nonprofit Alliances,* (San Francisco: Jossey-Bass, 1998).

16. Harold S. Williams, Arthur Y. Webb, and William J. Phillips, *Outcome Funding: A New Approach to Targeted Grantmaking,* (New York: The Rensselaerville Institute, copyright 1991, Second Edition 1995) p. 115.

17. The guide to outcomes measurement is found in the United Way publication, *Measuring Program Outcomes: A Practical Approach,* Item number 0989, United Way of America, 1996.

18. Christine W. Letts, William Ryan, and Allen Grossman, "Virtuous Capital: What Foundations Can Learn from Venture Capitalists," *Harvard Business Review,* March–April 1997, p. 38.

Chapter 4

LEADING, RETAINING, AND REWARDING PEOPLE ENTREPRENEURIALLY

Peter Economy, Associate Editor, Leader to Leader

IN THIS CHAPTER

Leading a social enterprise
Attracting and keeping great people
Motivating your team

Why do people choose to work for social enterprises, especially when pay and benefits are often much better in the for-profit world? Clearly, they do it because they have the chance to make a real difference in the world around them. Says Monica Drinane, attorney-in-charge of the New York City–based Juvenile Rights Division of the Legal Aid Society, "My experience from talking with young associates who come to us from other firms is that they are not getting a sense that they are more than just a cog in the wheel. They may have a piece of a project, but not ownership in the project [while at other firms]. The chance to have ownership and a sense of responsibility is something these individuals really thrive on."[1]

But there's more to it than just that. People are attracted (and loyal) to organizations with talented leaders, they are attracted (and loyal) to high-performing organizations that unleash the creativity and energy that lies within them, and they are attracted (and loyal) to organizations that give them the opportunity to do what they do best every day, free from managers who second-guess their decisions and frustrating and time-wasting policies and red tape that constrain their personal initiative.

Successful entrepreneurs—including *social* entrepreneurs—must be able to mobilize resources, and human resources are probably the most crucial resource to any organization. Social entrepreneurs are innovators, and, as such, they must motivate people to follow new paths. Lack of leadership skills will very likely doom would-be social entrepreneurs to failure (or, at least, mediocrity). In this chapter we'll explore some key aspects of leadership and building the kind of high-performance organization that attracts and retains talented employees. Finally, we'll take a look at employee motivation and the best ways to reward and recognize workers. One thing: Keep in mind that, while the focus in this chapter is on the *employees* who staff and run your social enterprise, these same principles apply equally well to your volunteers as well.

Leading a Social Enterprise

Ask 10 different people in 10 different social enterprises what the term "leadership" means to them, and you're likely to get 10 different answers. While most everyone will acknowledge the importance of leadership in organizations today, few people will agree on exactly what a leader is and what he or she looks like.

In theory, anyone in any organization can be a leader. Leadership is not something that depends on your job title, or how old you are, or what gender, race, creed, or color you happen to be. Not every executive director is a skilled leader, for example, and there are more than a few secretaries and mailroom clerks who are extremely talented leaders. There are accomplished women leading all kinds of organizations—from the American Red Cross, to computer maker Hewlett-Packard—and leadership comes in every possible color of the human palette, every religion, and every possible belief system and set of values.

No, leadership is far more than a label; it's the sum of many different traits that set leaders apart from others who follow in the steps that they so boldly make in the sands of change.

core concept

Some of the most common traits attributed to *leaders* include the following:

✔ *Charismatic.* Charisma—that special charm or allure that inspires fascination or devotion in others—compels many people to follow the direction that leaders set. The stronger the charisma of a leader, the more strongly the interest of potential followers is attracted.

✔ *Convincing.* Leaders are able to convince others to see their point of view, and often they are able to sway others' opinions into agreement with their own.

✔ *Credible.* Leaders are seen as being honest and trustworthy and as people who have integrity. People are willing to put their trust in leaders and follow their direction so long as they maintain their credibility and integrity.

✔ *Capable.* Skilled, talented, excellent at what they do. These terms are all indicative of someone who is capable in his or her job and able to lead others—inspiring those they lead to achieve their own high standards.

✔ *Visionary.* Leaders have the ability to paint a compelling picture of the future and communicate it to those around them—inspiring followers to work to help them achieve it.

✔ *Focused.* Leaders have the ability to focus their attention on specific goals while excluding distractions from other sources. This makes it more likely they will achieve their goals and earn the admiration of those around them.

Within the vast universe that comprises all leaders in all kinds of organizations, there is a wide variety of leadership styles. These styles can be summarized under two different major categories:

1. *Autocratic.* Autocratic leadership depends on pushing employees to accomplish an organization's goals through the use of authority. Workers are excluded from the organization's decision-making process and their ideas and suggestions are often ignored, leading them to shut down and withdraw from full participation in the organization. "It's my decision on how we'll proceed, and this is the way I want you to do it!"

2. *Democratic.* Democratic leadership encourages employees to be a part of the decision-making process, empowering workers and making them a vital part of the organization. This approach draws the best out of each employee and enables the organization to benefit from the full range of creativity, skills, and experience available from its workers. "I would like your opinion on how you think we should proceed in this particular situation."

practical tip

In the real world, a variety of legitimate leadership styles fall between these two extreme poles. The best leaders know when to make autocratic decisions (e.g., when time is short, or when group consensus is unlikely) and when it is wise to leave the decision to the group (true democracy). Leadership involves the wisdom to find the right style for the occasion and the humility to know that you do not always have the right answers.

Take a close look at yourself for a moment. Are you a leader? Do you exhibit some or all of these common leadership traits? If so, which ones? And which of these traits could use a bit of polishing? The more of these traits you are able to exhibit, the more likely it is that you will be seen as a leader by your coworkers and those who work for you. If you find yourself lacking in any of these areas, your leadership potential will be greatly enhanced by addressing them and taking steps to improve.

THE FIVE KEYS TO LEADERSHIP

Many people think that leadership is something that they either have or don't have, and there's nothing they can do to get it if they don't have it. This belief is just not true. Leaders can be made, and, in fact, they are made every day of the week.

Sure, leaders exhibit a variety of traits that give them an aura of leadership in the eyes of others, but in organizations, there's much more to leadership than simply having a charismatic personality, being trustworthy, or having a laser-sharp focus on the organization's goals. Tompeters! company chairman emeritus Jim Kouzes and Santa Clara University business professor Barry Posner have spent years studying leadership and looking for insights into what makes leaders leaders. The result, published in their book *The Leadership Challenge,* is a set of five things that leaders do.[2] These five practices are:

1. *Challenging processes.* Instead of being satisfied with the status quo, leaders make things happen. They continually push the limits of the organization by innovating and by taking initiative and risks. Social entrepreneurs question the status quo and find new ways to accomplish their social mission.

2. *Inspiring a shared vision.* Leaders have a clear and compelling vision of the future, and they are able to communicate this vision to others—both in and out of the organization. Social entrepreneurs have a vision of how to create social value, and they share it widely.

3. *Enabling others to act.* Rather than simply assign tasks to employees, leaders empower them with the authority that they will need to get the tasks done without any additional permission from management. Leaders also support their employees and help clear away organizational hurdles. Social entrepreneurs enable members of their team to find their own ways to accomplish the organization's goals.

4. *Modeling the way.* The best leaders walk their talk—they follow through on their promises, and they are willing to do the things that they say others should do. They have values and they exhibit them in their everyday organizational lives. Social entrepreneurs model entrepreneurial behavior: resourcefulness, accountability, and more.

5. *Encouraging the heart.* Leaders inspire those around them and encourage them to do their very best and to persevere in the face of adversity. Leaders celebrate successes—and those who brought them about—and they share in the inevitable failures. Social entrepreneurs encourage the members of their team to reach high and to never be satisfied with mediocrity.

Put these five practices to work for you and your leadership skills are sure to increase along with your ability to lead others. The more you use these practices, the better you'll get at it, and the sooner your leadership stock will rise. And this is a good thing—both for you and for your organization.

BALANCING LEADERSHIP WITH MANAGEMENT

So, what's more important for social entrepreneurs today—leadership or management? Actually, these concepts are not mutually exclusive—it takes both to make an organization run at its best. And some great leaders are also great managers—and vice versa. But leading an organization is definitely a different concept from managing an organization, and being a successful leader requires an entirely different focus from being a successful manager.

 Leadership focuses on *people,* whereas management focuses on *things.* As U.S. Navy admiral Grace Murray Hopper put it, "You manage things; you lead people." University of Southern California (USC) business professor Warren Bennis described the differences between leaders and managers this way:

- ✔ The manager administers; the leader innovates.
- ✔ The manager has a short-range view; the leader has a long-range perspective.
- ✔ The manager asks how and when; the leader asks what and why.
- ✔ The manager has an eye on the bottom line; the leader has an eye on the horizon.
- ✔ The manager accepts the status quo; the leader challenges it.[3]

Leadership is all about inspiring your team to do a terrific job; convincing, motivating, creating a compelling vision of the future; and doing all the other things that encourage a dedicated group of followers to make good things happen in an organization. We've all heard stories of the extraordinary efforts and accomplishments of workers who were inspired by a great leader. When people are sufficiently motivated to do something, there's little that can stop them from achieving their goals.

Management, on the other hand, is all about making organizations run better by designing and improving the processes, procedures, and policies that guide the actions of employees. These kinds of things are essential for making an organization work, but they rarely inspire people to go out of their way to provide extraordinary service to clients. When is the last time you've heard someone get very excited about a new absentee policy?

DELEGATING AUTHORITY

Smart leaders know that they can't do everything themselves—they can be much more effective and get far more done if they assign work to other members of their team. By leveraging themselves through others, leaders can focus on doing the things that only they are uniquely able to do, whether that means networking with potential clients, funding sponsors and regulators, or creating media opportunities to showcase the work of their organizations.

And delegation does more than simply farm work to employees—it *empowers* them to take on more responsible work and gives them the authority they need to do it effectively. This allows employees to tap into their own skills and creativity to solve an organization's problems—and take advantage of its opportunities—in ways that help them grow as employees while increasing their ability to respond to client needs quickly and in ways that are tailored to their unique situation. The result is happier clients *and* happier employees—a recipe for a terrific organization if ever there was one.

In an entrepreneurial organization, delegation does one more thing: It allows *every* employee the opportunity to be an entrepreneur—not just the owner, executive director, or top management. Imagine the energy, creativity, and client responsiveness that would be released by giving every employee the opportunity to be entrepreneurial in his or her job. The potential is truly awesome and inspiring. Delegation is the key to unleashing this wellspring of potential that remains untapped in far too many organizations.

tool of   Effective delegation is not automatic; it takes a conscious effort
the trade   on the part of the person doing the delegating—as well as the staff
                 member being delegated to—to make sure that the process works.
By following these six steps, you will ensure that delegation works for you and your organization.

1. *Communicate your expectations.* The work being delegated must be communicated to employees in a way that they can understand. Whether the work is delegated verbally or in writing, be sure to take time to explain the task in great detail and to encourage workers to ask questions and seek clarification for any part they are unsure about.

2. *Furnish context for the work.* Delegation is much more effective when you provide employees with the big picture—the background information that describes how the work fits into the rest of the organization and how it will further its goals. Employees can then make intelligent and informed decisions when required during the course of performing the work.

3. *Jointly determine standards.* Every project requires milestones, time lines, and goals to provide some way to measure progress. Standards provide this yardstick. To be most effective, they always should be mutually agreed to by both the person doing the delegating and the person being delegated to, and they should be finite and easy to understand.

4. *Grant authority.* Authority is the power necessary to get work done without constantly seeking permission from higher-ups. Effective delegation absolutely requires the granting of the authority necessary to get assigned work done—anything less will result in frustrated employees, ineffectiveness, and inefficiency.

5. *Provide support.* Every employee has different skill bases and levels of experience. When you delegate work to employees, you also should be prepared to support your employees in many different ways. One employee might need a quick training course in how to complete a specific task, another might need help in cutting the organizational red tape that threatens to stymie his or her efforts. Another might simply need someone to talk to.

6. *Get commitment.* Whenever you delegate work, be sure that you get a positive commitment from the employee that he or she has accepted the work and will complete it according to the standards that you have both agreed to. Without commitment, you really can't be sure that the work will be done at all, much less on time or within budget.

Make a point of delegating work to members of your team whenever possible. When delegation is done the right way, the benefits to the organization and its staff and clients can be considerable, while it frees up more of your time to do the things that only you can do.

ATTRACTING AND KEEPING GREAT PEOPLE

Attracting people to work for an entrepreneurial venture can be particularly challenging, as can be retaining them. Entrepreneurial ventures are inherently risky. While they may seem exciting in the abstract, it can be difficult to leave a secure job in a stable organization for a new venture that is just taking shape and that is inherently risky because it is challenging the status quo. And while the intrinsic rewards of helping others or giving back to their communities are highly motivating to many people, the extrinsic rewards—pay, benefits, work environment—are often significantly lower in nonprofit organizations than for similar positions in the for-profit arena.

All this makes hiring—and ultimately, retaining—talented people particularly difficult for social enterprises, especially when unemployment is low and for-profit organizations are forced to increase pay and benefits to attract new workers and retain current employees.

core concept   Attracting and retaining talented people is critical for the success of any organization. Fortunately, the approaches for accomplishing these goals aren't limited only to offering people higher salaries or increasing the size of their benefits packages. These techniques address the roots of employees' intrinsic motivation, appealing to their desire to be a part of an effective organization, to be encouraged to contribute their creativity and energy, to be granted some measure of autonomy and authority, and to be respected by managers and coworkers alike. By applying them in your own organization, potential employees will seek you out, and those already hired will feel compelled to stay.

PUTTING PEOPLE FIRST

By their very nature, for-profit organizations tend to put profits before people; that is, the creation of economic value for shareholders is given a higher priority than the employees themselves who create that value. According to Stanford Graduate School of Business professor Jeffrey Pfeffer, however, research increasingly points to a direct relationship between a company's financial success and its commitment to management practices that treat people as assets. In other words, companies today succeed not by putting their employees *behind* profits but actually by putting them first. Says Pfeffer, "Over the past decade or so, numerous rigorous studies conducted both within specific industries and in samples of organizations that cross industries have demonstrated the enormous economic returns obtained through the implementation of what are variously called high involvement, high performance, or high commitment management practices."[4]

Even social entrepreneurs can be guilty of neglecting people and focusing too much on performance, measurable outcomes, and the other mechanics of serving clients and constituents. Some readers may think that because social entrepreneurs—themselves included—care about society, they will automatically put people first. This does not seem to be the case. Nonprofit leaders can abuse people in the name of a greater mission just as easily as for-profit businesses can abuse people in the name of profits. If you care about your social mission, you will do better by putting people first.

In his book *The Human Equation: Building Profits by Putting People First,* Pfeffer lists seven practices of successful organizations—practices that put people first. These practices include:

1. Employment security
2. Selective hiring of new personnel

3. Self-managed teams and decentralization of decision making as the basic principles of organizational design

4. Comparatively high compensation contingent on organizational performance

5. Extensive training

6. Reduced status distinctions and barriers, including dress, language, office arrangements, and wage differences across levels

7. Extensive sharing of financial and performance information throughout the organization[5]

Take a close look at your own organization. Do members of your team feel secure that they will have a job tomorrow, or next week, or next year, or do they live under the constant threat of layoffs and downsizing? Do you spend as much time as you should recruiting and hiring the very best workers, and do you hire only when the needs of the organization dictate that you should do so? Do you encourage teams to manage themselves, and do you give people the authority they need to get their jobs done without being second-guessed by management? Are members of your staff paid well for what they do, and do you further invest in their career development by providing a wide variety of training opportunities? Is everyone in your organization "in it together," or do you have a distinct system of organizational haves and have-nots? Do you create quantifiable measures of your organization's success, and are the results widely publicized?

The answers to these questions will give you an idea of exactly how people rate in *your* organization.

BUILDING A HIGH-PERFORMANCE ORGANIZATION

Who doesn't want to have (and work for) a high-performing organization? High-performing organizations make much better use of their precious resources—including cash and human resources—and they tap the creativity and energy that lies within each and every employee. And when your employees are given an opportunity to unleash their creativity and energy on the job, their loyalty to the organization will increase as well.

core concept

According to USC business professor Edward Lawler, three key traits characterize well-designed, high-involvement organizations—organizations that are by nature high-performing ones:

1. *Individuals understand the business.* They know its strategy, how it is doing, and who their customers and competitors are. Successful social enterprises make open communication within and without the organization a priority—ensuring that employees and

stakeholders are well informed about the organization's workings, its priorities, and its progress toward meeting its goals.

2. *Individuals are rewarded according to the success of the business.* They are owners and share in its performance so that what is good for the business is good for them. While individuals in most social enterprises can't own their organizations in a truly financial sense, they can have psychic ownership of the organization by being involved in developing and implementing its vision and mission, by being involved in the organization's decision-making process, and by feeling that they are valued and respected members of the organization.

3. *Employees are able to influence important organizational decisions.* They decide on work methods, participate in business strategy decisions, and work with each other in order to coordinate their work. Every employee has something to offer his or her organization—it's often simply just a matter of asking them to get involved. But, once invited to participate, supervisors and managers must follow through by allowing workers to have real decision-making authority, not something less.[6]

Every organization has the potential to be a high-performing organization. And there's no reason that any nonprofit organization can't be the equal of even the best-run for-profit. By tapping the skills and talents of all employees, social enterprises can unleash large amounts of creativity and energy, vaulting their organizations into the top ranks of performance.

THE 12 HABITS OF HIGHLY EFFECTIVE ORGANIZATIONS

Of course, all the organizational initiatives in the world won't make a difference to employees if change isn't evident at their level. To become highly effective organizations, not only must organizations change the way that they *appear* to work, but they must change the way they *actually* work. After studying more than 1 million employees in hundreds of different organizations, the Gallup Organization polling firm identified 12 characteristics that exist in today's most productive organizations. According to Curt Coffman, global practice leader for Gallup, the presence of these workplace characteristics, which he calls Q12 conditions, lead to high levels of worker loyalty and performance:

1. I know what is expected of me at work.
2. I have the materials and equipment I need to do my work right.
3. At work, I have the opportunity to do what I do best every day.

4. In the last seven days, I have received recognition or praise for do-ing good work.

5. My supervisor, or someone at work, seems to care about me as a person.

6. There is someone at work who encourages my development.

7. At work, my opinions seem to count.

8. The mission/purpose of my company makes me feel my job is important.

9. My associates (fellow employees) are committed to doing qual-ity work.

10. I have a best friend at work.

11. In the last six months, someone at work has talked to me about my progress.

12. This last year, I have had opportunities at work to learn and grow.[7]

In fact, when the Gallup Organization asked employees the following question: "At work, do you have the opportunity to do what you do best every day?" the implications of the answers were clear and unequivocal. Employees who answered "strongly agree" were 50 percent more likely to work in business units with lower employee turnover and 44 percent more likely to work in business units with higher customer satisfaction scores.[8]

IMPORTANCE OF AN ORGANIZATION'S CULTURE

Every organization has its own unique culture. An organization's culture is the sum of its values, beliefs, policies, practices, and the knowledge and personality that each employee brings to work each day. Accord-ing to a survey of 150 U.S. executives by consulting firm Robert Half In-ternational, potential employees are very interested in the culture of or-ganizations they are considering for employment, and their perception of an organization's culture has a measurable impact on whether they will decide to work there. When asked the question, "Other than base salary and bonuses, what do most applicants ask about during job in-terviews today?" the surveyed executives reported the following replies:

Benefits:	36 percent
Corporate culture:	34 percent
Job security:	15 percent
Equity opportunities:	11 percent
Other:	4 percent[9]

How would your employees answer the above questions? How would *you* answer them? The more of these questions that your employees can answer in the affirmative, the higher their loyalty and productivity will be, and the better your chances of keeping them.

Motivating Your Team

When it comes to a desire to motivate people to give 100 percent of themselves to an organization and its customers and clients, social enterprises are no different from their peers in the for-profit sector. People who are motivated and give their all to the organization are much more effective and efficient—creating better products and services more quickly than those people who are unmotivated, and thus less effective and efficient. An organization with motivated employees often can get far more out of its limited financial and human resources than an organization with unmotivated, ineffective, inefficient employees.

But what makes people do what they do? Why are some team members more motivated to do a good job than others, and what can be done to help unmotivated team members become motivated team members?

These are questions that have long intrigued and even baffled supervisors and managers whose job it is to guide the efforts of staff or a team of employees. The fact is that employee motivation is not a simple topic—it is as complex as are people themselves. Decades of research on the topic have led to many theories that attempt to explain why workers do what they do, and none of these theories tells the entire story, nor does any one have a lock on the truth.

But one thing is for sure, what motivates motivates, and it's important for anyone in a position of supervising or managing people to figure out what it takes to get the most out of his or her employees—to unlock the creativity and energy that can take an organization to a much higher level than where it is today and to get more and better results for less money.

In the sections that follow, we'll take a close look at how to do just that.

Celebrate What You Want to See More Of

Most supervisors and managers know that motivated employees are a critically important ingredient in successful organizations—an organization's employees, after all, are the heart and soul of *any* organization, whether it's entrepreneurial or not. And most supervisors and managers also know that motivated, happy employees are less likely to leave the organization to seek out greener pastures. But, when it comes right down to it, many supervisors and managers fail to do even the simplest things to recognize and reward good employee performance.

Why is this the case?

According to recognition expert Arnold "Mac" Anderson, founder and chairman emeritus of the Aurora, Illinois–based worker motivation and self-improvement firm Successories, Inc., there are two key reasons why supervisors and managers don't do more to recognize and reward employees:

> *I think the main reason a lot of companies don't try to create a recognition culture is that, number one, they're afraid they might do something wrong—they don't totally understand it and don't want to hurt any feelings. And, number two, they're not sure how to present the return on investment they're going to get to top management. To start the recognition culture, you literally have to start at the top. The person at the top has to believe in it, he or she has to bring the managers together to say "Okay guys, what can we do at this company to create a recognition culture?" The key to making it work is the individual manager of each department because he or she has to do things that make employees feel important. As a manager, you have to make your people feel important because it's a basic human need to want to feel important.* [10]

The point is that building a culture of recognition—one that makes employees feel important to the organization and its customers and clients—is a key step in developing a team of happy, motivated employees. And the good news is that building a culture of recognition doesn't have to be a difficult task, and you won't have to break the bank in the process.

What's your first reaction when you hear someone in your organization (perhaps yourself) say something like this?

I just don't understand why they won't do what I ask them to do—what's their problem?

Morale here is the pits. How are we ever going to get our act together with the crew we have working here now?

I just wish I knew how to get everyone in the department to get more involved in their jobs and with our clients!

The tendency for many supervisors and managers is to first blame workers when they aren't engaged in their jobs, or when they do less than their best, or when morale suffers. In fact, most employees simply respond to their working environments. People who work in an environment that encourages and celebrates employee success tend to do more of the kinds of things that lead to even more success. Conversely, people who work in an environment that doesn't encourage and celebrate employee success will tend to do less of the kinds of things that would lead to more success.

It's simple human nature to respond positively to rewards and recognition. When people are rewarded for exhibiting a particular behavior—no matter what it is—they will tend to do more of it. For supervisors and managers grappling with ways to get employees to do more of the things that they want them to do, therefore, the answer is simple: Reward employees for doing exactly those behaviors.

gem of wisdom

In his book *Thriving on Chaos*, management expert Tom Peters explained this approach in a very simple way: "Celebrate what you want to see more of."[11]

action step

To put this approach to motivating team members into action, you've got to do two things:

1. Decide exactly what behaviors you want members of your team to exhibit more of. These behaviors could be anything from providing better customer service, to submitting more accurate reports, to missing fewer days of work.

2. Reward team members when they display these behaviors. A reward could be a simple verbal thank you, a written note of thanks, public recognition in a staff meeting, a certificate of recognition, or a variety of other methods of rewards and recognition.

Rewarding and recognizing the kind of behavior you want—whether it's giving great customer service or accomplishing a major organizational goal—is really quite simple. The hardest part for most supervisors and managers is setting aside the time to do it on a regular basis. But for the ones who do, the rewards to the organization can be quite profound and long lasting.

REWARDING PEOPLE: THERE'S A RIGHT WAY AND A WRONG WAY!

Is there such a thing as rewarding people too often? Probably not. But a word of warning: Be careful what behaviors you reward!

Think for a moment about this common situation: Let's say that you're an employee who not only does your job but often goes above and beyond the call of duty—going out of your way to complete projects ahead of time and solve client problems. And let's say that you have a coworker who does about half as much work and doesn't do it nearly as well as you do. So what does your boss do? Instead of pressing your coworker to improve his production and quality of work, your boss decides to give you half of your coworker's caseload.

What has happened here? Your underperforming coworker has been rewarded for doing a less-than-stellar job. How? Half of his workload has

INTERVIEW

REWARDING EMPLOYEES? SOCIAL ENTREPRENEURS HAVE A REAL ADVANTAGE

When it comes to rewarding employees, best-selling author and recognition guru Bob Nelson literally wrote the book. His blockbuster book *1001 Ways to Reward Employees* has sold over a million copies, and he speaks on the topic of rewards and recognition to all kinds of organizations, from small, community-based organizations, to Silicon Valley high-tech start-ups, to large, well-established nonprofit organizations and government agencies, all the way up to gigantic, multinational Fortune 500 companies. Many social entrepreneurs believe that they are at a disadvantage when it comes to recognizing and rewarding employees, but, according to Nelson, this is most definitely not the case. Social enterprises have certain assets and advantages that, when built into a well-designed recognition program, give them an edge over *anything* offered by the private sector. Let's find out how you can put the power of rewarding employees to work in *your* organization.

Q: Are there differences between rewarding people in a social enterprise and rewarding people in a for-profit organization?

Bob: Whenever I talk to people about employee rewards and recognition, their tendency is to focus on what they *can't* do instead of what they *can* do. And nowhere is that more prevalent than in nonprofits. They start off by saying "We're not private industry—we can't do that!" The first step in moving toward becoming a social enterprise is to stop saying how you're *not* like them and to start focusing on how you *could be* like them. When it comes to rewards, instead of saying what you can't do—"We don't have the money for this or authority to do that"—you could say "What do we have that could be rewarding to employees that isn't available even in private industry?" When you take that slant at the question, all of a sudden you'll find that you've really got quite a lot.

Q: Like what?

Nelson: Unlike most organizations in private industry, you have people in *your* organization who have come to you because they have an alignment with your mission—your purpose for being. In private industry, the purpose of most organizations is primarily to make money—something that's actually quite difficult to get employees excited about. Social enterprises have purposes—from feeding the hungry, to giving youth meaningful things to do with their free time, to running libraries, and much, much more—that have real meaning to people's lives and that get them excited to play a part.

(continued)

Q: How do you decide what rewards and recognition are best for a particular organization?

Nelson: You start by looking at what the purpose of your organization is and how you can reinforce people along the lines of your purpose. Take the Red Cross, for example. People work for the Red Cross because they are drawn to helping people and being a part of an international organization that rallies around people in their worst times of disaster. To determine the best rewards and recognition for people in the Red Cross, ask how you can help every employee feel that he or she is an important part of the organization's mission—especially an accountant or receptionist who is far away from the front lines. You could, for example, have a "First Response" award for the person or department who acts most like the organization's mission—doing the same thing as a unit in servicing their own organization. That would be a tremendous reward! You look for parallels, you look for the terminology, you make the link that way. You create rewards that allow employees to experience the organization's mission firsthand. Another terrific reward for a social enterprise might be to give team members two weeks to go to a different location to see front-line staff in action, to experience that. It's a learning thing, it gives people a piece of the bigger picture, and it creates a stronger tie to the mission of the organization, which, after all, is what attracted them to join in the first place.

Q: So tying into the organization's mission is an important element of an effective rewards and recognition program?

Nelson: Definitely. And equally good are rewards and recognition that parallel the organization's mission. You could sponsor a child in an employee's name, for example. While it's another organization, and another organization's mission, it's parallel to your own. And, while a private-sector firm might give an employee the use of a BMW for a month, chances are, that's not going to motivate the typical employee working for a social enterprise. If they wanted a flashy car, they would have worked for someone else. You want to get back to the roots of why your employees came to your organization—what drew them there and what's important to them. You could have a day every year where you encourage employees to volunteer with their favorite local charity. Or, for a more performance-based reward, when team members get an excellent rating in a performance review, then they get to take a day off of work to volunteer with a local charity. The idea is to give your performers the opportunity to do a related activity that makes them feel special.

Q: How about volunteers? Where do they fit in?

Nelson: Hands down, the most unappreciated group in all my experience is volunteers. Most nonprofits view volunteers as a kind of shadow population—"We've got our paid staff and we've got our volunteers." As such, they are often left out of an organization's rewards and recognition efforts. The key is getting them visibility within the organization. Bring in upper management to meet with the volunteer group, have an ice cream social, or have an open house where volunteers can bring their families and meet employees, board members, and clients. Tying volunteers into the pride and purpose of why they are there is an incredibly powerful motivator, and it's one that too often is overlooked.

been taken away, and he is still being paid the same amount of money—not a bad deal. You, however, have been punished. All of a sudden you are responsible not only for your own work but for that of someone who isn't doing his job—and you're not being paid a dime more for your effort. The result? Your coworker's behavior is reinforced—chances are he'll continue to do less than is required by his job. And you? Chances are you'll try to figure out some way to do less work, since in reality you're being punished for going beyond the basic requirements of your job.

practical tip   There's definitely a right way and a wrong way to reward employees. In his book *1001 Ways to Reward Employees,* Bob Nelson sets forth guidelines for rewarding and recognizing employees the *right* way. According to Nelson, you should:

✔ *Match the reward to the person.* One-size-fits-all rewards and recognition aren't nearly as effective as ones that are tailored to the individual. One employee may value time off, for example, while another may prefer a cash award or a gift certificate good for purchases at a local department store. Another employee may simply like a pat on the back for a job well done.

✔ *Match the reward to the achievement.* The accomplishment of large achievements or goals should bring with it larger rewards than the accomplishment of small achievements or goals.

✔ *Be timely and specific.* Rewards and recognition have their greatest effect when they are given soon after the behavior being recognized—ideally, on the spot. They also will be more effective when it is clear exactly what behavior is being rewarded. Sorry, this means that annual award ceremonies and award banquets are not the most effective ways to reward and recognize employee effort because they usually recognize employee behavior that occurred months before the event.[12]

While each of these points is critical to the employee rewards and recognition equation, it's particularly important to match the reward to the person who is going to receive it. We'll consider just how to do that in the next section.

WHICH REWARDS WORK BEST?

In 1999, St. Louis–based American Express Incentive Services (AEIS) asked 1,000 American adults a variety of questions regarding their personal experience with rewards and recognition on the job. The results of AEIS's *Achieve More* survey were surprising.

When asked if they had recently received any sort of reward or recognition at work, 18 percent of respondents—almost one-fifth of the total—

reported that they had *never* received a reward or recognition at work. That's *never!* This is particularly surprising considering the fact that giving rewards and other positive behavioral reinforcement will increase desired employee behaviors. Says Darryl Hutson, CEO of AEIS, "If employers are looking for new ways to keep employees happy and on the payroll, it could be as simple as rewarding them for a job well done."

The *Achieve More* survey went on to report some of the best and worst rewards mentioned by those who responded to the survey:

Best Rewards

✔ A verbal thank you for a job well done

✔ A letter of commendation

✔ A good performance evaluation

✔ A career-related gift or training

Worst Rewards

✔ Additional work

✔ Being fired or laid off

✔ T-shirt or clothing

✔ No recognition or being ignored[13]

The key to selecting rewards that work is to personalize them to individual employee preferences. Although, for example, the majority of respondents in the AEIS survey apparently considered T-shirts or clothing to be a poor reward for good performance, *your* case worker or receptionist might just think that a T-shirt emblazoned with your organization's name is a terrific reward for good performance. Everyone is different, and the impact of the universe of individual rewards and recognition possibilities varies from person to person.

So, how do you find out which rewards will work best for your employees? It's simple: Ask them. Says Janelle Brittain, executive director of Dynamic Performance Institute, "Remember, what one person sees as a reward, another may not. The best way for organizations to find out how their employees will feel rewarded is to ask what's important to them."[14]

Once you find out from your employees what kinds of rewards and recognition they find most motivating, then you can set out to build a culture of recognition that will have a positive impact on your employees, your clients, and your organization.

REWARDING PEOPLE FOR LITTLE OR NO MONEY

If entrepreneurial organizations are anything, they are willing to try out new ideas in hopes of finding a better way to solve an old problem, and they do their best to squeeze the most bang out of every precious dollar that they spend. These same attitudes extend to employee rewards and recognition in the context of social enterprises.

The fact is, you don't need to spend a lot of money to reward and recognize your employees. As the American Express Incentive Services *Achieve More* survey shows, the most effective rewards cost little or no money. And since this means that your budget won't have to be an issue when you give employee rewards and recognition, you're limited only by your imagination.

action step   Wondering what to do to reward your employees for little or no money? Why not give a few of these a try?

- ✔ Give out birthday cards with a cupcake and a candle.
- ✔ Throw a barbecue picnic at a nearby park.
- ✔ Send flowers home on the first day of work.
- ✔ Put gold stars on employee computers along with a note of thanks.
- ✔ Have a brown-bag lunch to welcome new employees and to introduce them to the team.
- ✔ Have an ice cream sundae break on a warm summer day.
- ✔ Sponsor a department pizza party.
- ✔ Read letters from satisfied customers at weekly staff meeting.
- ✔ Hold staff meetings outdoors when weather permits.
- ✔ Personalize employee business cards with nicknames.
- ✔ Give employees an extra hour off for lunch.
- ✔ Keep a well-stocked candy jar on your desk and invite employees to partake whenever the urge hits them.
- ✔ Create a special memo to recognize a notable team achievement; post it on the department bulletin board and fax it to all locations.
- ✔ Have a crazy hat day.
- ✔ Post letters of thanks from customers on break room bulletin boards.
- ✔ Attach thank-you notes to employee paychecks.

As you can see, when it comes to finding interesting ways to show your appreciation to employees, the sky's the limit. As a social entrepreneur, you are free to try out innovative new ways to make the most impact on your employees and your organization. The real secret is to be sure that whatever you do doesn't become routine and boring, and an employee expectation rather than a surprise. Be creative and mix things up. The result will be happy, motivated employees, and that's a very good thing for any organization to have more of.

Summary

No one ever said that leading and managing people was an easy thing to do, and indeed it's not. Social entrepreneurs face special challenges in this regard. They have to attract people to new organizations, lead them through the difficult process of launching an innovative venture, and they often have to do this on a shoestring. But the good news is that leading and managing are skills that can be learned, practiced, and perfected, no matter how old you are or how long you've worked for a particular organization. As you move forward in your career, keep these things in mind:

✔ Anyone in any organization can be a leader.

✔ Leadership focuses on people, whereas management focuses on things.

✔ The best leaders are able to communicate a vision to staff, clients, and the community while building high-performing organizations.

✔ Smart leaders know that they can get far more done by delegating duties and tasks—and the authority necessary to get them done—to members of their team.

✔ Today's most successful organizations put their people first.

✔ Effective organizations allow team members to do what they do best every day of the week.

✔ Celebrate what you want to see more of.

✔ Match staff rewards to the person, match the reward to the achievement, and be timely and specific.

✔ The most effective rewards cost little or no money.

Notes

1. Cited in Stephenie Overman, "Calculating the Rewards of Nonprofit Management," *Executive Talent,* Fall 2000, *www.aesc.org/executivetalent/nonprofit-mgmt.html.*
2. Jim Kouzes and Barry Posner, *The Leadership Challenge,* (San Francisco: Jossey-Bass, 1987), p. 8.
3. Warren Bennis, *Learning to Lead: A Workbook on Becoming a Leader* (Reading, MA: Perseus Books/Addison-Wesley, 1997), p. 9.
4. Jeffrey Pfeffer, *The Human Equation: Building Profits by Putting People First* (Cambridge, MA: Harvard Business School Press, 1998), p. xv.
5. Ibid., pp. 64–65.
6. Edward Lawler, *From the Ground Up* (San Francisco: Jossey-Bass, 1996), pp. 32–33.
7. Curt Coffman, "Gallup's Discoveries About Great Managers and Great Workplaces," The Workplace Column, February 4, 2000, *www.gallup.com/poll/managing/RightPeople.asp.*
8. Kathe Sorensen and Steve Crabtree, "The Flip Side of Talent," GallupJournal.com columns, July 30, 2001, *www.gallupjournal.com/CA/st/20010730.asp.*

9. *www.relojournal.com/CORPCULT.HTM.*
10. Interview with Arnold "Mac" Anderson, December 1998.
11. Tom Peters, *Thriving on Chaos,* (New York: Alfred A. Knopf, 1988), p. 311.
12. Bob Nelson, *1001 Ways to Reward Employees* (New York: Workman, 1994), pp. xv–xvi.
13. American Express Incentive Services, *1999 Achieve More Survey,* June 1999.
14. "Rewards May Reduce Turnover," *Flight School Business,* June 2000 *http://www.aopaflighttraining.org/newsletters/jun1_00.cfm.*

Chapter 5

MANAGING YOUR BOARD ENTREPRENEURIALLY

Jerry Kitzi, President, Social Venture Partners of Greater Kansas City

IN THIS CHAPTER

Understanding the role of the board

Life cycle of the board

Board functions

Creating an entrepreneurial environment

Alternative governance structures

Board recruitment

Orientation and development

Removing members of the board

Time for a change

Excellent social enterprises are characterized by excellent relationships between the board and the executive. The board is the single most important resource available to the executive. Conversely, the most entrepreneurially minded executive can become stifled and defeated by an ineffective board.

core concept   A social enterprise that chooses a not-for-profit structure is required by law to have a *governing board* of directors. The board has the responsibility of carrying out the mission of the enterprise. And the board is, in fact, the entity that holds the public's trust—the last source of protection for the clients and investors.

Boards differ according to the type of enterprise and stage of development along the life cycle of the enterprise. There are numerous alternative structures to help the board accomplish its objectives. And recruitment of board members is one of the most critical functions of the enterprise and directly related to the variables just mentioned.

The collective wisdom, energy, and connections of a group of committed volunteers is one of the important assets that social entrepreneurs have in their command. Successful entrepreneurs know what it takes to effectively grow this asset, and value it. Therefore, it is imperative that the board reflects an entrepreneurial spirit as well. Ultimately it's people who make the difference, not money.

UNDERSTANDING THE ROLE OF THE BOARD

Legally, the board owns the enterprise. The entrepreneur may have the ideas, passion and enthusiasm, and ultimately may be the one person whom others will look at to get the job done. But the board is the legally responsible entity for the enterprise if it is a not-for-profit corporation.

The board is the first resource an entrepreneur puts together to get the job done. In fact, aside from the entrepreneurial spirit, vision, and commitment that the entrepreneur brings to the table, there is no other entity that will stand as willing and as able to tackle the job over the life cycle of the enterprise. Over time, the relationship between the board and the executive becomes more like a partnership, and there is shared ownership and expectations. The relationship grows as long as there is clarity regarding roles and responsibilities and, of course, trust.

There are many similarities between the roles and responsibilities of for-profit boards and not-for-profit boards. However, consider these observations by Sharon M. Oster, from her book *Strategic Management for Nonprofit Organizations,* as an example of one of the basic differences between the role of a for profit board with that of a not for profit board.

> *In an ideal setting, we can characterize the role of the board in a typical publicly traded corporation as follows: The stockholders own the company. They delegate the responsibility for running the company to the board and it, in turn, delegates most of that operating responsibility to the management of the company. The board, however, retains ultimate control over the management. . . . In the for-profit sector, shareholders enforce their rights over directors, while customers protect themselves through their purchasing behavior.*

core concept Nonprofits are subject to a nondistribution constraint, meaning that they are not allowed by law to pass along any profits—net earnings or "surplus"—to those entities in control of the corporation (e.g., its directors, staff, or members). As a consequence, there are no stockholders in the nonprofit and there is no one with clear claims over any residuals. Thus the usual role of the board as a protector of stockholder rights over the interests of management is absent in the nonprofit.

On the other hand, the donor in the nonprofit may need some protection against the possibility of expropriation of the benefits of donations by internal management. In this sense, the nonprofit's board can be thought of as providing protection for one of the customers. In a broader sense, given the tax exemption of nonprofits, the board can be thought of as providing protection to the public who has indirectly contributed these tax savings.[1]

Generally speaking, foundation program officers, corporate-giving directors, or any other entity that has the responsibility for making investment decisions with a not-for-profit look to an organization's board for assurances that grant dollars will be spent prudently. Program officers believe that the entrepreneur will be responsible for getting the job done—the service delivered and the outcome achieved—but that the board will make sure it got done efficiently and effectively. Boards are the investors' primary source of protection.

Likewise, clients at the local level are in many cases accessing services that are subsidized or of last resort. They can't influence "quality" by refusing a service they may desperately need—a food kitchen for a homeless family, for example. These clients have little if any purchasing power and, without a board for protection, have little recourse against the practices of management and/or staff. This latter phenomenon is very common and should be considered a serious responsibility for the board. It is one of the driving factors behind the push to have clients represented on boards. And it necessitates a process for the board to have access to regular feedback from clients regarding the services and programs of the enterprise.

Brian O'Connell, author, founding president of the Independent Sector, and professor of public service at Tufts University's Lincoln Filene Center for Citizenship and Public Affairs, states in *The Board Member's Book:*

> *There are some universal truths applicable to every nonprofit organization, beginning with legal responsibility. Whether as board members you are called trustees, directors, governors, or something else, you are in essence the trustees in the literal and legal sense of the term. No matter how the organization is structured or the degree of authority delegated to staff, committees or affiliates, the board and therefore the trustees are ultimately accountable.[2]*

The board is the entity legally responsible for the enterprise. Beyond that fundamental responsibility, the board also holds the public trust and is the source of protection for customers and investors. Excellent working relationships, or partnerships, between the board and the executive characterizes successful enterprises. Social entrepreneurs understand the importance of this partnership. While it is the entrepreneur who is expected to produce results, it is the board that is ultimately held accountable.

LIFE CYCLE OF THE BOARD

Karl Mathiasen discusses this concept in his booklet for the National Center for Nonprofit Boards. Mathiasen contends that "Just as nonprofits pass through identifiable organizational stages, so do nonprofit boards. The first of these is the organizing board, the second is the governing board and the third is the institutional board."[3]

The life cycle of the board is related to the life cycle of the enterprise. The needs, roles and responsibilities, and board membership differ accordingly. Start-ups have very different needs from mature enterprises, and the level of involvement by the founding board members or organizing board, to use Mathiasen's terminology, is usually very intense. In essence, the board is used as volunteer staff performing many functions typically reserved for staff once the enterprise is up and running.

Established enterprises rely on the board to keep focused on the horizon, helping staff generate new opportunities and partnerships, and helping make tough decisions, such as putting to rest ineffective programs and/or services.

tool of the trade   An enterprise is typically in a start-up mode over the course of its first three to five years. However, once an enterprise matures, that doesn't mean the enterprise stands still. Numerous opportunities for growth and expansion require start-up activities anywhere along the enterprise life cycle. Exhibit 5.1 identifies how some of the board functions change as the enterprise matures.

The needs you have at any particular time over the life cycle of the enterprise should influence whom you recruit for the board. (Recruitment is discussed later in this chapter.) Also, as the enterprise matures, the types of governance and alternative board structures put in place give additional options that increase your ability to use these resources entrepreneurially.

BOARD FUNCTIONS

There are always gray areas that defy clear definition in terms of who does what for the enterprise. Many authors try to create charts and tables to assist boards and staff in the delineation of roles and responsibilities. No matter whom you read, most ultimately concur that it's the board's responsibility to set policy and direction for the enterprise and the staff's responsibility to manage the work of the enterprise.

gem of wisdom   If only the world were that precise. Consider the advice of Brian O'Connell:

The worst illusion ever perpetrated in the nonprofit field is that the board of directors makes policy and the staff carries it out. This is just

Roles and Responsibilities	Start-up Enterprise	Established Enterprise
Day-to-day operations	Heavy involvement. Board members are in essence volunteer staff.	Less involvement. Participation in special events, assignments, and other resource needs. Responsibility has shifted to executive and staff.
Budget and finances	Active involvement. Review purchases of equipment, leases, contracts, establishing budgets, and financial controls, etc.	Little involvement. Executive has authorization to expend resources according to approved budget, staffing needs, etc.
Long-range planning	No involvement. Activity focused on start-up functions reviewed against short-term benchmarks.	One of the primary responsibilities, done in conjunction with staff. Strategic plan looking five years out.
Resource development	Active involvement. Helps generate needed resources for operations and organization infrastructure—information systems, financial procedures, personnel policies, legal advice, benefit packages, etc.	Active involvement. Helps to generate new opportunities with the executive that build on organizational strengths and assets.

EXHIBIT 5.1 Life cycle of the board: roles and responsibilities.

not so. The board with the help of staff makes policy, and the board, with the help of staff, carries it out. Unless volunteers are committed and involved in the action phase of the organization, the agency cannot develop and, in fact, should not be characterized as a voluntary organization. Also it is naïve to assume that the staff doesn't have considerable influence—usually too much—on policy formulation.[4]

Generally speaking, you will call on the board to carry out two functional areas: governance and resource. Again, how these functions get carried out is very much dependent on the stage of development the enterprise is in.

GOVERNANCE

Some of the specific governance functions include:

✔ *Bylaws.* The initial board (sometimes called the founding board) establishes the bylaws. In short order the bylaws are the rules by which the board operates—the who, what, when, where, and how.

The bylaws should be reviewed by the board every so often to assure compliance. The board should make the necessary adjustments as the enterprise changes in a rapidly changing environment.

✔ *The executive.* The board has the responsibility of hiring the executive/administrator who will manage the operations of the enterprise. In start-ups, the person with the exciting idea or innovation may actually be putting together the board to support the work. However, any enterprise that creates social value and is meeting a need over time will experience turnover at the top. The ongoing responsibility for hiring, monitoring performance, developing, and firing the executive rests with the board.

✔ *Monitoring.* Board members must accept their official role as fiduciary agents of the enterprise who are legally responsible for the proper use of the resources and/or assets of the enterprise. The board has the legal responsibility to monitor the enterprise for compliance with the stated laws, regulations, and tax guidelines. Internally the board should establish processes for monitoring the goals of the enterprise, budget expenditures, policies, reporting, and the like. Externally the board should monitor the progress and effectiveness of the enterprise with the principal stakeholders/customers. Clear indicators of success and tools for monitoring by staff and board are critical.

RESOURCES

The board can be a tremendous source of knowledge, skills, labor, connections, and goodwill. Although governance responsibilities are pretty well spelled out in most organizations, an executive can be as creative as possible when designing ways to use board members as resources. When board members are used properly, the executive's effectiveness is extended dramatically and the board members experience a sense of meaningful contribution. The definitive words here are "meaningful contribution." Consider the perspective of Barbara E. Taylor, Richard P. Chait, and Thomas P. Holland, from their article, "The New Work of the Nonprofit Board":

> *The key to improved performance is discovering and doing what we call the new work of the board. Trustees are interested in results. High-powered people lose energy when fed a steady diet of trivia. They may oblige management by discussing climate control for the art exhibitions, the condition of old steam lines, or the design of a new logo, but they get charged up when searching for a new CEO, successfully completing a capital campaign, or developing and implementing a strategic plan. New work is another term for work that matters.[5]*

Think about your own experiences with volunteering. If you felt like just another warm body, you probably didn't stick around. If you felt you were valued and appreciated, you probably continued to volunteer with that organization.

The following list describes some of the potential functions for board members in the general area of "resource." But again, the quality of their performance in any one of those roles depends on the degree to which it is in fact "meaningful."

✔ *Fund raising.* This was once considered one of the most critical roles for a board member. It was expected that each member be actively involved—the old "Give, Get, or Get Off." But it's an old concept. Fund raising was much more related to charitable purposes and therefore can be a limiting concept for social entrepreneurs. Instead, consider *resource development* or *resource mobilization.* The governance function is approving budgets and monitoring the financial status of the enterprise. The resource function is generating resources—revenue, volunteer support, new partnerships. One aspect of fund raising, generating revenue for the enterprise, is still very important. Some board members are very good at it. Others are very good at contributing behind the scenes—contributing to the development of a business plan/proposal, participating in special fund-raising events, making connections that generate new funding relationships, educating policymakers. There should be an explicit expectation and clearly defined tasks for each board member to contribute to the sustainability of the enterprise. *The executive is not the sole person responsible for the financial security of the enterprise!*

✔ *Charting the future.* An established enterprise needs an entrepreneurial board that keeps its eyes on the horizon. The board has the responsibility for setting the direction—helping the enterprise develop an aggressive strategic or long-range plan. While the board has this responsibility, the most effective planning processes are a combined board and staff partnership. Ownership and buy-in are critical for growth and effectiveness. Provide opportunities for retreats or related activities that promote looking to the future. Make sure the members have materials that scan the environment or project future trends.

✔ *Cultivating brilliance.* Creating a board can be thought of as a tremendous opportunity to put together a collection of knowledge and skill sets that assure you of entrepreneurial know-how and programmatic expertise. As mentioned earlier, any enterprise, whether it's a start-up or a 100-year-old institution, has numerous resource needs.

✔ *Creating an inventory of needs.* Areas such as information technology, negotiating skills, marketing, financial investments, human resource, and programmatic experience, to name few, are skills that you can have access to from your volunteers and save valuable capital while still gaining the knowledge and information needed for the operations of the enterprise. If you bring on a board member who has connections or valuable knowledge and skills, tap them—big time. If you can attract a successful entrepreneur who also has passion for the mission, you now have one heck of a valuable resource!

✔ *Building relationships.* Relationships matter! The world revolves around a series of relationships. Yes, it is true we are all just six degrees away from knowing everyone else. It may be impossible for each board member to speak eloquently about the specifics of programs or services offered, but it should be expected that each could offer a passionate account of the social value of the enterprise and the difference it makes. Social gatherings, conferences, community meetings, and other special events are all opportunities to get the word out and gain support for the enterprise. Likewise, each board member should have the mind-set of opportunity recognition—constantly on the lookout for potential partnerships or connections that further the cause for the enterprise.

red flag   You can not do it alone. First, it's not legal, and second, it's physically impossible. The board is the legal entity responsible for the enterprise. Developed properly, the board is a tremendous resource to help carry out the mission. If you are a volunteer board member reading this, you can't do it alone either. The board needs an entrepreneurial leader to carry out the day-to-day functions of the enterprise.

CREATING AN ENTREPRENEURIAL ENVIRONMENT

Success in the nonprofit sector is not easy. In light of soft money from funders, changing political winds, and an increasing competitive presence from the for-profit sector, survival is difficult at best. It takes a strong entrepreneurial mind-set and commitment from both the executive and the board. Yet there is high turnover among not-for-profit executives, little attention paid to board development, too few programs that focus on board leadership, and a reluctance by board members to avail themselves of the training that does exist.

There are boards that function poorly—micromanaging staff, engaging in small "p" political infighting, forcing their own agenda, and struggling to achieve a quorum for regularly scheduled meetings. There are executives who spend more time selling the board than involving the board. Peter C. Brinckerhoff states in his book *Mission-Based Management,* "Too often boards either totally dominate an organization, thus blocking the staff's ability to do their jobs, or are so subservient to staff 'expertise' that the staff in effect manipulate the board at will. Neither are effective uses of resources, and both are counterproductive."[6]

An entrepreneurial leader suffocates in a dominating board environment and tends to burn out from being overextended in a subservient board environment. A number of contributing factors contribute to the right balance and ultimately affect the entrepreneurial spirit.

✔ *Culture.* The entrepreneurial spirit thrives in a culture that promotes it. While it seems obvious, in reality, creating an entrepreneurial culture in an nonprofit organization is easier said than done. If the board expects an entrepreneurial mind-set and rewards it, then management and staff usually will live up to that expectation. A board should place an emphasis on strategic operating plans, value-added partnerships and alliances, and results. The board should reward innovation, opportunity recognition, and responsible risk taking that furthers the cause of the enterprise.

✔ *Size.* The not-for-profit sector is notorious for large boards. Thirty-, 40-, and 50-member boards are not all uncommon. Size can create a bureaucratic nightmare if not structured and/or organized properly. Board effectiveness is based on a team function. Therefore, keep your board small, 10 to 12 at most. Use alternative structures like advisory boards, work groups, board teams, and task forces to attract other volunteer resources. (We talk about alternative board structures later in this chapter.) Remember, roughly 50 percent of an executive's time is spent relating to the board. Don't create structures that cause the executive to collapse under the weight of the board.

✔ *Stage of development of the organization.* As mentioned in the life cycle section, start-ups require greater day-to-day involvement by the board. Interaction with the staff subsides to some degree as the organization gets its feet under it. Sometimes, however, the board struggles with this transition and tensions develop. Established enterprises have experience and trusting relationships to fall back on whenever operational issues arise.

✔ *Relationship between the executive and the board.* Most boards and staff have set policies that guide the work of the enterprise. As long as there is trust, clarity of direction, and a good flow of information, the executive is free to run the organization with the board's blessing, not permission—a huge difference. This is where most young enthusiastic entrepreneurs falter in their relationship with the board, thinking that it is better to seek forgiveness than permission. That may be an effective approach, but not during the early stages of relationships. The answer is simple: Communicate! However, there must be history and trust in the relationship or there is liable to be trouble. An executive should never get out ahead of the blockers (board). Unfortunately, this is a lesson most young executives with a strong entrepreneurial spirit only learn the hard way.

✔ *Hierarchy.* Flat organizations are quicker. The "quality team" concept proposed by Edward Deming may have peaked, but the idea of the people closest to the work creating the innovation is still smart. Innovation is still the best source of opportunity for the enterprise. When new ideas from entrepreneurial thinkers within an organization have to travel though levels of hierarchy, they tend to die—as does the entrepreneurial spirit. Getting the board to support inverted organizational structure places the focus of the work of the enterprise on the front-line people. It is one of the best reflections of a servant leadership belief system. It's a very tough sell for old-school management types, but it is an internal structure that stimulates the entrepreneurial spirit.

Besides having a common understanding and commitment to the mission by the board and staff, they must have a commitment to the entrepreneurial spirit. Structures and policies that get in the way of entrepreneurs can be overcome in the short run, but over time they stifle the entrepreneurial spirit. Remember, for many entrepreneurs, rules are just temporary guidelines whose time for change have not yet been realized—at least not by people other than the entrepreneur who sees a better way! The board and the staff should and can develop structures and strategies that promote creative thinking and problem solving, encourage critical analysis and reflection, and reward responsible risk taking.

ALTERNATIVE GOVERNANCE STRUCTURES

By far, the best way to be appointed to a committee is to leave a meeting early. We all laugh at the suggestion during meetings. After all, this work, aside from being meaningful, is also supposed to be fun! Unfortunately, many times that's exactly how appointments occur. Committee work is just as important as any other function—perhaps even more so since it signifies a process that may delve deeper into an important issue or subject.

The point here is that the same thoughtful process that goes into the selection and care of a board member should go into the selection and support of committee members. Committees—or other forms of alternative structures—are the workplaces of the volunteer. It's where their contributions usually occur. Make sure expectations are clearly stated, including an emphasis on "out-of-the-box" thinking. Make sure the volunteers are well supported and their work valued and appreciated.

BOARD COMMITTEES

There are numerous board structures and equally numerous names for groups that do the work. Keep this as simple as possible. The question is: "What work needs to get done?" Again, consider the words of Brian O'Connell:

> It is a standard practice today for all kinds of organizations to go through the exercise of starting with a blank slate. If there were no committees, which ones would you actually recreate, and are there other ways to do the same business? You may want to write down the functions that must be performed and then decide on the simplest way of carrying out those jobs. Such functions might include bylaws, personnel, finance, annual meeting, fundraising, public relations, awards, nominating, legal, program(s), emergency decisions, and other business between board meetings.[7]

Before suggesting alternative structures, keep in mind that everything should flow from—or back to—a small governing board. This is the core group—the legally accountable group—and it should be small enough in number to work effectively and efficiently. As mentioned earlier, not-for-profits are notorious for large boards. And while many organizations have wonderful rationales for why that needs to be the case, large boards are just too cumbersome to maneuver. In today's environment, you need entrepreneurial speed. With that said, it's a great idea to have larger numbers of qualified volunteers available to meet the resource needs of the enterprise.

✔ *Standing committees.* A number of functions related to governance can be handled by a small group of board members. Typically, standing committees are described in the bylaws. They represent ongoing work versus time-limited special needs. A finance committee will be needed year in and year out. A special concept team looking into technology advances and program delivery should have a very short life cycle with definite deadlines for reporting back. Standing committees are pretty traditional. Keeping them outcome focused and timely with the expected results requires staff support and high expectations. Most often these committees are comprised of governing board members and staff. Some use of outside volunteers can occur when necessary.

✔ *Targeted action teams.* Short-term ad hoc teams represent flexible, special-need functions that can and should have a short shelf life. As these teams have clearly stated expectations and end dates, you have much greater flexibility in terms of recruiting additional volunteers. They are also represented by a shared responsibility of work by volunteers and staff working hand in hand. The old fears on the part of board members or an executive who wants to hold onto tight, hierarchical roles can sometimes result in the blurring of lines between the roles and responsibilities of board and staff. However, meaningful work requires meaningful participation.

ALTERNATIVE STRUCTURES

There are a number of ways to extend the reach of the enterprise into the community or into new fields of expertise. Many not-for-profits have applied a variety of alternative structures—some with great success. There is a trade-off, however, for the executive. More board structures provide greater reach and access to expertise, but at a cost in terms of time commitment. Good, honest discussion among the executive, board chair, and full governing board is absolutely essential to plan for the effective use and maintenance of alternative structures. And from a strategic point of view, alternative structures provide an opportunity to observe potential future board members at work. (We discuss board member recruitment later.)

✔ *Advisory boards.* Advisory boards—sometimes called auxiliary boards—have as their core function providing support and counsel relative to a specific aspect(s) of the enterprise. They are usually larger in number and have broader community/client representation than boards of directors. They can have formal structures and meeting ties or they can be more informal—a collection of advisors who agree to be available to the enterprise. A local YMCA might have a Youth Advisory Board or a local church might have advisory boards for each one of its ministries. One thing is for sure: The function and expectations of these boards need to be clearly stated to keep the group headed in the right direction. As a word of caution, consider the words of Cyril O. Houle in her publication, *Governing Boards:*

> *An auxiliary board may gain so much prominence and prestige that it is confused in the public mind—or, worse, in it own—with the board where controlling power lies. An auxiliary board may gradually take on more and more functions until it exactly parallels the controlling board; in such a case, there is in effect a two-house legislature, and every issue must be carried through both boards—to the eventual despair of the executive. Two boards may*

quarrel, or become deadlocked, or have any other kind of difficulties imaginable all to the detriment of the program they are supposed to guide and aid.[8]

✔ Again, establishing clear expectations and guidelines can avert these kinds of problems. Houle believes expectations and guidelines should be "set down in writing and generally understood." What must be understood is the function and the simple fact that the governing board may at any time (in full partnership with the executive) decide to end the function. According to John Carver in his book, *Boards That Make a Difference:*

> *Advisory boards can advise the governing board, the chief executive officer (CEO), or other staff. They can be positioned anywhere in the organization as long as they formally attach to some "proper" organizational element. Advisory boards are optional and have only as much authority as the authorizing point within the legitimate organization chooses to grant. . . . As long as some position within the organization can, even potentially, retract that authority, the group is not a governing board.*[9]

✔ *Operating boards.* There are examples of legal not-for-profit entities that have no staff yet plenty of work. In these situations, the board recognizes that is the governing board, auxiliary board, and more, all rolled up into one. Coalitions, councils, and other civic-interest groups that have, as their primary function, the provision of a forum for membership to meet and network often fall into this category. This is not to be confused with a "working board," a term usually used to describe an expectation of involvement for prospective trustees considering a position on a board.

✔ *Business enterprise board.* The emphasis on generating earned income in the independent sector has increased over the last decade. As a result, more and more social enterprises are focused on revenue-generating businesses. As long as the revenue-generating service or product is directly related to the mission of the enterprise, it is still tax exempt. When the connection isn't that clear, many not-for-profits elect to form a for-profit subsidiary corporation designed to generate profits that in turn support the ongoing operations of the not-for-profit parent corporation. When housed in the not-for-profit, the board can be considered an auxiliary board. When a new corporation is formed, a new board—the business enterprise board—is charged with the governance functions. However, in either case, the primary focus shifts from mission to profit—not to the exclusion of mission, just a greater emphasis on profit. Selecting volunteers for the enterprise board is especially important.

Volunteers serving on not-for-profit boards usually emphasize the public good. This often creates conflict with board members whose orientation is selling goods or services to the public.

Numerous structures and functions are associated with the work of the board. Keep it simple and follow the advice of O'Connell: "I believe in the principle of least number."[10] Small governing boards complemented by committee work and alternative board structures can enhance your organization's ability to achieve your mission. But don't forget that it doesn't happen without cost. Determine what is the right blend for you according to the type of organization, age of the organization, and purpose.

BOARD RECRUITMENT

Whether you inherited your board or are about to put one together, recruitment is one of the most important activities that will affect the future of the enterprise. It's just as important as the hiring process for staff—you, of course, want the best possible candidates for the position! The decision about whom you need is linked to what you need and why you need it. And those decisions are based on where you are along the life cycle of the enterprise.

Many potential board members are attracted to an organization's start-up phase, where uncertainty and conflict are all just part of the growth process and are not barriers in the way of the mission. Other potential members may feel less effective when serving on established boards even though they may absolutely endorse the vision and mission of the enterprise.

That isn't to say the work of established boards is mundane and boring. Quite the contrary, it's the functions that are different. And it's probable that with growth and expansion, start-up kinds of functions will appear all along the life cycle of the enterprise. As an entrepreneurial leader, you have the flexibility to establish committees or structures that are constantly exploring new opportunities and or value added partnerships.

In addition to the organizational need, there are the needs of the board members to consider—why they want to serve on the board. Consider their motivation, and gain an understanding of their personal strengths and preferences.

A word of caution before exploring the process of recruitment. Putting together a board of like-minded volunteers committed to a common vision has a downside: groupthink! Consider the advice of Sharon Oster in her book *Strategic Management of Nonprofit Organizations:*

Developing a common vision by recruiting board members who are already committed to the institution is not without its costs. This recruitment strategy typically reduces board diversity, and may encourage conformity, and resistance to change. Evidence suggests that homogeneous boards are conflict-averse, a feature that enhances board effectiveness in easy times, but may be a liability when change is needed.[11]

That doesn't mean that if you are an abortion-rights advocacy organization, you have to place the spokesperson for the local right-to-life organization on your board. It only suggests you should be careful of groupthink when considering the board's makeup.

THE RECRUITING PROCESS

The process of recruiting a board should be taken very seriously. Consider yourself the owner of a major league franchise when thinking about the board. What are the needs for the team to be a winner? Who are the best players out there? How will the potential player fit with the values and beliefs of the enterprise?

Usually a board committee—the nominating committee—organizes the process. A strong piece of advice for execs: Do not abdicate the responsibility for selecting members to the board. Board members, if you are reading this, do not exclude the executive from the recruitment process. This absolutely, positively must be a partnership process.

Some might argue that recruiting board members is strictly a board responsibility. Others argue that the executive alone should surface the candidates to the board. Remember, the board and the executive need each other to accomplish the mission and to provide leadership and continuity in the future as members rotate onto and off of the board.

A reliable method for determining who and what is needed is to chart it out using a mini-gap analysis such as the four-step one that follows.

1. *What are your needs?* Keep in mind a cross between "governance" and "resource" skills and experience. List the functional needs that exist for the board now as well as where you are going. (Is the strategic plan suggesting a direction that requires different expertise from what you have now?) Do the funding sources have specific requirements that mandate certain board membership criteria? Some federal and state contracts/awards require a percentage of clients be represented on the board. (Community health centers are an example.) The majority of a board must be community residents if certain state block grants have been received, and so on. List the mandates on the needs list. Be sure to include categories that will

provide diversity in terms of age, race, and gender. It is amazing how many social ventures that are targeting a certain population, say youth or the homeless, fail to recruit and develop these clients for board work simply because they are seen as not being capable.

2. *What are your assets?* An alternative to thinking about needs is to focus on strengths. What are the current assets of the enterprise? Prepare a list of strengths if you are an established enterprise and develop strategies to deepen and expand them. If you are strong at marketing, then you might develop a succession plan targeting an exciting entrepreneurial marketing firm for potential candidates to keep this asset strong and viable. If your strength is community trust, you might consider a succession plan that targets trusted community leaders who are supportive of your mission.

3. *Whom do you have?* Determine who on the board currently fills specific needs or provides specific assets, and don't forget to account for how long they will be around. Board membership is not a lifetime appointment. It doesn't matter how good they are; you must have board turnover. The board should have addressed this when establishing the bylaws—length of term, term limits, and staggered terms. In *Mission-Based Management,* Peter Brinckerhoff recommends the following:

> *My suggestion is a three-year term, with a maximum of two successive terms before a board member goes off for at least a year. Thus, one-third of your board is up for renewal each year, and this gives you a chance to evaluate them and recruit both new people and new skills regularly. Also, a three-year term works well with my recommendation on strategic plans, which include a planning retreat every three years or at least once in every board member's term of office.*[12]

Put a rotation plan into place that considers the review of the strategic plan (five-year plan gets reviewed and rewritten every three years).

4. *What are the gaps and who do you get to fill them?* The next step is generating the list of potential candidates. Keep in mind that alternative board structures provide an excellent opportunity to recruit additional volunteers in support of the work of the enterprise. And these volunteers are likely candidates for future board positions—first, because of their commitment to the mission demonstrated by their involvement, and, second, because you have had time to evaluate their performance in a teamlike setting. The reason it is so important to evaluate volunteers is that their values and beliefs need match the values and beliefs of the enterprise. Successful organi-

zations often have a strong culture that is founded on a core set of values and beliefs. It's not just getting results—it's how you get them that is the foundation of the not-for-profit sector.

 Volunteer Action Centers in most communities are a good source for volunteers, as are business schools (MBA alumni associations) and local entrepreneurial associations (such as the Young Entrepreneurs' Organization). United Way trains volunteers, and large corporations often encourage their employees to volunteer. And current board and staff probably have observed potential candidates. Consider a gentle reminder by Brian O'Connell:

Many boards and nominating committees want to go after the big names and new faces. After all, it makes us feel good to be serving on the board with Mr. or Ms. "Big" and to look down a bit on the organization's workers. On the other hand, one of the constant lessons of leadership is that people grow with responsibility and are capable of far more than appears on the surface. Many a leader has been amazed to discover that the people he or she has unfairly pegged at one level of output are capable of much more. An individual who has demonstrated faithful service and effectiveness at one level is the first source of leadership for higher levels of responsibility. This includes precinct captains and taskforce leaders who have worked faithfully and who often are overlooked for other responsibilities.[13]

Numerous resources present more in-depth processes for recruiting and developing board members. The National Center for Nonprofit Boards has great information.[14] You also might try *How to Recruit Great Board Members* by Dorian Dodson.

ORIENTATION AND DEVELOPMENT

Board development is the responsibility of the board and the staff. Both benefit from well-informed, committed volunteers, and, therefore, both should have active roles in their orientation and ongoing development.

ORIENTATION

The work of this sector is based on relationships. Therefore, the orientation process begins with connecting the new member to someone on the board.

✔ *Mentoring.* Mentoring by a second-term board member is a very effective strategy. It helps the new member feel connected to someone. An additional benefit is the impact on the mentor who is expected to help educate and interpret ongoing issues for the new member. Nothing board members do causes them to get more in touch with what the enterprise is all about as fully informing someone else. Discussing the structure of the board and the norms of the enterprise gets board members in touch with what they feel is good about the board and what isn't. It puts them in a perfect position to contribute to the next board assessment (assuming that you and the board have agreed to periodic assessments).

✔ *Reference materials.* Before the new member attends his or her first board meeting, the board member must have some sort of history of the organization. Provide the new member an opportunity to learn about the organization, tour the community being served if appropriate, and meet with community stakeholders. Also provide reference materials. Some people learn best by stories and by seeing and touching the enterprise at work. Some prefer consuming information by reading relevant materials that document the past and clearly articulate future direction. Provide both.

✔ The *Orientation Manual,* Board Member's Book, or whatever name you choose for housing the information that will help to educate the new member should contain some or all of the following:

- The history of the organization including the bylaws (vision and mission statements)
- Statement of values and beliefs
- Board member contract
- Membership profiles
- Glossary—the ABCs of your acronyms
- Staff profiles including the job description of the executive officer
- Program/services descriptions
- Annual report with a recent audit
- Strategic plan
- Operating plan with outcomes, marketing plan, and budget information
- Agency brochures/descriptive communication pieces
- Current financial statements
- Funding sources
- Meeting schedules
- Board committees and descriptions of committee chairman responsibilities
- Conflict-of-interest disclosure statement (to be filled out)

✔ *Board member contract.* An important first step in creating excellent board members is informing them of the expected behavior and having them formally commit to it. The norms by which you operate have to be clearly stated. The easiest way to remove ineffective trustees is to refer back to the expectations they signed off on when first committing to the enterprise. This document gets every member off on the right foot and protects you, the executive, from the negative effects of poor board performance. (The next section discusses removing ineffective board members.) Design your own form for a board member contract. The following is an example of what it might look like with some points of concern. Your contract should represent what you believe is important for your board to be entrepreneurial and an effective asset for the enterprise.

The contract should be reviewed carefully, signed, and placed in the board member's book and kept on file with the rest of the legal documents you file. It is highly recommended that the enterprise explicitly state the belief system regarding the principles of entrepreneurship in either the "values and beliefs" statement or the board member contract.

DEVELOPMENT

Board member development starts on day 1. It begins with orientation and ends with resignation. Everything in between is development. The high level of involvement by senior trustees and staff in the orientation should continue over the first year of board membership. Often, it may take a good year of committee work, board meetings, and special events for the new board member to feel as if he or she has made a contribution and is now ready to exert more leadership.

✔ *Debrief meetings.* Regular meetings, retreats, and committee work are development opportunities if select staff and/or the board mentor are willing to debrief the new member. Context and history are vital for perspective on issues discussed.

✔ *Participation in development activities.* When appropriate, board members should attend the same conferences and meetings that staff attends to complement the development process. That means having an adequate budget for board development. Unfortunately, some funders—especially foundations—tack programs onto agencies without the slightest regard for the strength of the internal workings of the enterprise, including the development of the board. Perhaps one of the best criteria included in a United Way review of an agency seeking funding is their extensive analysis of the internal workings of the agency, including board and board committee functions.

BOARD MEMBER CONTRACT

I will provide service to the organization to the best of my ability in accordance with the board member expectations listed below.

I will:

Attend and participate in board meetings and other related activities of the enterprise as appropriate.

Commit to promoting the principles of entrepreneurship at the board and staff level.

Commit to attaining a full understanding of the mission and strategies of the enterprise.

Uphold the responsibilities of a trustee in order to ensure public trust and proper legal governance.

Commit to staying informed on issues related to the mission of the enterprise.

Openly declare conflict of interest in relation to other personal and professional pursuits.

Listen carefully to and respect the opinions and positions of other members of the board.

Abide by the majority decision of the board in all matters relating to direction and policy.

Refrain from speaking "out of school" regarding decisions of the board in the community.

Agree to serve as a spokesperson to the community in a professional way consistent with the values and beliefs of the enterprise.

(Add or substitute as many as you wish.)

_____   _____
Board Member Signature   Date

_____   _____
Chair Signature   Date

✔ *Board member recognition.* Of course, one of the more enjoyable methods of development is recognition. Remember that board members have lives too. In most cases they have families, careers, and other interests. They are—in most cases—giving a considerable amount of their time and energy for the common good and need to be recognized for that. Great board members are typically modest, but being recognized is one of the fundamental human needs. "Pens and pins" for service and other forms of recognition should be a common occurrence at board meetings, special events, or social gatherings.

 practical tip   Tons of materials are available on building effective boards. Again, the National Center for Nonprofit Boards is an excellent resource. There are resources in your community, such as management assistance organizations, consultants, and an increasing number of nonprofit management schools across the country. However, it all starts with a commitment to create an excellent enterprise characterized by entrepreneurial principles and practices.

TIME FOR A CHANGE—REMOVING MEMBERS OF THE BOARD

Even in the best of circumstances, your organization is bound to make a big mistake: appointing a bad board member. A member who fails to attend on a regular basis, a member who despite signing the code of ethics has a personal agenda and sees the organization as a means to an end, or a member whose ego gets in the way of group progress are all examples of breakdowns that are extremely common.

red flag   Left unattended, poor performance or no performance can have cancerous effects on the rest of the group. Power struggles, disregard for roles and responsibilities, and inappropriate interactions with the staff can divert the attention of the executive and negatively impact the quality of services. And watch out—it can happen that fast!

So what do you do about it? If you have clearly stated the expectations of membership and reviewed carefully the code of ethics, you have a great place to start. You may be surprised to find that a struggling board member will be relieved to be relieved! Consider the words of Brian O'Connell:

Some people say you can't fire a volunteer, but that's not so. People who aren't performing should be given the chance to step aside and, in the extreme, must be asked to make way for someone who is ready to perform. If a bad situation is allowed to linger, it doesn't create a good atmosphere for others in the organization and certainly doesn't encourage up-and-coming volunteers to feel that this is a place they want to make their commitment. It has been my experience that the person who is not performing, and who's had all the proddings and hints you will have given, will be much more relieved than hurt to be taken off the spot.[16]

The executive and the chair of the board have to be in sync on what the concerns are and how they will be addressed. It helps if there is a stated policy on board absenteeism or misconduct. The board chair should be the first line of contact, clearly stating the case with expected performance changes. A clear statement of expectation with a clear statement of alternatives (resignation or dismissal) is the professional way to save face.

Excellent entrepreneurial enterprises are characterized by excellent relationships between the board and the executive. It begins with a firm commitment to recruiting the best volunteer support you can find and creating ongoing development opportunities for growth and multiple opportunities to make meaningful contribution. It sounds simple but does take a serious amount of time and energy.

Remember the definition of social entrepreneur. It includes "acting boldly without being limited by resources currently in hand." You may not have the financial or human resources to take on a new opportunity, but you do have the most valuable resources to help you figure out how to mobilize the additional resources you will need—the board. As long as you know that, and the board knows you believe that, anything is possible!

SUMMARY

Board members, carefully selected and developed, can be a real asset for a social enterprise in many different ways. Recruitment of the right board members is therefore one of the most critical functions of the organization. In this chapter, we considered the legal role of the board, its life cycle, and its functions. We took a look at how to work with a board to create an entrepreneurial environment and explored a variety of alternative governance structures. We found out the best ways to recruit new board members and how to orient and develop them. Finally, we addressed the sensitive issue of removing ineffective board members.

Key points to remember are:

✔ The board is the legally responsible entity for the enterprise.

✔ The board is the single greatest resource to help extend a social entrepreneur's ability to create or sustain the enterprise.

✔ Keep the governing board small yet diverse in composition and perspective—recruit successful entrepreneurs!

✔ Recognize that the functions of the board will change as the enterprise changes over its life cycle, and recruit accordingly.

✔ Create board turnover so fresh blood is pumping in the heart of the enterprise.

✔ Use alternative structures to extend your reach and opportunity to observe future board members at work.

✔ Provide opportunity for the board to keep its eyes on the horizon while doing meaningful work today.

✔ Create an entrepreneurial environment, endorsed and promoted by the board.

✔ Develop and recognize the board members for the important social value they create and sustain.

Notes

1. Sharon M. Oster, *Strategic Management for Nonprofit Organizations* (San Francisco: Jossey-Bass, 1990)
2. Brian O'Connell, *The Board Member's Book* (New York: The Foundation Center, 1985) p. 19.
3. The key stages of a board were excerpted from the work of Karl Mathiasen in a publication titled, *Board Passages: Three Key Stages in a Nonprofit Board's Life Cycle,* Governance Series, 7 (Washington D.C.: National Center for Nonprofit Boards, 1990).
4. Brian O'Connell, *The Board Member's Book* (New York: The Foundation Center, 1985) p. 44.
5. Barbara E. Taylor, Richard P. Chait and Thomas P. Holland, "The New Work of the Nonprofit Board," *Harvard Business Review,* September-October 1996, p. 36.
6. Peter C. Brinckerhoff, *Mission-Based Management* (New York: John Wiley & Sons, Inc., 2000) p. 42.
7. Brian O'Connell, *The Board Member's Book* (New York: The Foundation Center, 1985) p. 86.
8. Cyril O. Houle, *Governing Boards* (Washington D.C.: National Center for Nonprofit Boards, 1989) p. 174.
9. John Carver, *Boards That Make a Difference: A New Design for Leadership in Nonprofit and Public Organizations* (San Francisco: Jossey-Bass, 1990) p. 2.
10. Brian O'Connell, *The Board Member's Book* (New York: The Foundation Center, 1985)
11. Sharon M. Oster, *Strategic Management for Nonprofit Organizations* (New York: Oxford University Press, 1995) p. 84.
12. Peter C. Brinckerhoff, *Mission-Based Management* (New York: John Wiley & Sons, Inc., 2000) p. 44.
13. Brian O'Connell, *The Board Member's Book* (New York: The Foundation Center, 1985) p. 58.
14. National Center for Nonprofit Boards maintains a *Nonprofit Board Resource Catalog* with listings of a number of valuable publications that address recruitment and development of nonprofit boards. Washington D.C.: National Center for Nonprofit Boards.
15. Dorian Dodson, *How to Recruit Great Board Members* (Adolfo Street Publications, 1993)
16. Brian O'Connell, *The Board Member's Book* (New York: The Foundation Center, 1985) p. 65.

Chapter 6

TREATING YOUR DONORS AS INVESTORS

Kay Sprinkel Grace, Organizational Consultant

IN THIS CHAPTER

The new world of donor-investors

Moving from old sources of value to new ones

Identifying increased avenues for donor-investor/social enterprise partnerships

Getting ready for the entrepreneurial donor's involvement

Challenges in maintaining donor investment: Developing new stewardship

Ending "charity": Implications for creating value for donors

Guess what? If you want to be an effective social entrepreneur, you need to know how to build strong donor relationships. That's right—social entrepreneurship is not just about earned income and wealth creation. The most successful social entrepreneurs are adept at using a wide range of resources to achieve their social objectives. And, as you will see in Chapter 9, "Developing Viable Earned Income Strategies," earned income is not right for everyone and rarely will it create total independence from donors. If you want to be an effective social entrepreneur, you need to know how to attract and retain the right donors.

This chapter opens with an exploration of some of the basic new ideas affecting all philanthropy and then applies them to social enterprises. By providing the broader context for philanthropy, both the social enterprise and the potential investor can become more familiar with the vocabulary and ideas that frame social investment.

THE NEW WORLD OF DONOR-INVESTORS

gem of wisdom

In recent years, there has been a significant shift in the understanding of philanthropy. More than a decade ago, in an article in the *Wall Street Journal*, Peter Drucker sensed the true nature of this shift when he advanced a then-revolutionary idea that is now commonly accepted: "People no longer give to charity, they buy in to results."[1]

Philanthropy is more than just giving money. It is increasingly recognized as the social force that includes all voluntary activities we do on behalf of organizations that work to achieve social outcomes. In addition to this new perspective, there is increased recognition that the common thread that ties an individual's philanthropy together—whether it is for education, religion, the environment, social or human services, or culture or the arts—is the recognition that people act on their *own* values when they participate in philanthropy.[2] People do not give to, ask for, join, or serve any organization whose values they do not share. (Okay—maybe once if they are not sure of the values of the organization, but usually not twice!) Furthermore, when the values of the organization shift or no longer match the values of volunteers or donors, people will move on to find other organizations whose values are a better fit with theirs.

DONOR-INVESTORS

core concept

Perhaps the most significant change of all, however, has been the emergence of a new kind of donor—the donor-investor. A *donor-investor* is an individual or organization whose financial commitment to a nonprofit is undergirded by a belief in their shared values and in the ability of the investor and the organization to mutually benefit each other and the community.[3] *Donor-investors* differ from *donors* in the way that the individual or institutional funder is approached during cultivation, how the proposal for giving/investing is presented during the solicitation, and how the giver is treated after the gift is made (stewardship). Exhibit 6.1 details some of the most significant of these differences.

The donor-investor approach is dynamic; the donor, contributor, or giver approach *can* be dynamic, but most often is not. Why? Because donor-investors are much more involved in the organizations to which they decide to direct their contributions.

So why should you as a social entrepreneur spend any time at all considering the implications of donor-investors on your organization and responding to them?

One reason would certainly be because donors are increasingly expecting it—especially the donors who are naturally attracted to social entrepreneurs. But perhaps an even more important reason for taking this approach has to do with the fact that social entrepreneurs by nature

	Traditional Donor Approach	Donor-Investor Approach
Cultivation	Focus on what organization needs/wants from donor.	Focus on investor's needs/values/interests.
Solicitation	Presentation of organization's needs/goals and how the gift will help meet them.	Emphasis on social outcomes and how the investment is really an investment in the social outcome through the organization.
Stewardship	Emphasis on recognition of the donor immediately with little or occasional ongoing feedback about the continuing impact of the gift until the next gift is solicited.	Ongoing feedback to the donor about the impact of the investment on social outcomes and the way(s) in which they advance the donor-investor's values.

EXHIBIT 6.1   The traditional donor approach versus the donor-invester approach.

exhibit a heightened sense of accountability. This accountability in-cludes providing an appropriate and attractive "return" to investors on their money.

And there's one more reason for you to consider the implications of donor-investors on your organization: The revised attitude implicit in the approach leads to much higher renewal of gifts and a greater ease among nonprofit professionals and volunteers in presenting the concept of in-vestment to their donors. Funders are much more apt to reinvest if they know how well their investment is doing and if they are connected either actively or through steady information to the results of their philan-thropic investment.

red flag But remember: This change in how donors are viewed also carries a huge responsibility for nonprofits, many of which are concerned about what an investor may require as "return" on the investment. During the past several years, the rise of venture philanthropy—viewed as perhaps the ultimate donor-investor relationship—has caused both controversy and excitement and been both welcomed and resisted. The donor-investor approach to philanthropy offers tremendous opportuni-ties for social entrepreneurs, but we never said it was going to be easy!

CREATING A VALUES EXCHANGE

So, why isn't every nonprofit jumping on board the donor-investor band-wagon? Truth be told, many traditional nonprofit leaders worry that they will have neither the time nor the ability to engage appropriately those donor-investors who want increased involvement. If you're in this camp, understand that every donor seeks one thing in common from his or her contribution: a return on the investment. Not a monetary return, such as the profits or dividends that for-profit organizations provide to investors, but the personal satisfaction that comes from knowing that the contribution is furthering progress in the social outcomes in which he or she is most interested.

As a social entrepreneur, you will find that the donor-investor approach offers high value for your donors and high values return on donor investment.

core concept   A big part of the *values return* is how the donor-investor feels about making the gift: confident, satisfied, even joyful over making this investment. High values return means that the donor-investor, who may value dignity for elders, opportunities for youth to straighten out their lives, educational opportunities for the poorest of the poor, sees the organization acting on his or her values, creating a *values exchange*. A values exchange differs from the normal economic exchange we use in business in that donor-investors, in exchange for something valued (money and/or time), receive nothing tangible. Instead of a product or service that directly benefits them, they receive assurance that the values they hold are being advanced through programs and services that benefit others.

CASE STUDY

SAGE HILL SCHOOL: A HIGH RETURN ON INVESTMENT

In June 2001, the *Los Angeles Times* carried a story about Sage Hill School, an independent nondenominational high school that opened in Orange County in September 2000. In terms of return on values, the story could not have been more powerful. A guiding principle in the founding and fund raising ($35 million in the first phase and more to go) for the school was the emphasis on the school's values, particularly diversity. One donor-investor, in particular, placed his investment into financial aid with the aspiration that this school—although located in a very wealthy area of the county—would attract qualified students from all over the county regardless of economic, social, racial, or ethnic background. The story in the *Times* begins by describing one student— on full $14,000 scholarship—and how the experience of her first year there had changed her life. It then cites the number of students like her and balances the story with how well the school has served students from all areas and backgrounds, creating a true community. When coupled with visits to the school to see this phenomenal learning and social environment, this kind of feedback to the lead donor and others in the community who may have similar values can only lead to further investment by those who see the importance of diversity in education. This is exactly the kind of return that you, as a donor-investor, need.

Measuring the impact of this investment in the social outcomes through an organization is up to the organization, and requires both sound statistics based on solid program objectives and powerful stories that illustrate the impact of that investment on lives. It is your job to ensure both are an integral part of what your organization offers.

In a social enterprise, the donor-investor needs to be assured that the organization's values are not compromised by the increased emphasis on earned revenue. Some donors also need assurance that earned income will never be the sole source of income and that philanthropic investments will always be essential. (Of course, some donor-investors—particularly venture philanthropists—would welcome the development of a truly self-supporting organization, allowing them to turn their attention and money to another nonprofit that needs temporary help to become independent of donors.) Most of all, the donor-investor needs to feel that the investment is well used, has an impact, and is of value to the organization. If that information is conveyed, then the donor-investor will find satisfaction and be willing to reinvest.

MOVING FROM OLD SOURCES OF VALUE TO NEW ONES

Gone are the days when nonprofits could be vague about their financial or social impact: Donor-investors want numbers as well as anecdotal evidence of the value of their philanthropy. Accountability, which descended heavily on nonprofits in the 1980s, is not just expected—it is *demanded* by an increasing number of donors. This new source of value links directly with their own *values* and produces both satisfaction and desire to continue their investment in the nonprofit sector.

While donors are not the only ones to whom social entrepreneurs are accountable, they are critically important. Multiple tracking systems that monitor gifts and donors, accurately record and report financial transactions, including budgets, and provide quantitative service information for program outcomes are a must for accountability to work. But the commitment to being accountable to donors goes beyond just the hardware, software, time, and materials cost—the commitment also must include a willingness to be transparent. Transparency—the willingness to remove the barriers that cloak the inner workings of your organization, providing regular reporting on financials and program performance—is a very high value for many funders, and nonprofits that shy away from it discourage many donor-investors.

practical tip   As a social entrepreneur, it is critical that you understand the shift from the old sources of value for donors to new ones and design your organization's processes to accommodate the needs and desires of your donors—while increasing both the accountability and transparency of your organization.

TRADITIONAL SOURCES OF VALUE AND THE WAY THEY VARY AMONG DONORS

Despite the fact that many of your donors will consider the provision of feedback and transparency a source of value for them, many other more traditional donors may place less value on these newer ideas. In fact, they may have some very specific concerns and questions that you'll need to answer before you'll be able to attract their interest and earn their loyalty. Some of the most common questions for you to consider include:

✔ What about the donor who is still motivated by the value of altruism and the feelings of the heart? Will your social enterprise appear too "corporate"?

✔ What about the donor whose key value is "making a difference?" Will that donor feel less significant when considering the various sources of income your nonprofit may have?

✔ Will some donors question whether an increasingly corporate model strips your nonprofit of its ability to stand on its tradition as mission-driven and not succumb to the pressures of being overly market-driven? Will donors feel the integrity of your organization is compromised?

✔ What about the donor who values being the heroic rescuer, bridging the annual budget or the capital campaign gap with a gift that brings recognition and relief? Will that feeling change in an organization that no longer is so dependent on a donor or donors—one that generates revenue from other sources and thinks more entrepreneurially about its options for survival?

✔ Will your organization still believe that "every gift, no matter what size, makes a difference"? How will you honor those small donors whose gifts may not reach the aggregate total of one strand of earned income and whose values satisfaction has come from feeling as if "every gift counts"? Will some donors feel superfluous, caught between large philanthropic gifts and healthy earned income revenue streams?

✔ Because commitment to mission and values-based giving is a key traditional value, does a social enterprise, with its hybrid nature, provide the same mission value to a donor? Will the idea that some revenue that sustains your organization is not generated by philanthropic motivation, but by the desire for a product or service provided by the nonprofit, hurt the way in which the donor perceives your organization?

Traditional donors may well ask these questions. Responsible social enterprises must have the answers.

Donor education has to be part of every social enterprise's business plan. If you hope to earn the trust of your prospective donors, they need assurance that their values are not threatened or compromised by new operational models. They will need demonstrable evidence that these new models, in fact, have the potential for serving the social benefit sector more effectively. Established organizations making the transition to social enterprise need to talk with their donors and keep them informed about motivation, process, design, and benefits. New social enterprises need also to let their philanthropic investors know these things. Donors need to know that the social and funding context in which nonprofits operate has changed dramatically (higher community expectations, reduced government funding) and that new paradigms for revenue development and approaches to mission fulfillment can include a wide variety of entrepreneurial ideas.

At the end of the day, you must show that your social enterprise can generate more revenue and apply more creative solutions to chronic social issues, with the end result that your organization's mission thrives and its values flourish. Small gifts will have the same aggregate impact, and perhaps more: With income streams that support ongoing program operations, those small gifts may be the seeds for new and large projects that might otherwise not be possible. And for donor-investors concerned about the potential compromise of basic mission and values, proving that supposition to be false is up to you. You must:

✔ Know your mission.
✔ Define your values.
✔ Honor your values and promote them to your investors.
✔ Make your values a part of all of your strategies and all of your reporting to donors.
✔ Keep your values in the forefront of your decisions, and convey the ways in which entrepreneurship is enhancing, not compromising, the mission and values you share with your stakeholders.

By understanding what motivates a more traditional donor, you can build a bridge from the donor's values to your organization's vision—showing how the donor's values are in fact strengthened by increased revenue, nimbleness in meeting issues as they arise, and a growing presence in the community.

EXPLORING NEW SOURCES OF VALUE FOR DONORS

When researching donor-investors for *High Impact Philanthropy*,[4] one of the areas my coauthor and I focused on was the surge of giving in Silicon Valley. In the 1998 annual report of the Community Foundation Silicon

Valley, one donor (who had established a donor-advised fund), when asked what he invested in, had a one-word response: *Change.*

Increasingly, donors value their capacity to change chronic or emerging unsolved community problems (homelessness) or needs (shortage of performing arts space). Impatient to see results, they focus on getting things done as quickly as possible. Occasionally, in their zeal, they will leapfrog existing organizations and set up their own nonprofit to get the job done. They cannot understand why social change takes so long. This emphasis in change often pressures nonprofits inappropriately.

practical tip   Part of the education that leaders in both traditional nonprofits or those with a social entrepreneurship mind-set must do concerns the unique nature of nonprofit sector itself. Here are some key things you should be prepared to teach your prospective donors:

✔ How nonprofits work

✔ Why consensus-building is important but time-consuming when it comes to community and other issues and programs

✔ How nonprofit boards are constituted, organized, and operate, and why, even in the most entrepreneurial hybrid public benefit organizations, change probably will not happen as quickly as it would in a purely commercial model

The most promising outcome of this kind of donor and volunteer education is the growth of community partnerships based on mutual respect between the donor-investor and the nonprofit. Patience and tolerance are also pleasant by-products!

In exploring new sources of value for donors in social entrepreneurship, change looms as a very likely and exciting one. All nonprofits are, to some extent, change agents, although their structure and systems sometimes seem to inhibit their capacity to enact change. But innovative social enterprises have the capacity to accelerate the change process through their alternatives for revenue generation and their ability to implement more visionary management models.

Another new source of value that social enterprises can take advantage of is the opportunity for donor-investors to be more entrepreneurial in designating their gifts. Social enterprises, if positioned well for donor investment, offer more opportunities to donors to target their gifts in areas of interest to them. Potential donor-investors—uncomfortable with purely philanthropic investments that may feel ill defined or fuzzy to them—may welcome underwriting or sponsorship opportunities that provide a tangible benefit and recognition. This kind of targeted support is also easier to track and report—a high value added for many investors.

Embedded in both of the above values is another clear benefit also mentioned earlier: partnership. As communities face increasing needs, they require the partnership of the public benefit sector and donor-investors. The strength of this partnership will determine the health of the community. An increasingly entrepreneurial nonprofit or public benefit sector will accelerate the solution of community problems and the creation of community resources. In the process, it will attract donor-investors whose trust in the more traditional philanthropic sector may be challenged by a sense that they have made little or no progress in addressing these issues. Hybrid models—with aggressive programs rooted in mission and values supported by income-generating projects as well as philanthropy—can attract vital partners who might otherwise fail to participate.

What things do your current and potential donors value? If you don't know, then you need to find out. Take time to survey your donors to get a handle on their values and motivations, and then respond in kind.

IDENTIFYING INCREASED AVENUES FOR DONOR-INVESTOR/SOCIAL ENTERPRISE PARTNERSHIPS

If all nonprofits—from purely philanthropic to social enterprise—are viewed as *vehicles* through which people invest in social outcomes in which they are interested, it is apparent that social enterprises provide significant delivery value for the donor. People give as much *through* an organization as they give *to* an organization. Jim Lord, an early guru of nonprofit marketing, tells the following story: At Black & Decker, when they are training their sales associates, they ask them why people buy a Black & Decker drill. The answer seems obvious and comes easily to the trainees: because they want a drill. The trainers respond by telling them that people buy a drill *because they want a hole.*

An article in *The Economist* profiles the philanthropy of Bill Gates of Microsoft. It later refers to Larry Ellison, head of Oracle, saying "So far, he has declined to compete in largesse with Mr. Gates, his arch-rival. In his [Ellison's] view, the public's attitude to philanthropy is 'deeply bizarre. . . . We measure philanthropy by how much money you waste. We measure the size of your donation, not results.' " The article continues by noting "Even if it is an excuse for being tight-fisted, Mr. Ellison has a point. Results matter."[5] Important to this discussion is the relevance of creating that sense of partnership that says "Together we can get this job done."

Social entrepreneurs are by nature more interested in results than in the "size of your donation," which gives them a unique role in helping their donor-investors become more results-oriented. Social entrepreneurs work as partners with their donors—involving them in their mission and listening to (and acting on) their input.

The partnership feedback model requires an organization to listen as well as inform. While board member feedback is expected and implicit in traditional nonprofit governance models, there are new expectations among active donor-investors that they can provide ongoing feedback in the same spirit that the organization provides ongoing information. Both positive ("I heard such good things about our organization at a Rotary meeting last week") and negative ("Last week I got a call from the parent of one of our learning disability clients, and he was very unhappy that the previous counselor/teacher had been fired. What kind of response can I give him?") feedback should be welcomed by the organization, because it indicates the sense of partnership felt by the donor or volunteer. People who don't feel that engaged with the organization will be more apt to call three other people and pass along the complaint than bring it to the executive director for advice.

action step Create opportunities for donors to feel like donor-investors and partners in your social enterprise. Think of creative and appropriate

---

BUILDING PARTNERSHIPS AT SAGE HILL SCHOOL

reality check As partners in social enterprises, donors expect to be informed. They also may expect to be heard and to be involved. We found at Sage Hill School that the key investors—many of whom were young and from the high-technology community at a time when it was booming—wanted to be informed, and many of them wanted to be involved. This was hands-on philanthropy and an opportunity for them to do something few people are privileged to do: build a new school in the community that reflected their vision and values. Quite a few of these younger donors and other representatives of the community, through participation on advisory teams attached to a discipline (e.g., math/science) or value (e.g., diversity), got involved in helping create the media and technology center, the athletic program, the arts programs, and others. More traditional investors also had a large hunger for information: In addition to selecting an extraordinary head of school, whose commitment to the values of the founding visionaries was a complete match, an early investment in a top CFO from a school on the East Coast was one of the most important hires the school made. From the outset, the numbers have been there, accurate and immediate—and transparent for donors. Always coupled with the anecdotal information about the students and rich opportunities to get involved in both the creation of the school and to observe students and faculty as the school progressed, donors have been kept regularly informed about the financial situation. The sense of partnership has grown stronger.

ways to involve them, and then honor the partnership by both listening and informing. The resulting exhilaration of the donor—to be close and a part of something that is moving more quickly and innovatively toward social benefit—will help secure that donor as a long-term investor in your organization. The donor-investor engaged in this way may realize benefits unknown to others who give based on the traditional value-added donor benefits.

POSITIONING THE SOCIAL ENTERPRISE AS A BONUS FOR INVESTORS

tool of the trade Development marketing is changing, but not fast enough. In Chapter 10 of *High Impact Philanthropy*, I use the acronym IMPACT to describe effective nonprofit marketing for the twenty-first century. This acronym stands for:

- ✔ Impression
- ✔ Message
- ✔ Product
- ✔ Ability
- ✔ Case
- ✔ Timing

Powerful and convincing nonprofit marketing—particularly for social enterprises—needs to focus on the *issue(s)* embedded in the organization's mission, then on the way the organization is addressing the issue(s). Most nonprofits persist in marketing their organization rather than the issue(s) they are dealing with. How can you measure your impact if you don't focus on the issue (mission) you are trying to resolve?

At the Goldman Institute on Aging in San Francisco—formerly the Mt. Zion Institute on Aging—marketing is undergoing a dramatic remodeling. It is now going to focus on *issues of aging* (dignity, independence, health) rather than on the organization itself. As the oldest of the baby boomers reach their mid-50s—and those who used to be considered old in their 60s through their 90s are defying all previous expectations regarding their behavior or needs—an "institute on aging" was felt to have less appeal in the marketplace. However, an organization that markets programs and solutions around issues of *healthy* aging, promoting that idea widely in the community and then letting people know how they are responding to those needs, will find that the field of investors has widened. The institute—a highly entrepreneurial social enterprise—is entering into a new community partnership with a housing developer, building its new services center side by side with housing on land the organization has purchased and will lease a portion of to the developer. By focusing on the issues, before presenting the organization, the community's interest will be piqued.

Donors who are willing to make transforming investments in social enterprises are looking for new energy around mission and vision and faster solutions to community needs and problems. Marketing that focuses on issues and solutions—including entrepreneurial measures that bring fresh spirit—is attractive to donors who wish to transform organizations and communities (and, in the process, transform themselves into more satisfied donor-investors). They see innovative practices and entrepreneurial behavior as promising trends in a sector that many feel has been doggedly deliberate and slow to move. They also see opportunities to relate on a business-to-business level, and that provides a communication bridge between donor-investor and organization that can prove to be very exciting.

In Fresno, California, and nearly a dozen other communities in the United States and Canada, a pioneering innovative effort was made in the 1990s by United Way leaders to become the New United Way. Although the movement never caught fire, its intent is important to review. Two key entrepreneurial ideas framed their efforts:

1. *Organizing needs statements around the issue, not the organization.* Community organizations were invited to be part of a particular "table" (youth education, youth recreation/leadership, seniors, housing for poor, homelessness, etc.) with other agencies addressing the same issue. They were then asked to craft vision and solutions together for that issue for Fresno.

2. *Funding by issue, not just organization.* Distribution of United Way funds in the New United Way model was allocated to the issue, with each of the providing organizations indicating the programs they would offer to meet the community need. Traditional United Way funding has been by organization, with the pie cut smaller and smaller and high competition among agencies for their share.

The attraction for the donor in this model was the belief that these organizations would work together to solve an apparent community need or problem. The donors were encouraged to give to the United Way—rather than using the donor-designated option—because they were bringing the collective energy and wisdom of participating agencies together in a collaborative model. Programs like this struggle and too often fail because organizations cannot think broadly about the issues they and others are working with, and they think only about their organizational needs. The New United Way efforts have helped shape some traditional United Ways in some communities, but the progress is slow. The

Anchorage, Alaska, United Way is a beacon in this effort to unite organizations around issues in the community.

Traditional nonprofit marketing, which promotes the organization first and the issue(s) as subtext, is counter to social enterprise. It does not convey innovation, nor does it invite the entrepreneurial donor-investor who is more interested in results than in needs. The value added to an organization that is both entrepreneurial and collaborative, focusing on the issue and the best possible solution and structuring management and delivery systems that will accelerate that solution, is potentially extraordinary.

In a world where many nonprofits are viewed as being satisfied with the status quo through their resistance to change, donor-investors need to see the shift from change resistor to change agent—and then see it happening. Relating all marketing to defining the issue, quantifying the issue, describing what you are doing about it and what success you have had does one other very important thing: It quickly points out the things your organization values and invites those who value the same things to join you. Potential donors, seeking value and feedback for their investment, do not immediately see it just reading about your organization. You also must state the issues. Implicit in those issues are what you value and that can initiate the values exchange.

And that, after all, is the goal of engaging funders from the community in your enterprise. When donors see the things they value being acted on in innovative ways that engage people productively and appropriately, the value of the investment to the donors will increase.

GETTING READY FOR THE ENTREPRENEURIAL DONOR'S INVOLVEMENT

Entrepreneurial organizations attract entrepreneurial donors and volunteers. As mentioned earlier, many organizations worry about donors getting too involved with their organizations, particularly when venture philanthropists enter the picture.

Organizations that find themselves wincing over the degree of involvement desired or demanded by an investor need to consider carefully both why they are resisting and whether the degree of involvement requested is appropriate. Too often, organizations offered large gifts by funders who then want a seat at the table seem surprised by this request. One organization, on receiving notice it had been selected by a donor to receive a gift that would more than equal its budget for a year, seemed astounded when that same individual wanted a seat at the board table. The organization's leaders called me and said, "We don't sell board seats. He cannot expect to come on the board." My response was that this was not about selling board seats: This was about an investor wanting to be involved with the way his investment was used in the organization.

Among their policies, organizations need to define what roles donors can and cannot play. In one well-publicized incident, the Bass family of Texas made a gift to Yale for a core course on civilizations. The gift came with curriculum expectations attached that the Yale faculty was not prepared to support. Yale relied on policy to return the gift. The policy was sharply exposed by the appropriate response from faculty who did not feel that a donor should define academic programs. But the final measure was their policy.

action step Before you find yourself in a quandary over whether to accept a gift, ensure that your organization has policies in place that address the following:

✔ The sources from which you will not accept gifts (e.g., tobacco or liquor companies for youth or drug programs; oil, gas, or other corporate money for environmental organizations, etc.)

✔ The conditions under which you will make exceptions

✔ The agreements you will draft with the donor-investor so there can be no problems after the gift has been made

✔ The values premise on which the policy is based, and why it is intrinsic to the organization's mission and values

✔ The way in which the policy and values will be presented in the community to avoid a conflict over a gift that cannot be received

Accept gift??

THE IMPACT OF VENTURE PHILANTHROPY

In the venture philanthropy approach, investors view nonprofit investment in the same way that they would view a venture capital investment. Venture philanthropy usually entails multiple-year funding (this is good), participation on the organization's board (good or bad, depending on the people involved), and high standards for accountability (this is good). The downside is that the uninformed demands of the venture philanthropist may jeopardize the organization's stability.

Those who have cautioned regarding the venture philanthropy approach believe that donor expectations and involvement are unrealistic and inappropriate. Both Bruce Sievers, of San Francisco's Walter and Elise Haas Foundation, and Vartan Gregorian, of the Carnegie Endowment have written about the dangers inherent in the venture philanthropy model, citing in particular the difficulty of quantifying the impact of social, cultural, religious, and educational programs.[6] However, if this is the trend, and if the benefits are apparent to the organization, then one approach that has worked is for the organization to develop its goals and objectives for the period of funding, basing their expectations on the resources, opportunities, and constraints they know about and building in a margin for correction that is mutually agreed to by the funder and the organization. (Sage Hill School, for example, set objectives for enrollment, diversity, financial aid, and continued fund raising that were a stretch, but attainable, and have kept its hands-on investors engaged.)

Sievers and Gregorian both correctly submit that solving a community problem like hunger is not a likely outcome for a three-year venture philanthropy investment. However, putting 20 more feeding programs into marginalized neighborhoods, or developing relationships with 10 additional food providers, or, as happened in San Francisco, building a food bank that doubled the amount of food it processed within five years are all quantifiable objectives that no investor would dismiss. Nonprofits themselves need to distinguish their capacity to ease a problem from their ability to solve a problem.

Nonprofit leaders need to be clear with the investor about what is and is not possible. That puts the degree of involvement into a much more open forum: The investor can be brought increasingly to understand that even the most innovative approaches to nonprofit organization and management cannot completely change the playing field of the philanthropic sector. Certain processes, including the consensus model and community needs, are intrinsic to the sector. Without them, the sector is threatened.

THE DOWNSIDE OF VENTURE PHILANTHROPY?

While the overall, positive impact of venture philanthropy is certainly a very large net gain for the nonprofit sector as a whole, some people believe that when pushed too far, venture philanthropy can be dangerous to the traditional missions of the nonprofits that employ it. The problem is that, as involved, committed venture philanthropists push nonprofits to become ever more efficient and businesslike in their management and financial dealings, they may find themselves ignoring those "unprofitable" social outcomes and people with the greatest needs. Says Eugene Tempel, director of Indiana University's Center on Philanthropy, "Nonprofits are not bottom-line organizations. As some donors push for more and more efficiency, the organization may drop out services to the most needy because they're the most intractable problems and the most expensive."[7] The pressures on nonprofits to change the ways that they do things can be quite intense—and nearly impossible to ignore when a prospective donor is dangling the carrot of a large contribution. While this may not always be a bad thing, nonprofit leaders must ensure that, as they become more entrepreneurial, they do not lose sight of the very people and issues that they are "in business" to serve.

YOUR MOTHER'S PHILANTHROPY

Discussion here of donor involvement does not refer only to venture philanthropists: Donors don't have to subscribe to that model in order to want to be involved. Increasingly, investors are getting away from "checkbook philanthropy." I have previously theorized that this is no longer "your father's philanthropy"—it is more like your mother's. Early studies of women's philanthropy at UCLA and subsequent studies conducted by other researchers at the University of Wisconsin revealed that women get involved first and then give; parallel studies of new investors (male *and* female) show their need to be involved as well.

This result matches well with another phenomenon in philanthropy: the reversal of the donor search process. Increasingly, donors—keen on issues and not so knowledgeable about the organizations delivering on those issues—identify and seek out issues-focused organizations in which to invest their money. This has changed the whole arena of prospect research—prospects are now researching organizations at the same time as organizations are researching prospects! Entrepreneurial organizations are well positioned to attract the potential donor seeking an interesting nonprofit investment—their emphasis on the hybrid model of funding and management is more easily understood than the more traditional purely philanthropic model. People will find it easier to get involved and easier to find ways to give.

There is a parallel to be drawn between the way people invest and get engaged in their financial investments for income growth or retirement and the way they approach their philanthropy. It relates to the degree of activism they desire. (See Exhibit 6.2.)

Of course, few organizations will be populated with only one of these kinds of donor-investors; most have a mix of all types. An ideal arrangement for social enterprises is to have a mix of donors, with the majority in the lower-involvement categories and only a few in the most highly engaged category. Handling more than a few highly engaged donors can be a very real challenge for an organization—particularly if they pull in dif-

	Passive	Active	Highly Engaged
Equity Investor	Indexed mutual funds	Chooses own stocks	Shareholder activism with a voice in decisions and high level of influence
Donor Investor	Checkbook philanthropy	Seeks accountability	Seeks true partnership, including board seat or involvement in strategic issues

EXHIBIT 6.2 Variations among donor-investors regarding involvement parallels continuum with equity investors in financial markets.

ferent directions—and may require your constant attention to ensure that the organization stays on track.

Even if donors cannot be physically involved with the organization as volunteers, they still want to be treated as investors and involved through information and opportunities for visitation and meetings with leaders of the organization. And in arranging meetings between donor-investors and leaders, remember that the social enterprise investor wants and needs to connect with *program leadership.* Why do we persist in engaging our top investors only with administrators? Keep the product vital in their minds by connecting them as often as possible with program providers and clients (or their families) who have benefited.

A social enterprise, like any nonprofit, must be able to say to a potential donor-investor that there are too many strings or demands that come with the gift, or that the values of the donor and the organization are not compatible. Sometimes organizations have to let a gift—and the giver—go: either before the gift is given, or if the restrictions or demands that emerge after the gift is given become too great. Clearly, such dissolutions of relationships should be approached first from a negotiation posture and only later from the standpoint of "irreconcilable differences." Ultimately, the entirety of nonprofit development is about relationships—organizations need to guard them, nurture them, and promote them. When the relationships sours, then the gift will also. Usually these breaches occur around values: Sometimes we don't know the dimensions of our own values or the values of others until they are violated.

COMMUNICATING WITH YOUR DONOR-INVESTORS

red flag　It is well to remember that the very passion that inspires great investment in our social enterprises and the entire public benefit sector can convert to anger when the expectations of the donors are not met or the organization's pride or integrity are challenged. The solution is to communicate early and often with your donor-investors, ensuring that they understand exactly what the nature of their relationship with your organization will be and what they can and cannot expect in exchange for their contributions. This means that you should:

- ✔ Be sure the expectations are clear.
- ✔ Write a gift agreement that spells out the terms.
- ✔ Keep in touch with the donor.
- ✔ Not promise anything you cannot deliver.
- ✔ Not agree to demands independently of those who may have to be your partners in delivery (e.g., program staff or accounting personnel).

RULES OF ENGAGEMENT FOR DONOR-INVESTORS

practical tip   For the donor-investor—whether venture philanthropist or someone just weary of checkbook philanthropy who wants to be involved—here are the rules of engagement that will lead to a long and mutually fruitful relationship with a social enterprise or other nonprofit:

✔ Access the organization through the executive director and encourage him or her to connect you with the program people who are delivering on your investment; unless you are told to do so, don't connect first with the program person in a way that could be perceived as a threat to the executive director or other administrative staff.

✔ Don't allow yourself to become an agent within the organization, working behind the scenes to change personnel or policies, unless you are doing these things with encouragement and permission of the board or executive director.

✔ Be a good listener and observer, and if you see or hear things that bother you as an investor, use appropriate channels to discuss them within the organization—don't take them out to the community.

✔ If you see severe breaches of accountability, mission, vision, or commitment, go directly to the board chair or other appropriate person, ask tough questions, and expect truthful answers—and if you don't receive them, exercise your donor's rights and withdraw yourself and/or your gift from the organization.

✔ Ask to see existing policies, bylaws, articles of incorporation, and other materials that describe the mission and framework of the organization so you understand what basic precepts formed it.

✔ Be understanding that even the most innovative social enterprise is still a nonprofit and must act within the sometimes-slow policies of the sector.

Donor-investors must continue to set standards for the kind of accountability *they* need to feel their investment is well managed and spent. Organizations should present what is possible in terms of measures and accountability and not be held accountable for the impossible. Donor-investors should ask for results and carefully assess where they put their investments. Likewise, a social enterprise should be clear about the opportunities for donor involvement, and the limits.

Simply by communicating with your donors, you'll head off many minor issues before they have a chance to mushroom into major problems. Additionally, by educating your donors—providing them with a greater knowledge of and comfort with the nonprofit sector and its unique ways of doing business—you will ease many of their concerns and build the kind of trust that you'll need to ensure that your partnerships are as productive as they can possibly be.

While social enterprises work to a large extent within the standard business model, there are aspects of all nonprofits that will continue to fall outside of its boundaries. Donor-investors need to understand the strong values as well as the immense human and social capital involved in nonprofits. They should embrace those differences as the distinguishing, powerful, and value-added characteristics that identify the philanthropic sector. The breadth of potential philanthropy—and the wealth of mutual pleasure and benefit to organizations and their donors—has been barely tapped. The end of checkbook philanthropy is the beginning of hands-on philanthropy, a shift we applaud. The more donor-investors understand about the sector, and the more nonprofit organizations move toward management and delivery models that guarantee measurable results in the community, the greater will be the impact of philanthropy.

CHALLENGES IN MAINTAINING DONOR INVESTMENT: DEVELOPING NEW STEWARDSHIP

core concept Stewardship—which is defined as the continuing relationship between an organization and its donors that is based on mutual respect for both the source and impact of the gift—must be a part of social enterprises as well as traditional nonprofits.[8] Donor-investors in social enterprises will, perhaps more than donors to other kinds of nonprofit organizations, expect to have two kinds of "bottom-line" information: the financial performance of the organization and the performance on values. Both provide the return they are seeking for their investment. How is this best done? Here are some of the most effective ways:

✔ The Internet is a powerful tool for communicating quickly with donor-investors. A snippet of information about a new gift or program, or even a short note with an attachment that describes a problem or an achievement you want to share is a very positive use of technology.

✔ Be current and transparent with financial reports. See that donors get them and understand them—particularly those that reflect the management of their investment in the people and programs of your organization.

✔ Share stories. Combine a set of statistics with stories of the people those statistics represent, and people will multiply that single story by the numbers you give them.

✔ If you have a newsletter, evaluate its contents to ensure that it is not self-serving to the board or donors (people standing around with wineglasses or being photographed with celebrities) or merely a platform for the administrators, but instead focuses on stories about the impact of your programs on the community. (An excellent example of focus on impact is the newsletter "Give and Take" published by the San Francisco Food Bank.)

✔ Invite your donors to visit your site, if appropriate; if it is not (drug or psychiatric or other confidential programs), then find ways to connect your investors with people who have reason to value those programs from personal experience: Let them tell the story. One outstanding drug rehabilitation program, Walden House, invites its donors to its annual Celebration of Success (graduation).

✔ If donors do not want to get involved, don't pressure them. One foundation, responding to a question regarding the stewardship provided to it by an organization to which it had been very generous, said it was the best the foundation had ever experienced. Excited, the individual asking the question inquired about what the organization did to warrant such praise: "They leave us alone" was the answer. The foundation prefers to set its own timetable for visitations and requests for information, something it makes very clear to all organizations it funds. Only this organization, it said, seems to remember that.

✔ Find out how a person wants to be recognized and stewarded. A major museum, wishing to acknowledge an extremely generous gift from a new board member, offered recognition through membership in one of its donor benefit circles. The individual responded he had no interest in that. The board chair quickly asked, "What could we do to show our appreciation?" The response, to spend time with the curator responsible for the kind of art he and his wife collected, led to the formation of a relationship that has had huge benefit for the donor, the curator, and the museum.

✔ True stewardship is not a stop/start process; it is ongoing. It requires financial resources to keep it vital—funding that may be the first to go if things are tight in your organization. Be sure you communicate continuously with donors in a way that they find appropriate—Internet, letter, fax, newsletter, occasional "white paper" from a program staff member, personalized letters "From the desk of. . . (the executive director, program director, etc.)" giving feedback on a particular challenge or opportunity. Guard the stewardship funding zealously, remembering what we know from sales: It is easier and less expensive to renew an existing customer than it is to go out and get a new one. If your stewardship program is lifeless, you will not be able to sustain the values feedback that retains donors. You will have to keep identifying, cultivating, and engaging new donors over and over again. And that process, without a solid base of continuing investors, is exhausting.

Changing the profile of giving to nonprofits from the bell curve transaction model (where prospective donors receive lots of communication when the solicitation for their contribution is being made but very little after until another gift is needed) to the infinity loop transformation model (in which every time the lines intersect there is a renewed gift, commitment, understanding, or involvement) can be accomplished only with strong stewardship.[9] (See Exhibit 6.3.) In social enterprises, this is the heart of entrepreneurial success and the way in which the value added is communicated to the donor-investor.

ENDING "CHARITY": IMPLICATIONS FOR CREATING VALUE FOR DONORS

The results orientation of philanthropy—from Rockefeller to Drucker to Ellison—means that the concept of organizations as "charities" needs to be retired. Social enterprises are the leading edge of that retirement program!

Healthy and vigorous, the nonprofit sector must be an equal player in strengthening communities and in achieving the positive social outcomes that nonprofits are uniquely equipped to do. Innovative practices can only enhance that sense of vigor and cause nonprofits to be viewed as vital partners by communities and by donor-investors.

There is nothing wrong with the idea of charity: We can still believe that it begins at home and that charitable impulses or instincts are highly valued attributes of evolved individuals who understand their role in community advancement. We can still speak of charitable acts, charitable gifts, and charitable intent—indeed, they are measures of the nature of many gifts and often are part of a legal test for tax purposes (especially with estate gifts). However, to refer to an organization as a charity immediately puts it in the category of a needy organization, instead of an organization that pursues opportunities to improve the world.

While social enterprises infuse their activities with the new vigor of business models, they must also be certain that the messages that apply to the entire organization, including the philanthropic investment side, are free of "charity" messages. Social entrepreneurship can wrap itself comfortably around the way we position philanthropic investment as well: The value to

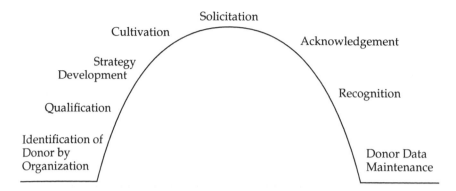

In this model, the curve begins again when a new gift is needed, and the cycle, with previous donors, begins with qualification and follows the same curve.

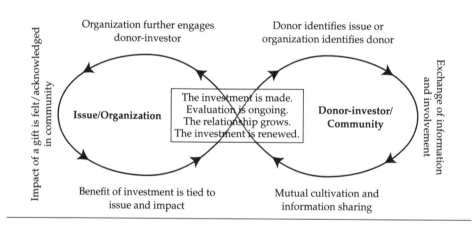

EXHIBIT 6.3 Moving the profile of giving from the bell curve transaction model to the infinity loop transformation model.

the donor is high. The movement toward calling the nonprofit sector the public benefit sector and nonprofits public benefit corporations is gaining momentum. Peter Hero, president of the Community Foundation Silicon Valley, uses every available platform to press for this shift in our perception and description of the sector. A public benefit corporation stands in sharp contrast to a charity. It is a welcome and needed contrast.

SUMMARY

Although many enterprises find themselves less reliant on the gifts of donors, donor issues are still an important—and often critical—issue for social entrepreneurs to understand. As donors become more engaged in the organizations in which they make their "investments," nonprofit leaders must rise to the challenge by moving their organizations from the old ways of delivering value to donors to new, more innovative and interactive ways. Remember:

- ✔ Social entrepreneurs are uniquely able to respond to the needs and desires of donor-investors, providing them with the accountability and involvement that they want.

- ✔ Be sure that the value you provide to prospective donors in exchange for their contributions is in line with their expectations.

- ✔ Be prepared to help your organization transition from the traditional sources of value to donors to the new ones.

- ✔ Develop and implement clear policies indicating when you will and when you will not accept certain kinds of gifts, and under what conditions.

- ✔ Communicate with your donor-investors early and often.

- ✔ Build long-term relationships with donors and provide them with the kinds of bottom-line information they need to be fully informed and engaged.

- ✔ The concept of the social enterprise is a fast-track way to get communities to view nonprofits not as charities with needs but as social benefit corporations meeting needs.

Notes

1. Peter Drucker, quoted in the *Wall Street Journal,* December 19, 1991.
2. Robert L. Payton, *Philanthropy: Voluntary Action for the Public Good* (New York: Collier Macmillan, 1988).
3. Kay Sprinkel Grace, *Beyond Fund Raising: New Strategies for Nonprofit Innovation and Investment* (New York: John Wiley & Sons, 1997).
4. Kay Sprinkel Grace and Alan L. Wendroff, *High Impact Philanthropy: How Donors, Boards and Nonprofit Organizations Can Transform Communities* (New York: John Wiley & Sons, 2000).
5. "The New Wealth of Nations: A Survey of the New Rich," *The Economist,* June 16, 2001, pp. 20–21.
6. Bruce Sievers, "If Pigs Had Wings," *Foundation News and Commentary,* Nov–Dec 1997.
7. Kirsten Haukebo, "High-Tech's Nouveau Riche Give Back in a New Way," *USA Today,* April 27, 2000, p. 7B.
8. Grace, *Beyond Fund Raising.*
9. Grace and Wendroff, *High Impact Philanthropy.*

Chapter 7

WORKING WITH COMMUNITY

Shirley Brice Heath, Professor, Stanford University

IN THIS CHAPTER

Defining community
Understanding why community is important to social entrepreneurs
Cultivating and continuing community connections

Everyone seems to agree that community is important for social entrepreneurs, but what is it and how does it come into play? This chapter explores the concept of community, its current complexities and challenges, and its key roles in determining and defining the success of social entrepreneurs.

DEFINING COMMUNITY

The idea of *community* is as much a part of American life as apple pie. But ask anyone what the word means, and answers will vary. Some believe their community is the neighborhood where they now live or where they grew up. Some find community in their voluntary face-to-face organizational memberships centered around key interests (Rotary Club, local opera company); others feel themselves part of a wide amorphous community (of Italian Americans, avid fly fishermen). Still others claim smaller networks tied to special events in their lives (breast cancer survivors, mothers against drunk driving). Regardless of the many definitions assigned to *community,* the word always brings to mind an ideal of relationships as well as an image of actual places or means of communication (face-to-face, chat rooms, mailings, and meetings).

Fundamentally, community makes us think of connections of place, people, history, and purpose. Community is a self-defined and self-limiting group of people who interact around their perception of shared goals, interests, and meanings. Often such groups determine ways to govern themselves or to manage tasks they see as essential to the group's purpose and integrity. Motivations of members come from reinforcement through effective communication, common assumptions about learning and teaching, and shared stories of success and failure. More often than not, communities also derive much of their sense of value in the group through their feelings of uniqueness or special qualities that set them apart from other such entities.

COMMUNITY IS . . .

core concept

Community is a group of individuals who decide that as a collective association, they can self-identify through shared experiences, values, goals, and sense of purpose in history.

Often membership and continuity come from identifying problems and working toward solving them together. Within any community, norms and expectations emerge, change, and sometimes overlap or conflict. Nevertheless, members of such groups remain connected through sustaining dialogue, a desire for action and change, and a sense of distinctive identity that sets them apart from other communities.

If social entrepreneurs are to become social change agents, they have to identify the people in the communities whose interests are most related to their purposes.

Being a social entrepreneur means being innovative, opportunity-oriented, resourceful, and value-creating. At the outset of any social enterprise related to economic, medical, educational, or social needs, social entrepreneurs are outsiders to those communities most affected. Therefore, attention to just what a community is, how it changes, and how needs are defined is critical to the success of any social entrepreneurial effort.

To think seriously about just how communities identify themselves within and around any specific interest, human collective, or geographic region calls for persistence and a willingness to learn. Each entity that calls itself a "community" is likely to start its self-definition from a set of needs, principles, or limits of space generated by insider views. For example, within an urban area, there may be no reality to "the homeless" as a general community; instead, transient individuals may align themselves by age, time on the street, or neighborhood. Similarly, any public housing projects may be seen by civic and police authorities as a single community, whereas local residents perceive certain spaces within the project as constituting different communities. It is easy for bureaucracies to define and identify "a community," but only rarely do such official labels come close to matching the self-designated idea of a group.

COMMUNITY TYPES

core concept

Community types vary by defining features and shifting boundaries, goals, and self-identities. As these alter, so do communication means and channels. Similarly, alliances among communities may shift. Therefore, social entrepreneurs have to spend a lot of time "staying in touch" with communities.

Exhibit 7.1 gives some idea of the many kinds of communities that include individuals who pursue shared purposes and who demand accountability. Most of these groups align themselves not only through a sense of common interests but also through perceptions that their achievements and needs are not adequately recognized by others. Over

Types of Communities	Defining Features	Examples
Geographical	Historically isolated and underresourced or abused areas	South Bronx, NY; bayou communities of lower Mississippi River; communities with abandoned toxic sites
Marginalized	Stigmatized groups often viewed as nonconformist particularly with regard to work, personal and residential maintenance, and sexual practices	Homeless groups, AIDS "victims," public housing residents
Age groupings dependent on working population	Populations segmented by virtue of their need for services, support, and control they seem unable to provide for themselves	Preschool age groups, school dropouts, youth too old for after-school care and too young for employment in the nonschool hours; the infirm and the elderly
Special interest groups	Affiliations that advocate for recognition, preservation, or expansion of issues or entities that cannot speak for themselves	Groups such as those urging preservation of virgin redwood forests, passage of a particular ballot measure, or ban of specific commodities or actions
Groups that self-identify through religious, ethnic, racial, or national membership	Alliances built through a sense of common history, often shared hardships, and hopes for a better future	Ethiopian Jews, Christian Indonesians, British Muslims, Native Americans, African Americans, Australian Aboriginals, Irish Americans, Polish Americans
Affiliate groups aligned through pursuit of similar activities	Devotion to what are often leisure activities or specialized ways of carrying out particular types of work	Medieval musical instrument groups, scuba diving clubs, bikers, artists or craftsmen such as organ makers or fine-print and handmade paper enthusiasts

EXHIBIT 7.1 Communities likely to work with or need social entrepreneurs.

time some of these groups split into smaller communities with more intensely specialized interests or a sense of loss of purpose of those advanced by the more general community. For example, recreational bikers who previously advocated creation of biking routes for leisure activities have in several urban areas, such as San Francisco, had break-off groups aggressively move to force the city to make it safe to commute to work by bicycle.

Maintaining open lines of communication with a community also means keeping up with how communities perceive other such entities. In addition to having a sense of themselves as a particular community, each also will have ideas about other communities that it sees as congenial, related, antagonistic, or destructive of its own. All communities also may hold firm ideas about those communities with whom they will build bridges or from whom they will accept help.

To create lasting influence, social entrepreneurs have to recognize that factors inside and beyond communities are always in flux. Often communities have had few successful ways to build ties to institutions, both public and commercial. Deprivation, marginalization, and absence of local role models for such bridging often keep members of a community locked in a cycle of interdependency and distrust of outsiders. They have little tolerance for outsiders who want to tell them what their needs and values *should* be. Social entrepreneurs have to be particularly alert, therefore, to see needs and capacities through community eyes. Doing so enables new opportunities for building social enterprises.

The success of such opportunities depends on acknowledging local felt needs. Such acknowledgment brings social entrepreneurs back to one of the earliest observations of community. The French count Alexis de Tocqueville noted on a visit to the United States in 1831 the "common" sense of groups that aligned around problems that they as key actors felt they had the power to resolve.[1] Both the creation and implementation of ideas for reform or changed values must be accountable ultimately to those most directly affected.

The history of each community and its point of emergence and peaks of intensification can tell social entrepreneurs a great deal about ways to access and mobilize resources from within the group. Often communities take special turns in their sense of purpose at points of crisis or threat to something they view as essential to their very being; many times several communities will be similarly affected by an external event and formerly distinct communities will then pull together.

For example, when underground fires from an oil refinery threaten the health of a public housing unit, a community of activists there may build bridges to an environmental group urging higher gasoline taxes, reduced automobile traffic, and safer routes for commuting to work by bicycle. Similarly, a community of professional artists working with local youth in housing projects may align with environmentalists urging low-density housing on the land of a former military base. The goal of the artists is to obtain rehearsal and performance space in an area scrambling to turn every possible vacant space into housing. The intentions of environmentalists are to limit growth, reduce automobile traffic, and keep open space. Social entrepreneurs have the opportunity in such bridge-building between communities to help develop innovative solutions.

WHY DOES COMMUNITY MATTER TO SOCIAL ENTREPRENEURS?

Communities make up social units that are neither government nor business. All human beings need community in one form or another. The history of humankind tells of the many ways in which communities have formed, shifted in structure, and adapted to local environments, from urban or rural, tropical to arctic. Whereas community was formerly inevitably tied to place and condition of birth and remained part of one's identity throughout life, today membership in communities is largely voluntary and can be changed quickly. But it is still the case that these groupings offer opportunities to shape values and work together, build social and ecological environments, and have a sense that their joint existence matters. Potentially, within communities, every member has the opportunity to make a difference.

For the profit-making world, the diversity of these communities can represent niche markets, such as religious groups, professional associations, recreational devotees, and age or social class groupings. For social entrepreneurs, these communities represent webs of relationships that embody communication capabilities and multiple kinds of talent and knowledge that can be assets for bringing about social improvement. Working with those resources that build the systemlike linkages within communities makes the difference as to whether social entrepreneurial efforts succeed or fail.

But social entrepreneurs have to believe that community matters. And this is made all the more difficult because often those communities most in need neither communicate nor function in ways familiar to outsiders who wish to work with them as social entrepreneurs. Respecting community needs and values has to remain just as vital as generating financial support and developing a smooth-running organization. This means that the efforts ordinary entrepreneurs put into developing their business—planning, doing market research, and mobilizing talents—must for social entrepreneurs be complemented by time-consuming resource-building with communities.

EFFECTIVE SOCIAL ENTREPRENURS NEED THREE CRITICAL ABILITIES

core concept

Effective social entrepreneurs need *three critical abilities:* the willingness to

1. See capacity where others may see ineptness and dependence
2. Bring disparate communities together around solutions no one else has tried
3. Maintain teamwork through mutual trust and sense of possibility, even in the face of overwhelming obstacles

As they work with clients all over Boston and with international groups, such as Amnesty International or national organizations such as United Negro Colleges Fund on specific projects, the young people at Artists for Humanity expand their ideas of just what constitutes a community. They hear other groups talk of common hardships and experiences that bond them, of their wish to be better known and supported.

Since young people come to Artists for Humanity from all parts of the city, they learn about one another's neighborhoods and how many adults in each area may be alike in their common disdain for the arts and artists. They think of ways to bring together constituencies that otherwise never acknowledge one another. A mural commissioned by the Museum of Fine Arts in Boston in connection with the opening of an exhibition of paintings by Monet allows the young artists at Artists for Humanity to link two such groups. They go to the museum, study Monet's work, and re-create a portion of his *Water Lilies* at the entrance to a bank located in a neighborhood of residents who otherwise might not have been reached by the Monet exhibition.

As they work on the mural, they meet residents who reveal their own past work in the arts and their enthusiasm for finding art from young people and within the museum reaching into their communities.

The young artists realize they are members of *many different communities.* In many cases they plan the work of Artists for Humanity with neighborhood members; they link their creation of outdoor murals with local summer day camps that use the mural creation as an outing for their charges. The students who helped found Artists for Humanity with Rodgerson remember their own days in middle school, and they plan a Saturday program primarily for youngsters who attend middle schools in the city. They find a community of curators and gallery owners throughout the city who share their interest in representing art in different places and in new ways. They link up with schools that offer the curriculum of the National Foundation for Teaching Entrepreneurship (NFTE) and become a site where students can see entrepreneurship at work in a social enterprise.

SUSAN RODGERSON SPEAKS

Old warehouses line the streets of the wharf area in Boston. Within one of these, young people from across Boston's poorest neighborhoods come in the afternoons to the studios of a nonprofit youth-based arts organization—Artists for Humanity. This social enterprise began in 1990 when Rodgerson was a visiting resident artist in Martin Luther King Jr. Middle School in Boston. There she worked with students to create a mural in the school library. Once Rodgerson's residency ended, six of the students sought her out to ask for more opportunities to learn and to do art.

These six students and Rodgerson created a nonprofit organization the next fall, and Artists for Humanity opened its doors to young people willing to come to their wharf warehouse three afternoons a week to learn with professional artists working in several media—photography, ceramics, painting, sculpture, and silkscreening. The young students who founded the group with Rodgerson learned along with others and also joined with her in planning just how the organization could work with paying clients. As each year passed, and the students stayed in school and continued to study art, Artists for Humanity brought in more and more contract work—murals in connection with special community events or exhibitions at the Museum of Fine Arts, commissioned portraits of key figures in the history of blues and jazz, and textbook cover and greeting card designs. After a period of apprenticeship, all new students coming to Artists for Humanity received an hourly wage for their work on both contracted projects and their own creative work.

Rodgerson brought together professional artists, students with poor schooling resources, and landlords worried about a deteriorating neighborhood. All benefited from creation of a social enterprise that no one had envisioned.

Q: What is it about Artists for Humanity that makes young people want to come here?

Rodgerson: Young people need positive ways to practice adulthood—to earn money, give of themselves, participate in a venture they invent. They value knowing they can play a part in the business world and in the community. Beyond earning income, the kids get pleasure out of sitting down in a board room and discussing who they were and what they have to offer society . . . how they fit into the world of business.

Q: What are the integral parts of your program?

Rodgerson: We teach microenterprise; we teach young people how to create a job for themselves, how to create a life for themselves. Young people come here to learn from the professional artists of our five studios. We require that young people who are interested in jobs here participate in a volunteer program for two months. At the end of two months, the

(continued)

young people who decide to stay have self-selected for this program. They study, learn, and are given opportunities to work on projects and a place to work on their own. At the end of four years, young people have really developed their own identities and their own vision.

Q: How did you come to the decision that Artists for Humanity could not be donor-driven, just another charity-supported nonprofit offering at-risk youth a place to go after school?

Rodgerson: We have to ensure some stability for the learning that young people from urban environments can do in the arts. Being solely donor-dependent puts us at the mercy of funders who often change their priorities every year. It's also the proverbial catch 22: No one wants to give you money if you need it; they only give you money when you have it. So we decided we needed to earn money. It's also necessary to realize that young people deserve full-time evidence of faith in them. What young people really need are adults who can participate with them in the process of educating and growing and becoming. We see ourselves as participating in an exchange that separates us from the traditional nonprofit in that we have a service to provide and we are willing to earn income. While we have a social, nonprofit, community value, and we'll always need income from foundations and grants to continue to grow, we realized we had to work toward a balance between earned income and foundation giving.

Q: What's your answer to your critics who feel that you should not pay young people who work at Artists for Humanity? What was the critical factor that led you to decide to expand your revenue base beyond the usual sources of government grants, foundation handouts, and corporate gifts?

Rodgerson: We have the voice of the youth at our fingertips. The foundation of our program is that we arrange for young people to be in a corporate environment, a business environment, be equals in a sense that they have something to give and they are reimbursed for that—not unlike a typical designer or a businessperson offering a product or a service. Year by year, these young people build a portfolio. We can benefit the young through real experience, through positive ways to practice adulthood.

Q: Who are the communities who work with you? How do you decide on community links and partnerships?

Rodgerson: These young people have worked with national and international companies, like Gillette and AT&T International. They've created T-shirt designs for students at the Sloan School of Management. They've also designed public service announcements for the Department of Public Health and public art displays for Amnesty International. I believe that you can turn a variety of business engagements to learning opportunities to benefit the youth through experience.

Q: How have your ideas of community changed since Artists for Humanity began in 1990?

Rodgerson: Artists for Humanity represents several different kinds of communities at work. Foremost to the young people who come here is the sense of community they create through their study and work in the arts, their exhibitions, and their contacts with the businesses of Boston. They see *community* as a sense of mutual commitment to the social enterprise they have helped build and want to continue for the next generation.

Their mission and goals—embedded in learning and earning through the arts for social improvement—can best be met by expanding their ideas of communities. While they value intensely their ability to earn money as they work in the arts during the after-school hours, they also see this ability as enabling neighborhoods, which gain positive role models in the young artists. Students who have worked with Artists for Humanity become impassioned when they talk of how important it is for young people to give something back to their community and to younger students.

IDENTIFYING COMMUNITY ASSETS

Rogerson's case illustrates many ways of identifying community assets and pulling communities together to meet several needs. Moreover, this case demonstrates the power of *the force of experience* within communities. Local knowledge provides the special understanding that can make solution of previously insurmountable social problems possible.

Community assets can be tapped by mapping those associations available within a local area and also by working to learn how associational groupings create networks or webs of interaction. How do youths who have dropped out of school connect and communicate, and with which other groups do they associate? Such questions are central for every target group of interest to social entrepreneurs. In addition, who are the guides to these associations in the local area? Who are those who know the history, purposes, places linked to communities? Who has the trust of the locals?

Community assets come in the form of leaders, local wisdom, inside knowledge about place and time, and means of communication. Is there a local newspaper certain communities read, or a Laundromat bulletin board residents regard as the place to learn what is going on? Are there trusted elders or key young people who know the pulse of community life? Such assets enable social entrepreneurs to know how to learn about needs and to build ideas into working projects of creativity and values.

But even with inside knowledge of assets, social entrepreneurs will quickly learn that targeted communities will by no means agree on what constitutes "social values." In addition, the idea of "value" for these communities may well differ markedly from the way that social entrepreneurs envision social value or improvement. Central to unlocking ideas about social value is the sense of *need* that different communities hold. What is it that these groups believe is most needed, and where do they see untapped resources? Drawing this information out before taking up the role of change agent is analogous to market research necessary for a commercial venture: What is it that people see as their needs, and what are they willing to do to meet these? In both cases, this early market investigation is critical. Finding ways to tap into this information helps ensure that social entrepreneurs also learn about opportunities as well as resources that may exist within the targeted communities.[2]

LINKING COMMUNITY PARTNERSHIPS
WITH INSTITUTIONS

Once social entrepreneurs have engaged with community members to identify needs and resources, forming *working partnerships* and *strategic alliances* across communities can be complemented by linking with institutions.

core concept   To link communities with *institutions,* social entrepreneurs need both imagination and patience. Institutions, such as government bureaucracies, schools, and transport systems, are often seen as alien or in opposition to community goals and needs. However, communities need to find ways to work with institutions in new ways, so that needless energy is not spent in railing against perceived "enemies." Social entrepreneurs can become the brokers who bring about innovative alliances between institutional forces and the needs, as well as the strengths, of the community. Often this bridge-building has never occurred before, because of limited inspiration, bureaucratic barriers, or long-held misperceptions between communities and institutions.

INTERVIEW

ANNA SJOLUND LINDSTROM SPEAKS

Halfway around the world, in a state system where the public sector provides much more substantial support for community activities than is the case in the United States, is a collection of buildings called The Dairy. In Lund, Sweden, this site is at the edge of a highly cosmopolitan city that is home to one of the oldest universities in the nation and a favorite tourist spot for Europeans.

Initiated 20 years ago as a way to save the dairy processing plant, today's social enterprise of The Dairy has become a laboratory for spawning entrepreneurial pursuits by young people of the region. Supported by a yearly budget of approximately $250,000 from the city, The Dairy houses a concert hall outfitted with the latest in sound and lighting equipment, 17 soundproof rehearsal rooms, a small theater, and a café with performing space. Three for-profit cultural organizations—a film group, an organization of musicians, and supporters of jazz and classical music, and a similar organization for rock and folk music—constitute the core of The Dairy's administration. These organizations have annual membership fees and bring film events, concerts, and recitals to The Dairy. Each organization has three representatives on the governing board, which was headed in 2000 by 20-year-old Anna Sjolund Lindstrom, a member of the rock and folk music organization.

Initiated and redesigned in 1990 as a place for cultural events for community members of all ages, but especially young people, The Dairy is open daily, with showings of two films every day except Monday, a café with three large television screens for viewing special sports events, concerts nearly every week, and several annual events, such as a Hip Hop Festival. A host of young volunteers usually headed by a teenager who works directly under Anna manage the cloak room, take tickets at the door, oversee the scheduling of use of soundproof practice rooms (for which each band pays approximately $60 each month).

Daily the venue buzzes with activity, as young people move in and out of practice rooms, come for instrument lessons, or stop by to check the upcoming calendar of events. Private music teachers may use the facility's practice rooms to teach lessons, but they must book these rooms in advance or operate on a regularly scheduled basis. Each month the facility's events range across the fields of interest of the three supporting cultural organizations, from classical music concerts to small jazz ensembles. Only the film program operates at all times; the administrative board otherwise ensures equitable programming and access to space by the other two cultural organization's members.

Q: What needs of the community did The Dairy set out to fill, and how was community defined by the founders?

Lindstrom: Several communities, as well as the city government, local police force, and tourist commission, had needs that The Dairy came to serve. Young people wanted to have their own local venue for music, to improve their technical and artistic skills, and to build professional connections for further learning. The city and related institutions wanted Lund to present a better image of its young people to local citizens and to visitors to the city. Without thinking of doing so in advance, The Dairy actually built new communities, such as those devoted to having certain kinds of films available, as well as improved the future prospects of certain communities, such as youth devoted to particular types of music.

Q: A major problem in urban centers is abandonment of large buildings that need substantial renovation and upgrading to meet current environmental and construction codes. How is it that the old dairy came to be such a rallying focus for reconstruction and shift of function in Lund? What have been the major revenue streams for The Dairy? And what about evaluation and accountability to your various supporters?

Lindstrom: Many in Sweden have hated to see evidence of the past economic history ripped away by modern construction. Dairies, including door-to-door delivery of dairy goods, figure in the memories of many civic leaders and prominent citizens. Therefore, interest in preserving the old dairy, or *mejeriet,* was high. We were fortunate also that one young man intensely devoted to popular music led the rallies and calls for the building to be used by young people as a venue and professional development site for their musical interests. Use of The Dairy as concert hall, theater,

(continued)

and music center has ensured that the young people who run the facility bring in revenue, but each year, the city of Lund provides several hundred thousand dollars as subsidy. However, we are accountable for responsible expenditure of these funds and to staying vigilant to the widest possible range of access to The Dairy by different communities (across ages, musical and film interests, and institutional affiliation). Annually, we provide to the city an inventory of equipment, record of types of uses and number of attendees and participants, and a written and oral accounting of the year's activities at The Dairy. Many young members take part in preparation of these materials, just as they hold primary responsibilities for security, maintenance, bookings, and new enterprise developments.

Q: As is the case in some other postindustrial societies, Sweden's young are attending universities in shrinking proportions to the youth population as a whole. You seem to feel The Dairy serves a critical educational role that helps launch young people into careers and simultaneously stimulates these individuals to remain aware of the importance of sustaining social entrepreneurship. How does this happen?

Lindstrom: The labor shortage brought about by the rapid expansion of telecommunications and high-tech industries has meant that employment and the opportunity to learn on the job draw Swedish youth away from universities. Here at The Dairy, young people, including many disaffected with schooling, find professional musicians and musical technicians to whom they can apprentice. In doing so, they gain valuable experience at a place that is known throughout Sweden, and they have no trouble moving into employment in other parts of the music and entertainment industry. Just as important, however, is their development here of habits and skills that transfer well to the job and often later into further learning in higher education institutions. The fact that The Dairy is the preferred concert venue for international artists who come to Sweden translates into invaluable experience and future reference. Moreover, becuse many come here as disaffected youth, as they move into professional roles, they tend to remain alert to social needs of different communities in areas where they work.

The young managers and technicians of The Dairy work in competition with entirely adult-run concert venues and music centers elsewhere in Sweden. They must compete for the big-name stars by maintaining a steady reputation of having the best sound projection equipment, the safest and most accessible facility, and the most competent public relations staff. The Dairy attracts its audiences from not only Lund and all of Sweden but also from Copenhagen and nearby regions in Denmark, easily accessible by the bridge completed in 2000. Managers of The Dairy must therefore stay consistently attuned to the interests and needs of their three core cultural organizations, while they also look ahead to new kinds of musical attractions and possible crossover groupings that will attract new and different communities as audience members. The strong sense of organizational memory over the decade of its existence serves as constant reminder of all the ways that within one decade communities of interests around The Dairy have changed, and they are certain to continue to do so even more rapidly.

reality check   Bill Strickland created the Manchester Craftsmen's Guild and later the Bidwell Training Center by staying close to his targeted communities—youth and displaced adults—and by learning their needs. As these communities changed and grew, Manchester's programs had to adapt and reach out to new partners for strategic alliance. To enhance their influence on youth, Manchester linked to local public high schools and to residency programs at local universities. Hence as these social enterprises worked as change agents for those caught in the cycle of poverty—the first constituency of need Strickland and others identified—they also played a role in changing education institutions. Through the arts, Manchester engaged public schools in innovative programs and processes by providing an arts director and leader from the guild. Higher education institutions were brought into the web of collaboration to help take learning opportunities in the arts to more professional levels than the public schools or Manchester alone could offer.

KEEPING IN TOUCH WITH CHALLENGES

core concept   Social entrepreneurs face five major challenges in the necessity that they work with communities. These can be thought of as the "*Dreaded Ds:*" disintegration, divisiveness, dinosaurs, diversification, and diversions.

Challenge #1: Disintegration

Since the end of World War II, experts have fretted over the disintegration of community. Since the mid-1980s, key writings have brought this concern to the public mind. Robert Bellah and fellow sociologists pointed out Tocqueville's concern that independence and individualism—especially as demonstrated in entrepreneurism—could pull apart community.[3] Sociologist Robert Putnam, through his studies of Italy and of the United States, identified civic decline or the loss of collective action in the face of several trends: the movement of women into the labor force, dramatic geographic mobility, and the technological transformation of leisure.[4]

Aside from raising the issue of general disintegration of community, these writings and others suggest the need to build "social capital"—networks of trust, values, and norms to facilitate cooperation. They also point out that formerly small tightly knit special-interest communities have now become massive groupings, such as the Sierra Club, with many members who define themselves only by paying annual dues or buying calendars.

Challenge #2: Divisiveness

Countering the move to larger and larger groupings is the splinter effect that develops when groups rally around narrower and narrower concerns.

These networks may be dense, but the membership may be so small that the work of keeping the group afloat falls to only a few.[5] Moreover, as the business world increasingly views niches and segmentation as positive market possibilities, a vision of the larger picture becomes harder to develop and maintain for voluntary communities.

Because social entrepreneurs tend to be action-oriented, divisiveness and the slow pace it inevitably brings tax patience. Remaining a good listener and a socially responsive partner in the face of the splintering of a community with whom one has worked to develop plans or implement strategies is difficult. It is tough to know when to introduce a reality check in such circumstances so that those threatening to splinter in the face of disagreement can foresee obstacles.

Challenge #3: Dinosaurs

While communities may be becoming more scarce or so divided as to be unable to maintain themselves in the eyes of some, organizations and institutions appear to be becoming larger. "Dinosaurs" has become a favorite term to apply to these entities, often charged with the inability to learn and therefore likely to become extinct but in the meantime to harm smaller units such as communities. Dinosaurlike attitudes on the part of governmental or financial institutions hurt communities when they are unwilling to lend money, permit long-term leases, or accept evaluations that do not show the usual "bottom line" in quantitative terms. The idea of "business as usual" within very large entities often works against the unusual ways that social entrepreneurs have to work—often with a lack of profitability, the absence of market growth, and few short-term demonstrations of success. Because social entrepreneurs often tackle hugely difficult social problems that have seemed intractable to the dinosaurs, the resistance of the latter to seeing new processes and patterns of development or means of accountability can be a tough challenge.[6]

Challenge #4: Diversification

Although diversification often is seen as a positive feature, excessive diversification creates instability. Sometimes a particular community finds its members' interests have gone in so many directions that splinter groups become the norm. Although social entrepreneurs must have talents for bridging, the overdiversification of interests and aims of communities can bring about a chaotic maze of conflicting groups. Moreover, it is extremely difficult to decide whether all these groups have legitimate claims to a separate identity and agenda and if all should have an equal standing in any move to innovate in solving social problems.

Community revitalization presents the most frequent case of conflicts among the diverse groups that feel they should have a major say in ways to renew physical spaces. Business and residential interests clash, as do practical goals that appear to conflict with artistic or aesthetic aims.[7] Intergenerational differences can present themselves as communities at odds over not only choices related to housing renewal but also such decisions as preserving parkland or forests or allowing continued development or logging. Environmental groups sometimes splinter in the name of protection of one animal over another.

Challenge #5: Diversions

Whereas working together in voluntary groups was for many decades a major activity during the leisure hours, many individuals now seek other kinds of diversion. Spectatorship and other passive activities, such as watching television or videos or surfing the Internet, have taken the place of community work, particulary for full-time workers.With the majority of women in the labor force, the largest segment of the population previously available for community development has no easy replacement. Moreover, as more work becomes information-based, many seek leisurely diversions that do not call for active engaged thinking; being "brain-dead" or wanting "to be just a couch potato" describes the preferred after-work state of many who work full time.

Therefore, social entrepreneurs working with communities in need may find few allies who are not members of those communities. Such assistance becomes more and more vital as market-based approaches and businesslike methods are increasingly expected of efforts to meet social needs.[8] Community members may lack necessary technical skills or experience for some specialized tasks essential to maintenance of a social enterprise.

As the cases of The Dairy and Artists for Humanity illustrate, young people may be becoming a key segment for building and sustaining communities engaged in social entrepreneurship. Their out-of-school hours exceed by a good bit those available to adults who work full time in the labor force, and the young are known to seek diversions that are unique, challenging, and high-risk—essential features of social entrepreneurs.[9]

KEY STEPS FOR CULTIVATING AND CONTINUING COMMUNITY CONNECTIONS

To identify opportunities for social improvement with communities as allies, entrepreneurs have to:

✔ Regard communities as assets for building any possible social enterprises

✔ Look to communities for their help in identifying needs and areas for improvement

✔ Be alert to the fact that an identified need does not necessarily create an opportunity

Once local community members identify and acknowledge potential opportunities, several key steps follow:

✔ Devise ways that key constituents from communities can see themselves as true resources.

✔ Work to distribute leadership and decision making among these constituents.

✔ Negotiate mission and goals at the outset, but remember these need to be readdressed periodically.

✔ Ensure that ways of evaluating both process and outcomes include community input and participation.

✔ Maintain communication among key players who in turn stay in touch with their constituents, so that change can be adaptive.

✔ Keep out front the need to agree on desired balance between social returns and investment and financial gains.

With the establishment of any social enterprise, social entrepreneurs must ensure ways to stay informed about demographic, economic, and cultural changes within communities. To gather this information, social entrepreneurs need to:

✔ Engage communities in ongoing appropriate opportunities for feedback.

✔ Be willing to find and use nontraditional means of communication.

✔ Remember that making fundamental changes in the ways things are done in meeting social needs within any community will not come easily.

No social enterprise can ever work with only a single community. Several communities—even at the local level—always will be involved, and more will emerge when social entrepreneurs seek out the underlying causes of problems and begin to build bridges to institutions. Because social entrepreneurs want to do more than offer quick fixes or treat symptoms, they have to go beyond the obvious and beyond single communities. They also have to pull together disparate players and think in creative ways to build and to sustain bold visions of social innovation.

Surrounding the core ideas of community for social entrepreneurs are the following direct reminders from the cases of Artists for Humanity, the Manchester Craftsmen's Guild, and The Dairy.

✔ Ventures that have a "social mission" often compete with fully commercial for-profit enterprises. Therefore, social entrepreneurship may need to be competitive and operate as any successful business must in a time of rapid technological changes and shifts in identities of niche markets and their interests in products and services.

✔ Community is almost never *local* primarily in the sense of immediate neighborhood; every community is inevitably interdependent, often with entitites not easily identifiable by outsiders.

✔ Communities shift not only in geographic and sociodemographic terms but also in tastes and interests.

✔ Social entrepreneurship efforts of all types are more likely than either government services or commercial businesses to have to take into consideration new ethnicities, stay keenly alert to local work and leisure patterns, and consider such matters as feasible transport access to their facility.

✔ Community building within any social enterprise needs to be a large part of the social entrepreneur's job; when established goals have to shift because of community changes, members may find new directions destabilizing.

✔ Exploration and invention of new groupings for responsive creativity will become increasingly the norm.

✔ Building local productive capacities will require imaginative and flexible ways of relating with the public sector and key institutions, such as schools, mental health facilities, and operations within the private and commercial sectors.

✔ Maintaining value often means staying ahead of the curve of technological change.

The struggle between institutions of depersonalization and services and the most desired features of social entrepreneurs has to move toward resolution through a vision of possibility. Positive relations of people working for a sense of well-being for themselves and those they identify as community will constitute the primary asset of social entrepreneurs. Broad goals and dynamic views of community identities and needs with regard to education, health care, social services, arts, and the environment provide the foundation for specific social enterpreneurial pursuits. New alignments of private capital and public need, as well as reduced provision of public programs and funds by postindustrial governments, will always act as dynamic forces for such efforts.

An enterprising business also must be an intelligent organization embedded in a network of other enterprising entities. This is especially the case for social entrepreneurs who want to meet community needs. At the heart of these efforts must be the time-consuming efforts that go into nurturing local talents, maintaining an alert posture toward possible new capital markets, and enabling organizational staff to sustain their own capacity for learning.

SUMMARY

This chapter has argued that community is integral to the work of social entrepreneurs—both those from within and from outside communities undergoing change through social innovations. The chapter addresses particularly social entrepreneurs who have not emerged from within the communities of social need with whom they work.[10] In these cases, understanding and accepting the types and features of communities, as well as the challenges they can present, is essential to the effectiveness and success of any social innovation. Since social entrepreneurs almost never have either policy or profit to help them along, communities constitute their greatest resource and best insurance for implementation of innovative approaches to opportunities.

action step   Every social entrepreneur needs to consider six fundamental action steps in working with community.

1. Become familiar with several successful cases of social entrepreneurship that rely on in-depth knowledge and understanding of community.

2. Undertake the exercise of listing all the various communities, their types and features, to which you belong. Sketch their interlinks, if any, and consider whether conflicting or overlapping aims occur. List the different leadership and decision-making styles reflected in the communities to which you belong. Then draw several generalizations about your own communities that could present challenges to outsiders trying to bring about social improvements for members.

3. Consider any ways in which you or someone you know has innovatively created social value by taking advantage of opportunities unseen by others. What was the relationship between initiation of the idea and actual implementation, and what role did affected parties play in either of these? Now ponder the extent to which maintenance of social value in these cases depended on strong buy-in and investment by the groups affected. How different would this situation be for communities in social need?

4. Spend time talking with members of one or more communities to which you are a definite outsider. Which types of questions work best in these conversations? What are some effective ways of drawing out of community members their list of needs and their sense of local resources and assets?

5. Assess your own tolerance for listening to groups whose lifeways differ from your own in patterns of work, uses of leisure time, and buying and maintaining goods and residential dwellings.

6. Schedule an interaction with members of one or more communities. Work out ahead of time ways to run the meeting, invite mem-

bers to express their needs, and maintain an ongoing dialogue with those in attendance. Make out an evaluation checklist before this interaction, so that you can record your perceptions of failed communication as well as expressions of willingness to move forward on a mutually agreed-upon set of goals.

Creativity in activities and means of communication will enable assets of social entrepreneurships to multiply and to generate a stronger base for collective efforts. Building capacity and enlisting new ways of extending this capacity will keep social entrepreneurial efforts constantly in change. Their dynamism and adaptive powers keep community at the center of the work and life of the enterprise.

Notes

1. McKnight draws on Tocqueville's observations for his definition of community. See John McKnight, *The Careless Society: Community and Its Counterfeits* (New York: Basic Books, 1995). Ironically, many of these same points are extended in discussions of the coming of community self-reliance in Great Britain by Dick Atkinson (*The Common Sense of Community* [London: Demos, 1994]) and Charles Leadbeater (*The Rise of the Social Entrepreneur* [London: Demos, 1997]). Both these writers emphasize the value of social entrepreneurs in tackling difficult social problems effectively and with accountability to involved communities. Other writers on community link these notions to effective leaders who work to overcome the loss of the nineteenth-century sense of community grounded in common experience in a local physical setting; see John W. Gardner, *On Leadership* (New York: Free Press, 1990), especially chapter 11. See also Frances Hesselbein, Marshall Goldsmith, Richard Beckhard, and Richard F. Schubert, *The Community of the Future* (New York: The Drucker Foundation, 1998), on the community of the future, and Peter F. Drucker, *Post-capitalist Society* (New York: Harper & Row, 1993), on the need to restore community through the social sector.
2. The mapping of assets within communities is now often a key component of workshops on social entrepreneurship. The most commonly used resource is John P. Kretzmann and John L. McKnight, *Building Communities from the Inside Out* (Chicago: Asset-based Community Development Institute, 1993) and related modules on specific topics, such as "mapping and mobilizing the economic capacities of local residents"; see Kretzmann and McKnight, *A Guide to Mapping and Mobilizing the Economic Capacities of Local Residents* (Chicago: Asset-based Community Development Institute, 1996).
3. Rarely has an "academic" volume produced such a wide readership as did *Habits of the Heart: Individualism and Commitment in American Life* by Robert Bellah, Richard Madsen, William M. Sullivan, Ann Swidler, and Steven M. Tipton (New York: Harper & Row, 1985). This volume drew heavily from Tocqueville's observations of the entrepreneurial spirit of the United States as well as its propensity to community.
4. Numerous articles as well as the seminal volume by Putnam trace the causes and consequences of the perceived loss of civic groupings. See the following by Robert Putnam: *Making Democracy Work: Civic Traditions in Modern Italy* (Princeton, NJ: Princeton University Press, 1993); "The Prosperous Community: Social Capital and Public Life," *The American Prospect,* No. 13 (1993); and "Bowling Alone: America's Declining Social Capital," *Journal of Democracy,* Vol. 6, No. 1 (1995).
5. Numerous works speak to the divisiveness of contemporary societies, especially those of postindustrial economies. Some point to the need for new kinds

of leadership; see Gardner, *On Leadership;* James M. Kouzes and Barry Z. Posner, *The Leadership Challenge* (San Francisco: Jossey-Bass, 1995); and Larry C. Spears, *Insights on Leadership* (New York: John Wiley & Sons, 1998). Others call for increased attention to collaboration and cultivating the "art of alliances"; see Rosabeth Moss Kantor, *Frontiers of Management* (Cambridge, MA: Harvard Business Review, 1997).

6. Those who tackle dinosaurs usually do so through promoting new kinds of bonds, often in spiritual terms, or innovative processes of organizational learning. Volumes that take the former approach often call on new metaphors—the "soul," "theater," and "the cathedral within"; see Alan Briskin, *The Stirring of Soul in the Workplace* (San Francisco: Berrett-Koehler, 1998); B. Joseph Pine and James H. Gilmore, *The Experience Economy: Work Is Theatre and Every Business a Stage* (Cambridge, MA: Harvard Business School, 1999); Shore, *The Cathedral Within;* and David Whyte, *The Heart Aroused: Poetry and the Preservation of the Soul in Corporate America* (New York: Doubleday, 1994). Donaldson and Dunfee argue strongly that belonging to a community creates ethical obligations and encourages societal responsibility; see Thomas Donaldson and Thomas W. Dunfee, *Ties that Bind: A Social Contracts Approach to Business Ethics* (Cambridge, MA: Harvard Business School, 1999). Processes of organizational learning are best known through the work of Peter Senge and the Society for Organizational Learning in Cambridge, Massachusetts; see his *The Fifth Discipline: The Art and Practice of the Learning Organization* (New York: Currency Doubleday, 1990) and *The Dance of Change: The Challenges to Sustaining Momentum in Learning Organizations* (New York: Currency Doubleday, 1999). But also see Douglas Hague, *Transforming the Dinosaurs: How Organisations Learn* (London: Demos, 1993), for a British perspective on dinosaurs.

7. Many softback, often short-lived publications recount diversities encountered in social entrepreneurial efforts, particularly those around housing and neighborhood revitalization; see, for example, Architects/Designers/Planners for Social Responsibility, *New Village: Building Sustainable Cultures,* Partners for Livable Communities, *The Livable City: Revitalizing Urban Communities* (New York: McGraw-Hill, 2000).

8. Some social commentators attribute this loss of volunteerism and willingness to "get involved" during the off-work hours to the "corrosion of character" that results from new forms of capitalism; see Richard Sennett, *The Corrosion of Character* (New York: Norton, 1998). Others feel that as longevity within a job becomes a decreasing feature of postindustrial life, the quest for diversion or the urge to jump from one thing to another is bound to affect more than the workplace; see Arie De Geus, *The Living Company: Growth, Learning and Longevity in Business* (London: Longview, 1997).

9. Shirley Brice Heath and Laura Smyth's *ArtShow: Youth and Community Development: A Resource Guide* (Washington, DC: Partners for Livable Communities, 1999), a guide for community organizations that involve young people in the arts for social enterprise, illustrates several cases in which community youth have taken charge of social innovation through entrepreneurial and educational efforts.

10. Although many of the same points regarding the importance of community to social entrepreneurship apply to insiders, most social entrepreneurs work with communities into which they were not born. Insiders share many of the challenges of those from outside the community, particularly when they have had to leave the community to obtain training, connections, and resources vital to the financial sustainability of their social innovation. Cases of "making things work" by both inside and outside social entrepreneurs illustrate the challenge common to both; see Stephen Thake and Simon Zadek, *Practical People, Noble Causes: How to Support Community-based Social Entrepreneurs* (London: New Economics Foundation, 1997), and Geoff Mulgan, *Connexity: How to Live in a Connected World* (Cambridge, MA: Harvard Business School, 1997).

Chapter 8

PERFORMANCE INFORMATION THAT REALLY PERFORMS

Fay Twersky, founding Principal, BTW Consultants-informing change and
Jill Blair, founding Principal, BTW Consultants-informing change

IN THIS CHAPTER

Defining value in the nonprofit marketplace
Developing a performance information system
Translating information into action

In the private sector, where the "bottom line" rules, there has long been an appreciation of the need for and value of accurate performance information. Businesses use performance data to assess financial health as well as the effectiveness of business and management practices. That performance information helps to guide private enterprise and contributes to profitability and viability in the marketplace. In the nonprofit sector, where "value" is a more ambiguous concept, generally less attention is paid to the consistent gathering and application of performance information. This is beginning to change and marks an important opportunity and challenge for the nonprofit sector.

In recent years there have been growing expectations among funders, both public and private, that nonprofit organizations have a responsibility to be more accountable for the outcomes of the programs and services they provide. These new expectations are associated with a shift in the economy that has yielded new wealth, given rise to a new breed of philanthropist, and established a new level of public accountability. These trends are bringing private sector principles to bear on social investments. Government and philanthropy are becoming less interested in the traditional notion of charity and more interested in the social return on investment.

At the same time that these shifts of focus and expectations have occurred among funders, another trend has taken hold as well—the emergence of a new type of entrepreneur: the *social* entrepreneur. The social entrepreneur is characterized by a strong commitment to positive social change and a sense of personal power to effect that change. A social entrepreneur has a social mission, but he or she also has a heightened sense of accountability both to the constituencies served and to the investors who support his or her efforts (for further discussion of accountability, see Chapter 5, The Accountable Social Entrepreneur, in *Enterprising Nonprofits: A Toolkit for Social Entrepreneurs*). It is fortuitous though not coincidental that the New Economy has given rise to both the social entrepreneur and the new investor whose expectations of nonprofits are shifting from one of compliance to one of performance. The social entrepreneur wants to demonstrate the quality of the program he or she develops as well as continuously adapt, learn, and innovate; these all require reliable and timely performance information. In this way, the social entrepreneur should be leading the call for accountability, not just following it.

In this chapter we discuss ways that nonprofits can position themselves to succeed in the twenty-first century as organizations delivering the highest-quality services in the most effective and efficient manner. We discuss how to define value in the nonprofit market place and ways to measure it. We review the steps to design and implement credible systems of measurement and, finally, discuss how to use performance information to achieve a social mission.

Defining Value in the Nonprofit Marketplace

In the for-profit sector, value is measured or defined in financial terms—and, in particular, according to the concept of "return on investment" (ROI). The value of an enterprise is defined by the people who pay for it. In the private sector, the value is defined by the consumer; in the nonprofit sector, value also has historically been defined by the people who pay for the services—namely the investors, either public or philanthropic. Value has not been defined by the consumers of those services, who are referred to, in a traditional model, as clients rather than customers. But why do philanthropic and public organizations make the investments they make? The answer is, to add value to the social fabric of society. While these investors do not expect a capital return on investment, they do expect a social one.

core concept   Value in the nonprofit marketplace is defined by *measurable social impact*. As a result of the changing landscape and changing expectations, it is no longer sufficient for nonprofits simply to assert their value in the absence of evidence. They now have to demonstrate value through measurable social impact.

WHY COLLECT PERFORMANCE INFORMATION?

Social entrepreneurs collect performance information in order to meet the needs of internal audiences (staff, board, and clients) as well as external audiences (investors, policymakers, media, competitors). Historically, nonprofits have too often focused exclusively on meeting the needs of the external audience without recognizing the value of and need for performance information within the organization itself as a means of maximizing efficiency and quality of services delivered.

In the nonprofit sector, there always will be multiple audiences for performance information. At different times audiences will require different information or information reported in different ways. It will not always be possible to meet the various, even conflicting demands for data. So the first question is: Who is the most important audience? An organization committed to social entrepreneurship should hold its own information needs as its first priority. This prioritization recognizes that the value of information is to inform practice, planning, and the quality of services to consumers. This organization will be better positioned to explain to external audiences what information it collects, how that information can be presented, and why it is important, stemming the tide on unnecessary or duplicative demands for information by outside audiences.

As a case in point, several years ago a large multiservice organization (organization A) located in northern California decided to undertake the development of a comprehensive information management system. This system, it decided, would serve its own need for performance information first while at the same time meeting the reporting needs and requirements of investors and donors. The organization invested more than a year and a half of staff time as well as using consultants and invested substantially in technological infrastructure. It developed a system that had a clear rationale for the collection and application of information to inform program design, practice, and service delivery. The comprehensive nature of the system and the forethought applied placed the organization ahead of the demand for information curve. On a practical level, this means the organization is less likely to be at the mercy of external requests for information and better positioned to define and defend the information to be collected and the value it holds.

This fact was best exemplified when the agency joined a multiorganization collaborative to provide welfare-to-work services. When the collaborative discussed information-reporting requirements, including information that would be useful to the agencies and the funding sources, organization A was able to set forth its own indicators and data collection practices as a model for the program; its ability to set forth a well-conceived approach meant that it avoided the need to comply with someone else's reporting requirements. Since the development of its own comprehensive information system, organization A has been invited by local foundations to advise on reasonable expectations for information and reporting requirements, helping to set the standard for others.

 In establishing the organization itself as the primary consumer of information, the social entrepreneur makes a commitment to use information to inform decision making.

WHY COLLECT PERFORMANCE INFORMATION?

✔ To inform practice
✔ To demonstrate accountability
✔ To improve planning
✔ To better manage programs and services
✔ To improve social impact of programs and services
✔ To meet funding requirements
✔ To inform the field
✔ To demonstrate cost effectiveness of services
✔ To raise public awareness of the issues being addressed
✔ To demonstrate "social return on investment"

WHAT IS PERFORMANCE INFORMATION?

 Performance information is any data that describe how well the organization is doing in terms of (social) impact and cost effectiveness as they relate to mission. But in order to assess how well an organization is doing, one must first clearly articulate what the organization is trying to do: what specific contribution the organization is making and how the world is different as a result of its existence and the programs and services it provides. To be most useful, performance information should be continuously gathered, analyzed, and shared so that it can be incorporated into ongoing planning and program development efforts.

There is no one right way to derive performance information; the best mix of performance information must relate to specific organizations and what they are trying to accomplish. In his article "Mission Impossible? Measuring Success in Nonprofit Organizations," John Sawhill describes how as the president and CEO of the Nature Conservancy he led the organization through a process of developing and then redeveloping performance information.[1]

Historically, the organization relied on a standard they called "bucks and acres" to measure their success in achieving their mission. Their mission was to conserve biodiversity and protect species from extinction. "Bucks" was shorthand for the dollars raised, and "acres" referred to the acquisition of land for the Conservancy. These measures reflected strategies the Conservancy had employed for five decades. These were easy indicators to measure; they made the Conservancy look good; and they were easily understood. As it turned out, however, "bucks and acres" alone, both as a strategy and as performance indicators, were not sufficient. Because despite outstanding results on both, species extinction was "spiraling out of control." Performance information has to be relevant to the unique contribution of the organization—what the organization is trying to accomplish. In the end, the Nature Conservancy engaged in a process to evaluate its strategies and performance measures to achieve greater alignment with mission. The process resulted in the development of a "family of measures" that were specific to the Nature Conservancy's overall goal of protecting species from extinction.

WHAT IS YOUR UNIQUE CONTRIBUTION?

core concept

What concepts currently exist that will help nonprofits define their value and their *unique contribution* in the marketplace? The concept of mission—the reason an organization exists—the concept of goals—the driving force of the mission—and the concept of objectives—the measurable milestones of progress toward the achievement of goals each play a critical role in defining the value of a nonprofit's efforts. (See Exhibit 8.1).

First, the concept of mission. A mission statement is not an action plan; it is a vision statement developed by the board of directors. It speaks to how different the world will look in the future because the

EXHIBIT 8.1   Organizational building blocks for a performance information system.

organization exists in the present. Goals are broad statements of intent that are developed by staff to help actualize the mission. They describe the work of programs and initiatives. Objectives, also developed by staff, are milestones toward the accomplishment of goals and are time-limited, specific, and measurable.

How do these concepts of mission, goals, and objectives help define value? When employed, these concepts specify anticipated social impact within a given time period. It is important to know what it is you are trying to accomplish in order to assess the effectiveness of your efforts. Articulating social mission, goals, and objectives is the first step in describing your organization's unique contribution to social change.

A THEORY OF CHANGE

core concept The relationship among mission, goals, and objectives should be clearly articulated in a *"theory of change."* Doing this will make explicit all of the assumptions that are embedded in the program design—the relationship between what you are doing and what you expect to happen as a result. By definition, the mission of the organization is lofty and visionary—it does not lend itself well to measurement in the short term; objectives, however, do. With respect to performance measurement systems, people often fail to articulate the assumptions that underlie their efforts. They measure objective x, which they take to be a good indicator of accomplishing goal y that serves mission z. But they fail to express the precise relationship among all three. Why do we believe that doing x will result in y, and why/how y will achieve (in the long term) z? Because it is not possible to measure the accomplishment of a mission in the short term, it is essential to describe exactly how you believe accomplishing your objectives in the short term will contribute to the achievement of your mission in the long term.

This was made clear in the Nature Conservancy experience. The organization had a performance measurement system in place, "bucks and acres." But when it questioned the assumptions about the relationship between what was being measured and the goals and mission of the organization, it discovered a disconnect. It found that it was "successful" according to the performance indicators but not with respect to the organization's goals. In other words, its theory of change was flawed. The system was developed on the assumption that dollars and land were the key indicators of progress in protecting biodiversity, but the organization discovered that in fact there were intervening variables that were not accounted for in this system. The theory of change is the foundation upon which all process and outcome objectives are crafted.

SMART Objectives

Once you have described your anticipated unique contribution, it is important to document it. In order to document impact, it is necessary to have very clearly defined objectives that can be tracked and measured over time.

tool of the trade   Statements of objectives serve as a road map for guiding the development and implementation of programs and services. In order for objectives to be helpful, they must be S-M-A-R-T:

✔ Specific

✔ Measurable

✔ Attainable

✔ Realistic

✔ Time-limited

core concept   There are two types of objectives—process and outcome.

1. Process objectives describe specific activities that are *performed*, by whom they are performed, and in what time period.

2. Outcome objectives describe what is anticipated to *change* as a result of these activities.

Recently there has been an increased emphasis on outcomes and outcome objectives and a shift away from using process objectives to describe programmatic accomplishments. The reliance on process to describe value of nonprofit services has been disparaged as a kind of "bean counting" that doesn't meaningfully express the impact of an organization or program. The notion is that this shift represents a higher level of accountability, having organizations ask themselves, "So what?" What impact did we have on reducing social problems in our society? This is distinct from asking "What services did we provide to how many people over what period of time?" The problem with emphasizing outcomes to the exclusion of process, however, is that outcomes alone fail to provide a complete picture of what has transpired.

In the private sector, if one were to focus exclusively on outcomes, one would be interested in only the bottom line (profitability) without examining the ingredients of success or failure. For example, what marketing strategies were employed? What staffing ratio was used? How many sales transactions occurred? All of these are essentially the *processes* that contribute to the bottom line. In other words, it is as important to understand the means (process) as it is to understand the ends (outcome). Documenting and measuring process gives insight into the relationship between what is being done and what is changing as a

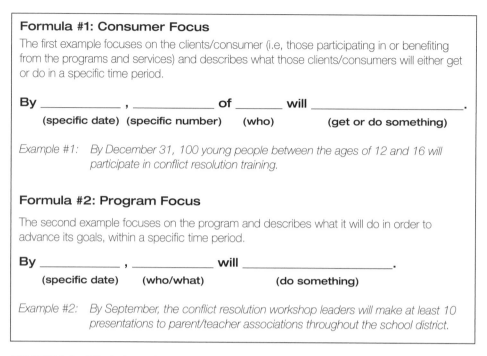

Formula #1: Consumer Focus

The first example focuses on the clients/consumer (i.e, those participating in or benefiting from the programs and services) and describes what those clients/consumers will either get or do in a specific time period.

By _____ , _____ of _____ will _____.
    (specific date) (specific number) (who)   (get or do something)

Example #1: *By December 31, 100 young people between the ages of 12 and 16 will participate in conflict resolution training.*

Formula #2: Program Focus

The second example focuses on the program and describes what it will do in order to advance its goals, within a specific time period.

By _____ , _____ will _____.
    (specific date)   (who/what)   (do something)

Example #2: *By September, the conflict resolution workshop leaders will make at least 10 presentations to parent/teacher associations throughout the school district.*

EXHIBIT 8.2 Worksheet for preparing process objectives.

tool of the trade   result. (See Exhibit 8.2.) Social entrepreneurs need to know both what happened and what changed in order to maximize their contributions and impacts.

THE PROCESS FOR DEVELOPING SMART OBJECTIVES

What is an effective approach for developing process and outcome objectives? There are different ways to approach this task. The most obvious is by talking with program staff who manage and operate programs and services in order to understand what they do, what they are trying to accomplish, and how they expect people will change as a result of the programs and services they are providing. (See Exhibit 8.3.) This approach can be cost efficient and draws on the specific expertise of the staff; it is best used when staff possess experience and knowledge about the "market" of services they are providing. Often process and outcome objectives are developed by a proposal writer who is seeking financial support for an organization. The proposal writer's goal, however, is to obtain financial support, and this can lead to an exaggeration of outcomes or, even worse, a misrepresentation of program design and expected impact.

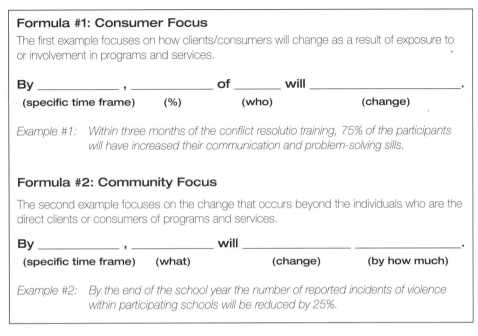

Formula #1: Consumer Focus

The first example focuses on how clients/consumers will change as a result of exposure to or involvement in programs and services.

By _____ , _____ of _____ will _____.
  (specific time frame)   (%)   (who)   (change)

Example #1: Within three months of the conflict resolutio training, 75% of the participants will have increased their communication and problem-solving sills.

Formula #2: Community Focus

The second example focuses on the change that occurs beyond the individuals who are the direct clients or consumers of programs and services.

By _____ , _____ will _____ _____.
  (specific time frame)   (what)   (change)   (by how much)

Example #2: By the end of the school year the number of reported incidents of violence within participating schools will be reduced by 25%.

EXHIBIT 8.3 Worksheet for preparing outcome objectives.

TIPS FOR INVOLVING STAFF IN SETTING OBJECTIVES

The involvement of staff in setting objectives is critical for their execution. Employees who are a part of the process of setting objectives are much more likely to internalize them—and, ultimately, to achieve them—than employees who are simply told what to do. Here are some ways to ensure your staff plays an important role in this process:

practical tip

✔ *Develop a uniform process.* Assign one person to gather objective-setting information from program staff across program areas so that there is consistency in the process.

✔ *Be inclusive.* Make sure to ask all staff for their thoughts and input when developing organizational objectives.

✔ *Be clear and concise.* Make sure that each objective relates to a single expectation for change. Don't say "Our youth program will provide arts and crafts for 200 children and our teen sports program will involve 10 students from five local high schools." These are two different statements of process objectives and will need to be measured separately.

At this stage in the process, it is important to ensure that what staff say they are trying to accomplish aligns with what the organization has promised and/or committed to its funders. If there is alignment, congratulations! You are one of the lucky few. In the more likely case that there is not complete alignment, the organization will need to reconcile differences.

For example, Youth Program staff indicated that the sports program has succeeded in reducing violence among participants. But the program was pitched to funders as a substance abuse prevention project, and funder expectations are that the program will demonstrate a reduction in substance abuse among participants. There are different ways to resolve the difference. One is to collect information on both indicators: violence and substance abuse. The problem with this approach is that if the intervention isn't specifically designed to address substance abuse, and if the population targeted for the intervention isn't at risk of substance abuse, you are about to collect performance information on outcomes that the program isn't really equipped to accomplish. Another option is to collect *only* information that responds to funder expectations. This option has the same flaw as the first, only worse, because now you are confining yourself to collecting performance data on only one outcome and it may be unrelated to program design. A third option is to go back to the funder and renegotiate the expected outcomes so that they align with the intervention as understood and implemented by staff.

The bottom line is that the process of staff consultation allows you the opportunity to bring the dissonance to light. In doing so, the social entrepreneur not only has the opportunity but the obligation to reconcile the differences that may have emerged and develop a meaningful list of objectives for all programs and services.

While it is always important to involve staff in the process of setting program objectives, one may want to enhance the process by employing "benchmarking." This is a technique that is comparative in nature. In *High Performance Nonprofit Organizations,* Christine Letts, William Ryan, and Allen Grossman describe benchmarking as an organizational process that links learning with results.[2] Frequently used in the private sector to evaluate competitiveness, benchmarking examines how an organization is doing in the marketplace of other similar organizations.

- ✔ *External benchmarking*—comparing one organization's performance or results against another.
- ✔ *Internal benchmarking*—comparing the results or performance of one division, program, or service within the organization with the results or performance of others within the organization.
- ✔ *Retrospective benchmarking*—using past performance as a standard to be met or surpassed in the future.

According to the authors, benchmarking focuses on "best practices" but is more than just discovering best practices. It includes comparative measurement, goal setting, and execution. In establishing benchmarks, it is important to draw on the literature that describes the relationship between interventions and results; this will help any organization set attainable yet ambitious goals and objectives for its own performance. In drawing on the literature to develop performance measures, you accomplish three valuable things:

1. You increase the credibility of the system being developed.
2. The literature will help in developing the theory of change for the program.
3. The literature will contribute to the development of objectives for the services and programs being provided.

"MISSION CHECK" YOUR PROGRAMS

It is important that there be consistency and responsiveness among the organization's mission, goals, and objectives. It is particularly important that programs do not extend themselves beyond the organization's mission. For example, if an organization has the mission to alleviate poverty within a defined geographic community, then the programs and services that are offered should be confined to that community. If there is pressure to expand beyond the geographic region, it will be necessary to revisit the organization's mission before launching new programs and services outside the original geographic boundaries.

It may be that such an expansion is warranted and the organization has the resources to do so effectively. But it may be that expanding beyond the original scope will compromise the quality and intensity of services in the primary geographic community.

If the organization determines that such a change is prudent, then it will be necessary to redefine the mission to reflect the change in geographic region and consequently the goals and objectives as well. On the face of it, this process of review and articulation of mission may seem cumbersome, potentially hampering the entrepreneurial spirit, but it is necessary to balance that spirit against the need to ensure program quality and effectiveness as well as fiscal responsibility.

ORGANIZATIONAL VERSUS PROGRAM PERFORMANCE

While this chapter has focused primarily on program-level performance, the concepts of measurement also apply to organization-level performance. The logic of defining goals and objectives that are grounded in the mission still apply when looking at the different aspects of organizational performance or effectiveness. Robert Kaplan and David Norton developed the concept of a "balanced scorecard" for the private sector to examine both financial and nonfinancial measures of performance. The "scorecard" allows a manager to examine business functions from four perspectives:

1. Financial
2. Customer
3. Internal business
4. Innovation and learning.[3]

The scorecard is now being tested in nonprofit settings.

The fundamental premise of the concept of a "scorecard" for nonprofits is that true assessment of performance for any organization requires an examination of *both* organizational and programmatic functions. Over the past three years, Berkeley, California-based BTW Consultants has evaluated an organizational effectiveness initiative sponsored by three northern California foundations. The initiative involves a cohort of 16 Bay Area nonprofits. To contribute to the cohort's understanding of the concepts of organizational effectiveness, BTW reviewed the literature and examples of other organizational effectiveness initiatives. Based on a synthesis of the literature and the initiative review, BTW identified six key functions that should be examined for the purpose of assessing organizational effectiveness for nonprofit organizations. These are similar to the topics included in the concept of the "balanced scorecard." They include:

1. Finance
2. Leadership/governance
3. Human resources
4. Strategic planning
5. Marketing/communications
6. Reflective practice

The same framework of goals and objectives applies to each of these areas. The first challenge for the nonprofit is to develop and articulate goals in each area and explain how those goals will contribute to the accomplishment of the agency's overall mission. The theory of change applies here as well. What is the organization aiming to accomplish financially? Financial goals can range from "diversifying the funding base," to "developing a three-year capital development strategy." The next step, once goals are established, is to develop process and outcome objectives for each area, using the same framework that was presented earlier for programs. If the goal is to achieve a diversified funding base, the theory being that diversity will contribute to sustainability, which will contribute to capacity in the long term, the SMART objectives associated with this goal could set out the specific proportional relationships sought between public and private funding sources and the time frame for achieving those relationships.

Social entrepreneurs who are interested in the double bottom line of achieving social and financial outcomes will be especially interested in measuring financial performance—both programmatically and organizationally. Is the organization delivering high-quality services cost effectively as compared with other similar organizations that have comparable outcomes? Are social enterprises able to retain hard-to-employ individuals while generating sufficient revenue to augment social service programs? These are critical questions that could be articulated in the framework of SMART objectives and then tracked and measured using a credible performance measurement system.

DEVELOPING A PERFORMANCE INFORMATION SYSTEM

As you might imagine, it can be incredibly difficult to get a handle on performance information if you don't have a system designed for the task. In this section, we'll learn how to design and implement a performance information system.

ASSESS CURRENT PRACTICES

Now that you know what you want to measure, how will you go about developing a system of measurement? What methods will you use? What system will you put in place? Before setting out on developing a new performance information system, it is important to know what information staff are already gathering on a regular basis and how that information is being used.

The social entrepreneur should use the opportunity to assess what currently is happening within the organization—how staff think about information, how they are already using information, and what challenges they encounter in doing so. Doing this will help inform the design of a performance system. Learn as much as you can about what has and hasn't been collected and what are effective information-gathering strategies within the agency.

tool of
the trade

✔ Begin by looking at the information the organization is already collecting on a regular basis—why it is being collected and how it is being used.

✔ Avoid the mistakes of the past by talking with staff about their experience gathering information—what has and has not worked from their point of view.

Exhibit 8.4 is a sample protocol that can be used in assessing current information collection and efforts on a programmatic basis.

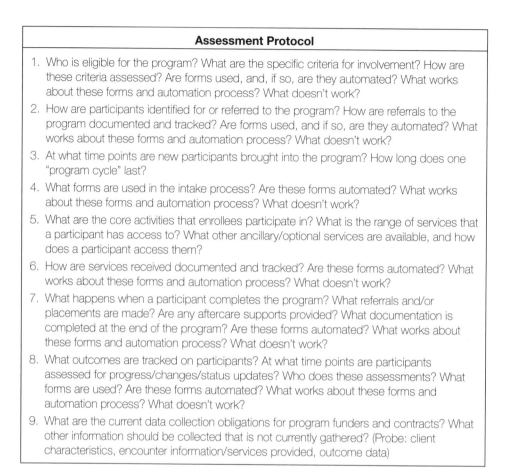

Assessment Protocol
1. Who is eligible for the program? What are the specific criteria for involvement? How are these criteria assessed? Are forms used, and, if so, are they automated? What works about these forms and automation process? What doesn't work?
2. How are participants identified for or referred to the program? How are referrals to the program documented and tracked? Are forms used, and if so, are they automated? What works about these forms and automation process? What doesn't work?
3. At what time points are new participants brought into the program? How long does one "program cycle" last?
4. What forms are used in the intake process? Are these forms automated? What works about these forms and automation process? What doesn't work?
5. What are the core activities that enrollees participate in? What is the range of services that a participant has access to? What other ancillary/optional services are available, and how does a participant access them?
6. How are services received documented and tracked? Are these forms automated? What works about these forms and automation process? What doesn't work?
7. What happens when a participant completes the program? What referrals and/or placements are made? Are any aftercare supports provided? What documentation is completed at the end of the program? Are these forms automated? What works about these forms and automation process? What doesn't work?
8. What outcomes are tracked on participants? At what time points are participants assessed for progress/changes/status updates? Who does these assessments? What forms are used? Are these forms automated? What works about these forms and automation process? What doesn't work?
9. What are the current data collection obligations for program funders and contracts? What other information should be collected that is not currently gathered? (Probe: client characteristics, encounter information/services provided, outcome data)

EXHIBIT 8.4   Data collection practices.

This preliminary assessment will inform the process of developing a measurement system as well as cultivate a sense of ownership and commitment among staff for implementing new ways of gathering and using performance information.

DEVELOP GUIDING PRINCIPLES

Once you have a clear understanding of current data collection practices and applications, it is worth discussing and agreeing on the kind of system you intend to develop. Is it a comprehensive system or a decentralized one? Does it provide information to line staff and managers or just to managers? How much staff time and money is available to invest in the system? Examples of guiding principles include:

✔ *Flexibility*—the system is dynamic, easily accommodates new data elements and new program components on a continuous basis

✔ *High level of rigor*—highly systematic data collection system, less flexible (subject to fewer changes) and more expensive

✔ *Integrated*—a single and consistent system of data collection that is used across all programs so that one program may be collecting information on another program's behalf

✔ *User-friendly*—tools are easy to understand and complete, potentially automated

✔ *Responsive to multiple levels*—a single system that collects data that is used by line staff to make service decisions as well as management staff to make resource decisions

There is no one right set of guiding principles for an organization's information-gathering efforts. The principles should be specific to the organization and consistent with its interests and capacities.

DETERMINE WHAT INFORMATION IS NEEDED

The information that is needed should be directly related to a program's process and outcome objectives. Before you can measure progress, you have to determine what the indicators of success are.

If your program is aimed at improving school performance, then the information needed will relate to indicators of school performance. Since there are many indicators of school performance, however, such as grade point average, attendance, standardized test scores, and graduation rates, it will be necessary to establish the relevance of the indicators to the specific interventions and services your program is providing. If you are a museum that is aiming to increase attendance not only generally but also among specific demographic groups, then your indicators will have to include pertinent demographic characteristics as well as general museum or exhibit attendance data. Selecting appropriate indicators becomes particularly important when resources are limited. To continue our example of school performance, if you do not have the resources to gather information on all school performance indicators, you will want to select those indicators that will tell you the most about the specific interventions you are using and the specific objectives that you hold in order to get the "biggest bang for the buck."

Things to consider when selecting performance indicators:

✔ What information will be most useful in planning and executing program efforts?

✔ What information do you need to share with other audiences, such as funders, your board of directors, and the community, in order to ensure the viability of your programs and services?

✔ What can you afford to spend on information gathering?

SUSAN CASTILLO, COLE STREET YOUTH CLINIC

At the time of the interview, Susan Castillo was the director of the Cole Street Youth Clinic, a community-based, comprehensive adolescent clinic located in the Haight Ashbury neighborhood of San Francisco.[4] The clinic is a public/private partnership between Huckleberry Youth Programs and the San Francisco Public Health Department. The clinic has served as a model of integrated services for youth at risk. It provides three types of services to at-risk and high-risk youth: primary medical care; psychosocial services, including case management and therapy; and health education, primarily peer education. The clinic was among the first in the country to institute ongoing successful AIDS prevention peer education programs.

When first approached in 1989 to be involved in an evaluation and information-gathering effort, Castillo responded with "Ugh, why are we doing this instead of providing [more] services?" Ten years later, Castillo had this to say about the process and results of collecting performance information: "I've learned a lot. I've become an 'information hag.' I want more and more information."

Q: What is the biggest challenge confronting nonprofits in the effort to collect and use performance information?

Castillo: It's the lack of funding . . . perhaps more important, the commitment of time required by the staff and sometimes clients/consumers can seem burdensome . . . even misdirected. Going through the process the first time . . . it is especially important to include time for learning, planning, and building ownership by the stakeholders. Once the process is in place, it seems necessary, even important, to continue doing it.

Q: What helped the Cole Street Clinic to overcome those challenges?

Castillo: We received funding from the California Wellness Foundation that allowed us to build an infrastructure for information gathering.

Q: Was your process of information gathering mostly responsive to external or internal demands for information?

Castillo: The grant from the foundation was to identify the program outcomes for young people using services, but we decided that the information-gathering process could have multiple purposes. In other words, while we were doing this for the funder, we asked ourselves: What do *we* want to know that will help us achieve our goals? We spent approximately one year developing the process for information gathering. We wanted to develop one database from which multiple reports could be prepared. This way the staff wouldn't be burdened with paper and everything would be in one place.

(continued)

Q: Who was involved in the planning process for your performance information?

Castillo: Everyone involved was included in the planning process. Managers wanted quality assurance and monitoring. For example, what is the staff doing? Is it appropriate for the kids? Is it clinically appropriate? Line staff wanted information from and about the clients so that they could better do their job. The young people wanted their problems to be evaluated, to be given what they need, to be engaged in the process. And, of course, the funder wanted to be given what it needed [to justify continued support of the program].

Q: Does the gathering of performance information detract from or impinge on the time available for direct program and service delivery?

Castillo: The intake process at the clinic changed significantly as a result of our information-gathering efforts. Every kid is asked to complete a questionnaire now at intake. It is 45 pages but takes only about 45 minutes. The old two-page intake form used by the staff took 45 minutes anyway because the staff had to ask follow-up questions in order to fully understand what was happening with the young person. The new intake has clear prompts, follow-up questions . . . things that a clinically astute staff member would ask. The new intake allows new and inexperienced staff to collect the same type of information, ensuring more consistency and quality in the information gathered.

Q: What have you learned from the performance information that you didn't know before, and how has it impacted the services you provide and the young people receiving those services?

Castillo: We've learned a lot. We learned that therapy provides a structured process for young people that helps them create structure in other parts of their lives. This led us to increase our outreach to recruit more young people into therapy because it was proving to be an effective strategy. We learned that there is a higher level of depression among our Latino youth than among clients from other ethnic groups. This raised our staff awareness about making assumptions about cultural norms. In some cases, performance information confirmed what we already knew. For example, few of our kids are involved in hard drugs; they are more involved in alcohol, tobacco, and marijuana. The clinic is working on more prevention, taking a psychosocial approach. Kids with the highest need, we learned, are receiving the most services, which is evidence that our assessment and case management systems are working as they should.

DESIGNING TOOLS AND PROCEDURES TO GATHER INFORMATION

Your organization has now articulated its mission, goals, and objectives and identified the purpose for collecting performance information. You also have articulated the guiding principles that will help you in developing your system and you have determined what specific information will be most useful. The next step is to develop a system for collecting information and measuring results.

At this time, you may feel that this process is labor- and time-intensive and taking a long time to get to the heart of the matter. But there is tremendous value in thoughtful preparation. The early investment delivers a long-term benefit.

Now you are ready to develop methods and systems for capturing information in a way that is not overly burdensome to the staff of the organization. In this phase you are designing information-gathering tools and operational procedures for implementing those tools.

At this juncture you also will have an opportunity to look across program areas and see if there are ways to integrate information-gathering efforts. The goal may be to maximize efficiency and consistency of information-gathering efforts across the organization. The organization will benefit to the extent that you are able to create one template that can be used for multiple programs and purposes. For example, having one encounter form used by all programs within an agency means that staff have to be trained in implementing only one tool, and the procedures are the same across the entire agency. Also, a streamlined system for gathering information will produce a streamlined system for analyzing and measuring results—fewer instruments often means fewer complications.

Methods

core concept Broadly speaking, there are two types of information: *quantitative* and *qualitative.*

Quantitative information uses numbers to express results. It is information that permits exact counting. The results of quantitative information collection usually are calculated in percentages, averages, dollars, and other numeric operations.

Sources of quantitative information may be primary or secondary. Primary data collection is data collection that you collect yourself on a first-hand basis. This could include surveys of or interviews with clients (or staff) or some other service-tracking process. Primary information typically is gathered by framing closed-ended questions—questions that have predetermined response categories (e.g., yes/no/maybe). Secondary data is collected from other sources, such as academic records, police reports, public health records, and the census.

Qualitative information uses words to describe results. It is gathered by observation, interviews, or focus groups. The information typically is gathered by framing open-ended questions—questions that elicit a narrative response (e.g., how is this job-training program different from others you have participated in?). The results of qualitative information collection usually provide descriptive accounts that emphasize either how or why people think or behave in certain ways. Qualitative information gathering may be more time-consuming than quantitative information gathering and is used more efficiently with smaller numbers of respondents. As a result, while it can provide rich descriptive information, it is often less generalizable than quantitative data.

Now you have all the pieces of the puzzle. The challenge is to put them together. How will you ask what questions of whom?

> *How:*   How will you ask the questions? You can ask questions in a one-on-one interview format—face-to-face, by telephone, or in writing—in a group interview or a focus group format, or through other techniques, such as observation.

> *What:*   What are the specific questions you need answered? Do the answers need to be quantifiable? Are they yes/no questions or multiple choice? Can they be open-ended questions that will yield narrative responses?

> *Whom:*   Who needs to answer which questions? Does everybody need to answer every question, or will some people know the answers to some questions and other people know the answers to other questions (two different instruments)? Does everyone speak the same language? Does everyone know how to read? Are there cultural issues that may suggest one form of information gathering over another?

How to ask what of whom is an interconnected issue. For example, if those who need to answer the questions come from different cultures and speak many different languages, this will influence how you ask which questions of which individuals.

The process of developing the instruments for gathering information works best as an iterative one. Develop the tool, show it to staff, redevelop it, and circulate it again. Now you have an instrument or a set of instruments for information gathering. Who will administer the instrument, when, and where?

For example, if you are tracking attendance for a particular program and the instrument is an activity log or attendance form, you will need to determine how the log will be completed. Will staff complete, it, or will program participants sign in or check off their names? What happens with the attendance sheets once they are completed? If you are conducting face-to-face six-month follow-up interviews with job-training participants, how will those individuals be contacted? Who will call them to establish contact? Will a postcard be sent out in advance of the interviews? Where and when will the interviews be conducted? In an office? In their workplace? What happens with "no-shows"? These are examples of procedural questions that need to be answered and documented as you develop your information system.

The same is true for secondary data collection. If a goal of a juvenile justice reform program is to reduce juvenile arrests in high-crime communities, how will you collect that data? In what time intervals? For which neighborhoods? Using what criteria? Over what period of time?

On what basis will you select the methods for information gathering? The following are the key considerations in making your selection:

✔ *What do you* need *to know?* Once you get started on the value of information, there will be many interesting questions to pose. It is important to distinguish between what is interesting to know and what is necessary to know in order to improve practice and demonstrate progress in achieving outcomes. Do you need to know how many people experienced change, which implies the need for quantitative methods, or do you need to understand how people experienced a particular program or service, which implies the need for qualitative methods? Or do you need to know both, which suggests that you will be combining methods?

✔ *How much flexibility do you have?* Often nonprofits are constrained by funding requirements. Have you made commitments to investors who prescribe the questions you ask and the information you gather? Are these commitments negotiable?

✔ *About whom or what do you need information?* Clients, staff, board, the general community? If you need information from clients or staff, or even your board, these are captive audiences that can be reached using primary data collection methods. If you are seeking information from the broader community, are there other institutions that are already collecting that information, and can you obtain their data set?

✔ *When do you need the information?* How quickly you need to turn information around often influences the methods you use and the scope of the information gathering.

✔ *What skills do you have in-house to collect information?* Often nonprofits hire people who have social service skills rather than social science skills. Certain tasks associated with developing a performance information system will require special skills. When thinking about the different stages of performance information system development, a nonprofit should consider hiring a consultant who has special expertise to help with the design phase and the analysis phase.

✔ *How much do you have in the way of staff time and financial resources to invest in the process?* Is there a budget that you are working within? Do any staff members have time to dedicate to the necessary tasks?

Testing Your Tools

Now is the opportunity to test your tools.

One of the most frequently forgotten steps in nonprofit evaluation efforts is the pilot testing step. What does a pilot testing step mean? First, let's discuss what it does *not* mean. It does not mean trying out an interview protocol with your colleagues or your parents. It does not mean asking program managers to role-play an interview process.

It means employing the instrument according to the procedures you have developed with the actual program clients/customers and doing it in such a way that maximizes your opportunity to learn from the experience. This may mean letting the client/consumer know that this is a pilot test and asking him or her to provide feedback on the instrument, the questions, and the procedures. The same is true for secondary data collection. If you have planned on gathering probation data or school data, it is important to test the processes and extraction tools you have developed. Gathering secondary data from institutional sources often is a laborious process, and pilot-testing procedures and instruments is essential.

- ✔ Build in time to test your information-gathering tools and processes.
- ✔ Refine the tools and processes based on your findings.
- ✔ Look at the information being gathered and assess whether it is in fact the information you want or need. If it isn't, try again.

Now that you have tested your tools, carefully document the finalized system of tools and procedures (with clear instructions) because the system must be able to stand on its own. It should not be dependent on any single individual within the organization. It should be designed to be implemented by anyone who is called upon to do so. Many systems go awry when people forget to carefully document process.

IMPROVING PROGRAMS THROUGH THE PROCESS OF INFORMATION SYSTEM DESIGN

As you proceed down the path of operationalizing the design of your information-gathering system, be prepared to confront the shortcomings of your current practice. Even before the information-gathering systems are fully operationalized, issues of program quality and consistency will emerge. For example, if a program has tried to be all things to all people and has not engaged in effective client referral, that will become clear when you are creating a system for tracking client encounters and staff activity. Staff may identify the services they are providing, and it may appear that some of those services fall outside of the scope of the program's goals.

This effort to capture the value of the programs and services your organization is providing will force you to confront any shortcomings or inconsistencies in the program design itself. There are two ways of dealing with these manifestations of truth. One is to avoid the truth—to ignore signs that programs are not aligned with the organization's mission or that programs lack quality control or are inconsistently implemented. Another is to embrace the truth and see it as an opportunity to improve.

Remember: Managing for results is about getting where you are going by having the courage to notice everything along the way and adjust course in order to get there.

CREATING A PERFORMANCE INFORMATION SYSTEM: THE ROBERTS ENTERPRISE DEVELOPMENT FUND EXPERIENCE

reality check　　The Roberts Enterprise Development Fund (REDF), based in San Francisco, California, maintains a portfolio of 10 nonprofit organizations that collectively operate 20 social purpose enterprises. Each enterprise operates with a double bottom line: a social mission to employ low-income and/or formerly homeless individuals and a business mission to operate profitably. REDF has invested considerable time and resources in working with its portfolio to develop an integrated approach to gathering, analyzing, and disseminating social impact information. What follows is an overview of its efforts to design a system that is intended to inform each organization's practice as well as the larger field of social entrepreneurialism. The information gathered in this system also informs REDF's efforts to measure its "social return on investment"(SROI), as described elsewhere in this book. (For additional information visit the REDF web site at www.redf.org.)

The first step in developing what REDF has termed "OASIS—Ongoing Assessment of Social ImpactS"—involved having each business manager and/or executive director develop a list of expected social outcomes. These lists were used to create a matrix of expected outcomes by enterprise. Using this list, REDF looked for an opportunity to create an integrated system that would provide consistent information across enterprises and a basis for more comprehensive analysis. REDF selected the outcomes where there was a critical mass of interest to be part of the core information set for the entire portfolio.

Once it was clear what information was needed across the portfolio, it was necessary to develop questions that would capture that infor-

(continued)

mation, using methods that would not be overly burdensome to any of the organizations. With the help of consultants, an interview instrument for the core social indicators was developed and distributed to the organizations for their review and comment. After incorporating changes, each enterprise was given the opportunity to develop more customized questions that reflected its specific areas of interest and additional social outcomes.

During this phase, groups had the opportunity to incorporate questions that were important to them as well as questions they needed answered for other contract reporting purposes. For example, one group emphasizes vocational training in addition to enterprise employment. It added questions about the development of specific job skills and employment history. Another organization works with high-risk youth and was interested in reducing drug use among its employees, so questions were included about the type and frequency of drug use for this group.

To ensure their utility, the interview instruments were pilot-tested in each organization. In some cases this resulted in a need to refine the core set of indicators, which was not an easy task. Changing questions because of one group's pilot test frequently had implications for other groups. This made for an iterative process of adaptation, with careful coordination and ongoing communications. In addition, the process of automation had to wait until the instruments were finalized. The alternative would have resulted in frequent modifications to the database programming effort.

Once the design process was complete, implementation became paramount. Baseline and follow-up interviews have been under way at participating organizations since 1998, data are regularly entered into customized databases, and each group has the capacity to produce customized reports on its target employee populations with the push of a button.

The process of rolling out this comprehensive system for measuring the social impact of enterprise employment inspired the organizations in the REDF portfolio to want to do even more ongoing measurement of social impacts within their organizations. REDF, along with five other philanthropic funders, is now investing in the development of the next phase of OASIS that is organization-wide, not just focused on enterprise employment. The next level of OASIS is an organizational planning process that results in a comprehensive and customized automated tracking system. These systems are being built to track services, activities, and outcomes in real-time, organization-specific, Web-based information systems. These systems are examples of entrepreneurial organizations pushing the information utilization envelope to inform their daily practice and their long-term vision.

TRANSLATING INFORMATION INTO ACTION

Knowing how to collect and gather information is an important part of determining the performance of an organization, but all the information in the world isn't going to do you or your organization a bit of good if you don't put it into action. In this section, we'll learn how to translate information into action.

MAKING SENSE OF THE INFORMATION GATHERED

It is often easier for people to collect information than to analyze it. Why? Sometimes it is because no one has been given the responsibility for analyzing the information that is gathered. Other times it is because someone has been given the responsibility but does not possess the skills to analyze the information; after all, nonprofits traditionally hire people with social service rather than social science skills. In both cases, the value of analyzing the information gathered has not been given high enough priority.

To resolve this, the organization must give priority to the analysis by building organizational capacity in this area. Organizations can hire information coordinators or planning and evaluation managers, contract with outside consultants who are information specialists, bring in technology experts who can assist in automating information systems, or some combination of all of these solutions. Having undertaken the effort to design and implement a system of performance information, it is imperative that adequate resources be devoted to analyze the information to render it meaningful.

How often do you analyze the information? Some information is analyzed almost continuously. Maintaining appropriate caseloads is one such example. There should be ongoing assessment of whether caseload levels are appropriate. To perform ongoing analysis, you will draw on technology. Other information that relates to longer-term social impact may be analyzed most appropriately annually or semiannually. In part it depends on how frequently you expect to see changes occur. And it also depends in part on the resources available for analysis.

In every case, information should be available for use in a timely manner. The system should be sufficiently dynamic to inform program practice. Unfortunately, too often information reaches its internal audience late or never, creating a credibility gap that makes it difficult to engage practitioners in any ongoing information-gathering effort.

So, be sure to:

practical tip ✔ *Make it timely.* Don't wait until a program intervention is over to assess its effectiveness.

✔ *Make it easy to understand.* Without compromising the integrity of the data, information should be presented in a way that is easy to understand and digest. This may mean the effective use of visuals, graphics, charts, and color.

THE PROCESS OF REFLECTION . . . THE PROCESS OF CORRECTION

At the core of the concept of managing for results is the expectation that an organization is open to learning about the ways in which its programs are effective as well as opportunities for improvement. It is essential that time be set aside for staff and board members to review and reflect on the performance information and have that process inform decision making and practice. For some organizations this will mean a culture shift. They must begin to express value for information and to engage board members and program staff in the process of informed reflection.

For program staff, organizations can facilitate the process of reflection by posing questions about the information that is being collected and analyzed. "What does the information tell you about your program?" "How do you intend to apply this information to improve services?"

For board members, the availability of performance information should inform strategic planning and decision making. Time should be set aside for board members to review performance information and to hear from program managers and staff about how that information is being used to improve practice.

practical tip

✔ *Make your audiences active rather than passive recipients of information.* Ask staff and board members to project the results of the information gathering that has taken place before sharing the actual findings. Doing this provides people with an opportunity to test their own assumptions; it is an effective tool for engaging people in active reflection.

✔ *Be inclusive in the process of interpreting the results.* Ask program staff, in particular program managers, to help find the meaning and explain the results. This includes asking such questions as, "Why do you think we have these results?" Or "What does it mean for our program design or staffing?"

By definition, social entrepreneurs embrace change. In this chapter, up until now, we have encouraged you to exercise restraint—systematically, methodically, and thoughtfully engage in a process to yield a clearly articulated vision for where you want to go and how you intend to get there. We have asked you to be detail-oriented—to imagine and then document

FREQUENTLY ASKED QUESTIONS

Q: What kinds of costs are associated with developing and implementing a performance information system?

A: There are three types of costs:

1. *Staff time*—Program staff will be involved in many aspects of the system's development—conceptualization, design, and ongoing implementation.

2. *Consultants*—In many cases, it is cost effective to bring in specific technical expertise to help in planning, instrument development, analysis, and automation.

3. *Technology*—In some cases, an information system will require purchasing new hardware or software. Often more robust information systems cost more and involve significant investment in staff time, consultant time, and technological resources. But perhaps an organization cannot afford the most state-of the-art performance information system but would benefit enormously from some programmatic information. In this case, assess the information priorities and the available resources and build a system that is sufficiently flexible to add new components, as resources become available.

Q: Do we have to use outside consultants?

A: Sometimes organizations don't possess all of the skills necessary to develop and implement a performance information system on their own. If that is the case, the best thing to do is to identify the gaps and hire consultants to supplement internal staff capacity. There is no requirement that you use outside consultants to develop a credible system. It is important to strike the right balance between relying on outside expertise and cultivating internal ownership, knowledge, and expertise.

Q: Can't we just buy evaluation software so we don't have to re-create the wheel?

A: Nonprofit organizations can purchase off-the-shelf software as a client-tracking tool. Even though the software has been developed, it still requires a significant amount of time and effort to meet the needs of specific organizations. The software cannot simply be dropped into any program and meet that program's needs. In general, the ratio of resources required to customize off-the-shelf software is 4:1—it takes four times the level of effort (resources) to customize a system as it does to purchase it. And the organization itself will still need to go through the process of articulating objectives, identifying indicators, and implementing a design.

Q: How long will it take until we get results?

A: It will depend on your design. It takes less time to see short-term performance results than long-term outcomes. The more comprehensive a system you develop, the more time it will take both to develop the system and use the results.

procedures. We have encouraged you to engage others in your vision—
to bring people in and bring people along. We have asked you to set pa-
rameters for performance and to measure results.

As the results begin to pour in, it is time to revert to where social entrepreneurs are often more comfortable: embracing change. As a responsible steward of public and private dollars, now you are in a position
to embrace change with confidence—to know that the change is well informed. Now you can pursue excellence through a process of continuous
and ongoing learning.

Get started in a manageable and affordable way—affordable is a state
of mind—and make this an integral part of the work that you do. Remember: No smart investor should support a program that doesn't include some dedication of resources to collecting, analyzing, and using information to inform practice and demonstrate results. While the
development of an effective performance information system may be
daunting to a social entrepreneur who is focused on changing the world
and seeing results, the effort will be well worth your while.

SUMMARY

More and more, funders expect the nonprofit organizations they support
to become more accountable for the outcomes of their programs and
services and to provide accurate and timely performance information. In
this chapter we determined how to define value in the nonprofit marketplace, and we learned how to develop and implement a performance information system. Finally, we considered how to translate information
into action.

Key points to remember are:

- ✔ Funders are less interested in the traditional notion of charity and
  more interested in the social return on investment.

- ✔ Social entrepreneurs collect performance information in order to
  meet the needs of internal and external audiences.

- ✔ Performance information is any data that describe how well the organization is doing in terms of social impact and cost effectiveness
  as they relate to its mission.

- ✔ SMART objectives are specific, measurable, attainable, realistic,
  and time-limited.

- ✔ There are two main types of information: quantitative and qualitative.

- ✔ It's often easier for people to collect information than to analyze it.
  Make analysis a priority.

Notes

1. John Sawhill, "Mission Impossible? Measuring Success in Nonprofit Organizations," *Social Enterprise,* Spring 2001.
2. Christine Letts, William Ryan, Allen Grossman, *High Performance Nonprofit Organizations: Managing Upstream for Greater Impact* (New York: John Wiley & Sons, 1998).
3. Robert S. Kaplan and David P. Norton, *Linking the Balanced Scorecard to Strategy* (Boston: Harvard Business School Press, 1996).
4. Susan Castillo left her position with Cole Street Youth Clinic in August 1999 to become the director of Technical Assistance for the San Francisco–based Tides Foundation.

PART II

GROWING AND EXPLORING NEW DIRECTIONS

Chapter 9

DEVELOPING VIABLE EARNED INCOME STRATEGIES

Beth Battle Anderson, Senior Research Associate, The Fuqua School of Business, Duke University,
J. Gregory Dees, Adjunct Professor of Social Entrepreneurship and Nonprofit Management, The Fuqua School of Business, Duke University,
and Jed Emerson, Senior Fellow, William and Flora Hewlett Foundation, and lecturer, Center for Social Innovation, Graduate School of Business, Stanford University

IN THIS CHAPTER

What is an earned income strategy?
Exploring the three different earned income paths
Developing a viable earned income strategy for your organization

So you want to generate more earned income? You are not alone. According to Lester Salamon of Johns Hopkins University, earned income was the largest source of growth in the nonprofit sector in the 1980s and early 1990s.[1] This chapter will help you explore your options in a rigorous manner. However, you need to go into this process with your eyes open. Finding and executing an effective and appropriate earned income strategy is no easy task. It may not even be right for your organization, at least not right now. In fact, after examining nonprofits engaged in a wide range of earned income strategies—everything from charging fees to their primary beneficiaries to launching full-scale businesses—Canadian researchers Brenda Zimmerman and Raymond Dart came to the following conclusion:

> *There is no single answer or authoritative conclusion possible concerning charities and commercial ventures. Rather, many different solutions will be equally possible, practical and ethically defensible. For some charitable organizations, commercial activity may be fundamentally improper*

because it would distract from the mission or refocus energies away from collective goods and services with long-run impact. For others, it may be precisely the lever that triggers useful organization-wide innovation and creativity.[2]

But isn't generating earned income what social entrepreneurship is all about? No! It is not. Social entrepreneurship is about finding new and better ways to create and sustain social value. It is about serving your mission, first and foremost. Funding strategies are a means to that end. Earned income should be pursued only when the net effect is an improvement in your social impact now or in the future.

The purpose of this chapter is to increase the chances that you will find an earned income strategy that will work for you. By covering a wide range of options, we help you identify potential strategies that you might not otherwise have considered. We also provide you with frameworks for evaluating their ultimate mission impact, determining their feasibility, and developing an action plan.

WHAT IS AN EARNED INCOME STRATEGY?

core concept

As we are using the phrase, *earned income* refers to revenue generated by the commercial exchange of a product or service between a buyer and seller. Earned income is distinct from grants and other charitable donations, which are gifts independent of any commercial exchange, even though they may be restricted or have strings attached. This chapter does not cover passive income generated by investments, although technically it counts as earned income.

core concept

An *earned income strategy* is any coherent plan of action that generates earned income, even if that income does not cover all the costs associated with producing it. Some strategies generate earned income directly for the nonprofit, when it sells products or services to paying consumers. Other strategies generate the earned income for a partner organization, with the nonprofit being paid by that partner, as in the case of corporate marketing partnerships.

Earned income strategies can take many forms. Suppose you are running a homeless shelter for teens and have decided to provide job training to your residents. You could try to fund this new effort entirely with grants, or you could consider possible earned income strategies to cover all or part of the costs. For instance, you might charge fees to the corporate employers who benefit from your training, placement, and retention services. You might start a temp agency to give your trainees some on-the-job experience, charging corporate customers for these placements. You might seek a government contract to provide training for teens who have been in the court system. You might start your own business, such as a bicycle repair shop, that will serve as a training ground and as an income generator at the same time. You might partner with Ben & Jerry's to open an ice cream franchise that would provide training and employment opportunities for your clients and income to your agency. Or you might cut a deal with a credit card company that wants to use your organization's good name and reputation to market its cards to socially conscious college students. The possibilities are limited only by your imagination.

However, before exploring some of these strategies further, we must dispel some dangerous myths and misconceptions about earned income that nonprofit leaders often harbor.

Myth 1: The ultimate goal of an earned income strategy is to generate funds. Most nonprofits start thinking about earned income in an effort to bring in additional revenues and improve the financial health of their organization. Indeed, some nonprofits may even turn to earned income as a potential solution to a financial crisis. This is highly risky. Earned income is not a panacea and most often will not bail you out of financial straits. In fact, many earned income strategies require financial stability for successful execution. *Reality: Mission impact is the ultimate goal. Funding strategies are a means to that end and should be assessed accordingly.*

Myth 2: Earned income is always more sustainable than donations or grants. Many nonprofits turn to earned income as part of their quest for sustainability. Don't fall into the trap of thinking earned income is inherently stable. It can dry up just as easily as donations. Businesses fail frequently. Your commercial activities will not be immune to market forces just because you are a nonprofit. Customers' preferences change, competition moves in, corporate and government policies are amended. Don't be fooled into thinking you can earn income "while you sleep," as one entrepreneurial leader we know once fantasized. Only endowment invested in safe securities offers that kind of sustainability. *Reality: Sustaining an earned income strategy requires significant time, energy, vigilance, and luck.*

Myth 3: Earned income is always a good thing because it helps to diversify your funding base. While diversification does reduce an organization's financial risk, it can be costly, leading to fragmentation and loss of focus. It may be a drain on scarce resources, such as your time and energy. The costs of any diversification strategy must be weighed against the potential benefits. Some earned income strategies do not even result in more diverse sources of income. They just result in different sources of income. Replacing a group of donors with one big state contract does not increase diversification. *Reality: Diversification alone is rarely a sufficient reason to pursue a particular earned income strategy.*

Myth 4: The best way to generate earned income is to start a totally separate, unrelated business dedicated to profit making. It is an appealing vision: a wealth-creating engine, off to the side, that generates cash to fund your core programs. In truth, creating a profitable business is very challenging, can take a long time, can require significant investment of capital, and often results in profits that need to be reinvested in the business. The best earned income strategies usually build on some strength or asset of your organization, and regardless, it is important to consider your full range of options. *Reality: Only on rare occasions will the best strategy be something totally unrelated to your core operations.*

Myth 5: By relying more on earned income, your organization exposes itself to valuable market discipline. It is true that earned income exposes nonprofits to market forces. Value must be created to generate revenue from paying customers. However, this market discipline enhances the creation of social value only if the value for your customers is aligned with serving your mission effectively. In some cases, these values will be aligned. In others, they may have nothing to do with one another or, worse yet, may provide incentives that could detract from your social value creation. The commercial success or failure of The Nature Conservancy's line of neckties tells us nothing about its effectiveness in preserving biodiversity. In some instances, tensions will arise between creating value for a paying customer and serving your mission. For example, a contract that pays you based on the number of people served may encourage you to focus on quantity rather than quality. In these cases, market discipline is not contributing to greater creation of social value. *Reality: Market discipline is healthy for your organization* only *when the market is well aligned with your social mission.*

EXPLORING THE THREE DIFFERENT EARNED INCOME PATHS

With those caveats in mind, let's consider the range of earned income strategies open to you. To help us navigate the wide array of options, we've grouped them into three major paths.

1. Getting paid for what you already do
2. Launching a new business venture
3. Building revenue relationships

Sometimes it's hard to draw a clear distinction between each path, and some ventures may be a blend of two, but it is useful to think about each category, its unique benefits, risks, and key success factors.

GETTING PAID FOR WHAT YOU ALREADY DO

You are already doing something valuable, so all you need to do is find people who will pay you for it! Many nonprofits fail to look in their backyard when first thinking about earned income. Admittedly, you may face compelling moral or practical reasons not to charge for your services. However, in many sectors, such as health care, education, and the arts, fees are quite common. In others, they are more rare but not out of the question. Social entrepreneurs contemplating charging fees have three options: (1) *charging their primary beneficiaries,* (2) *charging an interested third party,* or (3) *creating a hybrid pricing structure* that collects fees from both primary beneficiaries and third parties. Consider the following examples:

- Help The World See (HTWS) was created in 1987 to bring primary eye care and glasses to needy people in developing countries. It collected used glasses, cleaned them, and prepared them for distribution. It then recruited doctors and technicians to volunteer for short missions to provide exams and dispense the glasses on site. After several years of this approach, HTWS's leaders decided that a more permanent solution was still needed. They hit upon the idea of creating "self-sustaining" clinics in developing countries by charging a very modest fee for the glasses dispensed by these clinics. This fee was well below the market price of eyeglasses in the countries involved but was still sufficient to cover the cost of running the clinic once a reasonable volume was reached. The profits achieved once this break-even volume was exceeded could be used to subsidize care for the poorest residents who could not even afford the modest fee. By charging a fee, HTWS assured the ongoing provision of primary eye care to people who had no prior access, and it found a new way of serving its mission.

- When Glen Lopez finished his medical training in the United States, he wanted to return to Guatemala, where he grew up, to provide health care to the rural poor. Most of the government-provided health care was concentrated in the cities. After seeing how difficult it was to raise philanthropic funds to sustain this kind of effort, he developed a different idea. He reasoned that the farm owners who employed permanent and migrant labor had a vested interest in the health of these workers. He decided to ask the farm owners to pay for the construction of a clinic on their property and to pay a monthly fee for medical services to their workers. The workers made small copayments for services, but the third-party payments from the farm owners made it possible for Lopez to establish Guate-Salud as a self-financing organization.

- Canadian environmental organization Greensaver takes advantage of a hybrid pricing model to deliver a profitable service to customers. Greensaver performs energy- and water-conserving improvements for homeowners. Although homeowners desire these services, they are not willing to pay a price that would cover the full costs to the organization, much less generate a profit. Thus, Greensaver markets the service to energy companies, public utilities, and public works, which are willing to pay for part of the service based on the costs they avoid, such as infrastructure upgrades, due to reduced usage.[3]

Potential Benefits

Charging a fee, even a small one, can bring with it a number of benefits beyond the income created. Do any of the following potential results seem attractive? Charging a fee may have the effect of . . .

✔ *Empowering your clients.* Who wants to be seen as a charity case? Charging a fee may afford your clients more self-respect and dignity, changing the power dynamic in their relationship with your organization.

✔ *Screening out those who get less value.* Setting a price might help you reach the people who will get the most out of your services. Pricing can be a tool for triage, that is, for helping you determine who most needs your help.

✔ *Encouraging efficient use of a scarce resource.* Free goods and services often go to waste. The American Red Cross charges hospitals for blood to help avert this outcome.

✔ *Increasing commitment.* If customers have paid for something, they are more likely to do their best to put it to good use. Paying clients will likely think twice about giving up or walking away.

✔ *Providing a feedback mechanism.* Paying customers will let you know if you aren't delivering value—by either taking their dollars elsewhere or telling you directly. Paying clients have standing to complain.

✔ *Signaling quality.* People often assume that "you get what you pay for." Setting a price on a program can send a signal of high quality.

✔ *Providing subsidies for the truly needy.* By charging fees to those who can pay, you can create more resources to serve the truly disadvantaged.

If charging a fee to your clients is sounding increasingly appealing, you must be starting to wonder how you should price your goods and services. There are many options, but you should always remember three things:

1. *You don't have to make a profit for charging a fee to be worthwhile.* If you are charging for things that you would be providing anyway, any revenues you generate should free up other funds to do your work.

2. *You don't have to set a single price.* You can easily vary your prices and product offerings for different audiences or at different times. Have you ever taken advantage of a student discount or a senior citizen discount? Are your rates higher for long-distance calls made during the week rather than on the weekend? These are examples of selling basically the same goods or services at different prices. Many nonprofits can, and should, take advantage of similar opportunities to modify their prices based on differences in their target customers or in when and how their customers use their services. Common pricing tools used to assure affordability include:

   - *Sliding scale fees.* Does your clients' ability to pay range widely? Perhaps you can establish a sliding scale that allows you to charge different prices for the same product or service based on customer characteristics. For example, many day care centers set their rates based on the parents' income.

   - *Time-sensitive rates.* Do you have times of peak demand? Perhaps your program should cost more during those times, allowing you to charge less, or even nothing, during slower periods to attract customers who are less willing or able to pay. Discounts for off-peak usage can help level out the demands on your staff and facilities.

   - *Deferred payments.* Do your clients have limited financial resources currently but anticipate having more in the future? Think about asking them to pay you later, especially if you are providing them with skills that should increase their future earning potential. Education loans are perhaps the most common example.

3. *You can explore charging third parties.* If your clients really cannot afford to pay or should not be asked to pay for moral reasons, you still may be able to build some fee-based income by targeting third parties who have a vested interest in your target client population. Most often third parties will be the government or business owners who can contract with you to provide social services to their communities or employees in a more cost-effective manner than if they did it themselves. Third-party payments also can be priced and structured in different ways. You can charge a flat fee to make your services available to a specific population for a period of time. You can get reimbursed based on the actual services you deliver or the number of people you serve. You can get paid on results, such

as the number of homeless people you place in jobs. You can be a sole provider for a particular group or only one of many from whom the clients can choose. The key is to find a structure that fits well with your social mission. Of course, your ability to negotiate creative pricing structures is generally better with private payers than it is with government agencies, which often have strict contracting guidelines.

Risks and Challenges

Even when there seem to be very compelling reasons to charge for your services, you should be aware of the risks and challenges associated with this approach.

Encountering moral objections. Staff and board members may object to putting a price on charitable work. You must not ignore these concerns. They may well be legitimate. Probe to see whether the objections are grounded in sound moral reasoning and a respect for healthy relationships. Remember that moral considerations can cut both ways. Giving away services can subtly reinforce the power of the service provider over the recipient, and it can buffer your organization from the market test of whether you are creating value for your clients.

Getting seduced by the "low-hanging fruit." When you start segmenting your customers and charging them fees, it becomes a lot clearer and more obvious who costs more to serve and who can afford to pay. Don't be lured away from serving the most needy or most deserving clients just because it would improve your organization's financial health to avoid them.

Encountering resistance to change. Nobody likes being told she has to pay for something that used to be free. Beyond the philosophical and cultural objections charging fees might stir up, the introduction of a new fee-for-service policy can be challenging. Depending on the specifics of your organization and stakeholder community, consideration of and input from employees, clients, customers, and investors (foundations, individual donors, etc.) should be a part of your strategy. You may want to phase in the new structure or "grandfather" those already receiving your services, applying the new pricing scheme only to new clients.

Becoming too reliant on a small number of third parties. Overreliance on one or a few third-party contracts is just as risky as relying too much on one or a few donors. Your organization is vulnerable to shifts in government or corporate policy and potentially to improper influence if your third-party customers encourage you to serve clients or provide services that may not fit with your mission. To protect against this, it may be helpful to diversify your third-party payer base or to develop other sources of funding. In any case, it is wise to select third-party payers whose intrinsic interests are well aligned with your mission.

Key Success Factors

Introducing fees for your products and services can be challenging, but several factors can improve your chances of success.

Have a defined value proposition and discernible competitive advantage. As with any commercial transaction, you need to be clear about what you are selling and why customers should pay you, and not someone else, for it. What value do you give them? What are you asking in return? How does it stack up to alternatives offered by competitors? Making sure you are fully aware of these elements also will help you recognize when you may need to change your strategy due to a change in the environment.

Be flexible and open to experimentation. One of the benefits of pricing is providing opportunities for market feedback. You can gain valuable information on market response by instituting special offerings at time-limited price levels. You can convene focus groups to test out your proposed price levels. And you can assess what prices are being charged by your competitors in the marketplace, bringing your product to market at or just below a competitor's offering. If you do find that your prices appear to be substantially decreasing demand for your services, you certainly should ask yourself whether the price is too high for your intended clientele and, more important, whether you actually are offering something of significant value.

Understand your costs. In considering what price is most appropriate, be sure you have *all* your costs on the table. This is true even if you do not expect fees to cover all the costs for all your clients. It helps you understand the level of subsidy for each client group. Be sure to include fair portions of overhead and shared costs. Your pricing strategy may add costs to the process. You will have to create and manage systems for setting prices and collecting fees. You may need to spend more on marketing to attract paying clients. Your revenues from pricing generally should exceed the costs of implementing a pricing system.

practical tip   If you are already charging a fee for some of your goods and services, are you maximizing the potential of this revenue source? Consider the following questions:

✔ *Have you experimented with different pricing levels and strategies?* Try to think of at least one new pricing option you could test that might improve your impact by empowering individuals, increasing commitment, screening clients, encouraging efficiency, or generating additional funds.

✔ *Are you accounting for all of the associated costs when setting your prices?* This test is especially critical for goods or services you are providing in large part because you think they are profitable or self-sustaining. Could you raise prices to cover those costs? How would it affect your mission?

✔ *Are there any third parties you also could charge for the delivery of this good or service?* If your customers only cover a portion of the costs of delivering your program, make a list of any other entities that benefit from it. Could you possibly charge them as well? For example, an organization charging parents a sliding-scale fee for after-school programs for their children could consider trying to contract with school districts, local government, other educational organizations, or possibly even the parents' employers to earn additional revenues for their programs.

LAUNCHING A NEW BUSINESS VENTURE

When people think of earned income strategies, often the first thing that comes to mind is the idea of launching a business. Nonprofit business ventures include every thing from Girl Scout cookies and Goodwill Thrift Shops to the café in your favorite museum, the university bookstore, and the restaurant started by a homeless shelter to employ its residents. Thus, they come in all forms, shapes, and sizes. They may be structured legally as nonprofit or for-profit organizations. They may be more, less, or not at all related to the core mission of the organization. They may be integrated into the existing operations of the organization, established as totally separate operations, or somewhere in between. They may build to some degree on the existing assets and capabilities of the organization or require an entirely new set of skills and resources.

As you begin to think about what kinds of business ventures might be right for your nonprofit, it is helpful to consider four factors: your organization's *competencies, assets, relationships,* and *mission.* Each of these can serve as a basis for launching a new business. Of course, these four categories are not mutually exclusive, nor are they collectively exhaustive. Some enterprises build on more than one of these elements. Indeed, several of the examples we provide could easily fall under more than one category. This is generally a good thing. It is also possible to launch a venture that has no clear or direct link with your organization's current competencies, assets, relationships, or mission. Success in this sort of venture is typically more difficult, but it can be done. Remember that these four categories do not provide a classification for every possible idea. Rather, they are offered to stimulate your thinking about the kinds of opportunities that make the most sense for you.

Competency-based ventures. One place to start in looking for venture ideas is to ask "What do we do well that might be valuable to others?" Many organizations have found markets for the things they already know how to do by creating new products and services based on these capabilities. Consider the following:

- The American Red Cross, building on its expertise in dealing with disasters and traumas, has created a range of First Aid and Disaster Preparedness Kits and Supplies targeting different environments (household, workplace, automotive, and schools) and even different natural disasters (earthquakes, fires, floods, hurricanes, and tornadoes). The organization sells these products through a variety of channels, including online stores, retail outlets, catalogs, and local chapters.

- In Illinois, a church Sunday school asked a school for behaviorally challenged adolescents to talk to them about dealing with difficult teenagers. The session was a major success, and the school decided to develop a three-hour workshop on the subject and market it to other communities. The school rents space in various locales and charges admission, and nets nearly $65,000 a year.[4]

- Drawing on its years of experience developing a community service program for youth and working closely with corporate sponsors, City Year launched Care Force as a business division. Care Force offers professional consulting services specializing in community service and employee training experiences, specifically around strengthening diversity, team-building, and leadership skills, areas that are fundamental to City Year's core program.[5]

Since these strategies are building on the competencies, skills, and knowledge of program staff, staff may be less resistant and actually feel more valued and appreciated. In fact, while most nonprofits will need to acquire some business skills to capitalize on these types of ventures, as long as new demands are balanced with new responsibilities, developing such programs can provide appealing opportunities for career development and learning for program staff.

Asset-based ventures. Another question to ask is: "What do we own that others might value?" Asset-based ventures take advantage of underutilized or previously unrecognized assets that have market value to individuals or organizations that are willing and able to pay. Organizations usually have a wide range of assets, some of them intangible, that are not being used to their full potential. Think about these examples:

- The Breckenridge Outdoor Education Center (BOEC) offers ski lessons and wilderness programs for people with physical and mental disabilities. The organization has a beautiful lodge for its participants located on a pristine lake on prime real-estate property adjacent to the Breckenridge ski resort. The BOEC rents the lodge for weddings and special events during the off season, as well as occasionally to groups of skiers visiting Breckenridge during the winter. Since it is not a full-service lodge, the BOEC charges below-market rates for the area but nonetheless generates unrestricted cash flows by not letting its valuable property sit vacant for extended periods of time.

- The Clearinghouse, an advocate for the elderly in New York City, recognized that through its activities, the organization had amassed a wealth of valuable information. Thus, the staff assembled a guide that provided comprehensive information for individuals who were arranging nursing home care for someone in the city. Initially tying the cost of the publication to a $15 membership fee, the organization saw membership skyrocket and developed plans to expand the guide statewide and charge $25.[6]

Building an asset-based venture may provide many benefits, including the unique advantage of encouraging a new way of thinking within an organization. You are not "just a nonprofit," but you are an organization with valuable assets. Exploiting an underutilized asset might be a good first step for an organization looking to test the earned income waters.

Relationship-based ventures.   A third question to ask is "What relationships do we have that might have business value?" Nonprofits often have relationships with clients, donors, volunteers, alumni, staff, board members, and others that are potentially valuable. The value can be found in two ways. You can look at your relationships as providing potential markets for commercial products or services. Or you can view your relationships as a kind of asset that may be valuable to others. Consider the following examples:

- The Sierra Club organizes hundreds of outings and expeditions both nationally and internationally and markets these primarily to its sizable membership base. The operation is nonprofit but fully self-sustaining. Most of the trips are wilderness trips, and the organization only offers excursions that are in demand from members and that contribute to the overall conservation and environmental goals of the Sierra Club. The trips are run as cooperative ventures. Trip participants are expected to help out with camping chores and other work necessary to make the trip a success. Following the spirit of the purpose of the outings, all trip leaders are also club members who have volunteered their time to scout, plan, and direct the trips.[7]

- With the assistance of the consulting firm Community Wealth Ventures, the local chapter of a national youth services organization focused on inner cities capitalized on its close relationship with the

African American and Latino community. The organization created a focus group business that offers corporations, advertising, and marketing firms access to this desirable target market. Plans are now in motion to roll out this business in partnership with this organization's other local affiliates nationwide.

Clearly, the Sierra Club is building on its competencies as well as its relationships in its outings business. However, purely relationship-based businesses often require skills that are very different from those of the host nonprofit. In many cases, the best way to take advantage of these kinds of opportunities is to contract with an experienced provider, often a for-profit. For instance, it is common for museums that see an opportunity to provide food and drink to their visitors to contract with a food service provider to run the café. This is still a business venture for the museum. What it is selling is access to its visitors and space in which to operate.

Mission-based ventures. Finally, you can ask, "How could we use a business to directly serve our mission?" All nonprofit business ventures should further the social mission of the organization, at least indirectly by generating incremental funding for mission-oriented programs. However, some business ventures are specifically designed with the primary purpose of serving a social mission directly. These can be referred to as "social purpose enterprises." They generate and depend on earned income, but that income is not the primary goal. The most common type of social purpose enterprise is one that uses a business to train and employ disadvantaged populations. While this strategy is still relatively new outside of the employment and training area, some particularly entrepreneurial organizations have been developing other types of social purpose enterprises. Consider the following examples of mission-based ventures:

- As part of its strategy to fight poverty through promoting social purpose enterprises, Roberts Enterprise Development Fund invests in Rubicon Programs, a nonprofit that works with the economically disadvantaged to help them develop their assets and build their self-worth. Rubicon Enterprises, Inc., is a supporting corporation of Rubicon Programs. As part of Rubicon Enterprises, Rubicon Landscape Services, Rubicon Bakery, and Rubicon HomeCare Consortium provide job training and employment for Rubicon's clients while also generating revenue.

- The Benetech Initiative, a nonprofit venture that aims to provide social benefits by harnessing the power of technology, is in the process of developing Bookshare.org, a legal, Napster-style book-sharing community sharing scanned books among the over 30,000 users of Arkenstone reading systems for people with disabilities.

Several financial models are being considered, including some combination of a subscription fee, per-item charges, advertising, Internet link revenue, and in-kind or monetary contributions. The financial goal of Bookshare.org is to be operating at or above the break-even point within two years.[8]

- The International Women's Tribune Centre (IWTC) is dedicated to achieving women's full participation in shaping a development process that is just, peaceful, and sustainable. IWTC serves as an information, education, communication, networking, technical assistance, and training resource for women worldwide. One of its five major programs, Women, Ink., markets and distributes books on women and development, with a focus on the perspective of women from the Global South. The operation not only provides access to over 250 publications on a wide range of issues, but it also serves as a marketing outlet for publications produced by information-gathering groups and small presses in the countries of the Global South. Women, Ink., is funded by publication sales and a grant from United Nations Development Fund for Women (UNIFEM).[9]

Mission-based ventures have the advantage of appealing to staff and board members who worry about the appropriateness of a nonprofit running a business. The mission benefits are clear and direct. However, mission-based ventures can pose distinctive challenges as you balance mission and business considerations on a day-to-day basis.

Unrelated ventures. "Fine," you say, "but what if I have this terrific business idea that has nothing to do with my organization's competencies, assets, relationships, or mission?" Just be careful. Business is intensely competitive, and the landscape is littered with failed ventures based on what someone thought was a great idea. According to Amar Bhide, a professor of entrepreneurship at Columbia Business School, "Profitable survival requires an edge derived from some combination of a creative idea and a superior capacity for execution."[10] It is not enough to have a brilliant idea. Ideas are a dime a dozen. The hard part is putting the idea into practice. Starting with relevant competencies, assets, and relationships can help considerably on the execution. Linking the venture to your mission also can help. Doing so not only allows you to tap into the passion of serving a social mission, but it makes it easier to attract low-cost philanthropic funding, such as program-related investments or outright grants. That's why we urge you to start your search for business opportunities by looking at your organization's competencies, assets, relationships, and mission.

Can you succeed without any of this? Sure, but typically it will require a greater investment of time, energy, and money. You need to acquire or develop all of the competencies, assets, and relationships to assure successful execution. In certain businesses, this task can be daunting: The competencies are rare and hard to build; the assets are costly; and the relationships take a long time to develop. Think of oil refining or computer manufacturing. In others, a little bit of capital and a lot of hard work can go a long way. Consider bicycle repair shops or lawn service business. To borrow a term from Bhide, we can call these "hustle" businesses. Hustle businesses are most common in fragmented service industries.[11] The capital requirements are typically low; the market is not dominated by large entrenched competitors who will fight you off; and the necessary skills can be developed or acquired relatively easily. If you have a business idea that does not build on your organization's competencies, assets, relationships, or mission, you need to ask the following three questions:

practical tip

1. Can you compete in this business on hustle alone?
2. If not, what will it take for you to develop or acquire the competencies, assets, and relationships required to be competitive in this particular business venture?
3. Is it worth making the necessary investments of time, money, and energy, considering that the business will not directly serve your mission?

Potential Benefits

The potential benefits of launching a business venture are as varied as the different approaches and opportunities, but successful ventures may provide some of the following rewards:

✔ *Direct mission impact,* particularly in the case of mission-based ventures

✔ *Enhanced business and strategic skills* that also may contribute to better delivery of mission-related goods and services

✔ *Increased brand awareness and recognition* for your organization

✔ *A reenergized, entrepreneurial workforce,* if the staff is fully supportive of the business opportunity

✔ *Improved market discipline,* if the venture is aligned with the organization's social mission

✔ *Funds for serving the social mission,* if the venture is sufficiently profitable or the business itself directly serves the organization's mission

Risks and Challenges

No matter the category of a new venture, many of the risks and challenges facing the social entrepreneur are the same. This list is by no means exhaustive, but it should provide you with a good starting point.

MARIANNE WOODWARD AT ASK4 STAFFING, INC.

In 1998, Ask4 Staffing, Inc., was created as a for-profit corporation to serve as a source of earned income for the Children's Home & Aid Society of Illinois (CHASI). With an annual budget of over $36 million and 650 staff members statewide, CHASi serves children, families, and communities with an array of programs around adoption, counseling, education, foster care, residential treatment, and family, parent, and youth services. Ask4 provides staffing solutions to social service organizations, and a few years into its life, the company is well ahead of plan and positioned to prosper. But how did an organization like CHASI come to create a business like Ask4? To find that out, we spoke with Ask4 CEO and founder Marianne Woodward, and here's what she had to say:

> **Woodward:** CHASI was more equipped and ready for this business opportunity than most, and I think that is the only reason we are experiencing success thus far. First of all, they had very reasonable expectations about how long the process would take and how much money could be generated. Second, after completing a major long-term strategic planning process, they were determined to reduce their reliance on government funding via earned income, and they were very committed to developing a new business. They hired me, someone with years of business experience [Author's note: Ms. Woodward has over 15 years experience in the finance, banking, and venture capital industries], to explore opportunities for earned income full time. They also provided equity for the business, a real financial commitment that demonstrated their long-term dedication to this course. Finally, CHASI was a well-established, financially strong organization with a very strong board and management team. The leaders were enthusiastic about this undertaking and devoted their time, energy, and skills when needed. Additionally, they helped me set up an independent advisory board of experienced business leaders, lawyers, and venture capitalists to explore different business ideas and evaluate potential opportunities.

> **Q:** And how did you settle on creating Ask4 Staffing, a staffing service for social service organizations?

> **Woodward:** We began by establishing four criteria for identifying an earned income opportunity: (1) good risk/return trade-off; (2) low capital intensity; (3) ability to scale it up or roll it out; (4) competitive advantage. We weren't only focused on starting a new business—that was just one option and happens to be where we ended up after we explored and examined our options based on these criteria. We considered a wide range of opportunities, including starting a baby goods delivery service, acquiring a muffler franchise, producing a calendar, and creating a parent resource directory. But in the end, we chose Ask4 Staffing because we thought there was a lucrative business opportunity to be exploited and we thought we could do it better than anyone else given our affiliation with Children's Home & Aid Society. We did have a knowledge base and access to expertise about how nonprofits are run, how they make decisions, what their staffing needs are, and what the process is to interview, screen, and hire them. And the CHASI name carries some weight and gives us credibility in the marketplace. But that only helps us get in the door. Then it is up to us to deliver. So the business we are in does not directly further CHASI's mission (which is to help children and families), but it does help CHASI and other nonprofits achieve their mission-related goals by helping them solve their staffing needs.

Mission drift. Business ventures may inadvertently pull nonprofits away from their core social mission, especially if business success is not directly aligned with the mission. In the extreme case, an organization may find its business activities increasingly demanding more attention and coming to dominate much of its resources and focus, such that the tail has indeed begun to wag the dog.

Cultural conflict. Successful business ventures often require a culture that could be at odds with the kinds of cultures found in many nonprofits. Many nonprofit employees are uncomfortable with the language and operations of business. Depending on the magnitude of the venture and the degree to which it is integrated into the traditional activities of the organization, cultural conflict may result. Employees and volunteers may be skeptical of the values and motives of people with business training, put off by business concepts, or just generally offended by the idea of commercial enterprise potentially eroding the organization's mission focus.

Compensation clash. If your venture requires hiring new staff, you may run into compensation issues. Business management skills can be costly to acquire. Nonprofits often rely heavily on "psychic income" to attract workers for below-market rates. While some "businesspeople" might be willing to accept a lower than market wage in order to work for a nonprofit, their compensation requirements still may be much higher than your organization's norms. Bringing them on can cause conflict related to pay equity as well as strain the financial resources of the organization until the venture becomes profitable.

Confusing "need" with market demand. When considering commercial activities, you must be careful to distinguish between *community need* and *market demand.* You may see a need for some product or service in the community you serve, but that does not mean that there is adequate market demand to support a venture. Many years ago a food co-op in Berkeley, California, thought it had found an opportunity when it realized that its neighborhood was lacking good access to organic produce. However, before entering this market, it failed to adequately evaluate whether the residents of its community could afford such "high-end" products. In the end, the customers could not pay for the produce, and the venture failed.[12]

Counting too much on "feel-good" marketing. Don't count on your status as a nonprofit to increase sales in the marketplace! Sure, some people enjoy feeling like they are supporting a "worthy cause" when they buy a tie from The Nature Conservancy or a cake from Rubicon Bakery. But you cannot expect your charitable status to be your competitive advantage in the marketplace. In some cases, it actually could be detrimental.

Some people associate nonprofits with poor quality and low standards. Make sure you can offer a product or service that is attractive to customers on its own merits.

Not having a tax strategy. When planning any business venture, a nonprofit should consider its potential tax implications or whether any income will be subject to unrelated business income tax (UBIT). An activity is considered subject to UBIT if it is a trade or business, it is regularly carried on, and it is unrelated to the exempt purposes of the organization. As with many things dealing with the IRS, there is a lot of gray area. You should be cognizant of the law but not intimidated by it. You must report and pay tax on any UBI activities, but it will not jeopardize your exempt status as long as the activities are not so significant as to be considered your organization's primary activities.[13] And after all, having to pay taxes on *actual profits* may not be such a bad thing—at least you're making money! And you have a ready response to any businessperson who is concerned about the need for an "even playing field"—you pay taxes too! But regardless of how you approach the issue of taxes, you should consult competent legal and tax counsel for advice if you think UBIT might be a real concern for your venture.

Failing to do a comprehensive risk assessment for the venture. It's no secret that the majority of new businesses fail, and your key stakeholders should understand the risks before launching any new venture. In evaluating and planning your business venture, you should assess your risk exposure by paying close attention to the following key risk factors that may affect the probability of failure:[14]

Organizational Risk Factors

✔ *Quality of management.* "A good manager can succeed with a bad enterprise, but a bad manager will kill a good enterprise." Does your team have the necessary skills?

✔ *Quality of the workforce.* Can your employees perform at market level? This issue is especially critical for social-purpose enterprises seeking to employ a given target population.

✔ *Culture of the organization.* Does your culture affirm entrepreneurial approaches?

✔ *Strength of organizational infrastructure.* Does your organization have the capacity to manage a dynamic, market-based venture?

Enterprise Risk Factors

✔ *Basic enterprise concept.* Is the strategy tested and reliable or new and uncertain? Does it have greater risk than other similar enterprises? What factors make it risky?

✔ *Level of capitalization.* How much money will you need to launch this venture? Can you secure it? Are you taking on "risky" capital, such as debt that you have to service?

✔ *Prospects of long-term funding.* What do you need to support the enterprise? Are those funds readily available? What cash flow is necessary to support start-up and expansion?

External Environment Risk Factors

✔ *Changes in the marketplace.* Consider potential shifts in the capital markets, public policies, charitable interests of donors, and tastes or routines of consumers.

✔ *Changes in technology.* Think about effects on internal operating technologies as well as the potential impact of technological advances on your industry.

✔ *Stakeholder backlash.* We've said it before and we'll say it again— you may meet opposition from those who believe that "Charity is charity and business is business!"

✔ *Competitor reaction.* It will happen, so be prepared. Know your market segment and its players, understand the competitive advantages of each, and engage in competition yourself based on integrity and consistency with your core values.

Key Success Factors

While there are many challenges to keep in mind when considering whether to launch a business venture, paying attention to some key success factors can help position you for future success:

Focus on a genuine market opportunity. According to Jeffry Timmons, entrepreneurship professor at Babson College, "Good ideas are not necessarily good opportunities. . . . An opportunity has the qualities of being attractive, durable, and timely and is anchored in a product or service which creates or adds value for its buyer or end user."[15] In order to distinguish between an idea and an opportunity, you must do your homework. It is not enough for the venture to be built on your competencies, assets, relationships, and mission. You must have customers who are willing and able to pay for what you offer as well as a viable plan for reaching them. Market research is crucial![16]

Build on the natural resources of the organization. As our categories suggest, we advise starting with what you already know and have when thinking about developing an earned income business. Edward Skloot, executive director of Surdna Foundation and former president and founder of nonprofit consulting group New Ventures, argues that earned income activities are most likely to succeed when they build on what the organization is already doing. He offers Planned Parenthood Federation of America's development and marketing of a house-brand condom as one example. Staff members understand the connection, mitigating some of the potential tension around mission, and clients may welcome the product or service.[17]

Make sure you have strong management, financial, marketing, and communications skills. No matter what the venture, you will need access to strong management, financial, marketing, and communications skills throughout the planning and implementation stages. You must realistically assess your needs in these areas at the start and devise a strategy for acquiring the necessary skills. Can any of the skills you need be provided effectively by volunteers? What new staff may you need to hire? Can you develop relationships with others (consultants, contractors, suppliers) to provide any of them in a cost-effective manner?

red flag **Be careful about the use of volunteers.** Be careful in your assumptions about utilizing volunteers to play critical roles in your commercial venture. If they do not perceive it as closely tied to your mission, they may be less willing to volunteer their services. They may feel that they will not get the same "do-good" feeling of satisfaction from their volunteering. However, other volunteers may actually be attracted to the opportunity to take advantage of their hard business skills and put them to use for a good cause. Volunteers can be a very cost-effective resource, but you should be realistic in your expectations of the role they will play.

Look for "smart" capital. As a general rule, one dollar of "smart money" is worth more than five dollars of "dumb money." The key to finding "smart" capital is to identify capital providers whose capacities and interests match the character of your ongoing resource needs. Some issues to consider are the duration of your need; the size of your need relative to potential capital providers' capacity; whether the need is expected to grow, decline, or stay the same; and the risk you are asking the provider to take. But how can you attract this capital once you've "found" it? Do your best to cultivate and manage three of your intangible assets: *social capital* (in this case the goodwill and trust you've built through your existing relationships), *credibility* (the confidence you can create in your ability to make your venture a success), and *shared commitment* (the degree to which potential resource providers embrace your social mission's values and approach).[18]

Make sure the venture is understood and endorsed by the board. In the best scenarios, you will have full board support without inappropriate pressure. Ideally, there will be one or two "champions" on the board who ensure that you have adequate access to the financial expertise, business skills, and networks of all of the members. The board also must have a long-term commitment to developing income-generating opportunities and recognize the associated risks and potential liabilities.

 Be careful about pet projects. While board support is critical, you should not be swayed by pet projects of board members, even if they are offering their resources and think they have it all figured out. Earned income strategies need the commitment of all of your stakeholders and must not be driven solely by the board. Never forget that the plan ultimately must be executed at the staff level.

BUILDING REVENUE RELATIONSHIPS

Finally, some nonprofits have found value in partnering with a corporation to generate earned income that is shared. It may feel like selling your soul when you first think about it, but many nonprofits have found partners with whom they can work comfortably. Corporate-nonprofit partnerships can take many shapes and forms,[19] but here we are concerned only with those partnerships that are focused on generating earned income. These kinds of nonprofit/for-profit revenue relationships tend to fall into one of the following categories: *cause-related marketing, joint ventures,* and *licensing.*

> *Cause-related Marketing* (CRM). The marketing of a for-profit product or service in association with a nonprofit or a "cause." Sales trigger a payment to the nonprofit by the seller, thereby raising money and visibility for both the business and the nonprofit cause.
>
> *Joint Ventures*. Collaborations between nonprofit and for-profit entities to produce a unique program, product, or service by capitalizing on the strengths, assets, and capabilities of each.
>
> *Licensing Agreements*. A partnership in which a nonprofit sells the rights to use its name, logo, and images to a corporation for use in promoting its products or services.[20]

Consider these examples:

- American Express raised $1.7 million for the foundation overseeing the renovation of Ellis Island and the Statue of Liberty and increased usage of its card 28 percent by donating one cent for every transaction in the United States and one dollar for each new card issued during the last quarter of the year.
- KaBOOM!, a nonprofit devoted to building safe and accessible play spaces in distressed neighborhoods, partnered with Ben & Jerry's to develop and promote a new ice cream flavor, KaBerry KaBOOM! Ben & Jerry's committed a percentage of sales to KaBOOM!

Packaging for the pints of ice cream features information about KaBOOM!, and flyers in local retail stores as well as the home page of Ben & Jerry's highly trafficked web site promote the flavor and the cause.[21]

- As part of their collaborative relationship, in 1995 City Year and Timberland developed a new line of products called City Year Gear. Specially designed and marketed Timberland T-shirts, backpacks, and messenger bags promoted the values of both organizations with slogans such as "Give Racism the Boot" and "Hike the Path to Justice." The line was sold through Timberland's retail outlets, and profits from sales benefited City Year. In 2001, they introduced a new product, a red Timberland boot with a City Year logo.[22]

- The March of Dimes licenses its name to Kellogg to promote Product 19; the American Dental Association approves various oral hygiene products; the American Cancer Society licenses its logo to Smith Kline Beecham to promote its nicotine patch; Prevent Blindness America partners with a sports equipment manufacturer that produces shields that prevent eye trauma.[23]

Potential Benefits

In order to be counted as a success, these cross-sector partnerships must create benefits for both parties. With luck, a well-executed revenue relationship can help further your mission in a variety of ways.

✔ *Incremental funding.* It can generate a substantial amount of unrestricted funds to support mission-based activities.

✔ *Increased brand and cause awareness.* The increased public awareness can help attract new potential partners, donors, volunteers, and even clients for the nonprofit partner. It also can create a broader base of support for your general cause.

✔ *Logical division of labor.* Your corporate partner can focus on the business side of the deal, while you concentrate on what you do best—your core programs.

Your corporate partner can benefit in different ways as well.

✔ *Incremental sales.* This benefit accrues only if the link with you is valued by your corporate customer's customers.

✔ *Differentiation in a competitive market.* The partnership can help to create a distinctive brand image for the company.

✔ *An enhanced image as a good corporate citizen.* This image can help the company in a variety of settings.

✔ *Stronger customer loyalty.* Those customers who care about your organization and your cause may increase both their purchases and their loyalty to your corporate partner.

✔ *Better employee morale.* Employees may take more pride in working at a company that "cares."

 This is not corporate philanthropy! Companies typically are paying for these projects out of their marketing budgets and are expecting a return on their investment. Before you enter into any contract with a potential corporation, be sure that you understand fully the terms and commitments you're making within that contract. You should not fall into the trap of believing that because you're "just a nonprofit" companies will (or should!) cut you any slack in terms of your ability to fulfill your part of the deal. Remember: While many companies certainly secure some level of social benefit through such partnerships, they are primarily business relationships, so be sure you don't "let your mouth make promises your body can't fill," to quote an old blues tune.

Risks and Challenges

Shirley Sagawa and Eli Segal, coauthors of *Common Interest, Common Good,* an important book exploring business and social sector partnerships, identify the following obstacles that loom large in cross-sector partnerships:

✔ *Different language.* Communication may be difficult between entities that have their own jargon.

✔ *Different culture.* The stereotypical business with its time-is-money orientation may clash head-on with a slower-moving, consensus-oriented, and resource-poor nonprofit.

✔ *Different status.* Because of their greater resources, businesses may receive or expect greater deference than their nonprofit partners.

✔ *Different worldviews.* Nonprofits may consider business to be "part of the problem" and view a business partner as only a check writer; a business partner may receive or expect greater deference than its nonprofit partners.

✔ *Different bottom lines.* Because each sector measures success differently, cross-sector partners may clash over goals for the alliance.[24]

In addition to these challenges, the following risk factors should be considered when thinking about building a revenue relationship.

Damaged reputation. As pointed out earlier, tarnishing your reputation is a risk with all earned income ventures, but you must be especially careful when partnering with corporations. Alan Andreasen, Georgetown marketing professor and recognized expert on nonprofit marketing, relates the hypothetical story of a joint campaign against child abuse created by a child welfare organization and a women's clothing manufacturer. Six weeks into the campaign, a human rights organization in Bangladesh and Sri Lanka charges the manufacturer with exploiting children as young as 12 years old in filthy sweatshops. At the press conference exposing these allegations, the directors of the human rights organization holds up a poster from the child abuse awareness campaign and says, "Don't fall for it."[25] While this may represent the extreme, the situation is far from inconceivable. Make sure you understand the motivations of your potential corporate partners, and do a thorough investigation of their business practices.

Stakeholder objections. Nonprofit/for-profit partnerships can appear to undermine your social mission or compromise your integrity and independence, inciting objections from major stakeholders. Make sure your key stakeholders are on board before moving ahead. The American Medical Association (AMA) learned this lesson the hard way when it negotiated a revenue relationship with Sunbeam Corporation. The AMA agreed to "cobrand" a line of Sunbeam's home healthcare products, in effect endorsing the products. In return, Sunbeam would pay the AMA a royalty on sales of these products and distribute AMA-sponsored health information with them.

Members and the public were outraged by the idea that the AMA would endorse a particular line of products. In response to the outcry, the board of the AMA unilaterally decided to break the agreement with Sunbeam less than one month after that agreement was announced and created a new policy precluding product endorsements. Members felt better, but Sunbeam promptly sued for breach of contract. The AMA settled the suit for $9.9 million and reported an additional $3.5 million in costs related to the Sunbeam affair, including legal fees and executive search fees to replace those who were fired as a result of this decision.[26]

Loss of organizational flexibility. Corporations entering into agreements with nonprofits will want to make sure that they are maximizing their benefits, which may push them to add certain restrictions to the contract that might reduce your organization's flexibility to work with other businesses or organizations. Understandably, American Express would not want you to sign an agreement with it and then try to strike a deal with Visa. But it should not expect, or try to demand, to have a say in any partnerships you choose to enter beyond those with a direct competitor. And if possible, at least in the early stages of these relationships, nonprofits should aim for nonexclusive, shorter-term contracts to preserve their flexibility.[27]

Increased dependency on a single source. Like any major source of funding, there is the risk that the nonprofit will come to rely too heavily on its corporate partner. What if the corporation reduces or reallocates its marketing budget? If the nonprofit has devoted much of its fund-raising energy and resources to supporting the alliance, not pursued ways to sustain its marketing program without corporate support, and counted on its corporate partner to manage contacts with other businesses, the nonprofit could suddenly be at great financial risk.[28]

Market risk. Although revenue relationships typically do not require major financial investments on the part of the nonprofit partner, they do require significant time and energy from senior staff members. This investment may not pay off as expected, even with entrepreneurial nonprofit leaders, a terrific partner, and brilliant strategic advice. Timberland and City Year have an exceptionally close and effective corporate nonprofit partnership. Visionary entrepreneurial leaders head both organizations. They have strong shared values. When they decided to launch their first earned income project together, City Year Gear, they both had high hopes for the revenues it might generate for City Year. City Year wanted to diversify its funding base, which was about half from the government and half from corporate donations. The project benefited from the advice of a top consulting firm and a stellar advisory board with lots of business experience. But in the five years since this product line was launched, the net revenues to City Year have never exceeded more than 1 or 2 percent of its annual budget. That is not much diversification! City Year has benefited in other ways from this experience, but the financial impact has been well below the hopes of both partners. Markets do not always respond the way you expect them to.

Key Success Factors

There is no formula for success in entering into revenue relationships with corporate partners, but there are some qualities that should characterize any potential relationship.[29]

Have something valuable to offer. In order to be a viable partner in a revenue relationship, you must have a strong track record and something (i.e., relationships, programs, expertise, positive brand image, or credibility) of value to a corporate partner. One of the most famous revenue relationships is the American Express holiday "Charge Against Hunger" that involves Share Our Strength, the nation's largest hunger-fighting organization. According to Billy Shore, founder and executive director of Share Our Strength:

gem of wisdom

The main lesson for us in CRM [cause-related marketing] is that you have to have an asset to deploy—in our case it was our relationships with chefs and restaurateurs—rather than just assuming that a company will enter into a CRM campaign because of your name or goodwill or something like that. Companies can basically buy goodwill through advertising, and their names are bigger than yours. American Express didn't need to be affiliated with SOS; they did want to be affiliated with an organization that had tens of thousands of restaurants that would participate in different promotions.

While Shore was speaking specifically about CRM relationships, his advice holds true for licensing agreements and joint ventures as well. In order to go down this path, you must have something special to offer a corporate partner.

Establish a clear definition of and commitment to joint value creation. From the beginning, there should be a clear definition of goals of the relationship as well as a joint understanding of and commitment to what value will be created and how each party will contribute to creating that value. You have to be comfortable helping a company make money through its affiliation with your organization.

Build on shared values. Finding a partner with a commitment to the same, or very similar, values as your organization will greatly reduce the risks to both sides and improve the chances of significant value creation.

Develop and utilize negotiation and communication skills. This kind of earned income strategy is all about negotiation, from structuring the original deal, to addressing conflicts that may arise down the line. It will work only with open communication between partners, built on a mutual trust and respect.

Provide adequate top management attention. Even the most basic licensing or CRM deals require management attention and effort. Key staff members from both organizations must have the time, expertise, and commitment to make these deals successful.

Look for partners whose high product and program quality matches your own. Both parties must offer products and services of the highest quality for the deal to be equitable, for value to be created, and for risk factors to be mitigated.

Make sure you have adequate financial strength going in. It may seem paradoxical, but both entities should be in good financial shape. These relationships require resource commitments on both sides, and even the most valuable partnerships will not supersede the primary business and mission-related activities if one entity experiences a financial downturn. Neither an unstable business nor a financially needy nonprofit makes a good potential partner.

Getting Paid for What You Already Do	Launching a New Business Venture	Building Revenue Relationships
Charging your primary beneficiaries	Competency-based	Licensing agreements
Charging an interested third party	Asset-based	Cause-related marketing
Creating a hybrid pricing structure	Relationship-based	Joint ventures
	Mission-based	

EXHIBIT 9.1   Earned income strategy plan.

action step   Do you understand the different paths to earned income available to nonprofits? To test your comprehension and prepare yourself for developing your own strategy, try coming up with your own example of each type of strategy. Exhibit 9.1 should help you develop such a plan.

FIVE STEPS FOR DEVELOPING A VIABLE EARNED INCOME STRATEGY

Now that you're familiar with the three different paths for generating earned income, it's time to start the process of developing a viable earned income strategy for your organization. There are five critical steps.

STEP 1: REAFFIRM YOUR ORGANIZATION'S MISSION

Since positive mission impact is the ultimate goal of any earned income strategy, you should begin this process with your mission front and center in your mind. You must make sure that your mission is clearly defined and understood by all of your key stakeholders. If there is any disagreement or confusion, developing a viable strategy and achieving organizational buy-in will be extremely challenging. Your mission should be both the starting and the end point of any strategy—the touchstone of truth by which every strategy and decision should be tested and the supreme purpose against which performance and success should be measured.

action step   Ask at least five different employees, board members, customers, or other key stakeholders to explain your organization's mission to you in their own words, not just quoting the mission statement from your promotional materials (though they should be able to do that, as well!). If you get varying responses, or, worse yet, "I don't knows," you need to come to some consensus around the definition and meaning of your mission before moving forward.[30]

STEP 2: BRAINSTORM YOUR OPTIONS

After all of these examples, you must be brimming with ideas for your organization! Before you start unleashing them, here are a few guidelines for the brainstorming process:

✔ *Organization-wide participation.* Since your organization must buy into this strategy, it is wise to include a wide range of folks in the idea-generation process.

✔ *Write down every idea.* While brainstorming, no idea is a bad idea. Encourage creativity and active participation—you never know where the best ideas will come from!

✔ *Allow time for debate and discussion.* Once you've got a good list of ideas, encourage some debate and discussion, focusing on the idea's fit with your mission, culture, and values. Now is the time to air concerns and test the waters for organizational acceptance.

✔ *Parse ideas down to five or fewer.* While you should record every idea initially, before moving into the evaluative stage, narrow the list down to a manageable size. Keep only ideas that you really think have some potential for mission impact, organizational acceptance, and market success. At this point, it's usually safe to go with your gut.

Still not sure where to begin? Consider going through each of the three paths one by one. You've already thought a little bit about whether a particular path makes sense for you or not, so you may be able to save some time by ruling out one or more at the start. Looking for more guidance? Try out the following exercises.

Getting Paid for What You Already Do

Many organizations shy away from this option, but it would be a mistake not to give serious consideration to generating revenues from your core operations. Of course, some services can be ruled out due to moral problems. You are clearly not going to charge a drowning person for a life preserver. But most nonprofit services are not in this category, and even when it is inappropriate to charge your individual client, it may be feasible to charge a third party. Review the potential benefits of charging for your services mentioned earlier in this chapter, then think about each of your current products or services, and ask yourself:[31]

✔ *Does this service provide tangible and relatively immediate benefits to the individuals or organizations served?* What are those benefits? Do the recipients of the benefits recognize the value they are getting? It's much easier to charge fees for your services when these services benefit specific individuals or organizations in tangible ways that they can appreciate relatively quickly.

✔ *Are any of these beneficiaries both able and willing to pay without experiencing an unacceptable hardship?* Chances are, many of your clients could pay something without serious hardship. Do they spend money on other things that are far less valuable than what you have to offer? What would they have to give up in order to pay something for your services? Would they pay if you asked them to? If not, you have to ask why not? A number of explanations are possible. However, when the benefits are clear and the beneficiaries are able to pay, their reluctance may say something about the value you are delivering to them.

✔ *How great are the other "costs" to your beneficiaries for using your services?* Is it inconvenient for them? Is it psychologically difficult? You should not automatically avoid charging a fee just because the other "costs" are high, but you should be aware of them and assess whether a fee on top of these other costs will deter your most important clients from participating.

✔ *How could pricing be used to improve your organization's effectiveness?* For instance, could pricing create greater commitment on the part of your clients? Could it create a healthy shift in power to your clients? Could it serve to screen out those who get the least value from your services? Could charging some people allow you to use your philanthropic funding to serve the truly needy?

✔ *Is there a government entity or business that might have a vested interest in the service you are providing?* Do you offer a service that the government is interested in supporting? Will the benefits from your program in any way improve an individual's ability to perform on the job? Charging a third party may help you overcome some of the ideological barriers to charging your clients directly. You don't have to charge drowning people for life preservers; instead, you can charge the town that owns the beach for your lifeguard services. Can you specify and quantify the potential benefits to the third parties—in terms of cost savings, increased productivity, or reduced liability? What kind of deal might be appealing to them?

Launching a New Business Venture

Start with what you know. According to one study, over 70 percent of successful entrepreneurs started their ventures to solve problems they have grappled with personally as customers or employees.[32] Many of the best ideas are based to some degree on your existing knowledge and experience—recall the Ask4 Staffing example. In brainstorming possible venture opportunities, consider the following questions:

✔ *How can you build on your organization's distinctive competencies?* What do you do particularly well? Can you envision new products or services based on one or more of your distinctive competencies? Can you think of individuals or organizations that might be willing and able to pay for these products or services? Competency is often more important than assets or relationships in determining long-term success, so this is a good place to start.

✔ *How can you take advantage of your organization's (underutilized) assets?* Create an inventory of your organization's assets, including the intangible ones. Who might be willing to pay you for access to or use of those assets? What kinds of ventures might be built using these assets? Can you afford to use these assets for new purposes? Many assets are underutilized and can easily be devoted to other purposes when they are not being fully used by your core programs. Notice that intangible assets, such as knowledge, often can be used by any number of people, for different purposes, all at the same time without conflict.

✔ *How can you build a venture around the relationships you have with key stakeholder groups?* What ancillary products and services could you offer your current clientele or staff to make their experience more enjoyable, more memorable, or less difficult or frustrating? Common examples are food service, parking, and day care. Can you think of organizations that could benefit by getting access to the groups with whom you have a strong relationship? What kinds of business ventures could you build based on providing that access? How can this be done in a way that is respectful of and beneficial for your stakeholders?

✔ *How can you structure a business venture to serve your social mission directly?* What types of commercial activities could your clients execute? How could working in a business venture help them? Can you think of other ways a business venture might serve your mission directly? How can market forces be used to achieve your social objectives? Can you get people to pay you to do something that, by its very nature, will further your mission?

✔ *What other kinds of market opportunities do you see that you might be able to pursue effectively?* Unrelated ventures can present higher risks and generally are not recommended, but sometimes you recognize (or are presented with) an unrelated business opportunity that is worth pursuing. Do you have evidence of a genuine demand for this product or service? Is this a business venture in which success is more dependent on hustle than on prior experience, assets, or relationships? How can you acquire or develop the competencies, assets, and relationships needed?

Building Revenue Relationships

Keep in mind that these partnerships can take many forms. Begin by asking yourself the following questions. The first three are adapted from Alan Andreasen's article, "Profits for Nonprofits: Find a Corporate Partner."[33] We added the fourth and fifth.

1. *What kinds of value can your organization add?* Common examples include association with your image and brand, free publicity and public relations opportunities, credibility in certain markets, and access to your relationships with clients, staff, trustees, donors, alumni, members, and others. How can any of this be turned into profitable sales for a corporate partner?

2. *What are your organization's strengths and weaknesses?* Do you look like an attractive partner? How strong is your brand image? With whom? Is your cause or audience particularly appealing to a certain industry or group of people? Do you have a charismatic and well-known leader? Is your organization experienced and stable? Do you have weaknesses or an image that might trouble certain potential partners?

3. *Who are your potential partners?* Who could benefit most from what you have to offer? Would the partnership fit with their long-term strategy, business practices, and core values? Are their senior executives likely to be enthusiastic about the partnership over the long haul? Do they have the funds and people to devote to the alliance? Are they comfortable with your values? How would an affiliation with particular organizations or industries affect you? Which partners would fit best with your values and your stakeholders' values?

4. *Where do you have a good shot at getting to the right decision makers?* How will you get your foot in the door? Do you, your staff, or your board members have relationships with any of the potentially attractive partners? With whom, in which area? Existing relationships can help significantly. The corporate foundation or community relations office can be a way into the company, but ultimately you will want to get to the marketing department or even the CEO's office.

5. *What would your "sales pitch" be?* Once you've answered all of these questions, select the two or three potential partners with the best fit and develop the key points you would make in trying to "pitch" a revenue relationship deal to each potential corporate "customer." What is the value proposition you would put to them? What is in it for them? What do you want in return? Do you think you've got a chance to strike a deal?

STEP 3: ASSESS TOTAL MISSION IMPACT

We already established that positive mission impact is the ultimate goal of any earned income strategy. Some strategies are designed to help you serve your mission *directly.* Others are conceived to support the mission *indirectly* by generating resources, building capacity, enhancing credibility, and generally improving your ability to achieve your mission. Of course, just as a strategy may have a positive mission impact, there is also the potential for detrimental affects, such as pulling you away from your mission, draining scarce resources, and creating public relations problems. So how can you evaluate these various affects to assess the expected *total mission impact* of a given strategy?

core concept   When you want to assess *total mission impact,* just think about MOM: *Mission, Organization, and Money.* These represent the three dimensions of *total mission impact.* "Mission" refers to your direct social mission, and the indirect impacts are broken into two categories: "Organization" and "Money." In each area, you have to account for both negative and positive affects. The following sections explore each dimension further.

Mission: Direct Impact on Your Social Mission

Direct mission impact includes all those factors that you would consider in answering the following question: *Would this strategy be worth pursuing for mission reasons alone?*

To answer this question, it is useful to imagine that the strategy's other affects would be neutral at best. Assume that it would not improve your organization's capabilities, relationships, or reputation and that it would not generate any funds to support your other work. Would it still be worth doing because of the social value it would create? If so, how much good could it do? Would it create enough social benefit that you would be willing to subsidize the strategy if it did not cover its costs? If so, by how much?

Mission-based business ventures are usually the easiest to evaluate on this dimension. Other strategies are likely to be harder. Nonetheless, they may have direct impact on the mission, even if that is not the main purpose of the strategy. Their direct impact could even be unintended. In making your assessment, it might be helpful to look at the impacts of similar ventures in other nonprofits. Do cafés in museums typically draw more visitors to the museum and improve the quality of their experience? Or do they distract visitors from the exhibits, reducing the impact of a museum visit? It may be useful to think in terms of both *quantity* and *quality.*

   ✔ *Quantity.* Will the strategy directly increase the volume of mission-related service you deliver? Even if it makes no money for you, is it likely to result in your serving more clients in your rehab program, saving more whales, protecting more acres of wetlands, reducing greenhouse gas emissions, getting more people to quit smoking, or whatever your mission? How much of an impact do you expect, relative to the other strategies you are considering? Providing convenient and affordable child care could help attract single parents to your computer training classes. Running an ecotourism business could help you educate a few more people about the importance of rain forests and promote your cause.

✔ *Quality.* Will the strategy improve the quality of your mission-related service? Does it inherently improve the effectiveness of your programs? Does it help you reach those who will benefit most from your services? Your job-training program might have greater success if it involves on-the-job training in a business that you are running. Selling educational toys in your science museum might increase the educational impact on children who visit the museum. Charging a fee for a service actually may screen out clients who value your service less and create healthy pressure for you to improve the value of what you deliver.

red flag   **Beware! Not all direct mission impact is positive.** Earned income strategies can have negative effects relative to your social mission, even if they cover all their costs and are neutral in their affect on your organization. For instance, an environmental nonprofit might partner with a corporation to produce a candy based on nuts harvested naturally in rain forests only to learn that the candy must be packaged in a metallic-polyester pouch that will do significant environmental harm. Charging a fee for service actually might screen out some of the truly needy clients you want to serve, at least until you can find a way to subsidize them. It is worth trying to envision how a given earned income strategy might directly reduce the quantity or quality of your mission impact. Ask someone in your group to play "devil's advocate" by pointing up any possible detrimental direct affects on your mission.

Organization: Impact on Your Current and Future Effectiveness

The indirect affects of an earned income strategy on your organization can be more powerful in the long term than the direct affects. Admittedly, the organizational impacts of any strategy are varied and virtually endless. Some are subtle. Many are open to dispute. Still, it pays to think about them systematically before rushing into something. We recommend looking at the potential impact of each strategy on three of your most valuable organizational assets: *human resources, external relationships,* and *reputation.*[34] Once again, the impact can be positive or negative.

Human resources.   An earned income strategy could strengthen or undermine your staff, board, and volunteers. The following questions should help you determine whether the impact will be positive or negative.

✔ In implementing the strategy, will your staff, volunteers, and/or board learn skills that could be valuably applied to further your mission? What are the skills and how will they be used in mission-related work?

✔ Will the strategy serve as a useful tool for engaging your board members, by allowing them to contribute their business skills and networks? Will they feel more engaged and excited as a result?

✔ Will your management team or your most valuable staff members have to dedicate significant portions of their time to revenue-generating ventures at the expense of other mission-related activities?

✔ Do you have adequate human resources to implement the strategy? If not, how will the new hires affect existing staff? Will they be paid more? Will they be respected?

✔ Will your commercial activities create value conflicts and tensions among the staff, board, or volunteers? Could this undermine the esprit de corps? Could it lead to costly turnover?

External relationships.   An earned income strategy also can affect the character of your relationships with external constituencies that are important to serving your mission now and in the future.

✔ Will this new strategy cause conflict or concern with your primary beneficiaries, clients, or members? Or could it actually improve the relationship?

✔ How will your funders react? Will they see the strategy as appropriate, even admirable? Will this effort cause them to reduce their funding? Or might they become even more supportive, knowing that their philanthropic dollars are being "leveraged" with earned income?

✔ How will this strategy affect your key relationships in the communities you serve?

✔ Will pursuing the strategy help you attract new or more highly skilled board members, volunteers, staff, donors, or other supporters? Or will it make this process harder?

Reputation.   An earned income strategy also may have very beneficial or very detrimental affects on that reputation you've worked so hard to build. Reputation affects are one of the hardest things to predict, but it will help to consider these questions:

✔ Will the strategy help your organization establish or strengthen its "brand"? How, in concrete terms, does a stronger brand help your organization? What value does it add?

✔ Will the strategy expose your organization and cause to a broader audience? Will it bring favorable publicity? How can this be used to further your mission?

✔ Is this strategy potentially controversial? Is there a significant risk of negative associations with charging the needy, the potential of a failed business venture, or association with a partner with controversial values or business practices?

✔ Will the public view your adoption of this strategy as a signal that you are a well-run, innovative, and entrepreneurial organization? Or will people question your motives, your commitment to your social cause, and/or your ability to support our mission work?

Money: Financial Impact

Most people are drawn to earned income strategies for the financial benefits. In assessing the potential financial impact, it is important to remember that a profit is not necessary for the strategy to have a positive financial impact. For instance, charging fees for the services you would have provided anyway, using philanthropic funding, has a positive financial impact, even if the fees do not cover all the costs. If they cover half the costs, this potentially frees up a comparable amount in philanthropic funding for other uses. Similarly, a mission-based business venture may be deemed worthwhile as long as it is serving the mission in a way that is more cost effective than alternatives, even if it needs to be subsidized. Partially subsidizing a business that trains homeless youth for jobs may be more cost effective than classroom-based training that is by definition fully subsidized. Of course, this logic applies only when the strategy involves delivering mission-related services. Many earned income ventures do not fall into that category. Their financial impact needs to be measured in terms of the available financial surplus the strategy generates relative to the investment required and the risk of the strategy. The following questions should help you assess financial impact.

✔ Will this strategy generate revenues specifically to cover mission-related program costs that would have otherwise required philanthropic funding? Does this free up philanthropic resources to be used where they are more needed? Does it allow you to have greater impact with the same or fewer philanthropic dollars? Contracts, fees for service, and mission-based ventures tend to fall into this category. Be sure to include the costs of collecting fees and payments in your assessment of these options. These costs have to be covered before the strategy creates a net positive financial impact.

✔ Will this strategy result in a financial surplus that can be used to increase your organization's mission impact? How much is likely to be generated? This kind of surplus is required to justify any earned income strategy that does not produce significant mission or organizational benefits. An expected loss can be justified only by direct mission impact or significant organizational benefits.

✔ What kind of financial investment on your part will be required to implement this strategy? What are the start-up costs? How long will it take before the strategy is covering all its own operating costs and capital needs? How much of a subsidy will it require until then? In assessing strategies, you need to recognize that the level of investment required can vary widely. In general, you should expect a higher return for strategies that require greater investment.

✔ Will it reduce your dependence on less reliable or renewable forms of support? Are the funds generated by this strategy more reliable or renewable than the philanthropic funding it replaces? Does it represent a healthy form of diversification? Some revenue streams are highly risky, seasonal, cyclical, or otherwise volatile. They may not be more reliable than your philanthropic funding. Riskier ventures should be required to generate higher returns to compensate for the risk.

 red flag   **It is crucial to understand the economics of your earned income strategies.** Some earned income strategies make sense only if they generate significant surpluses that can be used to further your mission in other ways. In these cases, it is important to focus on "free cash flow" rather than revenue potential or even profits. Free cash flow is the amount of cash that you can take out of the venture each year without hampering its operations. It is important to keep two fundamental rules in mind.

 1. *Revenues do not equal profits.* Nonprofits launching these types of enterprises should be careful not to use market size and expected revenue as a surrogate for profitability. Different earned income strategies can have widely different profit margins. The profit margin is the net profits divided by the revenue. In the end, you need to understand all the costs associated with a given strategy, including the cost of your valuable time, then subtract these from the revenues to determine the profits you can expect, if any. But profitability only gets you part of the way to free cash flow.

2. *Profits do not equal free cash flow!* For most business ventures, it is common for a portion of the profits to be reinvested in the business to maintain adequate working capital, upgrade equipment, or fund expansion. In some cases, especially for startup ventures, all the profits and then some have to be reinvested, resulting in a profitable business with a negative cash flow. Strange, but true! Others require very little reinvestment. Different businesses have different cash dy-

namics. To understand the real financial impact of any venture, you need to make careful and realistic cash flow projections. You can take out only what is left over after the required reinvestment.

Consider this example: Assume you are considering opening a café. It is expected to have a 5 percent profit margin and requires half of these profits (or 2.5 percent of revenues) to be reinvested in the business. Under these conditions, for every $10,000 you expect to take out of this venture, you would need to generate $400,000 in sales, which produces $20,000 in profits, half of which are reinvested in the business. You could then ask yourself if it would be easier to raise an additional $10,000 in donations than to generate $400,000 in café revenue. The situation looks quite different if the café has a 25 percent profit margin and requires only one-fifth of this (5 percent of revenues) to be reinvested in the business. You would need to generate only $50,000 in revenue to produce $12,500 in profit, of which only $2,500 has to be reinvested, leaving your $10,000 in free cash flow. This kind of café is much more appealing—at least financially.

action step   Now that you understand the three dimensions of *total mission impact*—Mission, Organization, and Money—you can apply this framework to the ideas that resulted from your brainstorming session. Using the questions in this section as a foundation and reviewing what we said about each path earlier in the chapter, you can evaluate each potential strategy. Use your judgment to assign a rating of Negative, Neutral, Low, Medium, or High in each of the three MOM areas. Any strategy that is High across the board should definitely be carried on to Step 4. Any that rank as Negative, Neutral, or Low on all dimensions should be discarded. Those in the middle of the pack can be ranked roughly by averaging the three rankings to get a summary measure of their total mission impact.

STEP 4: EVALUATE FEASIBILITY

Now it's time to put each of your ideas to the feasibility test. This stage is important for any strategy, but depending on what path your organization decides to pursue, there are clearly varying degrees of complexity. Before pursuing an earned income opportunity, you should evaluate each idea according to its *internal* and *external* feasibility.

Internal Feasibility Test

This process will help you determine whether your organization is ready to take on the new strategy. You should evaluate each idea according to the following criteria:

✔ *Organizational culture and values.* Do you anticipate any cultural conflict arising from this strategy? Does this strategy fit with your personal and organizational values and goals? Did anyone raise any objections during the brainstorming or *total mission impact* evaluations? If so, these objections should not be ignored or glossed over since they are a key indication of how effective your most important resource, your human capital, may be in pursuit of the goal.

✔ *Core competencies.* How much does the strategy build on what you already know and do well? It's not that you can't implement a strategy that doesn't build on your existing capabilities, but it is more challenging to do so!

✔ *Management capacity and time.* Do you have the time necessary to plan for and manage this endeavor? Have you identified the staff members who will be responsible for it? Are they excited about the opportunity and capable of leading the effort?

✔ *Financial stability.* Is your organization stable and financially strong? Does this strategy pose much financial risk? If so, can you afford to take it on?

✔ *Willingness to take risks.* How great are the mission, organizational, and financial risks associated with this strategy? Is your organization, including your staff and board, prepared to take on that amount of risk?

✔ *Access to necessary business skills.* Do you anticipate having trouble attracting the necessary business and management skills? Does your organization have any staff members, or at least actively involved board members, with business expertise? If not, do you have funds or other resources available to acquire or develop any necessary skills?

✔ *Length of commitment.* Does this idea represent a long-term, ongoing concern or a one-time, short-term opportunity? If it's long term, is your organization truly committed to developing a new funding strategy for the long term? If it's short term, is it worth the time and effort that will be necessary to generate a one-time payoff?

External Feasibility Test

In evaluating the external market, you should begin by making sure you understand the industry in which each strategy would be operating, including a *quick* survey of recent trends. Is the industry growing, declining, or consolidating? It is generally easier to enter a growing market. You may not have to take business away from competitors. Is the pace of change and technological advancement fast or slow? Changes in technology can make it easier for you to get in. Are there any regulations, or any indications that there may be any on the horizon? Can you meet them? How will they affect your competitors? Once you have a basic understanding of the industry, you should focus a little more in depth on the four Cs: *customers, competitors, capital,* and *community.*

✔ *Customers.* Who is your target market? How easily can you determine their needs and wants? Are they an audience you already serve or a new one altogether? How would you reach them with your product or service? How many paying customers will you need? How hard will it be to get them?

✔ *Competitors.* Who are they? Are they nonprofit or for-profit or both? Are they local, regional, or national players? Are they all competing for the same target market, or are they fairly differentiated? How profitable are they? How will they react to you coming into this business? How will you stack up against them?

✔ *Capital.* What are your capital needs? Who are the likely providers? Would you be looking to raise a substantial, a moderate, or a small amount of funds? When would you need the financing? How much risk would you be asking investors to assume? Will pursuing this strategy pose a risk to any of your existing philanthropic funds?

✔ *Community.* How will the strategy be received by the community your nonprofit serves? Is this idea politically viable?

action step As with the total mission impact exercise, using the internal and external feasibility tests, you should be able to rate each strategy as Low, Medium, or High according to its feasibility. It may be easiest to give each strategy both an internal and an external score and then average the two to get the total feasibility rating. Include only those strategies that survived the total mission impact test. Once you have these assessments for all of the strategies still under consideration, you should pick out those that are most promising, considering both factors, their potential for total mission impact and their feasibility.

STEP 5: DEVELOP AN ACTION PLAN

At this point, you should know which ideas are the most feasible and potentially valuable for serving your mission. If you have more than one strategy that is promising on both dimensions, you need to be careful not to overextend your organization by trying multiple new ventures at once. Launching two strategies at the same time can be very difficult. New strategies always have an element of unpredictability. If both of them run into problems at the same time, you could find yourself in deep trouble.

One factor you might consider in selecting which one to try first is whether you are facing a limited "window of opportunity" with regard to either strategy. That is, will the opportunity go away if you don't act on it relatively quickly? If one of your most promising ideas also has a short window of opportunity, you should consider pursuing it before it evaporates. You can always go back to the other strategies.

Regardless of which strategy you select, here are some guidelines as you move into the planning and actions stage.

✔ *Focus your planning and analysis where it counts.* All new strategies have elements of uncertainty. It is tempting to analyze everything, but this is often a waste of time. Columbia Business School professor Amar Bhide argues that successful entrepreneurs tend to be "parsimonious" planners and analysts. They don't overdo it. They focus their research on getting information they can act on. They do not try to work out all the details. He says, "Entrepreneurs should concentrate instead on issues that they can reasonably expect to resolve through analysis and that determine whether and how they will proceed. Resolving a few big questions—understanding what things *must* go right and anticipating the venture-destroying pitfalls, for instance—is more important than investigating many nice-to-know matters."[35]

✔ *Integrate action and analysis.* Professor Bhide also advocates integrating action and analysis. You need to do some analysis; you also should develop an action plan; but you must not get hung up on these steps. Market research only goes so far, as does your internal assessment of your ability to execute a particular strategy. Some uncertainties will be resolved only by trying your strategy and fixing it along the way. You make assumptions and test them. Your action plan can reflect this by including milestones at which you will have tested key assumptions. You can do this by following three simple guidelines:

1. Define your performance targets for the first three years in terms of mission, organizational, and financial goals.

2. Make a list of the things that will have to be accomplished in order to achieve these goals, with a time line for completing each activity.

3. Identify the most critical assumptions you have made about your strategy. For each one, establish a milestone on your calendar for when you will revisit each assumption and test it in light of your actual experience.[36]

✔ *Be smart about how you use consultants.* You can get help, but do not turn the planning over to a consultant or, worse yet, to an intern from a local business school. You need to own and understand this strategy. You may need the most help with execution. Take it from one of the leading consultants in the field. In reflecting on his experience consulting with numerous nonprofits on revenue strategies, Billy Shore, chairman of the Community Wealth Ventures consulting firm and founder of Share Our Strength, says, "The biggest issue we've found is one of execution. Most nonprofits thought that they were engaging us to write them a business plan, and in fact, that is what we thought we were selling when we started. And then we realized that they needed to write the plan. . . . Moreover, the place where they need us most is not in the development of ideas but in the actual execution—how do they launch it? How do they capitalize it? How do they meld it into their organization? What kind of capacities do they need?"[37]

✔ *Manage your risks constantly.* In addition to testing your key assumptions along the way, you should pay close attention to managing your risks as your strategy unfolds. Testing your assumptions and assessing your progress against milestones will help you mitigate risk. But you also should protect yourself by planning for the unknown. Do not make large, irreversible investments until you have some confidence in your ability to execute this strategy successfully. Envision scenarios different from the ones for which you've planned and anticipate the effect of those scenarios on your approach, trying to avoid those with substantial downside risks. Create contingency plans for dealing with the unexpected.[38]

✔ *Be flexible and open to changing course.* Once you've started down the path of developing an earned income strategy, don't ever fall into the trap of feeling that you've committed to that course of action and can't turn back. You should be clear with regard to exactly how much time and money you're willing to lose before deciding whether to radically change plans. The process should be a test of your organization's commitment and ability to actually do what it's trying to do, and if you are failing the test, don't be too proud to admit it! Earned income strategies are challenging and not right for every organization or at every point in an organization's life. Some persistence is required as you try to make this work. Be open to changing course. And don't be afraid to read the writing on the wall and just say "Enough!"

✔ *Keep your eyes on the prize—the creation of social value.* Throughout all of this, as you plan, analyze, act, assess, and try to manage your risks, make sure that you stay focused on your mission and goals. Change will happen—no strategy ever develops exactly as planned. But each time you see the need to alter your plan or revise your assumptions, consider the impact of these modifications on your ultimate mission and creation of social value. This is all about mission impact—direct or indirect. Don't lose sight of that!

SUMMARY

This chapter has provided tools and frameworks to help you develop a viable earned income strategy for your organization. While creating some form of earned income may not be the best option for every nonprofit, all social entrepreneurs should at least consider the possibility when developing a comprehensive strategy for achieving, and funding their social mission. In doing so, you should remember the following:

- ✔ An earned income strategy is not primarily a financial strategy. It is first and foremost about improving your mission performance, not solving a financial crisis, diversifying your revenue base, or pursuing sustainability.

- ✔ There is a wide range of options for pursuing earned income: getting paid for what you already do, launching a new business venture, and building revenue relationships.

- ✔ Mission drift and philosophical objections are major risks common to most earned income strategies, and you should address these issues up front and manage them closely from the start.

- ✔ When brainstorming ideas, involve as many stakeholders as possible, encouraging them to think creatively and broadly. Then evaluate the best ideas in terms of total mission impact and feasibility to identify the most viable opportunities for your organization.

- ✔ Developing a viable action plan is just as important as identifying an attractive opportunity, and often it is more challenging. Be sure to analyze parsimoniously, identify and test your assumptions, manage your risks, and stay focused on your mission and goals.

- ✔ Earned income is not for everyone, and it is just as important to get to no as to get to yes. If you've read this chapter and determined none of the three paths is right for you, then you've done yourself and your organization a great service.

Good luck!

Notes

1. Lester M. Salamon, *Holding the Center: America's Nonprofit Sector at a Crossroads,* (New York: Cummings Foundation, 1997).
2. Brenda Zimmerman and Raymond Dart, *Charities Doing Commercial Ventures: Societal and Organizational Implications* (Ontario: Trillium Foundation, 1998), p. 13.
3. Ibid., pp. 24–26.
4. Peter C. Brinckerhoff, *Social Entrepreneurship: The Art of Mission-Based Venture Development* (New York: John Wiley & Sons, 2000), p. 16.
5. *www.cityyear.org.*

6. Edward Skloot, *The Nonprofit Entrepreneur: Creating Ventures to Earn Income* (New York: The Foundation Center, 1988), p. 150.

7. *www.sierraclub.org/outings/national.*

8. *www.benetech.org/projects/bookshare.shtml.*

9. *www.womenink.org/about.htm.*

10. Amar Bhide, "How Entrepreneurs Craft Strategies That Work," *Harvard Business Review,* March–April 1994.

11. Amar Bhide, "Hustle as Strategy," *Harvard Business Review,* September–October 1986.

12. A number of Roberts Enterprise Development Fund documents address this example and others. Visit *www.redf.org.*

13. Bruce Hopkins, "Social Entrepreneurs' Brief Guide to the Law," Appendix A in *Enterprising Nonprofits: A Toolkit for Social Entrepreneurs,* ed. J. Gregory Dees, Jed Emerson, and Peter Economy (New York: John Wiley & Sons, 2001).

14. Jed Emerson, "Understanding Risk: The Social Entrepreneur and Risk Management," Chapter 6 in ibid.

15. Jeffry A. Timmons, *New Venture Creation: Entrepreneurship for the 21st Century,* 4th ed. (Boston: Irwin McGraw-Hill, 1994), p. 87.

16. For some guidance on market research, see Kristin Majeska, "Understanding and Attracting Your 'Customers,' " Chapter 8 in *Enterprising Nonprofits.*

17. Edward Skloot, "Enterprise and Commerce in Nonprofit Organizations," in Walter W. Powell, *The Nonprofit Sector: A Research Handbook* (New Haven,CT: Yale University Press, 1987), p. 384.

18. J. Gregory Dees, "Mobilizing Resources," Chapter 4 in *Enterprising Nonprofits.*

19. For more extensive, practical discussions of productive, strategic alliances between for-profits and nonprofits, see James Austin, *The Collaboration Challenge* (San Francisco: Jossey-Bass, 2000), and Shirley Sagawa and Eli Segal, *Common Interest, Common Good: Creating Value through Business and Social Sector Partnerships* (Boston: Harvard Business School Press, 2000).

20. Community Wealth Ventures, "Creating Community Wealth," *www.communitywealth.org.*

21. "Ben & Jerry's Pops New Flavor for KaBoom!" *IEG Sponsorship Report,* August 21, 2000, *www.kaboom.org.*

22. Austin, *The Collaboration Challenge,* p. 27.

23. Dennis Young, "Corporate Partnerships: A Guide for the Nonprofit Manager," *www.nationalcne.org.*

24. Sagawa and Segal, *Common Interest, Common Good,* p. 180.

25. Alan R. Andreasen, "Profits for Nonprofits: Find a Corporate Partner," *Harvard Business Review,* November–December 1996.

26. Sarah Klein, "AMA Sunbeam Suit Settled," *amednews.com,* August 17, 1998.

27. Andreasen, "Profits for Nonprofits," p. 6.

28. Ibid., p. 7.

29. Inspired by Sagawa and Segal, *Common Interest, Common Good;* Austin, *The Collaboration Challenge;* and Rosabeth Moss Kanter, "Collaborative Advantage: The Art of Successful Alliances," *Harvard Business Review,* July–August 1994.

30. See Rob Johnston, "Defining Your Mission," Chapter 2 in *Enterprising Nonprofits.*

31. This list is inspired by Zimmerman and Dart, *Charities Doing Commercial Ventures,* and by V. Kasturi Rangan, Sohel Karim, and Sheryl K. Sandberg, "Do Better at Doing Good," *Harvard Business Review,* May–June 1996.

32. Amar Bhide, "How Entrepreneurs Craft Strategies That Work," *Harvard Business Review,* March–April 1994, survey of 100 founders of the 1989 Inc. "500" fastest-growing private companies.

33. Andreasen, "Profits for Nonprofits."
34. For a discussion of emergent outcomes of earned income strategy, including the categories of reputation and relationships, see Zimmerman and Dart, "Charities Doing Commercial Ventures."
35. Bhide, "How Entrepreneurs Craft Strategies That Work."
36. For a more thorough discussion with expanded steps for planning your strategy, see Dees, "Mobilizing Resources," in *Enterprising Nonprofits,* pp. 78–81. This section, as well as the section in Dees's chapter, was inspired by McGrath and MacMillan's "Discovery-Driven Planning," *Harvard Business Review,* July–August 1995.
37. Phone interview with Bill Shore, July 2001.
38. See Jed Emerson, "Understanding Risk: The Social Entrepreneur and Risk Management," Chapter 6 in *Enterprising Nonprofits.*

Chapter 10

THE QUESTION OF SCALE: FINDING AN APPROPRIATE STRATEGY FOR BUILDING ON YOUR SUCCESS

Melissa A. Taylor, PhD candidate, Martin School of Public Policy and Administration, University of Kentucky;
J. Gregory Dees, Adjunct Professor of Social Entrepreneurship and Nonprofit Management, The Fuqua School of Business, Duke University;
Jed Emerson, Senior Fellow, William and Flora Hewlett Foundation, and lecturer, Center for Social Innovation, Graduate School of Business, Stanford University

IN THIS CHAPTER

The seductive appeal of going to scale

Why scaling up is not for everyone

"Scaling deep" rather than scaling up

Different pathways for spreading the benefits of success

Guidelines for deciding whether and how to scale up

You've started your new social venture, made your vision a reality, and exceeded your goals. It's been hard work, but you're gaining due recognition. Stories are showing up in local, perhaps even national, media. Letters of congratulations are coming in from the mayor, the governor, maybe even the White House. Your funders give you a prominent spot in their annual report. How do you build on this success?

To some the next step is obvious. Your organization should "go to scale," taking your programs into other communities. But scaling up is not for everyone! It's certainly not the only way to build on your success, and the personal challenges that go along with scaling up are not within the scope of this chapter. This chapter will, however, help you understand the benefits and risks of scaling up, introduce you to alternative strategies for building on your success, and guide you in making smart decisions about the right strategy to pursue.

THE SEDUCTIVE APPEAL OF GOING TO SCALE

core concept   *"Scaling up"* or *"going to scale"* means creating new service sites in other geographic locations that operate under a common name, use common approaches, and are either branches of the same parent organization or very closely tied affiliates of a parent organization.

Going to scale is an enormous undertaking and may not be the right path for you. But challenging as it is, scaling up has potential benefits that can't be ignored.

SUCCESS CREATES PRESSURES AND TEMPTATIONS TO SCALE UP

"Grow or Die!" is a common slogan in business. It reflects the belief that bigger firms are stronger competitors. They drive out or buy up the small firms. Of course, there are exceptions to this rule—small, "lifestyle" businesses such as lawn cutting services, art galleries, or hair styling salons. It's possible to stay small and survive in business, but think of all the local drugstores, cafés, and banks that have been replaced by chains. Competition hasn't had the same effect in the social sector. Even so, successful social entrepreneurs face their own pressures to scale up.

✔ *Moral imperative.* If you offer a socially beneficial service, you're likely to feel an obligation to make that service available to as many people as possible. Whether you teach literacy or clean up the environment, if you've found a better way, you'll feel a duty to share it.

✔ *Demand-side pressures.* Even without the moral imperative, once word gets out, people may ask you to bring your program into their community. It's hard to ignore the requests from communities for your help.

✔ *Organizational needs.* If your organization doesn't grow in some way, it may be difficult to provide the necessary challenges and career advancement opportunities to keep good people. Creating a national organization opens up opportunities for career development.

✔ *Funder expectations.* Remember when you wrote that grant proposal saying that your program would become a "national model"?

Your funders may remember too! If others aren't starting up similar ventures on their own, your funders may expect you to do it.

✔ *Personal ambition.* You've had success locally, so why not conquer new territory? Although this may sound like hubris and egotism, it can be a good thing. In fact, two leading business writers have called ambition "the root of all achievement."[1]

ACHIEVING SCALE DOES HAVE POTENTIAL BENEFITS

Behind these pressures are some real benefits of scaling up. Many of these come once a significant scale is achieved, not during the process of scaling. If you aren't successful in addressing the challenges of scaling up, your organization may not be around to see the benefits.

The most obvious benefit is *social impact:* reaching and serving more people. This is the main rationale for scaling. However, advocates also point out that scale can increase an organization's chances of survival, improve its efficiency, and enhance its effectiveness.

Increased Chances of Survival

According to organizational theorists, larger organizations have better chances of survival because they tend to be more resilient.[2] Scaling up helps you to:

✔ *Spread the risk.* If you stay local, your support may be heavily dependent on your local economy. A downturn may have the tragic effect of increasing the need for your services while simultaneously reducing your financial base. A multisite organization has more diverse sources. Setbacks in one region can be offset by stronger results in another, and the national office might provide some support to local affiliates in tough times.

✔ *Create more stakeholders.* Larger organizations create a network of people and institutions that are dependent on them. Because so many people rely on them, funders, including the government, are less likely to let large organizations die.

Improved Efficiency

Scale also could increase your efficiency—your cost per person served—provided that the savings from scale exceed the costs of a central office. Scaling up makes it possible for you to:

core concept

✔ *Capture "economies of scale."* The most straightforward economies of scale come from spreading shared costs over more operating units. In a scaled-up organization, many costs—accounting systems, fund-raising materials, marketing programs, human resource systems, and new program development—can be shared across different sites. Local sites don't have to reinvent the wheel. Economies of scale also can come from increased purchasing power—the ability to get discounts by buying in bulk.

core concept ✔ *Enjoy "experience curve" effects.* Cumulative experience usually leads to productivity improvements. The organization learns how to do its work more efficiently. Fewer mistakes are made. Systems are put in place to guide new employees. As organizations move along the *experience curve* (also called the "learning curve"), per unit costs decrease. Scaling up helps your organization build its cumulative experience faster.

red flag **Economies of scale are typically less significant in service organizations** than in manufacturing firms. This is because the largest cost item is typically the direct labor of providing the service, which can't be shared across units or purchased in bulk. However, cost structures vary. Yours may allow for economies of scale. Although nursing homes, day care centers, and legal aid societies offer few economies of scale, educational institutions, research centers, and business associations offer more.[3]

Enhanced Effectiveness

Scale also can improve your effectiveness—your ability to have the desired social impact. Scaling up makes it possible for you to:

✔ *Promote innovation through local experimentation.* If local operations are given autonomy and encouraged to experiment, a multisite organization can be more innovative than a single site. For instance, a Girl Scout troop might try out a new leadership training program. If it works, the program can be shared with troops around the country. Sharing new practices across units can be a powerful vehicle for organizational learning.

✔ *Use specialization to develop greater expertise.* As organizations grow, they develop a division of labor. Specialization leads to greater expertise in important functional and program areas. For instance, a larger organization can hire top-notch fund raisers, marketers, and other functional experts, leaving program staff free to focus their energies on delivering services. This allows everyone to do what they do best.

✔ *Capitalize on name recognition.* By scaling up, a nonprofit can create a recognized "brand" name. Establishing a strong, trusted brand in multiple locations or on a national level can improve your effectiveness by helping you to:

- *Reach the people who benefit most from your services.* When an organization has an identifiable brand name, potential clients have a better idea of what to expect. This reduces the amount of time they must spend searching for the right service provider and increases the number of appropriate clients walking in your doors. Trusted brands also convey a sense of reliability. Incentives to assure consistent quality are high because a nationally recognized organization is putting its name on the line.

- *Attract resources and find partners.* Brand name organizations are more visible and appear more stable and legitimate. These features are attractive to potential employees, volunteers, and funders. Having multiple sites also may make your organization more attractive to potential partners who otherwise would not be interested, including other nonprofits with national objectives, federal agencies, and large corporations.

- *Serve as an advocate on relevant issues.* A scaled-up organization with a trusted brand name also exercises more power in the public policy process. When it comes to advocacy efforts, there is strength in numbers and in visibility. A national organization with many affiliates and a recognized brand is likely to wield more weight than a small local organization when its leaders speak out on public issues related to its mission.

✔ *Find systemic solutions to systemic problems.* Many social problems are systemic and require a systemic solution. Environmental problems are the prime example of this. Pollution in one area tends to affect everyone who is downwind or downstream. Other social problems, such as youth violence, also may have spillover effects and systemic causes that cannot be addressed simply by focusing on one location. Working in a single neighborhood may not solve the problem if youth violence is affected by outside factors. In such cases, a scaled-up organization may have a better chance of having a lasting impact.

action step

ASSESSING YOUR POTENTIAL BENEFITS FROM SCALING UP

Whether you actually can achieve these benefits depends in part on the character of your organization. Before launching any effort to scale up, you should conduct an inventory of whether and how you might achieve the potential benefits just outlined. This inventory will help guide your scaling strategy. Ask yourself these questions:

✔ Can you identify specific economies that could be achieved if you scaled up?

✔ Do you have systems to capture lessons learned so that you can enjoy experience curve effects?

✔ Can you think of specific ways that establishing a brand name in different communities could be helpful to your clients or your organization as a whole?

✔ Has being local limited your access to important resources or prevented you from forming productive partnerships?

✔ Is your organization a provider of government-funded social services? Would you benefit from being a large-scale organization in terms of negotiating for these contracts?

✔ Does your organization address a systemic problem that cannot be handled sufficiently on a local basis?

If you answered no or I don't know to more than a few of these questions, then scaling up may not be right for you. Read the sections on scaling deep (pp. 242–245) and on different pathways for spreading the benefits of your success (pp. 245–250) to find some alternatives to consider. If you answered yes to many of these questions, read the next section carefully. It explains the costs and risks of scaling up that may offset these benefits.

WHY SCALING UP IS NOT FOR EVERYONE

Going to scale isn't the only way to build on success and may not be the best avenue for your organization. Scale has costs and risks. In some cases small is beautiful.[4] Consider how U.S. public housing design has changed over the years. In the late 1950s and early 1960s, the effort was made to design huge complexes. These eventually became poverty warehouses and centers for crime and despair. By contrast, today's designers of affordable housing are literally blowing up the structures of the 1960s and replacing them with smaller units of higher quality.

SCALING UP HAS SIGNIFICANT COSTS AND RISKS

There's a downside to everything. And going to scale is no exception.

✔ *Scaling up can pull your organization away from its original mission, vision, and values.* Many social ventures are founded with an explicit mission that may specify a geographic focus. In scaling up, an organization can change and evolve into something far removed from the original vision. For social ventures, any diversion of resources, including management time, away from the original mission and community may create a serious resistance from the organization's core stakeholders—those who helped build the organization.

✔ *Scaling up strains scarce financial and human resources.* You may get economic benefits once scale is achieved, but getting there is costly. You have to build the infrastructure to perform the functions of a central office, such as marketing and site selection, development of systems for coordinating and communicating across sites, and provision of technical assistance to new sites. Start-up costs may not be covered by new funds raised for each new site. It's easy to underestimate the cash needed for expansion, and a cash shortage could put a significant strain on your organization. Perhaps more important, as the organization's leader, your time is a valuable and scarce resource, as is the time and attention of others who know how your venture or program works. Your team may already be stretched to its limits. If team members get stretched too thin, morale and productivity are likely to decline and your organization's performance, locally and in the new sites, could suffer significantly.

✔ *It's easy and dangerous to overestimate both the need and the demand for your programs.* It's only natural, especially when you are getting positive results locally, to assume that the same need exists in other communities and that you could serve it better than current providers do. The slightest expression of interest confirms this. Scaling into new communities without objective confirmation of an unmet or poorly met need can be a serious waste of your resources and harmful to other providers addressing the same needs in that community. Even if you are sure about the need, you also must assess demand—the willingness of key stakeholders, such as local funders, potential clients, partners, and public officials, in the new community to support your entry. Without adequate demand, you won't be able to create viable new sites.

✔ *Effectiveness can suffer if the focus is on growth, not quality.* By scaling up you can serve more people, but you run the risk of serving them with lower quality. The focus on growth can draw attention away from effective service delivery. Attempts to control quality through regimentation can leave clients feeling like they are being "processed."

✔ *Your reputation could be harmed by poor performance at a renegade site.* Poor performance in one new site can affect the reputation of the whole organization. As a result, quality control is a major management issue. In the social sector, because the desire for local autonomy is so strong, control is even harder to exercise. It can take years to build the value of a brand name and only a very short time to undermine it.

✔ *Concerns about control can lead to excess bureaucracy and stifle innovation.* Larger organizations tend to be more bureaucratic and resistant to change. Employees may become more concerned with organizational maintenance than with social change or justice. The tendency toward stagnation can be exacerbated when you're trying to coordinate multiple locations of an organization. Quality control rules can limit local experimentation.

✔ *Scaling up can lead to an inappropriate "cookie cutter" approach.* Solutions to social problems often must take into account the distinctive aspects of each community, including demographics, culture, economic climate, and politics. An approach that has worked in your home community may not be applicable in another community. One of the greatest challenges of scaling up is deciding how much local tailoring to allow while maintaining consistency and quality. It's easy to err on the side of too much standardization.

action step   Later we will take you through a more detailed process for deciding whether and how to scale up. As a prelude, you may want to answer a few quick questions.

- Is your current mission consistent with the idea of scaling up into new communities?

- Do you feel in your gut that your organization has the resources or could mobilize what it needs to scale up?

- Have you identified funders who are strong prospects to finance the infrastructure and skill building needed for scaling up?

- Can you present any solid evidence that other communities have sufficient need and demand for your organization's services?

- Do you know who your "competition" is in these communities? Can you say how your approach would be better than what they are doing?

- Is your organization ready to manage the tensions inherent in scaling up, balancing growth and quality, consistency and local autonomy, control versus innovation?

If you answered no or I'm not sure to one or more of these questions, you may not be ready to scale up. You should give serious thought to the alternatives to scaling up that are discussed in the next two sections.

"Scaling Deep" Rather Than Scaling Up

"Scaling deep" is about being the "best of breed" in your field. It requires building your internal capacity to increase social value, looking for the best practices and lessons learned by others in your field, and adapting those lessons to your community's needs. It's also about setting an example that can help others.

core concept   *"Scaling deep"* means focusing your energies and resources on achieving greater impact in your home community by doing one or more of the following: improving the quality of your services, achieving greater penetration of your target client population, finding new ways to serve your clients, extending your services to new client groups, developing innovative financial and management approaches, and serving as an example for others in your field.

Scaling Deep Can Have Some Powerful Benefits

Scaling deep has several potential benefits for your organization. It allows you to:

✔ *Build on your intangible assets.* If you're successful in your local community, you will have developed some intangible assets, namely your knowledge of this community and a local reputation. Scaling up doesn't take advantage of these. By contrast, scaling deep can help you create greater social impact, reaffirm your connection to your home community, and concentrate on what you know best.

✔ *Penetrate your home market.* Of all the people in your home community that you could serve, what percentage are you serving? Probably a very small percentage. Don't be tempted to scale up because of the attractions of becoming a national player before you've significantly penetrated your home community. By directing attention elsewhere, you're missing exciting challenges and opportunities in your own backyard. The lessons you learn from increasing your local market penetration could benefit not only your community but also organizations trying to do the same in other communities.

✔ *Improve your program's quality and effectiveness.* Of equal if not greater importance than the question of how *many* people you serve is the question of the *quality* of your service delivery. Are you the "gold standard" in your sector? Could you provide better, higher-quality services to your clients? Scaling deep allows you to focus your energies and resources on becoming the best that you can be.

✔ *Strengthen your operating systems and culture to improve effectiveness.* Even successful local programs often don't have the management systems or culture in place to make sure their organization runs as effectively as it could. Do your staff members have the management information systems and resources they need to maximize the value of their life's work? Are they empowered in their efforts? How is your organization striving for continual improvement? Remember that

Case in point. Focus: HOPE began its efforts to address poverty in Detroit as a food program for mothers and children. Instead of taking its successful food program to other communities, Focus: HOPE expanded its services in Detroit. The food program was expanded to the elderly, but it became clear that providing food was not enough. Focus: HOPE shifted into job training and education. The organization added day care, machinist training, an engineering degree program, and manufacturing operations serving the auto industry. Although its services have expanded over the years, the organization has remained focused on issues of poverty in its home community. It has served as a beacon and training ground for people who want to do similar things in their communities. Focus: HOPE provides a strong example for others because it scaled deeper into its community.[5]

happier employees working with supportive systems are more productive and creative.

✔ *Use technology to gain some of the benefits of scale.* You don't need to forgo all the benefits of scaling up if you choose to scale deep. Today, through websites, online discussion groups, and listserves, local social entrepreneurs in different communities can work together, sharing their resources and knowledge. Local organizations can benefit from the experiences and innovations of peers operating in other communities. In addition, application service providers (ASPs) make it possible for small nonprofits to access operating infrastructure formerly available only to large organizations. By purchasing such services on a subscription basis, nonprofit organizations can access accounting, planning, and client tracking systems. ASPs make it possible for nonprofit organizations of any size to maximize communication and operating system capacity. In effect, they can enjoy economies of scale.

Scaling Deep Does Have Its Own Risks and Costs

Scaling deep isn't immune from costs and risks.

✔ *Organizations can become too focused on internal affairs.* Scaling deep involves organizational soul searching and self-improvement. However, organizations going down this road should be careful not to become too focused on improving management and financial systems at the expense of serving their clients. Investments in infrastructure have to be justified by the social returns they generate. It's not about having all the latest technology or the fanciest systems. It's about the social value you're trying to create.

✔ *Harder-to-reach clients can be more costly and harder to serve.* Increasing your market penetration may be very costly. You can reach a point of diminishing, even negative, returns. Some clients may not want to be "served" by you. While extending your services to new client groups, you can overextend your organization. If you currently serve first-time juvenile delinquents, be aware that services for repeat offenders may not be the same and could be a lot more expensive.

✔ *Providing new services to existing clients is likely to require new resources and skills.* Providing counseling services to abused women is one thing. Providing job training is another. Just because you understand the needs of your clients doesn't mean you automatically know how to serve them. Building the skills to offer new kinds of services can be costly and may not be wise if it puts you in competition with others in your community who could do it better.

action step When considering scaling deep, explore the following questions with your board, staff, and community members. They should help you identify promising opportunities for scaling deep.

- How can you improve your current program offerings for existing clients?
- Should you consider offering new services to existing clients?
- How can you cost-effectively get more people to use the services you currently offer?
- Should you consider serving some different client groups? What would you offer them and how would you reach them?
- Is your mission consistent with these forms of local expansion?
- Does some portion of your programs duplicate those of other organizations in the area?
- Could you assist another organization in building a program that isn't your strong point?
- Do you have the systems in place for the continual improvement of your organization?
- Are you adequately networked with your peers in other communities?

DIFFERENT PATHWAYS FOR SPREADING THE BENEFITS OF SUCCESS

"Scaling deep" may not satisfy your sense of moral imperative to spread the benefits of your success. You can serve as a role model for others, but what if they don't really understand how your organization works? Poor imitation may be worse than no imitation at all. You may need to be more proactive, but scaling up may be too much for you. You might consider some different paths for spreading the knowledge you've developed. We discuss three such paths, arranged in order of the degree of central control, starting with the least demanding.

PATH 1: DISSEMINATE YOUR OPERATING PRINCIPLES AND LESSONS

You can spread the word and serve as a catalyst for others. The core of dissemination involves actively sharing stories, lessons, principles, methods, programs, and ideas with others. Beyond information sharing, you also can offer guidance through handbooks or technical assistance to interested organizations.

Key Success Factors

Although dissemination is the least demanding form of spreading your innovation, doing it effectively requires you to:

✔ *Conduct a critical self-assessment.* Dissemination can't be about blowing your own horn or offering unrealistic panaceas to audiences eager for quick fixes. It must be built on an honest and critical assessment of your success. The first step is to build your own knowledge about what you've done, what has worked, what hasn't, and what accounts for your success. In order to assure objectivity, it may be helpful to bring in an outside consultant.

✔ *Frame a moving yet candid message.* While spreading your ideas, don't simplify your prescriptions and exaggerate the benefits.

Case in point. The Roberts Enterprise Development Fund (REDF) funds nonprofits that create businesses to train and employ individuals from disadvantaged backgrounds. In 1996, they published *New Social Entrepreneurs: The Success, Challenge and Lessons of Non-Profit Enterprise Creation.* This book offered a candid assessment, which inspired and informed numerous nonprofits (both in the U.S. and abroad) considering business enterprise creation. REDF has continued to widely share information about its lessons, successes, and failures through its website *(www.redf.org).*

Move people to action but prepare them for the work ahead. In some cases, you need to help people see that your ideas may not be appropriate for them.

✔ *Develop or acquire strong communication skills.* Dissemination requires strong writing, speaking, and probably Web-design skills. If you don't have these skills, develop them or find someone who has—a ghostwriter, designated spokesperson, or Web designer.

✔ *Use effective, targeted communication channels.* Dissemination is more effective if it reaches the right people through credible, high-impact channels. Define your target audience—the people most likely to use the information you can provide. Then select the most effective vehicles and venues for reaching them or making it easy for them to reach you.

✔ *Special variation: Disseminate now and unify later.* It's not uncommon for social entrepreneurs to spread their ideas informally through dissemination, then formalize relations with interested organizations at a later date. Dissemination serves as a market test of the concept. If it's replicated in enough places, it may make sense to consolidate these efforts by creating a national umbrella organization. This way the infrastructure of a national organization isn't built until there are enough affiliates to justify it.

✔ *Powerful combination: Scaling deep and disseminating the results.* Those who choose to spend their energy and resources on scaling deep could combine this effort with a dissemination strategy to ensure that others learn from their valuable experience. It addresses the moral imperative and allows you to stay focused. In fact, our case in point, REDF, has effectively used this combination.

PATH 2: CREATE A LEARNING NETWORK WITH SHARED PRINCIPLES AND GOALS

The main drawback of dissemination is that often you have little knowledge about who is using your ideas and how. Unless they seek you out, they learn from you without returning the favor. To avoid this problem, consider creating a learning network. This is especially appropriate when you feel more confident about the applicability of your operating principles than you do about the transferability of actual practices. These networks spread the principles and provide a conduit for sharing lessons learned as the principles are applied in different locations. This method allows for experimentation and local tailoring. Managing a network is more demanding than dissemination, but it has the potential for much greater returns.[6]

> **Case in point.** The Coalition of Essential Schools (CES) is a learning network built around 10 "Common Principles" for restructuring education and redesigning schools.[7] CES was established in 1984 and now includes over 1,000 schools, 24 regional centers, and a national office. Through a newsletter, a website, an annual conference, and the regional centers, CES helps member schools implement the Common Principles and share ideas and lessons with each other.

Key Success Factors

Creating a network is different from running a successful program. It requires you to:

✔ *Articulate the core principles and goals on which the network is based.* The core principles and goals are the glue that holds the network together and provides its reason for existence. As the organization's founder, you may want to articulate the principles and let people select in or out depending on whether they agree. If you're less confident about your ability to get the principles just right, it may be wise to allow the founding network members to formulate the network's principle as they search for common ground.

✔ *Recruit the right members for the network.* The quality of a network and its effectiveness is determined in large part by members' skills and commitment. You should consider having requirements for joining the network or at least for remaining a member in good standing. You want organizations with the will and ability to implement the core principles in creative and effective ways. In addition, you want members who will share their experience with others and are open to learning.

✔ *Establish pathways of communication and information dissemination.* The primary value added by a network is its ability to facilitate communication and learning. You need mechanisms that make communication easier and more effective. The ideal network would be structured to help members find patterns, recognize when the lessons of others apply to them, and engage in a constructive, rigorous dialogue. Members of the network should be able to capture some of the benefits of each other's learning curves and innovations.

✔ *Create a viable membership agreement and governance structure.* Organizations need a reason to join and remain involved. What should members expect out of the organization, and what should they be required to give? Who will control the network, and how will they be selected? How much say will members have? Should you offer different types of membership to reflect different levels of commitment?

✔ *Find a reliable funding mechanism.* The initial organizing effort might be supported by grants, but eventually the issue of membership fees and other revenue sources will arise. Membership fees are an attractive option because they put the network to the market test; willingness to pay is a good sign of value creation.

PATH 3: PACKAGE AND SELL YOUR PROGRAM(S)

If what you really want to replicate is a program, rather than just principles, you may need more than a network. If it's only a program and not an entire organizational structure, you don't need to go to scale. Innovative programs can be packaged and sold to existing organizations in other communities. Those organizations generally are in a better position than you to assess the need and demand for your program in their communities. They also should have a better sense of how the program needs to be adapted in their communities.

Key Success Factors

This approach to replication requires new skills and capital, but it's not as demanding as scaling up. Packaging and selling your programs requires you to:

✔ *Create a usable package, including follow-up customer service.* It's one thing to operate a successful program and another to document how you do it in a way that is transferable to other locations. Determine what's essential, what can be changed, and the level of follow-up support you're willing to give. You need to build or attract skills in documentation, product design, and training to support successful transmission of the program.

✔ *Pick the right local partners.* The understanding, commitment, skills, and reputation of local partners can make or break you. You have to develop or acquire skills in marketing, partner assessment,

---

Case in point. Success for All is an organization based primarily on an innovative curriculum for developing early reading skills. The founders could have used this innovation to start a chain of charter elementary schools or independent learning centers. Instead, they packaged their curriculum, teaching methods, and support services as a bundle to be sold to existing schools. In this case, the rationale wasn't to permit local adaptation but to reach the most students in the most cost-effective way. Since Success for All's founding in 1987, it has grown at a rapid pace, reaching some 1,800 elementary schools by the 2001–2002 academic year.[8]

and partner selection. The commitment of a potential partner can be tested in a number of ways. Success for All, for instance, requires that at least 80 percent of the teachers in a potential partner school vote in favor of adopting the curriculum.

✔ *Structure a mutually beneficial contract.* Decide the terms on which you will share your programs with other organizations. Elements include pricing, use of brand name, quality control procedures, and conditions of termination by either side. Product design, economics, and the needs of your partners should drive the design of the agreement. A lawyer experienced in licensing or franchising can be helpful in raising important issues and offering different options for achieving your objectives.

✔ *Develop systems and skills for quality control and support.* Once you have a contract specifying how you will service and audit those who use your programs, you need to create the systems and structures to support this activity. You also need staff members who have the skills to provide assistance or engage in quality control. The people who have done well running your local program may be able to grow into quality control and service roles, but it may not be an easy transition. You may have to look outside for these skills.

action step Before going further with the idea of scaling deep, you should stop and ask yourself whether any of these less demanding pathways would be right for you. If you don't think about this now, you may find that the analysis in the next section sends you right back here. Assuming that you want to spread the benefits of your success, the following questions may help:

- Do you need new stand-alone organizations to spread your success to other communities? If so, go to the following section on whether and how to scale up.

- Do you have well-defined programmatic innovations that could be implemented effectively by peer organizations in those communities, with your help? If so, you may want to consider packaging and selling your programs.

- Are you more confident about the transferability of your principles than of your programs? Could you learn from others who share these principles? If you answer yes to both, consider creating a learning network.

- Do you think there are social entrepreneurs in other communities who are willing and able to learn from your experience? Could they put this knowledge to work on their own, without much help from you? If so, consider following a dissemination strategy.

GUIDELINES FOR DECIDING WHETHER AND HOW TO SCALE UP

If you're still considering scaling up, this section will walk you through a process for deciding whether and how to proceed. Going to scale is like launching a new venture. It involves developing new capabilities and requires significant financial, organizational, and personal investments. You must make the case for scaling up and devise a feasible scaling plan. We recommend taking the following steps:

Step 1. Define specifically what it is you want to scale and determine its replicability.

Step 2. Conduct an honest assessment of the opportunity.

Step 3. Evaluate your organization's readiness to take on the challenges.

Step 4. Formulate a scaling strategy that fits.

In the sections that follow, we'll take a close look at each one of these steps.

STEP 1: DEFINE WHAT YOU ARE SCALING AND DETERMINE ITS REPLICABILITY

The first step is getting clear about exactly what it is you have that's transferable to other communities.

What Do You Have to Offer?

Define the key elements that make your operations successful and distinctive. Harvard professor and nonprofit consultant Jeff Bradach calls this your *"minimum critical specification—the fewest program elements possible that produce the desired value."*[9] This may be a whole organizational structure, a specific program innovation, or a set of operating principles. Creating a bare-bones description helps you answer two key strategic questions:

> ✔ *Is it possible to spread this innovation without growing your organization?* If your minimal critical specification is less than a full-blown organization—if it's a program or a set of operating principles— you may spread it more effectively by other means, as discussed in the previous section. Scaling up makes more sense if your minimum critical specification involves a more complete organizational structure or if its successful replication rests on factors that are hard to transmit to others, such as a distinctive organizational culture or tacit knowledge.

✔ *Which elements must remain the same, and which can be adapted to local conditions?* With local autonomy such a crucial issue for social sector organizations, it's essential to know the dimensions on which you can offer local sites flexibility and those that have to remain constant to maintain program integrity and value.

How Replicable Is Your Success?

Once you've identified what to scale, determine how transportable it is. This is a degree-of-difficulty measure, ranging from near impossible to quite easy. To determine the level of difficulty, you should ask:

✔ *To what degree has your success depended on unique people?* How much of your organization's local success depends on your distinctive capabilities, leadership style, reputation, contacts, and experience? How easy is it to replace you? Once you've gone through this thought process for yourself, do the same with key staff and board members. If your success is dependent on hard-to-duplicate individuals, you may want to postpone scaling up. If you move ahead with scaling up, your site selection should be driven heavily by the quality and character of local leadership.

✔ *To what degree has your success depended on unusual operating conditions?* Identify the external factors that have played a role in your success; then ask how important they were and how easily they can be found elsewhere. Are there enough communities with the right conditions to justify a scaling effort? You may have benefited from rare circumstances, such as unusual forms of support from local government, local corporations, or a major donor. You may have benefited from complementary organizations or partners that would be hard to find in other locales. Again, if your success is dependent on unusual circumstances, you should be cautious about scaling up. If you do it, pick your sites accordingly.

STEP 2: ASSESS THE OPPORTUNITY

Just because you have something that's replicable doesn't mean that it *should* be replicated. You have to size up the opportunity. Is it big enough to justify scaling up?

Can You Document a Significant Level of (Unmet or Poorly Met) Need Elsewhere?

Social needs and problems are rarely confined to one community. However, even when a need is nearly universal, the intensity can vary widely from community to community, as can the quality and extent of existing service provision. The combination of a high level of need and weak existing service provision is necessary to ensure that you have an attractive scaling opportunity. You need to show that a sufficient number of communities have enough need to justify a local site and that current service providers can't meet the need as well as you can.[10]

✔ *Is there sufficient need in other communities now or will there be in the near future?* Quantifying the need can be a powerful persuader when you go to funders and other resource providers with the idea of scaling up. To put some rough numbers on the potential need, identify relatively easy-to-collect, reliable indicators. The key question is how many communities have a critical mass of people to serve or problems to solve. What constitutes a "critical mass" depends in part on the level of investment required to start and operate a new site—the higher the investment, the higher the threshold. Look at trends and projections. Is the need growing or declining? Will some communities that don't meet the threshold now meet it soon? Does the answer vary from one community to the next?

tool of the trade Here's a hint: You can *estimate the minimum critical mass* of need by looking at your local program. How many clients or projects would be too few to justify the creation of your organization? Remember that you're probably only serving a small portion of your potential market in your home community; that number is your "market penetration rate." When looking at other communities, use that penetration rate as an optimistic estimate of how much of the need you'll be able to serve. For instance, if you feel 50 participants are necessary to justify the cost of starting a new program for kids with AIDS and your penetration rate in your home market is just 5 percent, look for communities that have at least 1,000 such kids.

✔ *How well is this need currently being met?* If existing service providers in your target communities are doing a good job, the opportunity to scale may not be that great. Of course, if there's a strong case that you can do the job better, your entry may be a form of healthy competition. Before assuming that you would be more effective than potential competitors, an honest assessment is in order. If some strong providers already exist, it might make more sense to work with, rather than against, them. They might become your local affiliates. Or, rather than scaling up, you could sell your program to them or create a learning network with them.

 High need does not always indicate an attractive opportunity. You may find that sites with high levels of need don't provide the best opportunities because the high need has already attracted strong local social entrepreneurs or other national organizations. Sites with emerging needs may provide greater opportunity for a new entrant. Emerging-need sites are communities in which (1) the need is just beginning to register on the radar screens of civic and nonprofit leaders and (2) the need is expected to grow significantly. Growing markets are always easier for new entrants.

Don't forget to look in your own backyard. Don't just look at other communities. Analyze the unmet need in your home community. If your home community has more unmet need than other communities, ask yourself whether your energies would better be spent trying to get a greater penetration at home. Maybe you should *scale deeper*!

Will Key Stakeholders in the Target Communities Support Your Entry?

Consider the actual demand for your services. Are key stakeholders in your target communities ready? Do they recognize the need, or can they easily be brought to see it? Do they care enough to take action? Make a short list of potential communities, based on your needs analysis and prior expressions of interest. Then assess the demand in some of the communities on the list.

✔ *Whose cooperation do you need to enter these communities?* Since you'll be coming in as an "outsider," you must build a base of support in these communities. Key stakeholders include not only the users of your services but anyone whose cooperation or support is important to your success—civic leaders, complementary organizations, potential nonprofit and business partners, business leaders, and any local staff you may need to attract. Some regions are cosmopolitan and open to outsiders. In others, outsiders are distrusted, so you'll need a local champion who has the standing and credibility to invite you in.

✔ *How receptive and committed are these stakeholders?* How do you judge their willingness to provide support? Communities with an emerging need are likely to be more receptive. Expressions of interest, particularly in writing, from prominent leaders in local government, the business community, the philanthropic world, or your social sector field count as evidence of openness. Another indicator is a change in leadership in key public or nonprofit institutions. New leaders are often more open to new approaches.

Talk is cheap. Keep in mind that it's easy for key stakeholders to express support when they have nothing at stake. You have to make sure that they understand what is required of them to get this new site off the ground. Will they go on the record publicly supporting your entry into the community? Have they taken actions to support other innovative approaches brought from the outside? Did they provide sustained support for those efforts? Or were they just looking for the "solution of the month"?

STEP 3: EVALUATE YOUR READINESS

Even if the external conditions are right for scaling, make sure your organization is ready. One key variable is organizational and personal readiness. You don't have to start the scaling process with all the capabilities, systems, and processes that you'll ever need. However, it's reckless to start the process without a solid base on which to build.

Do You Have the Systems and Documentation in Place to Become Multisite?

Many entrepreneurs start out with informal organizations and develop systems only as needed. When you grow your organization, you must take a more formal approach.[11] Scaling up is a developmental turning point. Old informality and flexibility must give way to more formal systems. Operating procedures must be documented in a way that allows them to be easily transferred to other locations, and new systems must be established to coordinate multiple sites.

✔ *Have you formalized your operating procedures?* What kind of handbook would you give a management team who wanted to start a branch of your organization in another community? Do you already have it? If not, what would it take to produce it? Defining what it is you want to scale (Step 1) provides a starting point. According to Bradach, you also must "routinize key activities" and "standardize inputs."[12] Routinizing key activities means documenting how to do them and codifying the required knowledge and skills. Standardizing inputs means defining the resources required, including staff, clientele, and funds.

✔ *Have you laid the groundwork for developing management systems?* The central office plays at least two new roles: facilitating learning and exercising quality control.[13] It also can offer centralized services.[14] Each of these roles requires new systems and procedures. Are you ready to develop them? Do you have systems now for capturing lessons learned and sharing them internally? Do you formally evaluate your performance to ensure impact and maintain quality standards? Centralized services can include many things, such as training, bulk purchasing, marketing assistance, fund-raising assistance, computer systems development, strategic planning assistance, and public policy information. What systems does your organization have in each of these functional areas? If your local experience hasn't laid the foundation for many of these central functions, scaling up may not be prudent.

Do You Have the Organizational Competencies and Capacity Needed?

Scaling up requires new competencies in marketing to new communities, selecting promising new sites, recruiting local teams, negotiating with local affiliates, evaluating local affiliates, and managing central services. Few local social ventures have these competencies in place. Readiness to scale requires either having the necessary competencies or having a viable plan for acquiring or developing them.

✔ *Which competencies do you need to build?* As you visualize the scaling process, identify the key competencies needed at each step along the way. Then assess your organization against these needs. Where it comes up short, plan to develop the competency. By thinking of the process in stages, you can set priorities. You also should flag those competencies that are likely to be hardest to build from your current base.

✔ *Are you prepared to do what it takes to build them?* Hiring is the quick way to bring in new skills, but it also can lead to resentment from existing staff. New staff members still have to learn about your organization and its culture. They may not be productive immediately. Developing the skills in your existing staff can be appealing because it provides internal promotion opportunities, but it can be costly and time-consuming. Existing staff may not be ready to grow into the new roles. Even if you can hire or develop the needed skills, keep in mind that organizational capabilities are more than individual skills. Organizational competency requires an institutionalization of the skills through systems and processes.

Are You, Your Staff, and Your Board Ready for the Change?

Evaluate your personal readiness. Your role will change and so will your staff's and board's. Even those who continue to run the home site will now be part of a larger organization, and this will impact their work. Do you want to play on a national stage? Are you comfortable representing the organization in new cities and with national funders? Are you willing to let someone else take over day-to-day operations of the original site? You also should assess the willingness and ability of key senior staff and board members to be part of a scaling effort. Talk with people in other organizations who've been through the process to get a realistic sense of what it will take. If enough people aren't ready, you should abandon or postpone the effort. If you proceed anyway, expect some turnover.

The founder's dilemma.   What if your organizational founder has the will to scale up but not the ability to lead that effort? Some people are great initiators and work well in small, informal organizations but don't have the skills required for managing a growing, more professional, and more complex organization. Sometimes new leadership must be brought into a growing organization, and the role of the founder may need to change. This can be traumatic for both the founder and the organization.

STEP 4: FORMULATE A SCALING-UP STRATEGY THAT FITS

The last step is to develop a strategy that fits with your findings so far. You must answer four questions to formulate that strategy.

1. How quickly will you roll out, and what are the key milestones or checkpoints?
2. How will your organization be structured as it scales up?
3. How will sites be selected as you scale up?
4. How will you build the necessary capabilities and acquire the resources?

The order of these questions doesn't imply a linear process. After addressing the last question, you may need to return to the earlier questions to revise your answers.

How Quickly Will You Roll Out, and What Are the Key Milestones or Checkpoints?

The heart of any scaling strategy is the rollout plan. It defines the sequence of steps and the pace at which to move. The appropriate pace and sequence will vary widely.

✔ *Adjust the speed to fit your situation.* The main factors that should drive your rollout plan fall into three categories: the nature of your replicable innovation, market conditions, and your readiness.

- *How easy is it to replicate?* If what you're replicating is relatively simple, easy to explain, and can be implemented without special knowledge or expertise, you can move faster. The rollout pace will be slower when the core of your innovation is complicated, hard to explain, and/or dependent on intangibles, such as culture or hard-to-find skills.

- *Is the market ready for you? How is it expected to change?* Need, demand, and window of opportunity can affect the pace of your rollout. An urgent or compelling need provides a strong moral argument for rapid expansion. If you could save lives by moving fast, consider how to make that possible. If demand is low, scaling up will require more education and marketing in each site, and this will slow your pace. High levels of demand make a faster pace possible but don't require it, unless the window of opportunity is closing. A closing window means that the demand for your services is expected to shrink, because of reduced needs, the entry of other organizations, or the shift of stakeholder attention to other issues. With emerging needs, the window may just be opening.

- *How quickly can you develop or acquire the necessary competencies?* The closer you are to having the necessary skills, resources, and systems in place, the faster you can roll out. The pace of scaling is influenced by the time spent attracting resources, building competencies, developing systems, and strengthening your team.

✔ *Think in terms of stages.* A realistic pace for scaling depends on both your organizational capacities and market acceptance. Bradach outlines the organizational capacity process in four stages: (1) refining the model, (2) designing the network, (3) building corporate capability, and (4) growing the network.[15] The first stage is a "proving period" in which you test, improve, and refine your service so that it can be replicated.[16] You also can use it to test replicability, demand, and readiness. It may last several years and include up to 10 sites.[17] In terms of market acceptance, stages can be defined around the innovation adoption curve.[18] In this approach, Stage 1 involves working the bugs out with the help of "Innovator" communities—those that welcome experimentation. Stage 2 rolls out the refined version to "Early Adopter" communities—those with high demand or emerging need. Stage 3 involves "crossing the chasm" to "Early Majority" communities—those that are more conservative, with moderate levels of need and demand. This stage requires a strong brand image and a well-tested approach. Stage 4, if it occurs, involves penetrating "Late Majority" communities—those that are less motivated.

✔ *Creating milestones to test key assumptions.* Make your assumptions explicit, identify those that are most crucial, and find ways in your rollout plan to test them.[19] Go through each element of your scaling strategy, and ask yourself how confident you are about your judgments. Could you be wrong, and would this make a difference to your strategy? If it would, how and when can you test the assumption? Some assumptions can be tested with more research. Others can be tested only by action, trial and error, or trial and success, if you are lucky. Set milestones for assessing key assumptions and adjusting your pace accordingly.

How Will Your Organization Be Structured as It Scales Up?

Scaling up, as we defined it at the beginning of this chapter, involves creating new service sites in other geographic locations that are either branches of the same parent organization or very closely tied affiliates of a parent organization. Will you choose branches or affiliates? How will you divide responsibilities? The answers to these questions may change as you move through different stages in your rollout plan.

✔ *What will be the relationship of the local sites to the parent?* Will your new local sites be branches of a single nonprofit organization, or will they be legally independent organizations that operate under a strong affiliation agreement? In the business world, this is the difference between company-owned operations and franchises, which are locally owned but tightly controlled through a franchise agreement.

- *Independent affiliates promote local autonomy.* With the strong emphasis on local autonomy in the social sector, it's not surprising that most large national nonprofits are organized as franchiselike operations, which are bound together by an affiliation agreement and common brand name. This structure has several advantages.[20] Independent affiliates improve access to local capital, provide strong incentives for the local leaders to make the program work, and attract more volunteers. This structure is more likely to attract social entrepreneurs as local leaders. They tend to prefer autonomy. Independent affiliates can offer greater legitimacy in their communities. They're not outsiders coming in; they're local people using knowledge developed elsewhere for the benefit of their own communities. Overall, this structure permits a more rapid pace for scaling up, as the local affiliates take on chores, such as local fund raising and recruiting, that otherwise would fall to the central office. This structure also can provide a good market test of the value you're creating for your affiliates, but affiliates are harder to control than branches. They must be persuaded rather than directly managed. Having affiliates can stimulate learning and innovation, but change is harder to drive through an affiliate network than it is through a branch system. These factors have to be anticipated and managed.

- *Centrally owned branches allow for greater control.* Control can be more important during the early "proving period" while the model is still being refined and formalized. It also can be important when success depends heavily on intangibles, such as culture, leadership style, or tacit knowledge. These intangibles are easier to transfer to branches than to independent affiliates. If you choose a centrally owned branch structure, you must develop mechanisms to ensure local ownership and credibility. This can be done, for instance, through local advisory boards, local staffing in key positions, regular meetings with community leaders, and partnerships with respected local organizations. City Year, a prominent AmeriCorps program, opted for the branch approach to make it easier to transmit the strong culture that its leaders and advisors see as essential to the program's success. City Year works hard in each community it enters to build a strong sense of local ownership, although it still maintains central control. However, it is unclear that a branch structure is conducive to operating a large number of sites. Among large multisite nonprofits, branch structures are more common when the number of sites is small. A recent study by Sharon Oster at Yale University found that organizations with branch structures had on average only nine sites, compared to 461 for those with franchise structures.[21]

- *A combination structure may allow you to capture the benefits of both.* You could mix these two structures by having some branches that are directly owned and operated by the central organization and other sites that are independent affiliates. This kind of mixed structure is rare in the social sector but common in some businesses. For instance, Jeff Bradach found that 79 of the top 100 restaurant chains had a mixture of franchises and company-owned sites, a structure he calls the "plural form."[22] The plural form enhances opportunities for learning and provides incentives for performance improvement. Branch sites can be used to test ideas before affiliates are asked to adopt them. The central office would gain credibility by operating local sites. This might help bridge the gulf that sometimes exists between the central office "bureaucrats" and the local front-line staff. Having affiliates in the mix adds an independent voice that can challenge central office thinking. Branches and affiliates can set performance benchmarks for one another. Of course, managing a mixed structure has its costs. It's more complex and doesn't solve the control issue. You have to manage both kinds of relationships. If you're going to use branches to set benchmarks, you should operate them with the same constraints that you place on franchisees. Otherwise, branches will be perceived as having an unfair advantage.

✔ *What will be the division of responsibility between local sites and the central office?* Whether you have branches or affiliates or both, you must decide on the respective roles and responsibilities of the central office and the local sites. The right division of labor maintains the right balance of central control and local autonomy and ensures that you capture the benefits of going to scale. Finding the right division is especially crucial before taking on independent affiliates. With branches, you can change the division of labor much more easily. Areas to consider include, but are not limited to, the following:

- Various aspects of fund raising
- Establishment of local operating standards and procedures
- Recruiting, training, and development of local paid staff and volunteers
- Network-wide strategic planning
- Local-level strategic planning
- Governance of local sites and of the central office
- Provision of management support to new affiliates
- Purchasing of various supplies and materials
- Development of marketing materials
- Marketing the organization and its programs, nationally and locally
- General public relations
- Public policy advocacy
- Quality control policies and audits
- Evaluation of central office performance
- Financial auditing of local sites
- Filing IRS Form 990 for independent affiliates
- Facilitation of networking among local site leaders
- Selecting future sites[23]

One especially crucial area is financial roles and responsibilities. Will the central office contribute to start-up expenses of local affiliates? Beyond start-up, when, if ever, will the central office provide support for local activities? What fees, if any, will the local site pay to be an affiliate, use the brand name, and enjoy the benefits of being part of a national organization? In addition to membership fees, will the central office charge fees for specific services, such as training programs, networking events, or technical assistance? If local affiliates are allowed to fund-raise outside of their immediate communities, how will this be coordinated? How will potential conflicts of going after the same donors be managed? The central office may need to play a role in preventing and resolving conflicts.

How Will Sites be Selected as You Scale Up?

Regarding site selection, you need criteria and a selection process, which are likely to change as you move through different stages of your rollout.

✔ *How should the initial sites be selected?* For good testing grounds, you want communities that have sufficient demand, welcome innovation, and are open to outsiders. In the early sites, you may need to exercise more control by keeping them under your legal umbrella and putting some of your experienced staff into key positions. Local stakeholders need to understand and accept this fact. It may be wise to start with sites that are geographically close to your home base and similar to your original location in ways that are relevant to your program's success. As you develop more confidence, you'll want to test your approach in different kinds of communities to show that it's robust. Evaluate potential sites, approach them, and manage expectations through the selection process. If demand for your innovation isn't high enough for you to be selective, you may need to take what you can get. In the case of low demand, this turns from a selection process into a sales process. The other criteria for selecting prospects remain the same.

✔ *How will the selection criteria change as you move beyond the proving period?* Ultimately, site selection should be driven by the social return on your investment in a new site. This is largely a function of three factors: (1) the potential benefit you could create in the community, (2) the probability that your program will actually achieve that benefit, and (3) the amount of investment required to assure success. If a particular site requires extraordinary investment, it should offer the chance of a correspondingly greater impact. The specific criteria you use to assess these factors will depend on kind of service you provide. The site selection process at this stage can become more open and formal, constrained only by your capacity.

red flag   **Risky sites and your brand.**   When using this kind of risk/return assessment, remember that the reputation of your brand may be affected by local failures, so weigh these costs into your site selection. You might want to set a limit on the number of high-risk sites you'll take. A high-risk site is one with a large potential benefit but a low probability of success. You also could adopt strategies to reduce the risk by taking on a knowledgeable partner, recruiting a particularly skilled team, cross-subsidizing the site with national funds, or even initially operating the site under a different name.

How Will You Build the Necessary Capabilities and Acquire the Resources?

You need a resource mobilization plan for scaling, just as you do for a new venture. You should start with a definition of the capabilities you will need, then work your way back to resources.[24]

✔ *What capabilities do you need and when?* Based on your readiness assessment, you should have identified specific competency gaps. When you need these competencies will depend on your rollout plan and your organizational structure. With those decisions in mind, create a competency development schedule to ensure you have both the capabilities and the capacity to scale up.

✔ *How will you build the needed capabilities on this timetable?* Based on the schedule, create a specific plan for how to develop the competencies. Elements of this plan should include specific personnel decisions, such as job changes for existing staff and new hires. It should involve decisions about what to contract out and what you might get pro bono. It also should include necessary training as well as time to translate individual knowledge and skills into an organizational capability. This is done by developing systems, using teams, and cross-training personnel.

✔ *Is this development plan feasible?* Before developing your resource plan, do a reality check. Is it realistic for you to develop the needed capabilities quickly enough to follow your rollout schedule? Setting unrealistic expectations can lead to burnout and poor morale. The rate of sustainable growth depends on how hard it is to build the new competencies for the central office and the new sites.

✔ *What resources are needed to develop these capabilities and deliver on your plan?* What will you need to build your capabilities and start up the new sites? Create your resource shopping list of the things money can buy and a list of the resources that money can't buy, at least not easily, such as credibility or trust.

✔ *How will you acquire (or develop) the resources you need?* Create a resource acquisition strategy. Where will you get what you need and on what terms? How will you create or acquire the resources that can't be bought? A key decision in scaling up is how much responsibility local sites should take for mobilizing their needed resources, particularly at start-up. This is especially important when working with franchises. The answer is largely a function of the level of demand among local resource providers, the degree of local autonomy you want to encourage, and what tasks are easier for the central office to do. Requiring local leaders to raise all their resources is a powerful test of their entrepreneurial skills, but initial assistance from the central office can help create a greater sense of mutual commitment. This decision sets the stage for ongoing relations with the local sites and should be consistent with your overall philosophy about local autonomy.

✔ *Is the resource mobilization plan feasible?* Based on the details of this resource plan, is it realistic for you to attract the needed resources? If not, either you need to be more creative about your use of resources—finding ways to do more with less—or you need to change the rollout plan. Once you have a plan that seems feasible, articulate the key assumptions and include them in the assumptions that will be tested and revised as you reach your milestones or checkpoints.

red flag   **Scaling raises special funding challenges.**   Ultimately, membership fees may cover the cost of the central office, but during the scaling up process you're likely to need philanthropic support. Scaling may give you access to some new sources of funds, but growth capital isn't easy to come by. Some funders are geographically focused and reluctant to support national expansion. Many of the large foundations like to fund replicable innovations, but they rarely want to fund the replication process beyond a couple of test sites. The federal government has helped some organizations scale up, but this has become increasingly rare. It's probably wise to count on local fund raising to support as much as possible of the operating costs of each site and to contribute some amount to the central office. During the period when central office growth and costs outstrip the amount of support that can be expected from affiliates, you need to find national sponsors. These are likely to be organizations or individuals who have a national agenda, share a strong commitment your cause, and are not bound by bureaucratic limits on the amount and duration of their support.

tool of the trade   One way to lower the costs of geographic expansion is to *piggyback* on another organization that already has a presence in the communities you want to move into. This partner can provide facilities, access to financial and human resources, and credibility in the new communities. Since many of today's large nonprofits grew out of religious traditions, it's not surprising that some of them piggybacked on churches. For instance, Goodwill Industries was essentially a program of the Methodist church in its early days. In addition to churches, consider piggybacking on national nonprofits or corporations.

SUMMARY

Success of a new social venture inevitably raises the question of scale. If your program is working, why not take it to new areas or new markets?

In fact, some would say that successful social entrepreneurs face a moral imperative to make sure more people have access to their innovations. However, achieving geographic scale in the social sector has historically been a difficult and slow process. This is because social entrepreneurs face a distinctive set of challenges in deciding how to spread their innovations and build on their success. This chapter has provided frameworks for thinking about your strategic options for building on success, including alternatives to scaling up. As you make your own decisions about how to build on success, keep the following points in mind.

- ✔ Scaling up successfully requires very different organizational skills and resources from running a great local program.

- ✔ Before "going national," you need to assess your readiness and your organization's readiness for such a move.

- ✔ If you scale up, you need to define the "core" of your program and decide on some key strategic issues concerning local autonomy and organizational structure.

- ✔ Throughout this process, you should keep in mind that there are attractive alternatives to scaling up that might be more appropriate for your organization at this time.

- ✔ Scaling deep in your original community or market may be a more powerful and effective way to grow your organization.

- ✔ The ultimate criterion for determining how to build on your success is social value creation. Ask yourself: How can we get the greatest social impact relative to the energy and resources required—the greatest social return on our investment?

Good luck!

Notes

1. James Champy and Nitin Nohria, *The Arc of Ambition* (Cambridge, MA: Perseus Books, 2000).
2. Jeffrey Pfeffer, *Organization Design* (Northbrook, IL: AHM Publishing, 1978).
3. Burton A. Weisbrod, *The Nonprofit Economy* (Cambridge, MA: Harvard University Press, 1988).
4. E. F. Schumacher, *Small Is Beautiful: Economics As If People Mattered* (New York: Harper & Row, 1973).
5. See Chapter 12 in Ram Charan and Noel M. Tichy, *Every Business Is a Growth Business* (New York: Times Books, 1998).
6. For a provocative discussion of the power of networks, see Kevin Kelly, *New Rules for the New Economy* (New York: Penguin Books, 1998), especially Chapters 2 and 3.
7. Ted Sizer, a leading educator and visionary, first articulated these principles in his book *Horace's Compromise: The Dilemma of the American High School: The First Report from a Study of American High Schools,* cosponsored by the National Association of Secondary School Principals and the Commission on Educational

Issues of the National Association of Independent Schools (Boston: Houghton Mifflin, 1984).

8. *www.successforall.net/about/who we are.htm.*

9. Jeffrey L. Bradach, "Going to Scale," Harvard Business School Working Paper, Social Enterprise Series, No. 9, forthcoming in *Harvard Business Review.*

10. For guidance on low-cost market research methods, see Alan R. Andreasen, *Cheap But Good Marketing Research* (Homewood, IL: Dow Jones-Irwin, 1988).

11. For an excellent discussion of how this evolution to more formal systems works on the for-profit side, see Amar V. Bhide, *The Origin and Evolution of New Businesses* (Oxford: Oxford University Press, 2000).

12. Bradach, "Going to Scale."

13. Christine W. Letts, William P. Ryan, and Allen Grossman, *High Performance Nonprofit Organizations: Managing Upstream for Greater Impact* (New York: John Wiley & Sons, 1999), p. 157.

14. Bradach, "Going to Scale."

15. Ibid.

16. Letts, Ryan, and Grossman, *High Performance Nonprofit Organizations*, pp. 157–161.

17. Bradach, "Going to Scale."

18. J. Gregory Dees, "Mastering the Art of Innovation," Chapter 7, *Enterprising Nonprofits: A Toolkit for Social Entrepreneurs* (New York: John Wiley & Sons, 2001), pp. 178–181.

19. This approach to planning is described in Rita Gunther McGrath and Ian C. MacMillan, "Discovery-Driven Planning," *Harvard Business Review,* July–August 1995.

20. See Sharon M. Oster, "Nonprofit Organizations and Their Local Affiliates: A Study in Organizational Forms," *Journal of Economic Behavior and Organization,* Vol. 30 (1996).

21. Ibid.

22. Jeffrey L. Bradach, *Franchising Organizations* (Boston: Harvard Business School Press, 1998).

23. Adapted from Dennis Young, Neil Bania, and Darlyne Bailey, "A Study of National Nonprofit Associations," *Nonprofit Management & Leadership,* Vol. 6, No. 4 (Summer 1996).

24. J. Gregory Dees, "Mobilizing Resources," Chapter 4, *Enterprising Nonprofits.*

Chapter 11

MANAGING ORGANIZATIONAL CHANGE

Betty Henderson Wingfield, Senior Consultant, Executive Development Associates

IN THIS CHAPTER

What social entrepreneurs should know about organizational change
How to prepare to lead organizational change
What happens when organizations experience change?
Your role as the leader of organizational change

Today, more than ever, organizations in the social sector are facing major change; the organizations that are able to manage this change effectively will be the successful ones. And successful organizations will not only invite change, they will use the energy it creates to drive their results and outcomes. Since the level of change today is like nothing organizations have experienced before, there is a need for a different kind of leader—one who is a change agent, courageous, and who possesses the characteristics of an entrepreneur.

This kind of leader can be found in leadership positions in many changing organizations as well as in many levels within these organizations—the staff, board members, volunteers. Known as social entrepreneurs, they are key to the growing trend of how nonprofit organizations are changing their behaviors to thinking and acting like for-profit businesses. In fact, British prime minister Tony Blair put it this way, when speaking about social entrepreneurs, "[They] bring to social problems the same enterprise and imagination business entrepreneurs bring to wealth creation."[1]

Of course, making the transition to an organization that is more entrepreneurial is much easier said than done; we all know that many organizations (and the people within them as well as key stakeholders) are resistant to change. From a board perspective, there may be the sense that it is their prerogative to set the policy and vision—and social entrepreneurship may run counter to your board's goals. From a staff perspective, the notion of applying any business frameworks within the organization may be viewed with suspicion. And through the eyes of a community stakeholder, social entrepreneurship may be viewed as taking away from the core mission of an agency that has been a mainstay of the neighborhood for years. All of these reactions (and others as well!) may be understandable, but all must be addressed if you're to successfully advance an entrepreneurial agenda within your nonprofit.

This chapter will help provide you with the tools you'll need to successfully institute change in your organization while strengthening your change management skills as you strive to meet social needs in new and innovative ways.

WHAT SOCIAL ENTREPRENEURS SHOULD KNOW ABOUT ORGANIZATIONAL CHANGE

Social entrepreneurs, by their nature, are tenacious and focused. They see a social need that requires a solution, and they find innovative ways to address the need. This kind of behavior is energizing for many of the individuals who make up an organization but at the same time is frightening for those struggling to adjust to the affects of the changes they are facing.

RESISTANCE TO CHANGE

Organizations in general are resistant to change, especially organizations that have been around for some time. The immune system of mature organizations automatically seeks out new ideas and gets busy wiping them out as they arise. There is always a strong desire to return to the status quo. *After all, we know what is best. We have stood the test of time.* This belief used to give cause for pause, but, today, more and more organizations are disappearing or are being swallowed up in mergers and acquisitions. Many of these organizations were the stars of the business world at one time. Remember Digital Equipment Corporation, Bank of Boston, Eastern Airlines? Each of these once-stellar organizations has either fallen by the wayside or been swallowed up by a more successful rival.

While this process is not occurring in the same way in the social sector, many nonprofits are fighting for their survival. Others are in need of serious revitalization as they try to provide the same level of support and services as conditions change all around them. Some are underfunded, many are understaffed, and some have simply lost their way. Others need to look at new opportunities to manage the impact of change in order to create a viable future. With such pressing needs, it would seem reasonable for organizations in the social sector to be major champions of change. However, some key issues can make such an objective difficult.

ISSUES UNIQUE TO THE SOCIAL SECTOR

A number of issues unique to the social sector can make it difficult to embrace an entrepreneurial mind-set. The response to change can be widely different among some of the key stakeholders. For example, organizational change can be frightening for staff and volunteers, who have invested time, energy, and resources to organizations they believe in. Perhaps they chose to work or volunteer in the social sector because of a deep commitment and identity with certain causes. They know they make a difference for millions of people every day—in good times as well as tough times. Acceptance of a scarcity mentality as normal day-to-day practice has become the modus operandi. And changing directions and pursuing new opportunities may seem like "bait and switch" to board members who dedicate their time and expertise.

Now, you might ask, "Aren't some organizations open to change?"

The answer is yes. Some organizations are change-hardy, having weathered numerous changes in order to survive. They have evolved to a place where change is continuous, gradual, and almost unnoticeable. The description of the unique issues is meant to serve as a reminder to social entrepreneurs of the complexity of managing change in nonprofit organizations. Individuals within organizations must modify certain behavior in order for change to happen. With a bold vision and determination to see it realized, social entrepreneurs have the needed fortitude to manage organizational change.

HOW TO PREPARE TO LEAD ORGANIZATIONAL CHANGE

red flag When addressing urgent needs, there is always a tendency to "just get going." Therefore, it is easy to overlook the importance of preparation before beginning a change effort. Here's a piece of advice: Don't! The real keys to managing change are to know where you are headed and that you can get others committed to come along with you. You may have to win individuals over one at a time—and, at times, it will be hard and quite frustrating—but if you're up to the challenge, you'll be presented with even more opportunities to improve social conditions and to do the things that you are passionate about.

Whether the change you are leading is for survival or for continuous improvement, you will need to prepare if you are to see your vision realized.

THE SPECIAL CHALLENGES FACING SOCIAL ENTREPRENEURS

There are a number of reasons why turning your nonprofit into an enterprising nonprofit—becoming more entrepreneurial in the process—can be a challenge for even the most vigorous change leader. Here are some of the most common:

- *Social entrepreneurs, like all entrepreneurs, are driven more by opportunities than by threats or crises.* In many cases, organizational change is driven by serious competitive or financial threats, maybe even a crisis. The status quo is failing. In this case, people may have little choice but to change. Opportunity-based change has some different dynamics from threat-based change. When the status quo is not under threat, change leaders may encounter more inertia and skepticism. How do they motivate people to change when they are comfortable with the way things are?
- *Social sector organizations tend to draw staff who are passionate about the mission and hold strong values that are reflected in their work. It is not uncommon to find an antibusiness bias.* Many staff members accept below-market wages because they believe in what the organization stands for. They may have left the business world or avoided it because they find it offensive in some way. Many social sector organizations rely heavily of volunteers who are there primarily because of values. Revolutionary change can threaten the values that hold the organization together, or at least appear to threaten them. Values-based resistance may be the most intense and difficult form of resistance. At Bennington College in Vermont, for example, when faced with the prospect of an administration that wanted to make fundamental changes to curriculum to attract more students, some faculty were so committed to the old ways that they would rather declare 50 years of victory and close the doors than change some core aspects of the college. If the change involves being more "businesslike," the resistance can be particularly strong. This places a special burden on social entrepreneurs. On the flip side, this feature of the sector can become a tremendous asset. Social entrepreneurs may be able to tap into those strongly held values and use them to motivate change.
- *The board tends to play a more crucial and active role in the social sector, and, legally, it is in charge.* Nonprofit boards tend to be more hands-on (though of course this varies widely). Some boards view their role as making the major strategic decisions. There are no stockholders to whom the board is responsible.

(continued)

Nonprofit CEOs may not even have a vote on their board. Many social entrepreneurs have run into major board-level roadblocks. Social entrepreneurs need to be more adept at bringing their board along and giving the board a sense of ownership.

- *The local community or the general public may feel that they have more of a stake in social sector organizations.* Because of their missions and the tax breaks they receive, nonprofits tend to be viewed as operating for the benefit of the public at large or at least the communities in which they do their work. Communities can be a factor in business change efforts, but it is generally recognized that businesses are operated for a profit and have owners who can decide whether and how they change to pursue that profit. Politics and public relations are likely to be more important skills for social entrepreneurs as they manage potential external resistance and build community support.

- *It can be hard to demonstrate results in the social sector, especially in a timely way to validate your change hypothesis.* Every change effort has a change hypothesis that says: "If we change in X way, we will get Y results that are better than the result we are currently getting—making the change worthwhile." However, results are notoriously difficult to measure in the social sector. Making the case for this proposition can be hard in the absence of clear performance data, even about current operations. Demonstrating successes, even early wins, can be very hard. This makes it easier for resisters and critics to work against the change. Measurable surrogates need to be found that serve as reliable indicators of success. Social entrepreneurs need to look for convincing ways to demonstrate improved performance.

- *The social sector tends to have a culture of tolerance that can make staffing and board membership decisions even more difficult.* When businesses restructure, they usually have little trouble letting people go who do not fit in the new organization. Of course, the better firms will help people find new jobs and offer generous severance benefits, but they have no trouble making tough decisions. People who impede the change are usually gone. Many nonprofits find it very hard to fire staff members. How do you fire a volunteer, a friend, a comrade-in-arms, someone who has given something to the organization (and perhaps not been fully paid for this contribution)? Removing board members, who typically are volunteers and often donors as well, is also very difficult. With the board, term limits can help. Change may require new people with new skills and a commitment to the new approach. "Leaving a few behind" is a special challenge for social entrepreneurs.

Although there is no single failsafe process, the following five steps will serve as a guide as you prepare to lead change.

STEP 1: ASSESS YOUR PERSONAL READINESS

Do you have your seat belt fastened for the turbulence that may await you up ahead? Leading major change does not exempt you from being affected.

Ask yourself the following questions:

- ✔ Why is this particular opportunity right for your organization?
- ✔ Is the timing right to introduce this change?
- ✔ How does your organization deal with change?
- ✔ Where might the greatest resistance to your ideas surface in the organization?
- ✔ What, if any, significant risks will this opportunity impose upon the organization?
- ✔ How do you personally deal with change?
- ✔ What is your tolerance for those who will become your adversaries?

Having the right answers to these questions does not ensure success. Thinking through the questions and acting on them will better position you for building a change team to join in the long march you have embarked upon.

STEP 2: ASSEMBLE YOUR CHANGE TEAM

practical tip It is impossible to manage an organization through change without enlisting a group of dedicated and, it is hoped, willing people to work with you. They must know what your vision is and how committed you are, and feel that you are confident that your dream can come true. Your team should include those who support you, those who could be resistors, and those who are representatives of the informal leadership system that exists in all organizations. This team will help carry the change messages to places beyond your reach, no matter how driven you are.

Depending on the expected impact of the change effort on the organization, it may be important to seek board involvement. The best change teams include a mixture of staff, volunteers, board members, and other critical constituencies such as clients, patrons, and community leaders. This team becomes your guiding coalition.

John P. Kotter, a professor of leadership at the Harvard Business School, puts it this way: "In most successful cases, the guiding coalition is always pretty powerful—in terms of titles, information and expertise, reputation and relationships. . . . Efforts that don't have a powerful enough guiding coalition can make apparent progress for a while. But, sooner or later, the opposition gathers itself together and stops the change."[2]

reality check   For example, there is a well-known midwest cultural arts organization whose executive director is a true social entrepreneur. She has ridden the waves of change with her organization many times. In looking for ways to expand the vision of her organization, she found a new opportunity that was a bold strategy for survival and competitive positioning—a cultural arts charter school. Some board members found her idea intriguing but thought the idea had little chance to be realized. As it became evident that she was steadily moving toward realizing the vision of the charter school, board members began to resist, questioning the soundness of her vision. While she never intended to leave the board members in the dark—or perhaps even thought they were natural allies— too much of her time had been spent lining up other key constituencies, and she took her board for granted. Because the executive director and her board had worked together for years, she naturally thought she had their support.

This unintended oversight created major division among staff, board, and volunteers. The executive director—with some outside consultation— was able to regroup and begin the process of building a team to make her vision reality. A couple years later, the charter school is in the final stages of opening its doors.

STEP 3: CREATE A TEAM VISION

Once you have assembled a team, it is then necessary to make sure you are all headed in the same direction—in other words, you must have shared vision. Make sure to dedicate time to assessing the organization's readiness for the change effort. The vision and ideas that you brought to the team may shift, perhaps—in the long run—for the better.

tool of the trade   A recent report from the National Center for Social Entrepreneurs titled "Managing Mission & Money" posed these important questions that change teams must consider:

- ✔ *What is our vision?* Critical to any change effort is clarity of the vision. In other words, what change are we trying to lead and why? What will it look like? Shared vision is the goal.

- ✔ *What is our mission?* How will the change happen? Who needs to be involved? What is our game plan?

- ✔ *What are the core values that guide us?* What will keep us together when the going gets tough, as it surely will? What are the new values that we must share?

✔ *What forces are driving us to take part in this process?* Is everyone clear about the marketplace trends or the organizational issues that are driving these needed changes?

✔ *What outcomes do we expect?* How will the future differ from today? Know that the picture of the future may change slightly, but it must remain "in focus" to keep change efforts on track.[3]

reality check   Three years ago the YWCA—an organization well over 100 years old—was in danger of becoming obsolete, or at least that is what about 400 participants at a preconvention meeting believed when they decided to launch a change effort. In true entrepreneurial style, they moved quickly to establish a change initiative team to raise the money needed to lead this change effort. After their initial planning meetings, they reached out to 500 more participants—board members, executives, staff, volunteers—and brought them together to help identify the issues they were facing.

At this meeting, the participants voted to have a special convening of their convention the following year to insure greater involvement of local associations. They emerged from this special convention with a transition team to help shape a plan for organizational change. Needless to say, this was not an easy process as there are over 400 YWCAs around the country, but these women were driven to breathe life back into an organization they believed deserved to exist. What took place were many meetings, loads of volunteer time, trust building, time for resolving conflict—all leading to bringing a change plan to the delegates at the next scheduled convention. They went on to research and shape the key issues over a two-year period and developed a document outlining the change plan, "Steps to Absolute Change," in time for their convention. At their thirty-sixth national convention, the first real step in their transformation to the new YWCA for the twenty-first century was accomplished—85 percent of the member associations approved the change plan.

Now the real test, of course, is whether the YWCA can, as the chairperson of the transition team said, "lead, act and risk. We will never cross the ocean if we are afraid to leave the shore."[4]

The YWCA's change initiative is a powerful example of just how long and how many iterations an organization must undertake in order to get to the point of just agreeing to a change plan. Still more time is needed to actualize the plan.

STEP 4: CRAFT A COMMUNICATION STRATEGY AND EXECUTE IT RELIGIOUSLY

As leaders of this change, you and your team must use every possible communication vehicle in every possible way to communicate on a continuous basis. Technology tools such as e-mail, intranets, and the Internet are inexpensive and can speed the communication process. If you don't have adequate technology access in your organization (look for ways to find it), don't let that stop progress—form telephone trees, send broadcast faxes, make face-to-face visits. Don't leave anyone out! Know that the same messages will have to be repeated numerous times. Some say it takes at least eight times for a message to be heard. One of the major reasons change efforts are derailed has to do with messages not getting to the folks who are affected the most in a way that is useful to them. Having this strategy in place will create the "buzz" that is needed to demonstrate that things are going to be different.

STEP 5: DRAW UP A PLAN OF ACTION

You will need to hold a series of meetings to put in place a plan that the team can use as a guide. This plan should not be carved in stone but rather one that can change based on what is and is not working as you move toward implementation.

These steps will serve as preparation for the journey. Good judgment and common sense will be essential to the credibility of the work that your team does. Along the way expect lots of meetings, disappointments, and setbacks until you reach the point of implementing your change plan.

When you are ready to implement the change, simply go back through the steps and choose the ones that would help you execute implementation.

Remember, it is not necessary to overplan. There will be unforeseen situations no matter how much time you devote to trying to predict the future. Having a commitment to the vision and its outcomes is much more important.

WHAT HAPPENS WHEN ORGANIZATIONS EXPERIENCE CHANGE?

Change is here to stay. It will become more demanding and create more pressure, but it will not go away. The change effort you implement will evolve into other needed changes, because change is never finished. One change is simply preparation for the next, much like life. But, as William Bridges, an expert on change management, reminds us, it's not the change that does us in, it's the transitions.

Change is everywhere, and it takes many shapes and forms. Specifically, organizational change varies in both scope and intensity. The intensity of change ranges from incremental, which is simply a refinement of the status quo, to evolutionary, which moves the organization in a significant way along an anticipated development process, to revolutionary, which results in an organization that is different in fundamental ways—skills, competencies, values, and culture. When social entrepreneurship is first introduced to an organization, it may be revolutionary, involving a fundamental shift in vision: "We can do and be so much more by fundamentally changing the way we operate." In this chapter, we are not talking about incremental change of relatively narrow scope, affecting just one small part of the organization. You do not need a major change effort or team for that. We are talking about significant evolutionary or revolutionary change that has widespread scope in the organization. The more widespread and revolutionary the change, the more resistance it is likely to generate and the more carefully it has to be managed.

There are numerous ways to look at the psychological impact of change on individuals within the organization. Some experts relate it to the stages of grieving; others relate it to taking a journey. All of these models have one thing in common: They attempt to acknowledge the strong feelings that are invoked during change and the transition it brings.

core
concept

In this chapter, the stages of change (see Exhibit 11.1) will be identified as:

Stage 1: Letting go of the old

Stage 2: Facing the unknown

Stage 3: Moving forward

It would be a lot easier to manage change if these stages always progressed in a linear manner, but, as you might expect, they don't. We sometimes can get stuck in one of the stages, and, without support and

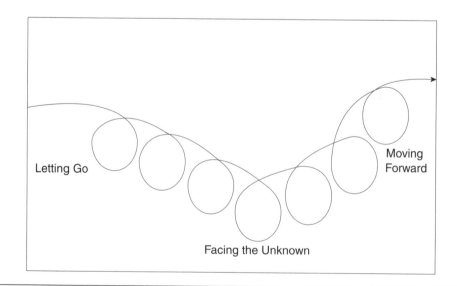

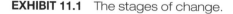

EXHIBIT 11.1 The stages of change.

a grasp of reality, we can linger there for some time. It is important that you understand what is happening when things don't seem to be moving as quickly as they should or could. Rosabeth Moss Kanter warns us that "change compelled by crisis is usually seen as a threat, not an opportunity."[5] While all change is not driven by threat as much as by opportunity, change often does contain a threatening element.

PHASE 1: LETTING GO OF THE OLD—COMING TO TERMS WITH WHAT NEEDS TO CHANGE

core concept

During the letting-go phase, certain dynamics are observable. The following story is a classic example of how issues surface during the letting-go stage.

When a Protestant church in the Southwest decided to incorporate a McDonald's franchise as part of a new lifelong learning center, the organization immediately heard concerns from their local community—everything from traffic issues to unhealthy eating habits. The church entered into a limited partnership with an entrepreneur who also happened to be a member of the church. The minister, a social entrepreneur in his own right, was looking for innovative ways to bring a convenient service to members and economic development to an underserved community. While this is a very different approach for a church, it's not surprising that a social entrepreneur would take a leap of faith. The church has spent $150,000 on equipment, will pay all additional operating costs, and will receive 100 percent of the profits. The member/entrepreneur will manage the business. He said, "It's my church and I believe in what we're doing. It will mean jobs for the community, and that is the blessing for me. It's a service I am glad to provide for the church."[6]

Members of the church's community did not have a problem with the learning center or the large numbers of people who were expected to attend traditional weekly services. These are the traditional activities that are expected at a church but, in reality, may be equally responsible for increased traffic. Rational thinking does not always determine the way organizations experience change in how things are "supposed" to be done.

practical tip

Change Strategies for Letting Go

If you want to help members of your social enterprise let go of the past, here are some essential strategies for doing just that.

Tell and retell the story driving the change; make sure it is compelling. Articulate the reality driving the change. After all, you do not want this to sound like another "flavor of the month." This is the time to get real! Change programs have come and gone under many different names, and many people are tired of poorly planned interventions that never seem to live up to expectations while needlessly traumatizing the organization. There is little tolerance because the hours are too long and the work is very hard (but rewarding) in the social sector. No matter how great the opportunity, individuals in the organization must believe what they are being told in order to let go of the way things used to be.

Be up front and acknowledge the reactions you are observing. If you've had similar reactions in the past, acknowledge as much. Self-disclosure by leaders is a powerful tool for people who are struggling with change. It helps them see that others have similar experiences and feelings. Provide verbal and visible support to help those dealing with their sense of loss. Create opportunities for people to express their feelings, and listen to what they are telling you. Although you may be uncomfortable or impatient at times, don't discount their feelings.

Communicate, communicate, communicate. Write it down, talk about it, use electronic support to deliver the change message in as many ways as will meet individuals' readiness to listen. The information should be clear, direct, and repeated regularly. Use hot lines, open forums, newsletters, and chat rooms to communicate during change. Persuasive speeches to try to motivate positive thinking will backfire—they will be seen as insensitive and patronizing.

Outline in specific terms what needs to be done. Put together time lines and tools for measuring progress. This will help move the organization along at a steady pace that is not too jarring and prepares for a greater push later on.

Get everyone involved in some way as quickly as possible. Keep the focus on the "what" before the "why" or "when." Discussion groups, focus groups, and change teams are but a few of the ways you can begin getting the organization involved in the change. There may be a need for training to help inculcate some of the new behaviors and skills that will be expected in the changing environment. This is another way to provide information and get valuable input. It gives members of the organization an opportunity to be heard and to influence the direction of the change.

red flag **Prepare for a drop in productivity.** Productivity often drops during the course of a change process, and the severity of this drop will depend on how well prepared you are to execute some of these strategies. Nonprofit organizations can ill afford the detrimental consequences when productivity is down and morale is low. The slowdown can be devastating and make it very difficult to get things back on track.

No doubt, it is hard to let go of what is familiar and comfortable when faced with the uncertainty of the unknown, even if it means better opportunities for your organization. There is a certain comfort in the fantasy of how "good" things used to be. Stay focused, and stay in touch, so situations don't spin out of control and prove that the change efforts were unnecessary in the first place.

PHASE 2: FACING THE UNKNOWN

core concept

At this stage your organization is *"facing the unknown."* As a social entrepreneur, you will have sound management and business skills and solid research to promote the new opportunities you are bringing, yet it often serves as little or no consolation to those who are struggling with change. Nothing will do, short of the *answer*. If you don't have a readily available answer—the answer everyone wants—it can be a very frustrating time.

In order to move forward when facing the unknown, change leaders must communicate their vision with conviction while understanding the human dynamics of change. Social entrepreneurs at all levels are ideal for leading an organization during this time. *Your dedication, decisiveness, and ability to engage key stakeholders can serve as a living model for those who need to see visible signs.* You have the key ingredients: a vision of what could be and the ability to go for it. This is what others need to see to get through this phase. They are looking to your team to tell them how you will help them. Support, encouragement, caring, and empathy will earn a lot of credibility for change leaders and move people through this phase at a reasonable pace.

Addressing Resistance

core concept

Resistance will be at its peak during this phase. Organizations resist change for many reasons:

- ✔ There have been many fits and starts and people are skeptical.
- ✔ Fear of the unknown sets in, and memories of similar situations emerge.
- ✔ Fear arises that the values and mission of the organization will somehow be destroyed or disregarded.
- ✔ Lack of respect for the cultures that already exist is evidenced.

If it is not clear that the changes you are leading will make noticeable improvement, they will be resisted—and rightfully so! Repeat over and over the case for change and talk about the behaviors that will drive the outcomes. If the information needed is not forthcoming in a straightforward manner during this phase, people will make up their own story, and usually it will not be in line with what you are doing. The result is people working *against* your efforts rather than *with* your efforts.

*red
flag*   Although resistance can slow you down, if it is not managed well, not all resistance is bad—it is not always an obstacle thrown in the way to prevent you from carrying forth the vision for the change effort. Resistance can provide a voice of reason and point out possible problems ahead. It is critical to listen to the concerns of resisters, try to answer questions, get at the core issues, and tease out what is worth paying attention to and what is just noise in the system. However, do resist the pressure to stop or curtail the change process. Take the advice, make the course corrections needed, and move forward. Resist the pressure to stop or curtail the process simply because it goes against conventional wisdom.

Symptoms of Organizational Resistance

✔ Increased absenteeism

✔ Lower productivity

✔ Poor communications

✔ Little or no teamwork

Symptoms of Individual Resistance

✔ Withdrawal

✔ Anger

✔ Complaining

✔ Apathy

✔ Frustration

Symptoms of Hidden Resistance:

✔ Withholding information or dribbling information out bit by bit

✔ Taking steps to personally protect the organization from change

✔ Coming late and leaving early

✔ Creating extra work, extra processes, extra time to do the simplest task

✔ Revisiting previous issues that were or were not resolved satisfactorily

Resistance that is out in the open is hundreds of times better than mindless compliance or passive resistance. Hidden resistance has a bottom-line impact on the services and support that the organization provides.

Change Strategies for Facing the Unknown

If you want to help members of your social enterprise face the unknown, here are some essential strategies for doing just that.

practical tip

When you don't know the answer, say so. This is when the acronym *IKIWISI* (I'll know it when I see it) becomes a part of visionary conversations. Check in with all of your different stakeholders. Hold frequent meetings to announce what you do know and report progress or setbacks. You don't want the organizations creating their own stories in a vacuum you have created by poor communication. Just tell them what you know, as honestly as possible. It will go a very long ways toward shutting down the rumor mill. A saying goes "During change the truth keeps changing." What this aphorism forgot to add is "But you better make sure everyone knows."

Use rituals to help individuals get through this difficult time. Studies show that people will let go of things much more readily when they have an opportunity to acknowledge the loss in some way. For example, when we complete college, we graduate—a rite of passage to another stage in life. The graduation ceremony marks the occasion and provides opportunities for us, as well as for others who are significant to the event, to celebrate our accomplishments and acknowledge the change we are facing.

During the reorganization of a major bank, members of an operations team were transferred to other departments. To help ease the transition, the organization held a graduation ceremony. Each person was declared to have successfully matriculated the requirements of the team and was deemed ready to go on to "higher learning"—the new department. The team members were able to celebrate their successes and prepare to face the unknown in the new department they were joining.

Saying good-bye or bringing closure to the past is a very tangible way of helping people face the unknown.

Encourage new ideas, new ways of thinking. Promote an environment where trial and error is accepted. This brings much-needed energy and creativity to the organization and helps to raise morale.

Leading and managing through change usually requires, among other things, heightened levels of creativity to deal with new challenges change reveals. Since information is the raw material of creativity . . . do everything possible to open the information flow. Only then do we maximize the chances that creative solutions will present themselves.[7]

This is a telling quote from a change leader as he mused about what his theater company learned when it embarked on a change effort after almost seeing the curtains come down for a final time.

Keep the focus on "why" this change is needed and "what" you expect the future to look like. Even though the answer may evolve as more work is done and more information is known, you should be repeatedly answering the question "Is this change going the way it's supposed to go?"

Take a look at the organization's management structure. Entrepreneurs have shown us time and again that a few engaged and committed individuals can move ideas forward with incredible speed and create amazing breakthroughs. "There is no time, money, or patience to afford employees who contribute little or nothing to an organization's [vision]."[8] Breakthroughs often happen when "new blood" is inserted into the organization. Why? Because people who are new to an organization ask great questions and are not vested in old ways of doing things. Just remember to protect them until they gain credibility.

Let go of overdependency on job descriptions. Concentrate on the work that needs to be done. Who can do it? Are there opportunities for board, staff, volunteers to work together? What has to get done is more important than who does it or what their job title is. During change efforts, resistance is often evident in the resounding phrases: *Whose job is it anyway?* or *That's not my job!* or *That's not what I do!* These comments are simply ways of slowing down the process.

Pick up speed. Although recklessness is not encouraged during change efforts, it is essential that things not slow down because all the details are not yet clear. Keep the emphasis on short-term goals and the focus on long-term goals. This will help ensure that the momentum of your change effort continues to move in a forward direction.

reality check   A small organization undertook a change effort to streamline the process and reduce costs by automating expense reports. When the change team introduced its plan, there were few complaints or concerns. Training was provided, and again there were few major concerns expressed. However, when the new system was rolled out, the outcry and confusion was deafening. According to troubled members of the organization's staff, there were too many bugs in the system and the new process took far more of their time than the old one did.

The change team was stunned by the uproar. Meetings were held to assess the situation. Not all of the concerns were without validity; indeed, there were glitches. But the change team decided that once the glitches were corrected, they would proceed according to plan and continue to provide support as requested. They communicated the final date for submitting paper expense reports and held firm. In less than 18 months, a slow-moving, small but bureaucratic organization made a significant (and highly successful) change. Especially telling is the fact that many people in the organization now look back on and wonder why they didn't do it sooner. The speed in which expense reports are processed has made believers out of many who were formerly diehard resisters.

Continue to keep everyone involved. What are the ways you can involve the board, volunteers, or communities? The YWCA change team referred to earlier used weekly e-mail newsletters, monthly newsletters, a change initiative website, and telephone trees to keep over 1,500 people around the country informed. They asked for feedback, formed task forces and project teams involving hundreds of people, and conducted surveys. The level of staff involvement will be limited only by your team's ability to think of creative ways to do so.

Be an example of the change you are leading.   In other words, walk the talk. If you want the organization to buy into an entrepreneurial mind-set, they need to see entrepreneurial behavior in how the change process is led. Why, after all, go through all of this "new way of thinking" simply to return to the old ways of doing things? If you are leading the change—as you should—everyone can see what you are doing anyway. Your visibility is critical to the success of the change effort.

Take a look at your board structure.   Is this the right board to lead the organization once the changes have been completed?

David Espinoza, president and CEO of La Causa, Inc., a large bilingual, multicultural child care and family social service agency in Milwaukee, did just this when he took over the reins of the organization more than 20 years ago. David was an entrepreneur in the Hispanic community where La Causa is located. He was given six months to get the child care agency shaped up. As he went about this task, he had an entrepreneurial mind-set but was not an expert in child care agency management. He soon realized that if La Causa was to thrive and live up to expectations of its mission, the board and many of the organization's behaviors and practices needed to change.

There were 21 members of the board at the time. They were tired; they had lost their enthusiasm for trying to keep afloat the child care agency for the Hispanic families in the community. David decided the board should consist of working committees, which caused several board members to leave. Those who stayed and worked with David through the change came to respect the direction he was leading La Causa. Today's board is made up of 15 members, representing a cross section of the communities the agency serves. Through steadfast focus on the mission, the board has grown in its commitment and sense of dedication. And La Causa has grown from 17 children to well over 400—and is still growing. Additional fee-for-service programs have been added along with an import/export business.

Keep score and measure results.   Results matter. They help others see that their contribution and investment in the change vision was of value.

Returning to La Causa, under David's leadership there has been steady growth. When he took the helm of the organization in 1981, the annual budget was around $50,000; today it is around $26 million. Drawing on his skills as an entrepreneur, David found ways to provide services; partner with unlikely supporters; hire, train, and promote people from within La Causa and its community; and keep more than $2 million in economic impact within the community. When the community, staff, board, and others look at La Causa, they can see the difference the changes have brought. Recently, in a Milwaukee newspaper, one of the customers of the import/export business said, "The social service end of their business is one of those feel good things that make you want to spend money with them."[9]

Understand that you may have to leave behind a few people who can't or won't get with the program. Time and energy are critical resources that must be budgeted and allocated in ways that move the change efforts toward your vision.

reality check   Clara Miller, president of the Nonprofit Finance Fund (NFF), a national nonprofit financial intermediary with $39 million in assets and six offices serving eight markets, learned this lesson as her organization's assets grew 100 fold while revenues increased by a factor of 30. As the focus of the organization changed, so did staffing needs. Some staff were vested in the efforts at certain points in time. (In the past, the organization's focus was on providing financial products and services for energy conservation as well as cultural facilities.) As the focus has changed, some staff felt the need to move on. Other staff did not have the skills to function in the new environment. However, some did stay, retooled, and have been joined by other needed talent to help realize NFF's vision to "ensure an enduring and effective nonprofit sector, whose organizations deliver services to their communities for years to come."[10]

gem of wisdom   **Set a clear vision and stick with it.** Revise it if there is a compelling need to do so. It is the rallying call to keep teams focused and committed.

"You must be maniacal about your vision," said Arthur Mitchell, who has been the social entrepreneur behind Dance Theatre of Harlem, a world-class ballet company, for over 30 years. Through incredibly innovative ways, DTH has remained true to the company's vision—that diverse, talented, and well-trained ballet dancers who might not have the opportunity otherwise can perform to accolades for national and global audiences.

Celebrate small achievements along the way. Doing so is another way of keeping score. It helps measure progress and demonstrates that change is possible. With a few hurdles successfully navigated, it makes the rest of the journey possible. It is also another way of showing genuine appreciation for all the work that has been done and provides motivation for staying the course and becoming more invested in the outcome. There is, however, a caution sign that must be raised here. John P. Kotter correctly states, "While celebrating a win is fine, declaring the war won can be catastrophic."[11]

PHASE 3: MOVING FORWARD—WHEN THE ORGANIZATION CAN LOOK TO THE FUTURE AND EXPLORE THE OPPORTUNITIES THAT CHANGE CAN BRING

At this point you can see through some of the fog that was so thick during the second phase, facing the unknown. But don't even think of taking a breather because you are not there yet. Now is when you will experience the kind of chaos that is the precursor to creativity. It is because people are searching, testing, experimenting, and exploring new ways of doing things.

Good People Will Leave

Bailout will occur just when you think you can take a deep breath. Change agents very often move on to new challenges and opportunities. Others simply need to rejuvenate or find other interests. Board members may feel that it is time to move on because the changing organization needs a different kind of board. Staff might realize that the changing organization is no longer where they want to work. New players may come on the scene, bringing their enthusiasm for the new directions while creating insecurity or discord with those who might feel they are being discounted by these new faces. Know who the people are that are essential to keep in the organization and try to re-recruit them. Let them know how much they are valued. But don't be disappointed; for some it is simply time to move on.

The journey is not over, but some progress toward the vision has been achieved.

How can you keep the energy level up and the commitment high? By making results visible to those who are charged with achieving them. This is exactly how the organizations we have visited throughout this chapter—the mandate for a new YWCA, the McDonald's on church property providing economic development for an underserved community, completion of La Causa's new 60,000-square-foot building and expanded services to children and their families—were able to rally the support and active participation of the members of their teams.

reality check   The following scenarios may provide snapshots of what might happen with some of your stakeholders during the "moving forward" phase.

✔ *Board members.* If they have been involved and kept in the process, they may be champions for the opportunities entrepreneurial thinking can bring to the organization or they may be asking themselves, "Are we the kind of board needed to guide this changing organization?"

✔ *Donors and funders.* They are still with the organization because they see the value of the opportunities that social entrepreneurship brings and see that this change is revitalizing the social sector. Who doesn't want to have their name connected with innovative, powerful change efforts that help address issues for the common good? Some may have withdrawn because the fit is no longer there for them or they are still skeptical about how effective social entrepreneurship is to the social sector.

✔ *Staff and volunteers.* New skills have been developed in change management and, perhaps, leadership skills too. Staff and volunteers know the value of entrepreneurial ways of doing things. Maybe they now realize that you did not "throw the baby out with the bathwater." However, as previously stated, people may leave because the "new" organization no longer meets their needs. A few will always stay around to preserve the "culture." Don't expect the naysayers to disappear. They may go undercover for a while, but they will always emerge to keep the organization on its proverbial toes.

✔ *Clients and communities.* The services and support that you visualized are available and benefiting those in need. When the new facility opens at La Causa, more of the community will benefit in ways that put children and families first through job creation and more child care and family support. And as an added bonus, they will have a beautiful building whose architecture celebrates the culture of the Hispanic community.

So, what can you expect as you move forward? Almost any setback—no matter the size—can send people whom you thought were fully committed spiraling back through the abyss to behaviors experienced when facing the unknown. Events and situations can upset the status quo at any time: New programs, a downturn in the economy, a budget crisis, new board members, and new staff all have the potential to throw your efforts off track.

Change Strategies to Help Move Forward

 practical tip

If you want to help members of your social enterprise move forward, here are some essential strategies for doing just that.

Acknowledge the "pain" of the journey. These observations from Clara Miller of NFF are useful to remember:

 gem of wisdom

✔ Fail early and often.

✔ Get used to messing up.

✔ Be willing to admit when something is not working and encourage others to do the same.

Stay focused and don't backtrack.   Make the needed adjustments but keep focused on your organization's vision. Typically, the funds for a change process in nonprofit organizations are hard to come by (witness the YWCA change team's efforts), so it's vital that you keep the main focus on critical priorities.

Reward those who have helped make the change possible.   Find tangible ways of showing appreciation for their sacrifices and struggles. A genuine "thank-you" is still one of the most powerful ways of showing gratitude. Organize special events. Ann Fudge, former group vice president of Kraft Foods, said this about the Dr. Seuss' book, *Oh, the Places You'll Go!* that she has distributed to all the people in her division: "What I love about the book is that it starts in one place and takes you through a dark stage. Eventually you come out of it, but the book makes it clear that to get where you need to be, you have to make your own path."[12]

Set long-term goals.   Once people have experienced what is possible, there is enough traction that achieving long-term goals seems more attainable. The new YWCA is possible because "thousands of women have come forward to take leadership roles to bring about the changes needed to keep our organization vital to the millions we serve," said Myrna Deckert, the chairperson of the Y Change Initiative.[13] They can now work toward the long-term goals of the organization—racial justice for all and economic empowerment for women.

Acknowledge the new ways individuals have learned to work together. Often the change that really takes root in an organization is that change that has been driven by teams representing all segments of the organization that have worked and learned together. The limited resources of many nonprofit organizations often do not allow devoting the time or resources to classroom training; however, going through a change effort provides "real" training and learning opportunities that are as valuable as classroom learning. Don't forget to document your experience; it will be a valuable tool for ongoing change initiatives.

Take care of yourself.   Create opportunities to help people see that the organization benefits by having people who can take care of themselves. Acknowledge the stress, provide opportunities for people to unwind, and encourage healthy behaviors. An organization of sick people has little value.

This stage of moving forward can be a great time for an organization— people experience a sense of renewal in having let go of what is no longer useful, having faced the uncertainty of the unknown, in order to move forward, realizing that change is possible. Take time to reflect on what happened. Just as we are sometimes in denial about the need for the change, we are often as selective in our thinking about the ups and downs experienced along the way. There's absolutely nothing wrong with having these feelings; they are human.

YOUR ROLE AS THE LEADER OF ORGANIZATIONAL CHANGE

Having the ability to lead your organization successfully through change is of immense value to every single human being who is helped by the support and services the social sector provides day in and day out. Your leadership gives hope and brings much-needed innovation to the social sector.

tool of the trade The following principles that combine an adaptation of the advice of Rosabeth Moss Kanter and John Kotter provide a useful checklist for the role social entrepreneurs play in leading organizational change.

✔ *Establish a sense of urgency* for sustaining the social values and mission that are critical to your organization.

✔ *Build a powerful guiding coalition* to ensure you have others who feel a sense of ownership for the change as well.

✔ *Create a compelling vision* of what the future can be for your organization.

✔ *Communicate the vision* by demonstrating your determination and commitment to making the vision work.

✔ *Empower others to act on the vision by transferring ownership to a working team.* Run interference to remove the obstacles that will impede their success. You are adept at getting others to take the responsibility and the credit for successful implementation.

✔ *Plan for and create short-term wins* so others will remain optimistic and see evidence that your vision for change is possible to achieve.

✔ *Integrate improvement into the day-to-day actions of the organization* so the organization can see the benefits of the change as the effort continues.

✔ *Institutionalize new approaches* by modeling the new behavior that will be needed with the changes.

✔ *Tune into the environment* and take advantage of your ability to assess what is and is not working in your quest to find a better way.

✔ *Challenge the prevailing organizational wisdom* by demonstrating the value business skills bring when looking for opportunities to create social change.

✔ *Learn to persevere.* Perseverance is something that comes naturally to you. Help others see what happens when they stick with the vision and see a change effort through to completion.

✔ *Make everyone a hero.* Be there to recognize! reward! celebrate! the implementation of the vision.[14]

THE ADVICE OF TWO CHANGE LEADERS

Throughout this chapter, stories about different nonprofit organizations have been used to illustrate key concepts. Two of the social entrepreneurs you met along the way were Clara Miller and David Espinoza. When asked what lessons they have learned as change leaders who continue to transform their organizations, they offered the following sage advice.

gem of wisdom

Advice to Change Leaders from David Espinoza, La Causa, Inc.

✔ Don't be afraid to take risks.
✔ Be honorable. Do what you say you are going to do.
✔ Take responsibility for mistakes. Find out what is not going well and fix it.
✔ Be smart enough to know when and how to take calculated risk.
✔ Don't be afraid to make a strategic move, because if you hesitate you are dead!

gem of wisdom

Advice to Change Leaders from Clara Miller, Nonprofit Finance Fund

✔ Learn from your mistakes and move on.
✔ Attract the talent you need as you grow. Sometimes these are individuals who have worked in larger organizations or in the business world and bring a fresh perspective.
✔ Don't be afraid to bring in staff that has expertise that you don't have. Once you do, listen to them, give them responsibility, and hold them accountable.
✔ Organizations and teams want leaders that can tell them what to do during tremendous change. They want you to provide the necessary information so they can get the job done.

SUMMARY

Change efforts should leave organizations in a better place—not wounded and in disarray because of poor planning, lack of insight, and disregard for the human factor. Social entrepreneurs who are skilled in change management are invaluable to organizations that are harnessing the forces of change. They bring a well-rounded perspective to managing change in nonprofit organizations: sound management practices, strong business skills, and visionary leadership for a better world.

Key Points to Remember

✔ To remain viable, the social sector must face the fact that change is here to stay and that the organizations that survive in the twenty-first century will be the ones that learn to manage change effectively.

✔ Social entrepreneurs are change agents who, with a "guiding coalition," are ideal for leading organizations undergoing change.

✔ You cannot overcommunicate when managing change. Remember the *Rule of 8*—messages must be repeated at least eight times before they are taken seriously during change efforts.

✔ Institutionalizing change in an organization requires involvement by everyone: board, staff, volunteers, and ultimately the customers.

✔ No matter how well planned your change efforts may be, you can expect people to react and for there to be resistance.

✔ Call them phases, or call them stages—people will have to let go of the old, face the unknown, and move forward in order for change to take place in an organization.

✔ Organizations that embrace social entrepreneurship will transform themselves over time—not overnight, but over years. The organizations in this chapter have provided examples of this.

Notes

1. "What You Won't Hear in the Debate," *Arianna Online,* October 2, 2000, SeaChange website: *www.sea-change.org.*
2. John A. Kotter, "Leading Change: Why Transformation Efforts Fail," *Harvard Business Review,* March–April 1995, p. 59.
3. Jerry Boschee, "Managing Mission & Money," The National Center for Social Entrepreneurs, Summer 2000, *www.socialentrepreneurs.org.*
4. "The New YWCA Is Born," *Transition Newsletter,* July 16, 2001, *www.changeinitiative.org.*
5. Rosabeth Moss Kanter, "The Enduring Skills of Change Leaders," *"Leader to Leader,* the Peter F. Drucker Foundation for Nonprofit Management, Summer 1999, *www.pfdf.org.*
6. "McDonald's Goes to Church," *Black Enterprise,* September 2001, p. 24.
7. Bruce E. Rodgers, "Change as Crisis and Recovery," *National Arts Stabilization Journal,* Spring 2000, p. 13.
8. J. Gregory Dees, *Enterprising Nonprofits: A Toolkit for Social Entrepreneurs* (New York: John Wiley & Sons, 2001), p. 17.
9. Tannette Johnson-Elie, "Mexican Artistry Helps Fund Inner City Programs," *Journal Sentinel Online* (Milwaukee, WI), March 13, 2000.
10. Nonprofit Finance Fund annual report, 2001.
11. Kotter, "Leading Change."
12. *Oprah,* "Ann Fudge Reads Her Way to the Top," May 2001, p. 251.
13. "The New YWCA Is Born."
14. Kanter, "The Enduring Skills of Change Leaders," Kotter, "Leading Change."

Chapter 12

GROWING WITH AN ENTREPRENEURIAL MIND-SET

Steve Roling, Senior Vice President, Ewing Marion Kauffman Foundation

IN THIS CHAPTER

Developing an entrepreneurial mind-set
Creating an entrepreneurial environment
Developing entrepreneurial leadership
Dealing with growth
Teaching values and support
Summary

Many of us who have studied business in college, or who have worked in the for-profit world throughout our careers, were taught by professors and business mentors that most individuals who work in the social sector mean well, but they cannot be counted on to bring about measurable or sustainable results. On the other hand, those of us who studied social sciences in college, or who have worked in the not-for-profit sector throughout our careers, were taught by our professors and not-for-profit mentors that individuals from the business community lack the compassion and commitment to address the problems of the underprivileged. The business community is seen as focused on achieving monetary results as opposed to creating social value. Unfortunately, this divisive thinking continues to exist today in both the business and the not-for-profit sectors.

The good news is that a growing number of both for-profit and not-for-profit leaders are realizing that we can no longer afford to operate in our academic and practice silos where we blame others for society's lack of accomplishments. Over the years, both sectors have been coming to the same conclusion: We can solve the problems facing society today only if we all work together, seeking common solutions.

In this light, many of us who work in the social sector are beginning to take a closer look at the concepts and skill sets used by for-profit entrepreneurs to achieve success in their businesses.

✔ In the introduction to this book, we addressed the definitions and characteristics of entrepreneurship and social entrepreneurship. In this chapter, we discuss the *mind-set* of a social entrepreneur, that is, the attitudes, behaviors, beliefs, and values that characterize successful social entrepreneurs.

✔ Entrepreneurship is not a science of exacting checklists to follow in order to be successful. Rather, entrepreneurship is an art. It can be messy, exhilarating, frustrating, and full of paradoxes.

✔ For some, it seems natural to speak about entrepreneurship only when they are talking about new ventures or organizations. However, an "entrepreneurial mind-set" can be crucial throughout the history of an organization, in all stages of growth and development.

✔ How can an entrepreneurial mind-set be maintained as a new venture grows or an existing not-for-profit matures? Growth and success pose potential obstacles to maintaining that mind-set. Different managerial and leadership skills are needed as an organization becomes larger and more complex.

core concept   An *entrepreneurial mind-set* is not easily defined. It is a complex way of thinking about, planning for, acting in, and reacting to situations that makes social entrepreneurship become a reality. As you read this chapter, keep these key questions in mind: As an organization grows, how does a social entrepreneur: (1) maintain passion for and continue to achieve her social mission? (2) develop and continually energize an organization? (3) insist on continuous innovation that is not limited by current resources? and (4) show accountability in achieving sustained results?

Of course, not everyone is cut out to be an entrepreneur. This applies to both the for-profit and not-for-profit worlds. We therefore address the following questions as well: What are the attributes of the successful entrepreneur? Are certain technical and administrative skills needed to be a successful social entrepreneur? How important are feedback and peer support in this entrepreneurial process?

By the end of this chapter, we hope you will have a clearer understanding of the entrepreneurial mind-set of the social entrepreneur. While you will be given valuable information and personal examples that can be used to improve and make a more effective not-for-profit organization, it is important to realize, from the outset, that an entrepreneurial mind-set is one that is always looking to improve, to create, to innovate, to start, and to change for the purpose of achieving the social mission. Social entrepreneurs are revolutionaries who take action. It is their entrepreneurial mind-set that causes them to think and act differently from the rest of us.

DEVELOPING AN ENTREPRENEURIAL MIND-SET

Ewing Kauffman (Mr. K) was a businessman, sportsman, and philanthropist who made his money in the pharmaceutical business. Upon his death, he left most of his life proceeds to the Ewing Marion Kauffman Foundation. Mr. K often called Marion Laboratories an "uncommon" company. Plaques located throughout this vast organization explained what Mr. K meant by uncommon:

gem of wisdom

We have a responsibility for excellence and innovation. We do all that we do to the very best of our ability and with the strongest enthusiasm we can generate. It is the very nature of our business to do things that have never been done before and for which there are always reasons they cannot be done. Success for us requires the ability and the spirit to find a pathway through any obstacle, even when no pathway is visible at the start.

By this statement, and the actions he took to implement it, Mr. K was creating an entrepreneurial environment. The mind-set he established permeated every individual and every decision made throughout the organization. The entrepreneurial mind-set he created could be described by words such as self-starter, innovation, passion, growth, high energy, results, customer focus, creativity, ambiguity, curiosity, opportunity, vision, feedback, and fairness.

Greg Dees, Adjunct Professor of Social Entrepreneurship and Nonprofit Management at Duke University, often tells the story about Ellen Langer, a colleague from Harvard University who, after showing her class a picture of a quadriplegic person using a wheelchair, asked the following question of her students: "*Can* this person drive a car?" As you would imagine, the answers were without exception "No," because of the person's obvious disabilities. In her next class, Professor Langer showed the same picture and asked a slightly different question. "*How* can this person drive a car?" This class had a very different kind of discussion. After several minutes of interaction, the students came up with many innovative alternatives and devices that would allow the person to safely drive through the streets of Boston.

The small difference in the question succinctly describes the entrepreneurial mind.

Entrepreneurs, both for profit and not-for-profit organizations, are always asking themselves and others questions of how to make something happen, just as the professor asked of her students and just as Mr. K nurtured his uncommon company. The entrepreneur's curiosity, passion, innovation, creativity, and ability to network cause him to look at a situation differently from someone who does not think entrepreneurially.

As not-for-profit leaders, we work with budgets, boards, clients, and employees, and we consider our job to be managing the resources provided. An entrepreneur starts with these same factors, but he or she also constantly questions and seeks input from clients, customers, employees, and board members on how to offer better service, how to improve performance, how to improve the workplace culture, and many other aspects of the business. An entrepreneur is always looking for improvement and breakthrough solutions. An entrepreneur is optimistic and self-assured that he or she can accomplish the goals set forth.

CAN ENTREPRENEURSHIP BE TAUGHT?

Can entrepreneurship be taught, or are some people simply born and blessed with an ability to think and act like an entrepreneur? This question has been debated over the years by researchers throughout the country and around the world. Now, as we think about the skills of entrepreneurship being applied to the not-for-profit sector, it is an important question to consider.

We have all seen children who are particularly gifted in sports, reading, music, math, or science and who, at a very early age—with seemingly no effort—are naturally blessed with extraordinary talents and abilities. Qualities of leadership and entrepreneurship are often recognized in young people, and some seem to have innate talents. What about the rest of us? Can we learn these skills?

Of course we can! While we may never become the next Mozart, Einstein, Mother Teresa of Calcutta, Lou Gehrig, Colin Powell, or Bill Gates—and enjoy the level of success these individuals achieved—we *can* learn and practice the skills they more naturally possess.

The vast majority of baseball players who make it to the major leagues, for example, were never considered natural athletes in their younger years. Many were considered to be gangly, seemingly had no coordination, and appeared to be uninterested. But something happened as they developed over the years: Their passion for the sport caused them to be mentored and coached, to develop practice habits, and to become obsessed with being the best they could be.

This very same scenario can work for entrepreneurs. Many of us have been blessed to be raised in families full of entrepreneurs. Always being curious and always looking for the next innovation was the way these lucky individuals were brought up. But the rest of us, if we are fortunate enough to find mentors among our professors, friends, and colleagues, can learn these very same skills. There's no question that, with determination, practice, and a strong self-belief, entrepreneurship can and is being taught *and* learned.

Entrepreneurship is not something you can learn out of a book or by memorizing a checklist. The skills that have been described in this and other chapters of this book must be discussed and practiced consistently. Feedback must be obtained from peers and friends. "The making of an entrepreneur occurs by accumulating the relevant skills, know-how, experiences, and contacts over a period of years and includes large doses of self development."[1] After some time—often many years—success *can* be achieved. Some of the most successful for-profit and not-for-profit entrepreneurs in the world failed in the first two, or three, or even more opportunities in which they were involved. It is almost unheard of for any for-profit or not-for-profit entrepreneur to be successful in every opportunity she seizes. But persevere they did, and the rewards of success made the challenge that much sweeter.

PARADOXES OF ENTREPRENEURSHIP

If entrepreneurship can be learned, although probably not by everyone or from everyone, why is it so difficult? Entrepreneurship is not a science. There are no formulas, recipes, or prescriptions that, if used repeatedly, will provide the same results. John Eggers, Professor of Entrepreneurship, University of Western Ontario Richard Ivy School of Business, and Raymond Smilor, President, Foundation for Enterprise Development, state that the "most compelling aspect of the entrepreneurial process is its paradoxical nature."[2] Some of the many paradoxes facing entrepreneurs are summarized in Exhibit 12.1.

core concept How one approaches and manages these *paradoxes* in the start-up or growing organization is what separates the effective entrepreneur from the one who never reaches full potential. For entrepreneurs

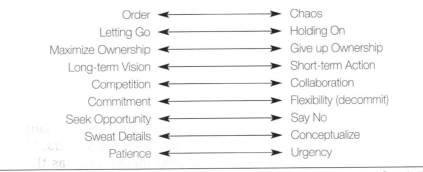

Source: John Eggers and Raymond Smilor *Leadership and Entrepreneurship: Personal and Organizational Development in Entrepreneurial Ventures* (Westport, CT: Quorum Books, 1996) p. 19.

EXHIBIT 12.1 Paradoxes facing the entrepreneur.

to reach their full potential, these paradoxes must exist at the same time. Success cannot be achieved by focusing on only one side of this ledger. Eggers and Smilor explain this paradox in the following way:

> In the entrepreneurial organization, order exists side by side with chaos. The very purpose of structure is to try to bring order out of chaos as a company grows. Yet too much order kills the energy and creativity of the building process. The entrepreneur must find a way to hold on to the spirit, purpose, and direction of the company while simultaneously letting go through delegating, allocating responsibility, and letting others make their own mistakes. By giving up ownership in the company through stock options, equity sharing, and incentive plans, the entrepreneur actually maximizes his or her ownership. The entrepreneur must take short-term actions while maintaining long-term vision. This may require that the company collaborate with others, even competitors, through strategic alliances in order to be competitive in the marketplace.
>
> Thus, entrepreneurs commit quickly to a course of action and then decommit or "pull the plug" on that course of action if it proves ineffective. Entrepreneurs must sweat the details, focusing on each activity day by day while conceptualizing and keeping the big picture in front of them. They must be patient, practicing urgency while striking the precarious balance between getting things done now and waiting for the right time and circumstances to act.[3]

These paradoxes can explain many of the tensions of growth. Growth puts pressure on the balance between the two sides. For example, growth favors order over chaos, letting go over holding on, and saying no over being opportunistic.

An entrepreneur thinks differently from those who are trying to simply "manage and control" a business or not-for-profit. Excitement, joy, frustration, anxiety, commitment, determination, and simple hard work allow entrepreneurs to achieve a level of success far beyond what most of them thought was possible. Nothing comes easily, even for the natural athlete, if he or she does not hone those skills with mentorship, practice, feedback, commitment, and determination. Even the most gifted businesspeople or not-for-profit leaders might not be successful and truly achieve their full potential if they do not develop the entrepreneurial mind-set, which allows them to seek constantly to improve the human condition and to make life better than they found it.

CREATING AN ENTREPRENEURIAL ENVIRONMENT

In creating an entrepreneurial not-for-profit organization, a leader must create an organizational climate that establishes how employees work together and treat each other. Often this culture is an outgrowth of the organization's values and beliefs statement. If the climate is not consistent with the statement, serious internal conflict will exist because employees will consider the organization to be hypocritical.

Any discussion about entrepreneurship would be incomplete without paying serious attention to the work of Jeffry Timmons of Babson University. Timmons has written nine books on the subject and is considered by many to be one of the premier entrepreneurship educators in the world. His most recent book, *New Venture Creation: Entrepreneurship for the 21st Century,* is believed to be the largest-selling book used to teach entrepreneurship in colleges and universities in America.

core concept   In *New Venture Creation,* Timmons writes that *entrepreneurial climate* can best be described along six basic dimensions:

1. *Clarity:* Organizational clarity in structure, procedures, and measurement. People need to know what to expect and what they are trying to accomplish.

2. *Standards:* Expectations and potential pressure that management puts on staff to perform at the highest level possible. What are the consequences for meeting and exceeding the standards? What are the consequences for falling below what is expected?

3. *Commitment:* Shared determination between leaders and staff who work together to achieve the goals and objectives of the organization.

4. *Responsibility:* Employees' personal commitment and responsibility to achieve goals and to help others in the organization achieve the goals. No worrying about being micromanaged or constantly second-guessed.

5. *Recognition:* Celebrating and rewarding staff for meeting their goals. This does not necessarily mean money, but always appreciation. Celebrating successes rather than punishing failure says a lot about the work environment of the organization.

6. *Esprit de corps:* An environment that is team-oriented and fun. Employees do their best work when there is a sense of cohesion and goodwill shared in the workplace.[4]

RESISTANCE

In an entrepreneurial organization, change is your constant companion. Growth, for example, is a form of change. While some team members thrive in this kind of environment, others in the organization might look at change as something to be avoided or, at the very least, resisted.

Entrepreneurs understand that one of the paradoxes of leading and managing an organization is seeking balance between the need for stability and the need for change. According to Barry Dym, nationally recognized teacher, lecturer, and author:

> *Resistance wears many faces. They include outright refusal, denial, skepticism, lethargy, incompetence, pessimism and helplessness. At times people resist by questioning the confidence, credentials or motives of their leaders, or behind the scenes lobbying. To others they may become secretive, entering a bunker-like mode until the siege of change passes.*[5]

To handle resistance effectively in an organization, Dym offers five practical approaches:

1. *Anticipate resistance:* Change is difficult for many people, including board members. No matter how well prepared, well thought out, or well communicated the reason for the change, resistance at some point is almost certain. Because resistance is part of the change process, don't perceive it as a negative. Instead, consider it useful feedback in the entire process of bringing about change.

2. *Explore the problems for which resistance provides feedback:* If you are sincere in considering resistance as a form of feedback, then it is crucial for you to get to the bottom of the reasons behind the resistance. This is done by asking a *lot* of questions—of those who are actively resisting the change, of those who are actively supporting the change, and, most important, of those who seem to be in the middle and who may be the most helpful allies in eventually bringing about the change.

3. *Join and validate the resistance, thus empowering those who resist:* In order to overcome resistance, managers must acknowledge that they truly understand the reasons behind it and must reassure people that they want to understand other points of view. The worst thing to do is to ignore or get angry with the resistance. Managers must become part of the problem-solving approach that always accompanies change.

4. *Form a partnership to solve the problem addressed by the resistance:* After you have listened, ask questions that help you understand the deeper meaning behind the resistance. It is time to join together with some of the resisters and some of the middle-of-the-roaders to seek a way to bring the conflict to a close.

5. *Problem solving:* No matter what you find to be the underlying cause behind the resistance—misunderstanding, breakdown of authority, relationships, conflict of interest—a mutual problem-solving approach (sometimes with outside facilitators) offers the best chance of buy-in as you begin to implement the change process.[6]

PETE LEVI, PRESIDENT, GREATER KANSAS CITY CHAMBER OF COMMERCE

The Greater Kansas City Chamber of Commerce has a 110-year history of championing the interests of business. As the only metropolitan chamber, the organization works to build a strong climate and help businesses grow. The chamber, representing 3,000 businesses and some 250,000 people in the 10-county area, is a leader in all areas that are important to business in the region.

At the head of this organization is Pete Levi, a man who has helped turn the chamber into one of the most powerful advocates of social services in Missouri. As a result of Levi's leadership, the chamber is a leading force for school reform, welfare-to-work programs, child care, cost-effective environmental solutions, and much more. We spoke with Pete Levi to get a better perspective how an entrepreneurial approach has affected his organization.

Q: Is the Greater Kansas City Chamber of Commerce becoming more entrepreneurial?

Levi: Yes, definitely. We have made the move for two key reasons. First of all, we needed more money to do more work. Second, the revenue that we brought in solely from chamber member fees was not enough to accomplish our goals.

Q: What is an example of an entrepreneurial program that you're particularly proud of?

Levi: Our incentive compensation plan is one that I'm very proud of. The plan rewards employees when net revenue increases. Every staff member has a personal performance plan through which they earn points that contribute toward their incentive compensation. Not only has the plan made our organization more businesslike in its operations, but it sends a strong message to our members that they are receiving value from the membership and other fees that they pay. Growth of net revenues is very important to our organization in many different ways. It allows us to grow our fund balance. This not only allows us to provide funds of a capital nature for community opportunities, but it gives us a cushion to get through lean times, which provides the chamber with a measure of stability.

Q: Incentive compensation plans are not typical in nonprofit organizations. Was the board hesitant to approve it?

Levi: No, the board actually drove the adoption of the plan. In the first year, the plan applied only to the management team. After the first year, it was offered to everyone. Initially, our 45-member staff was unsure about it. They were concerned that they would make less compensation in total. A common question at the time was "How can the chamber make more net revenue?" I explained to them that, sure, there was a risk that they would earn less money, but that they had a very real opportunity to make even more.

(continued)

Q: What are the results of this program?

Levi: Our gross revenues have increased from $3.5 million a year to $5 million, and the fund balance has grown from $300,000 to $2.5 million. Each year we have maxed out on our goals—we have to keep setting them higher and higher to keep up.

Q: How does the chamber go about doing its mission?

Levi: About two-thirds of our members are in Missouri. In addition, the Greater Kansas City Chamber of Commerce is not only the umbrella chamber for the metropolitan area, but also the chamber for Kansas City, Missouri. Thus, the chamber is more involved in advancing the interests and addressing the problems of Kansas City, Missouri. Nearly every city in the metropolitan area has a local chamber that meets many of the routine membership needs. Thus, the chamber is able to keep a higher-level, big-city perspective.

Q: How did school reform, welfare-to-work, child care, drug-free workplace, and so on become important issues for the chamber?

Levi: Businesses traditionally did not recognize these issues as business concerns and tended to ignore them. However, two megatrends—the tightening labor market and the changing demographics of the workforce—forced area businesses to address some of the most pressing social issues. As the attitude of our business members has changed, so too has the focus of the chamber's efforts. And we have been fortunate to have the help and input of the community. In child care, for example, I have to give credit to Staci Goffin at the Kauffman Foundation. She has a vision of the way the system should work in her mind. She's then able to convert and convince business leaders to see at least a part of the vision and to get on board. Staci is able to instill the notion that these are business issues. For example, the Metropolitan Child Care Council is a cross-sector initiative that addresses a very important need in our community.

Q: How do you handle resistance to change within your organization?

Levi: It's mostly through a "one-on-one" with those who need to deal with the change. I'll tell them, "Wait and see, and give the new process a chance." One of the challenges that I constantly deal with is demonstrating to staff that it is not inherently bad to be in a nonprofit. I tell them that they can match common sense with idealistic values and that it is okay to take the opportunity to make more money. The key is innovation, finding new and better ways to serve the members and finding partnerships to make things happen. The best entrepreneurial nonprofits are those in which the volunteers can feel good about being involved and that have a tremendous impact.

As with other processes involved in managing people and operating your business with an entrepreneurial approach, every situation dealing with resistance is different, and the results can be messy and frustrating. However, listening and trying to understand root causes for the resistance, involving people in the problem-solving process, and looking for solutions will clearly tell your staff that you value their opinions and want to involve them as active and important participants in the change process.

THE ENTREPRENEURIAL LEADER

Of course, not everyone is cut out to be an entrepreneur, but research shows that individuals who have certain attitudes and behaviors—which can be acquired, developed, practiced, and refined—have the best chance of success as entrepreneurs. Not everyone learns at the same pace, and, often, repeated failure precedes success.

SIX THEMES: DESIRABLE AND ACQUIRABLE ATTITUDES AND BEHAVIORS

Jeffry Timmons suggests that research has developed a consensus around six dominant themes that describe what successful entrepreneurs do and how they perform. (See Exhibit 12.2.) Obviously, there is no single set of attitudes and behaviors that guarantees your success as an entrepreneur.

These six dominant themes are very important ingredients in the recipe that makes a successful entrepreneurial leader. Let's consider them in more detail.

1. *Commitment and determination.* Timmons suggests that commitment and determination are seen as more important than any other factors. Building a new not-for-profit venture from scratch or changing its course in midstream requires its leaders' commitment. For entrepreneurs to be truly successful, their focus has to be almost totally on what they are trying to accomplish, often demanding great sacrifice of personal time and lifestyle. Entrepreneurship is a "contact sport"—you don't just throw your hat into the ring and see what happens. You must be strong-willed, persistent, and totally immersed in what you are trying to accomplish. Hard work over a long period of time is almost always required.

2. *Leadership.* Ewing Marion Kauffman, the founder of the Kauffman Foundation, said that he owed all of his success as an entrepreneur to one simple principle: "Treat others as you want to be treated." If you practice this behavior without worrying who gets the credit, you will provide your organization with the kind of leadership it takes to be successful. Obviously, leaders need to inspire teams. Leaders must understand that no one can be successful on his or her own. It is up to entrepreneurs to attract people who complement

Theme	Attitude or Behavior
1. Commitment and Determination	Tenacity and decisiveness, able to decommit/commit quickly Discipline Persistence in solving problems Willingness to undertake personal sacrifice Total immersion
2. Leadership	Self-starter; high standards but not perfectionist Team builder and hero maker; inspires others Treat others as you want to be treated Share the wealth with all the people who helped to create it Integrity and reliability; builder of trust; practices fairness Not a lone wolf Superior learner and teacher Patience and urgency
3. Opportunity Obsession	Having intimate knowledge of customers' needs Market driven Obsessed with value creation and enhancement
4. Tolerance of Risk, Ambiguity, and Uncertainty	Calculated risk taker Risk minimizer Risk sharer Manages paradoxes and contradictions Tolerance of uncertainty and lack of structure Tolerance of stress and conflict Ability to resolve problems and integrate solutions
5. Creativity, Self-reliance, and Ability to Adapt	Nonconventional, open-minded, lateral thinker Restlessness with status quo Ability to adapt and change; creative problem solver Ability to learn quickly Lack of fear of failure Ability to conceptualize and "sweat details" (helicopter mind)
6. Motivation to Excel	Goal-and-results orientation; high but realistic goals Drive to achieve and grow Low need for status and power Interpersonally supporting (versus competitive) Aware of weaknesses and strengths Having perspective and sense of humor

Source: Jeffry A. Timmons, *New Venture Creation: Entrepreneurship for the 21st Century,* 5th ed. (Boston: Irwin/McGraw-Hill, 1999), pp. 220–225.

EXHIBIT 12.2 Desirable attitudes and behaviors.

their strengths and weaknesses. Successful entrepreneurs have high integrity and trust, which inspire loyalty. They have high standards and a sense of urgency, while at the same time having patience and the understanding that perfection is something for which to constantly strive rather than something that must be achieved every day.

3. *Opportunity obsession.* Ideas are a dime a dozen, especially if entrepreneurs are talented in listening to the needs of their clients. Successful entrepreneurs are obsessed with the process of searching through all of these ideas, looking for one or two opportunities that would create value for their clients, are market-driven, and are sustainable. This is no easy task, and many of the chapters in this book have been written to help readers improve skills in assessing the difference between a viable opportunity that will make a difference and the preponderance of other ideas that are simply ideas.

4. *Tolerance of risk, ambiguity, and uncertainty.* If you are not able to enjoy and thrive on ambiguity and lack of structure, the paradoxes and contradictions, and the stress and the conflict that always accompany any entrepreneurial activity, then maybe entrepreneurship is not your cup of tea. On the other hand, if you enjoy calculated risk-taking, realize that change is a constant companion, have ability and a tolerance for problem-solving, and listen well to people, then maybe entrepreneurship is for you. There are no rules or guarantees of success, but entrepreneurs have an excitement and a passion that causes them to thrive, grow, and develop in times of uncertainty.

5. *Creativity, self-reliance, and ability to adapt.* Entrepreneurs have a lot of confidence in themselves and their ideas. They also have confidence in their ability to surround themselves with people smarter than they from whom they will learn. Entrepreneurs have an inherent restlessness with the status quo and are always looking for better ways to serve their clients. While no one likes to fail, entrepreneurs consider failure a learning experience rather than a total defeat. They can't wait to get up the next day and apply what they learned from their failure to the next opportunity. Entrepreneurs have the uncanny ability to conceptualize big-picture ideas and still sweat the details, because they are well aware that no matter how good the idea, without effective and efficient implementation, the idea is useless.

6. *Motivation to excel.* Entrepreneurs are action-oriented people who set high but realistic goals and devote themselves to achieving those goals. Successful entrepreneurs are acutely aware of their personal strengths and weaknesses, and work to build teams that complement those strengths and weaknesses. They set up an atmosphere

and a culture within their organizations that seek to achieve excellence and to support the notion of the all-for-one-and-one-for-all mentality. Entrepreneurs simply do not want to be "pretty good" or offer an "OK" service. They want to be industry leaders and are constantly motivated to improve. In order to achieve this kind of success, entrepreneurs and those around them have to maintain a healthy sense of humor and perspective. Balance-of-life issues must also be considered, but, at the close of each day, entrepreneurs must feel that they have made a difference and that they are closer to achieving their desired goals.

THE NONENTREPRENEURIAL MIND

red flag

Jeffry Timmons also believes there is such a thing as a "nonentrepreneurial mind." These characteristics—which can become more problematic as an organization grows—are summarized in the following list.

✔ *Invulnerability.* This thought pattern suggests that "no matter what I do, I will be successful." People with this trait are likely to take unnecessary risks. This is particularly troublesome for someone who has had some early success; because she believes that she is on a roll, she will, without proper due diligence, "bet the house" and lose everything that has been achieved.

✔ *Being "macho."* This describes the person who always has to be the biggest and the "baddest." This is someone who is supremely overconfident and headstrong. He considers himself always right because he believes that he is generally better than anyone else is. The problem is, macho individuals aren't always right, and they tend to ignore the truth—much to the detriment of their organizations.

✔ *Being antiauthoritarian.* Some people believe that one of the advantages of being an entrepreneur is that you don't have to listen to anyone else—you are your own boss. This type of behavior becomes problematic as the organization grows. The truth of the matter is that a good entrepreneur listens to everyone. She listens to the staff, board, clients, and family, and makes decisions accordingly.

✔ *Impulsivity.* "Ready, fire, aim." Some people are inclined to make a decision as soon as a problem has presented itself, without proper thought and discernment. Sometimes this impulsivity seems necessary to survive. Or it might be needed to seize opportunities. As the organization grows, the entrepreneur must be less impulsive and more systematic. For example, experienced entrepreneurs can complete the proper discernment process quickly enough so that the fear of losing an opportunity can be minimized.

✔ *Outer control.* Some people have a "victim mentality." They believe that they have no control over what happens to them. If something bad happens, it's not their fault because some outward condition is responsible for their lack of success.

✔ *Perfectionist.* In the human services field, it is imperative that we have high standards and measurable quality control so that we can deliver valuable services to our clients. However, entrepreneurs who insist on perfection may be wasting valuable time and missing golden opportunities in new areas while looking to perfect a program or activity that is already very good.

✔ *Know-it-all.* Some people feel that they have to be the smartest—they have to have all of the answers. Successful entrepreneurs realize what they know and what they don't know and surround themselves with people who can help them be successful.

✔ *Counterdependency.* This extreme and severe case of independence keeps the entrepreneur from trusting anyone else to provide the same quality of service to clients. Counterdependency can be a result of the founder of the organization seeing it as his "baby" to be protected. This can be a trap for the entrepreneur as he is trying to grow the organization. Often this type of entrepreneur burns out staff quickly, or perhaps even destroys his agency. Sometimes this type becomes a sole practitioner in order to avoid the difficulty of trusting and/or controlling others.[7]

In a *Harvard Business Review* article, Manfred F. R. Kets de Vries, the Raoul de Vitry d'Avaucourt Professor of Human Resource Management at INSEAD, observes that creative entrepreneurs possess the positive side of many of these traits. The traits become problems only if the entrepreneurs do not have the ability to adapt as the social enterprise grows.[8]

THE IMPACT OF GROWTH

An individual exhibits his or her entrepreneurial mind-set through the attitudes and behaviors described in the previous section. In order to achieve entrepreneurial success, he or she must also have critical skills that complement the various stages of growth of the social enterprise.

gem of wisdom

"Managers craft an approach to the task at hand. Yet, as the firm grows, growth changes the fundamental nature of that task and the approach the manager has developed. The search for a new solution generates a new mode of management, and requires a transition from the old to the new." Thus begins Michael Roberts's chapter on managing growth in the book *The Entrepreneurial Venture.*[9] Roberts continues with the observation that growth increases the demands on the entrepreneur's time and energy, which are fixed resources. Yet the entrepreneur is generally unwilling to limit the range of activities over which she has influence. So she has to find new management approaches that are less time-consuming, yet still allow her to have influence.

Roberts suggests four "modes of management":

1. *Context:* Create the organizational culture.
2. *Results:* Specify the desired results.
3. *Behavior:* Prescribe the behavior that is designed to lead to the results.
4. *Content:* Do the work itself.

Roberts explains that with growth, the entrepreneur generally moves up the modes of management, from content to context. However, Roberts suggests "good managers do not use only one mode. On any given day, certain groups or individuals might require the content mode while others want the context mode." For example, content is appropriate when the risk of the entrepreneur not being involved in an activity or a decision seems too high. The context mode is reasonable when the entrepreneur's team is composed of professionals assumed to possess the skills and values needed to do the right thing.

tool of   Neil Churchill, Professor Emeritus of Entrepreneurship at INSEAD,
the trade   and former Harvard Business School Professor Virginia Lewis observe, "Categorizing the problems and growth patterns of small businesses in a systematic way that is useful to entrepreneurs seems at first glance a hopeless task. . . . Yet on closer scrutiny, it becomes apparent that they experience common problems arising at similar stages in their development."[10] They describe the stages as: existence, survival, success, takeoff, and resource maturity. In the existence stage, "the entrepreneur *is* the business," doing or directly supervising everything. In the success stage, functional management has been added. In the resource maturity stage, the entrepreneur is concerned about "retaining the advantages of a smaller size, including flexibility and entrepreneurial spirit."

While Churchill and Lewis emphasize organizational life-cycle issues, other authors reject the simple stages-of-growth models but still recognize the importance of transitions. In "Building a Self-Sustaining Firm," Amar Bhide, Professor of Business at Columbia Graduate School of Business, states that a social enterprise "has to grow in order to support the organizational infrastructure it needs to function without the day-to-day intervention of the founder."[11] As described in the "Values and Ethics" section later in this chapter, entrepreneurs should hope to build a culture that lives beyond their presence in the enterprise. Bhide makes a similar observation: To attain sustainability, entrepreneurs should focus on the capabilities of the organization as a whole, not just their own skills. Bhide suggests that the organizational capacity has to be "broadened and deepened. For example, through more qualified personnel, specialization of functions, decentralized decision-making, systems to cope with the larger and the more complex . . . and employees oriented towards a common long-term purpose."[12]

Bhide believes that most enterprises fail to achieve "basic operational sustainability: the ability to function without the day-to-day intervention of the founder and/or owner." He adds that if an enterprise is perceived to be self-sustaining, it can attract capital, customers, employees, and other resources that further solidify its position.

ENTREPRENEURIAL SKILLS

Entrepreneurs can form teams that collectively have the required skills for entrepreneurial success. This book has described many of the skills required for entrepreneurial success. Here we highlight an example of how growth affects the set of skills needed.

Social enterprises experience growth for many reasons, such as new markets, new services, customer service, leadership, and innovation. A common challenge to all growing enterprises is the management of human resources. John Kotter, Professor Emeritus at the Harvard Business School, and Vijay Sathe, Professor of Management at the Claremont Graduate University, outline common problems:

- ✔ Important decisions must be made rapidly.
- ✔ Job demands expand continually.
- ✔ Recruiting and training needs are significant.
- ✔ Constant change is inevitable.
- ✔ Resources are scarce.

The challenges are intertwined. For example, "Growth makes . . . management more difficult because the number of relationships to be managed increases more rapidly than the number of employees." Also, growth "requires more employees, which require more recruiting and training." Employees "do not have the time to do anything but what is immediately required," so planning, information, control, and operating systems are neglected. To meet the challenges of growth, Kotter and Sathe recommend that entrepreneurs force themselves to take the time to establish effective recruiting, training, and planning processes, build teams, and manage the culture.[13]

This example of growing human resource management along with growing the enterprise is applicable to all functional areas, such as planning, service development, operations, and finances. Aligning interpersonal and team skills with growth is also important. The following are examples of the skills that will support entrepreneurs in pursuing the mission. At the same time, entrepreneurs must adapt these skills, in both themselves and their team, so that growth can be pursued.

✔ *Personal values.* The underpinning of any individual is her personal values and beliefs and the framework in which she lives her life. It is important for individuals and organizations to have values and belief statements.

✔ *Leadership.* Providing direction and clarity in the vision and mission of the organization. Developing a culture, process, or structure that effectively and efficiently carries out the programs that support the vision and mission.

✔ *Developing subordinates.* The ability to delegate responsibility and authority to subordinates and to mentor them in their development of management skills.

✔ *Conflict management.* The ability to create an atmosphere where open discussion of conflict is seen as healthy, and all parties agree to participate in this discussion in a professional manner until a resolution is reached.

✔ *Teamwork.* Realizing that nothing is *ever* done by one individual. Acknowledging the importance of being able to work together with others in pursuing the common vision.

✔ *Feedback.* The ability to both give and accept constructive feedback on individual and organizational performance. Recognizing feedback as constructive and not becoming defensive or argumentative.

✔ *Motivation. Of others* to do their best, which allows them to achieve results far beyond what they thought possible. Motivation *of self,* which allows a leader to always give 110 percent and maintain a can-do attitude.[14]

✔ *Honesty.* The ability to trust someone and not worry about hidden agendas or half-truths. Establishing an atmosphere that creates loyalty and collaborative support.

✔ *The Golden Rule.* Treating others as you want to be treated. This is the most powerful and easiest-to-understand attribute. It causes organizations to become uncommon. Employees understand that they have both rights and responsibilities and are held accountable for their actions. What you do and what you accomplish are important. How you accomplish it is equally important.

VALUES AND SUPPORT

Any discussion about an entrepreneurial leader has to include values and ethics. We've all heard stories about organizations that change dramatically for better or worse every time a new leader is chosen. But according to Joseph Badaracco Jr., John Shad Professor of Business Ethics at *gem of wisdom*

Harvard Business School, and Richard Ellsworth, Associate Professor of Management at the Claremont Graduate University, in their book, *Leadership and the Quest for Integrity:*

> *A leader's actions must serve purposes and reflect basic values that followers identify with personally. Followers must become committed to organizations instead of their leaders. . . . what separates a leader from a competent professional manager is the ability to build an organization that is a source of self-fulfillment and personal integrity for its members. The main task of leadership is energizing followers to take actions that support higher corporate purposes and not their own self-interests.*[15]

What Badaracco and Ellsworth are suggesting is that, while it is crucial for entrepreneurial leaders to have a value system and ethical standards that everyone understands and follows, what truly makes a leader outstanding is when those values and ethics continue after he or she leaves the organization. These values and standards become part of the culture. For example, values are passed down by supervisors who tell stories about past staff who exhibited the organization's values in an exemplary way.

VALUES AND ETHICS

People want to take pride both in their work and in where they work. They want to work someplace that helps them to develop their fullest potential—a place that will fully challenge them, a place where they can accomplish more together with others than they ever could accomplish on their own. They also want to put their personal "stamp" on the work, to contribute in a significant way to the purpose of the organization, and to know that their efforts are making a difference. Finally, they want to work with those whom they like, respect, and trust.

Values and ethics can and must be taught within an organization. While the services you provide to your clients may change over the years, what should never change are the values that guide the leadership of your organization and your relationships with your staff and clients.

Who determines the organization's values and ethics?

The organization's leader has primary responsibility. However, for a values and beliefs statement to be practiced—and not just talked about—the creation of the statement should be a shared responsibility between the leader and staff. Over several weeks or months, the leader should guide these discussions, asking such questions as: What is really important in how the staff treat clients and each other? What rights and responsibilities should be in place for staff to provide service to clients in a value-centered way?

A values statement is a living document that should be reviewed, discussed, and updated on a regular basis. It is not something you simply hang on the wall. It should be the heart and soul of the organization. The leader's primary responsibility is to make sure every employee in the organization understands what is expected of him or her in practicing the intent of the values and beliefs statement.

PEER SUPPORT AND FEEDBACK

What do these famous athletes have in common: Joe DiMaggio, George Brett, Nolan Ryan, Willie Mays, Hank Aaron, Stan Musial, and Roberto Clemente? These are all players in the Baseball Hall of Fame, who excelled at their sport and are considered some of the best in baseball history. Even these legends had mentors and coaches, not only in the early years when they were in little leagues and minor leagues, but even after they had established themselves in the major leagues as outstanding players. Every year coaches would watch them field, throw, and hit, and offer suggestions on how to improve.

Feedback for entrepreneurs is just as important as it is for athletes. None of us can improve without effort and commitment, but we also need feedback: from our staff, boards, clients, and colleagues. We need mentors to take an interest in us. Often for a seemingly unexplainable reason, they are willing to devote an extraordinary amount of time to help us be successful. There are very few shortcuts to success, and no entrepreneur, either for-profit or not-for-profit, has led an organization on his or her own. Without feedback we do not learn and grow; we will become stagnant and eventually deteriorate. An entrepreneur's lifeline to the future is to continually learn and listen to others, because entrepreneurs are always looking for a new or better way to serve clients in the marketplace.

SUMMARY

One of the greatest challenges an entrepreneur faces is maintaining an entrepreneurial mind-set as the venture grows and matures. Here are some points to consider as you create and nurture your own entrepreneurial mind-set:

- ✔ Growth and success pose threats to the entrepreneurial mind-set.
- ✔ Most scholars believe that the skills needed to successfully start a venture are different from the skills needed to grow it, even to grow it with an entrepreneurial mind-set. This means that the entrepreneur must grow and develop personally, or leave.

✔ In growing their ventures, entrepreneurs should anticipate certain challenges and organizational transitions.

✔ The entrepreneurial mind-set is useful throughout the organizational life cycle.

✔ To maintain that entrepreneurial spirit, the entrepreneurial leader must master some key paradoxes.

✔ The entrepreneurial leader also must grow personally, develop new skills, let go of control, and nurture future entrepreneurial leaders for the social enterprise.

✔ The entrepreneurial leader needs to know when to move on.

Notes

1. Jeffry Timmons, *New Venture Creation: Entrepreneurship for the 21st Century* (Boston: Irwin/McGraw-Hill, 1994).
2. John Eggers and Raymond Smilor, *Leadership and Entrepreneurship: Personal and Organizational Development in Entrepreneurial Ventures* (Westport, CT: Quorum Books, 1996).
3. Ibid.
4. Timmons, *Entrepreneurial Venture: Entrepreneurship in the 21st Century* (New York: McGraw-Hill, 1999) p. 524.
5. Barry Dym, "Resistance in Organization," *Organizational Development Practitioner* Vol 31, Issue 1, 1999.
6. Ibid.
7. Jeffry Timmons, *Entrepreneurial Venture*, p. 226.
8. Manfred F. R. Kets de Vries, "The Dark Side of Entrepreneurship," *Harvard Business Review*, November–December 1985.
9. Michael J. Roberts, "Managing Transitions in the Growing Enterprise," in William A. Sahlman and Howard H. Stevenson, *The Entrepreneurial Venture*, 2nd ed. (Boston: Harvard Business School Press, 1999).
10. Neil C. Churchill and Virginia L. Lewis, "The Five Stages of Small Business Growth," *Harvard Business Review*, May–June 1983.
11. Amar Bhide, "Building a Self-Sustaining Firm," in Sahlman and Stevenson, *The Entrepreneurial Venture*, 2nd ed. (Boston: Harvard Business School Press, 1999).
12. Ibid.
13. John Kotter and Vijay Sathe, "Problems of Human Resource Management in Rapidly Growing Companies," *California Management Review*, Winter 1978.
14. John Eggers and Raymond Smilor, *Leadership and Entrepreneurship: Personal and Organizational Development in Entrepreneurial Ventures* (Westport, CT: Quorum Books, 1996) pp. 15–38.
15. Joseph L. Badaracco Jr. and Richard R. Ellsworth, *Leadership and the Quest for Integrity* (Boston: Harvard Business School Press, 1993).

APPENDIX

FOR FURTHER READING

Chapter 1: Developing a Strategic Service Vision

James C. Collins and Jerry I. Porras, *Built to Last* (New York: HarperBusiness, 1994).

James L. Heskett, *Managing in the Service Economy* (Boston: Harvard Business School Press, 1986).

James L. Heskett, "Lessons in the Service Sector," *Harvard Business Review,* March-April 1987, pp. 118-126.

James L. Heskett, W. Earl Sasser, and Leonard A. Schlesinger, *The Service Profit Chain: How Leading Companies Link Profit and Growth to Loyalty, Satisfaction, and Value* (New York: Free Press, 1997).

W. Earl Sasser, Jr., Christopher W. L. Hart, & James L. Heskett, *The Service Management Course: Cases and Readings* (New York: Free Press, 1991).

Chapter 2: Developing an Entrepreneurial Competitive Strategy

Shona L. Brown, Kathleen M. Eisenhardt, *Competing on the Edge: Strategy As Structured Chaos* (Watertown, MA: Harvard Business School Press, 1998).

Paul J. Stonich, *Implementing Strategy: Making Strategy Happen* (New York: Harper Information, 1982).

Burton Weisboard, *The Nonprofit Economy* (Cambridge, MA: Harvard University Press, 1988).

Boris Yavitz and William Newman, *Strategy in Action: The Execution, Politics, and Payoff of Business Planning* (New York: Free Press, 1982).

Boris Yavitz and William Newman, *Strategy in Action* (New York: The Free Press, 1984).

Chapter 3: Cooperative Strategy: Networking and Building Partnerships and Alliances

"Ben's Big Flop," *Inc.,* September 1998.

Rollin Glaser and Christine Glaser, *Negotiating Style Profile, Organization Design and Development, Inc.,* 1996 revised.

Shirley Sagawa and Eli Segal, *Common Interest, Common Good,* HBS 2000.

Ron Shapiro, "The Power of Nice," *Fortune,* October 1998.

Leigh Steinberg, "Winning with Integrity," *Fortune,* October 1998.

Chapter 4: Leading, Retaining, and Rewarding People Entrepreneurially

Kathleen Allen and Peter Economy, *The Complete MBA for Dummies* (Foster City: IDG Books, 2000).

Katherine Catlin and Jana Matthews, *Leading at the Speed of Growth* (New York: Hungry Minds, Inc., 2001).

Peter Isler and Peter Economy, *At the Helm: Business Lessons for Navigating Rough Waters* (New York: Doubleday, 2000).

Bob Nelson, *1001 Ways to Energize Employees* (New York: Workman, 1997).

Bob Nelson, *1001 Ways to Reward Employees* (New York: Workman, 1994).

Bob Nelson and Peter Economy, *Managing for Dummies* (Foster City: IDG Books, 1996).

Harvey Seifter and Peter Economy, *Leadership Ensemble: Lessons in Collaborative Management from the World's Only Conductorless Orchestra* (New York: Times Books, 2001).

Chapter 5: Managing Your Board Entrepreneurially

John Carver, *Boards That Make a Difference: A New Design for Leadership in Nonprofit and Public Organizations* (San Francisco: Jossey-Bass, 1990).

Peter Drucker, *The Drucker Foundation Self-Assessment Tool* (San Francisco: Jossey-Bass, 1998).

James Hardy, *Developing Dynamic Boards: A Proactive Approach to Building Nonprofit Boards of Directors* (Erwin, TN: Essex Press 1990).

Brian O'Connell, *Powered by Coalition* (San Francisco: Jossey Bass, 1997).

Chapter 6: Treating Your Donors as Investors

Ken Burnett, *Relationship Fundraising* (University Heights, OH: Heights International, 1996).

Kay Sprinkel Grace, *Beyond Fund Raising: New Strategies for Nonprofit Innovation and Investment* (New York: John Wiley & Sons, 1997).

Kay Sprinkel Grace and Alan Wendroff, *High Impact Philanthropy: How Boards, Donor-Investors and Volunteers Can Transform Communities* (New York: John Wiley & Sons, 2000).

Chapter 7: Working with Community

"Architects/Designers/Planners for Social Responsibility," *New Village: Building Sustainable Cultures,* Issue 1, 1999.

Atkinson, Dick, *The Common Sense of Community* (London: Demos, 1994).

Robert Bellah, Richard Madsen, William M. Sullivan, Ann Swidler, and Steven M. Tipton, *Habits of the Heart: Individualism and Commitment in American Life.* (New York: Harper & Row, 1985).

Alan Briskin, *The Stirring of Soul in the Workplace* (San Francisco: Berrett-Koehler 1998).

Arie De Geus, *The Living Company: Growth, Learning and Longevity in Business* (London: Longview, 1997).

Thomas Donaldson and Thomas W. Dunfee, *Ties that Bind: A Social Contracts Approach to Business Ethics.* (Cambridge, MA: Harvard Business School, 1999).

Peter F. Drucker, *Post-Capitalist Society* (New York: Harper, 1993).

John W. Gardner, *On Leadership* (New York: Free Press, 1990).

Douglas Hague, *Transforming the Dinosaurs: How Organizations Learn* (London: Demos, 1993).

Shirley Brice Heath and Laura Smyth, *ArtShow: Youth and Community Development: A Resource Guide,* (Washington, DC: Partners for Livable Communities, 1999).

Frances Hesselbein, Marshall Goldsmith, Richard Beckhard, and Richard F. Schubert, *The Community of the Future* (New York; The Drucker Foundation, 1998).

Rosabeth Moss Kantor, *Frontiers of Management.* (Cambridge, MA: Harvard Business Review, 1997).

James M. Kouzes, and Barry Z. Posner, *The Leadership Challenge* (San Francisco: Jossey-Bass, 1995).

John P. Kretzmann, and John L. McKnight, *Building Communities from the Inside Out* (Chicago, IL: Asset-Based Community Development Institute, 1993).

John P. Kretzmann, and John L. McKnight, *A Guide to Mapping and Mobilizing the Economic Capacities of Local Residents* (Chicago,IL: Asset-Based Community Development Institute, 1996).

Charles Leadbeater, *The Rise of the Social Entrepreneur* (London: Demos, 1997).

John McKnight, *The Careless Society: Community and Its Counterfeits* (New York: Basic Books, 1995).

Geoff Mulgan, *Connexity: How to Live in a Connected World* (Cambridge, MA: Harvard Business School, 1997).

Partners for Livable Communities, *The Livable City: Revitalizing Urban Communities* (New York: McGraw Hill, 2000).

B. Joseph Pine and James H. Gilmore, *The Experience Economy: Work Is Theatre and Every Business a Stage* (Cambridge, MA: Harvard Business School, 1999).

Robert Putnam, *Making Democracy Work: Civic Traditions in Modern Italy* (Princeton: Princeton University Press, 1993).

Robert Putnam, "The Prosperous Community: Social Capital and Public Life." *The American Prospect,* no. 13, 1993.

Robert Putnam, *Bowling Alone: America's Declining Social Capital. Journal of Democracy,* Vol. 6, No. 1, 1995.

Peter M. Senge, *The Fifth Discipline: The Art & Practice of the Learning Organization* (New York: Currency Doubleday, 1990).

Peter M. Senge, *The Dance of Change: The Challenges to Sustaining Momentum in Learning Organizations* (New York: Currency Doubleday, 1999).

Richard Sennett, *The Corrosion of Character* (New York: Norton, 1998).

Bill Shore, *The Cathedral Within* (New York: Random House, 1999).

Larry C. Spears, *Insights on Leadership* (New York: John Wiley & Sons, 1998).

Stephen Thake and Simon Zadek, *Practical People, Noble Causes: How to Support Community-Based Social Entrepreneurs* (London: New Economics Foundation, 1997).

David Whyte, *The Heart Aroused: Poetry and the Preservation of the Soul in Corporate America* (New York: Doubleday, 1994).

Chapter 8: Performance Information that Really Performs

Robert S. Kaplan and David P. Norton, *The Balanced Scorecard: Measures that Drive Performance, Harvard Business Review,* January-February 1992.

Christine W. Letts, William P. Ryan, and Allen Grossman, *High Performance Non-Profit Organizations: Managing Upstream for Greater Impact,* (New York: John Wiley and Sons, Inc., 1999).

Elaine Morley, Elisa Vinson, and Harry P. Hatry, *Outcome Measurement in Non-Profit Organizations: Current Practices and Recommendations* (Washington, DC: Independent Sector, 2001).

Sawhill, John C. *Mission Impossible? Measuring Success in Non-Profit Organizations,* paper, 1999.

Fay Twersky, *An Information OASIS: The Design and Implementation of Comprehensive and Customized Client Information and Tracking Systems,* REDF, 2001.

Chapter 9: Developing Viable Earned Income Strategies

Sutia Kim Alter, *Managing the Double Bottom Line: A Business Planning Guide for Social Enterprise* (Washington, DC: Save the Children Federation, 1999).

Alan R. Andreasen, "Profits for Nonprofits: Find a Corporate Partner," *Harvard Business Review,* November-December 1996.

James E. Austin, *The Collaboration Challenge: How Nonprofits and Businesses Succeed Through Strategic Alliances* (San Francisco: Jossey-Bass, 2000).

Amar Bhide, "How Entrepreneurs Craft Strategies That Work," *Harvard Business Review,* March-April 1994.

Amar Bhide, "Hustle as Strategy," *Harvard Business Review,* September-October 1986.

Peter C. Brinckerhoff, *Mission-Based Marketing* (Dillon, CO: Alpine Guild, Inc., 1997).

Peter C. Brinckerhoff, *Social Entrepreneurship: The Art of Mission-Based Venture Development* (New York: John Wiley & Sons, 2000).

J. Gregory Dees, "Enterprising Nonprofits," *Harvard Business Review,* January-February 1998.

J. Gregory Dees, Jed Emerson, Peter Economy, *Enterprising Nonprofits: A Toolkit for Social Entrepreneurs* (New York: John Wiley & Sons, 2001).

Jed Emerson and Fay Twersky, *New Social Entrepreneurs: The Success, Challenge and Lessons of Nonprofit Enterprise Creation* (San Francisco: The Roberts Foundation, 1996).

Robert Hisrich and Michael Peters, *Entrepreneurship: Starting, Developing and Managing A New Enterprise* (Chicago: Irwin Press, 1995).

Rosabeth Moss Kanter, "Collaborative Advantage: The Art of Alliances," *Harvard Business Review,* July-August 1994.

Rita Gunther McGrath and Ian MacMillan, "Discovery-Driven Planning," *Harvard Business Review,* July-August 1995.

Mike McKeever, *How to Write a Business Plan* (Berkeley, CA: Nolo Press, 1992).

National Center on Nonprofit Enterprise: *www.nationalcne.org*

V. Kasturi Rangan, Sohel Karim, Sheryl K. Sandberg, "Do Better at Doing Good," *Harvard Business Review,* May-June 1996.

Roberts Enterprise Development Fund: *www.redf.org.*

Shirley Sagawa and Eli Segal, *Common Interest, Common Good: Creating Value Through Business and Social Sector Partnerships* (Boston: Harvard Business School Press, 2000).

Bill Shore, *The Cathedral Within: Transforming Your Life by Giving Something Back* (New York: Random House, 1999).

Bill Shore, *Revolution of the Heart: A New Strategy for Creating Wealth and Meaningful Change* (New York: Riverhead Books, 1995).

Edward Skloot, *The Nonprofit Entrepreneur: Creating Ventures to Earn Income* (New York: The Foundation Center, 1988).

Jeffry A. Timmons, *New Venture Creation: Entrepreneurship for the 21st Century,* Fourth Edition (Boston: Irwin McGraw-Hill, 1994).

Dennis Young, "Corporate Partnerships: A Guide for the Nonprofit Manager," *www.nationalcne.org.*

Brenda Zimmerman and Raymond Dart, "Charities Doing Commercial Ventures: Societal and Organizational Implications," (Ontario, Canada: Trillium Foundation, 1998).

Chapter 10: The Question of Scale: Finding an Appropriate Strategy for Building on Your Success

Alan R. Andreasen, *Cheap but Good Marketing Research* (Homewood, IL: Dow Jones-Irwin, 1988).

Amar Bhide, *The Origin and Evolution of New Businesses* (Oxford: Oxford University Press, 2000).

Jeffrey L. Bradach, *Franchising Organizations* (Boston: Harvard Business Schools Press, 1998).

Jeffrey L. Bradach, "Going to Scale," Harvard Business School Working Paper, Social Enterprise Series, No. 9, forthcoming in *Harvard Business Review.*

James Champy and Nitin Nohria, *The Arc of Ambition* (Cambridge, MA: Preseus Books, 2000).

Ram Charan and Noel M. Tichy, *Every Business Is a Growth Business* (New York: Times Books, 1998).

Malcolm Gladwell, *The Tipping Point: How Little Things Can Make a Big Difference* (Boston: Little, Brown and Company, 2000).

Kevin Kelly, *New Rules for the New Economy* (New York: Penguin Books, 1998).

Christine W. Letts, William P. Ryan, and Allen Grossman (*High Performance Nonprofit Organizations: Managing Upstream for Greater Impact,* New York: John Wiley & Sons, 1999).

Rita Gunther McGrath and Ian C. MacMillan, "Discovery-Driven Planning," *Harvard Business Review,* July-August 1995.

Sharon M. Oster, "Nonprofit Organizations and Their Local Affiliates: A Study in Organizational Forms, " *Journal of Economic Behavior and Organization,* vol. 30, 1996.

Dennis Young, Neil Bania, and Darlyne Bailey, "Study of National Nonprofit Associations," *Nonprofit Management & Leadership,* vol. 6, no. 4, Summer 1996.

Chapter 11: Managing Organizational Change

John A. Kotter, "Leading Change: Why Transformation Efforts Fail", *Harvard Business Review,* March-April 1995, p. 59.

The National Center for Social Entrepreneurs, *www.socialentrepreneurs.org.*

The Peter F. Drucker Foundation for Nonprofit Management, *www.pfdf.org.*

Chapter 12: Growing with an Entrepreneurial Mind-Set

Joseph L. Badaracco, Jr. & Richard R. Ellsworth, *Leadership and the Quest for Integrity* (Boston, MA: Harvard School of Business Press, 1989).

J. Gregory Dees, Jed Emerson, Peter Economy, *Enterprising Nonprofits: A Toolkit for Social Entrepreneurs* (New York: John Wiley and Sons, Inc, 2001).

Peter F. Drucker, *Innovation and Entrepreneurship,* (New York: Harper & Row, Publishers, Inc., 1995).

Peter F. Drucker, *Managing the Nonprofit Organization: Principles and Practices* (New York: HarperCollins Publishers, 1990).

John DuRand, *The Affirmative Enterprise* (St. Paul, Minnesota: MDI Press, 1990).

Ronald A. Heifetz, *Leadership Without Easy Answers* (Cambridge, MA: The Belknap Press of Harvard University Press, 1998).

Douglas C. Henton, John Melville, Kimberly Walesh, *Grassroots Leaders for a New Economy* (San Francisco: Jossey-Bass Publishers, 1997).

Frances Hesselbein, Marshall Goldsmith, Richard Beckhard, *The Leader of the Future* (Jossey-Bass Publishers: San Francisco, 1996).

Paul Heyne, *The Promise of Community: Strengthening Civil Society* (Indianapolis, Indiana: The Philanthropy Roundtable, 1994).

Rosabeth Moss Kanter, *The Change Masters: Innovation and Entrepreneurship in the American Corporation* (New York: Simon & Schuster, Inc., 1984).

John J. Kao, *The Entrepreneurial Organization* (Englewood Cliffs, New Jersey: Prentice Hall, 1991).

John R. Kimberly, Robert H. Miles and Associates, *The Organizational Life Cycle: Issues in the Creation, Transformation, and Decline of Organizations* (San Francisco: Jossey-Bass Publishers, 1980).

Christine W. Letts, William P. Ray, Allen Grossman, *High Performance Nonprofit Organizations: Managing Upstream for Greater Impact* (Canada: John Wiley & Sons, Inc., 1999).

Thomas A. McLaughlin, *The Entrepreneurial Nonprofit Executive: The Myths, The Money, The People* (Rockville, MD: The Fund Raising Institute, 1991).

Thomas A. McLaughlin, *Nonprofit Mergers and Alliances: A Strategic Planning Guide* (New York: John Wiley & Sons, Inc., 1998).

Steve Mariotti, *The Young Entrepreneur's Guide to Starting and Running a Business* (New York: Random House, Inc., 1996).

Robert H. Rosen, Ph.D. with Lisa Berger, *The Healthy Company: Eight Strategies to Develop People, Productivity, and Profits* (New York: The Putnam Publishing Group, 1991).

William A. Sahlman and Howard H. Stevenson, *The Entrepreneurial Venture* (Cambridge, MA: Harvard Business School, 1992).

Jeffry A. Timmons, *New Venture Creation: Entrepreneurship for the 21st Century* (New York: Irwin/McGraw-Hill, 1977, 1985, 1990 and 1994).

Jeffry A. Timmons, *The Entrepreneurial Mind* (Andover, MA: Brick House Publishing Company, 1989).

INDEX